ECONOMIES OF WRITING

ECONOMIES OF WRITING

Revaluations in Rhetoric and Composition

Edited by
BRUCE HORNER
BRICE NORDQUIST
SUSAN M. RYAN

UTAH STATE UNIVERSITY PRESS
Logan

Published by Utah State University Press
An imprint of University Press of Colorado
5589 Arapahoe Avenue, Suite 206C
Boulder, Colorado 80303

Manufactured in the United States of America

The University Press of Colorado is a proud member of
The Association of American University Presses.

The University Press of Colorado is a cooperative publishing enterprise supported, in part, by Adams State University, Colorado State University, Fort Lewis College, Metropolitan State University of Denver, Regis University, University of Colorado, University of Northern Colorado, Utah State University, and Western State Colorado University.

The paper used in this publication meets the minimum requirements of the American National Standard for Information Sciences—Permanence of Paper for Printed Library Materials. ANSI Z39.48-1992

ISBN: 978-1-60732-522-2 (paperback)
ISBN: 978-1-60732-523-9 (ebook)

Library of Congress Cataloging-in-Publication Data

Names: Horner, Bruce, 1957– editor. | Nordquist, Brice, editor. | Ryan, Susan M., Ph.D., editor.
Title: Economies of writing : revaluations in rhetoric and composition / [edited by] Bruce Horner, Brice Nordquist, Susan M. Ryan.
Description: Logan : Utah State University Press, [2016] | Includes bibliographical references.
Identifiers: LCCN 2016005516 | ISBN 9781607325222 (pbk.) | ISBN 9781607325239 (ebook)
Subjects: LCSH: English language—Rhetoric—Study and teaching (Higher)—Economic aspects. | English language—Rhetoric—Study and teaching (Higher)—Political aspects.
Classification: LCC PE1405.U6 E325 2016 | DDC 808/.042071173—dc23
LC record available at http://lccn.loc.gov/2016005516

CONTENTS

ACKNOWLEDGMENTS

Many of the ideas and insights presented in this volume emerged out of work accomplished at the University of Louisville English department's 2012 Thomas R. Watson Conference on Rhetoric and Composition, "Economies of Writing." We are grateful to Min-Zhan Lu, the conference director, for designing and organizing that conference, and to Dr. Thomas Watson, whose bequest made the event possible.

We thank the University of Louisville's Committee on Academic Publications and the College of Arts and Sciences at Syracuse University for providing funding in support of this project. For their support and encouragement, we are grateful to the University of Louisville English department's former chair, Susan Griffin; its current chair, Glynis Ridley; and other colleagues at the university, as well as Lois Agnew, chair of the Department of Writing Studies, Rhetoric, and Composition at Syracuse University.

Thanks go to Michael Spooner of Utah State University Press for his early interest in the project and for his support and guidance throughout, and to Allie Madden, Laura Furney, and Kami Day, also of Utah State University Press, for helping us see the book through to completion. Thanks also to the press's anonymous reviewers, who provided valuable suggestions on earlier versions of this collection, and to Kathryn Perry, Laura Tetrault, and Sara Alvarez for their helpful research and editorial assistance. Portions of chapter 10 originally appeared in T. R. Johnson's *The Other Side of Pedagogy: Lacan's Four Discourses and the Development of the Student Writer* (2014). SUNY Press has kindly granted permission to reprint.

Most of all we wish to thank our contributors, without whose efforts this book would not exist. Finally, we thank our families and friends for their patience and support as we worked on this book.

ECONOMIES OF WRITING

INTRODUCTION

Bruce Horner, Brice Nordquist, and Susan M. Ryan

Enduring economic recessions, growing economic inequality, the emergence of a corporate state, and increasing privatization of education at all levels have made the economic a seemingly inevitable point of departure, if not an assumed premise, for those of us committed to the study and teaching of writing and rhetoric. For, like it or not, the economic as force and framework shapes the conditions, direction, and purpose of our work. There is thus ample exigency for a collection like this one that investigates economies of writing: how the economic defines, limits, and thereby shapes the work we do, how we do it, and to what ends and with what effects we do it. But a further exigency for this collection is the need to rethink the economic itself as force and framework by challenging the values of our work. We seek, then, to offer counterframeworks and forces alternative not to the economic but rather to how the economic is commonly understood—as a predictable, all-powerful monolith. Such representations work in concert and intersect with a notion of globalization as an inevitable, if not already completed, *shift* from a fordist to a postfordist, fast-capitalist economic regime to provoke reforms to the ways in which work is conceived and conducted in all sectors of the economy. Fueled by the values and ideologies of market fundamentalism, such reforms are perhaps most evident in the increasing efforts to regulate the work of education. For example, the Bill and Melinda Gates Foundation's *A Path to Alignment Report* asserts that "in today's global age—an era in which a well-educated citizenry is absolutely vital to economic success and social progress—a truly aligned education system has become all but indispensable. Without such a system, it will be next to impossible for us to forge the necessary human capital—the talent—that can power our economy and ensure a thriving democracy" (Conley and Gaston 2013, 2).

According to this appeal, a conflation of economic, social, and national progress depends upon the design and deployment of systems that can transport individuals from cradle to career and thereby

DOI: 10.7330/9781607325239.c000

efficiently and effectively transform them into human capital. Students are convinced to undergo this transformation with a promise that as long as they are willing to be molded by the needs of capital, they will be granted a secure and desirable place in the economic hierarchy. And educators are tasked with facilitating this transformation by predicating the value of their work and the work of their students solely upon potential payoffs in the future (typically in the form of individual earnings). Thus academic activities are valued primarily in terms of success at achieving such payoffs.

It is difficult for educators and activists, including teachers and scholars in rhetoric and composition, to engage the debate on the shape and value of our work in terms set by these representations of the economic. But as Katherine Gibson and Julie Graham (Gibson-Graham 2006) have argued, without discounting the effectivity, on the ground, of dominant "capitalocentric" discourse maintaining capitalism as an undifferentiated and all-powerful force, it is also possible to know the economic differently, outside that framework, by recognizing and investigating the diversity of economic activities and practices flourishing unrecognized by that discourse and (thereby) the vulnerability, and invalidity, of hegemonic representations of capitalism. For, as Gibson-Graham observe, noncapitalist activities are invisible only because "the concepts and discourses that could make them 'visible' have themselves been marginalized and suppressed" (xli).

Following such a strategy, while chapters in this collection do engage dominant economic discourse by investigating processes of commodification, conditions of labor, models of production, managerial measures, and so on and contend with changing articulations of writing in an age of globalization, digital communication, and late capitalism, the work gathered here refuses to accept unchallenged the terms and ideologies of dominant economic discourse for the production and valuation of writing and rhetorics. Instead, the collection approaches the economic as plural, contingent, and political, exploring the ways in which dominant ideologies of the economic obscure the full value and meaning of the work of writing and its teaching and study. Following Pierre Bourdieu's (1986) model of the interdependent and contingent relations among various forms of capital, the chapters in this collection explore the complex dynamics of economies by which writing, rhetoric, and composition both are produced and contribute to producing specific, contingent values.

The influence of Bourdieu's (1977, 1984, 1986, 1991a, 1991b) conception of symbolic capital linking the economic with the cultural, and specifically with language practices, is evident in the convergence of two traditions in the scholarship of rhetoric and composition: first, a long-standing tradition of attending to the economics, and economic imbalances, of writing programs, college admissions, social class, and labor, including concerns with the status of rhetoric and composition as an academic field; and second, a tradition of approaching and understanding the writing undertaken within as well as outside such programs as a material social practice.[1] *Economies of Writing* addresses this convergence explicitly. The chapters assembled here consider how specific forms of language and writing (broadly defined), writing pedagogies and programs, and public rhetorics can be understood in terms of economies that are inherently political rather than politically neutral, self-producing, and self-sustaining structures.

While many of the chapters in the collection trace threads connecting economies of writing across educational, professional, and civic contexts, the book is divided into sections coalescing around four unifying themes. Part 1, "Institutional and Disciplinary Economies," considers the circulation of value at the level of the writing program, the college catalog, and the discipline as a whole. Tony Scott's account of writing program assessment at a large public four-year university (chapter 1) addresses the difficulties of attempts to effect meaningful institutional change within daunting constraints: how, Scott asks, can a writing program administrator design and implement modes of assessment that value the labor of both instructors and students while simultaneously satisfying larger institutional and accreditation-agency imperatives that tend to commodify and dehumanize those very actors? Katie Malcolm reports on the efforts of part-time instructors at a Seattle community college to pilot an innovative redesign of the institution's approach to basic writing—efforts, she argues, that demonstrate how "the most insidious economic structures of our institutions can become conduits for their own change" (chapter 2). Continuing this attention to the intersections among ethical, economic, and pedagogical considerations, Steve Lamos (chapter 3) articulates ways in which the field might counter the competitive and rhetorical pressures that for-profit institutions have introduced in recent years by attending to the "dwelling work" that face-to-face writing instruction allows (and that might be done more effectively). Joan Mullin and Jenn Fishman (chapter 4) address a conflict between the principles and practices espoused within the microeconomy of writing studies, on the one hand, and, on the other, the ideological valuation of labor in academe's macroeconomy. They pose as an intervention in that conflict the Research Exchange Index—an expanded and democratized form of peer-reviewed digital publication that incorporates research projects undertaken by individuals in a range of positions within postsecondary settings. Finally, shifting the scope of analysis from writing studies to English as a composite discipline, James Zebroski (chapter 5) invites us to think through the political economy of English to better grasp rhetoric and composition's necessary, albeit fraught and uneven, interdependencies with literary studies and creative writing.

Part 2, "Economies of Writing Pedagogy and Curriculum," sharpens the focus brought to bear in part 1 by addressing the ways writing and, more broadly, language itself circulate within postsecondary classrooms and curricula. The opening chapter by Anis Bawarshi (chapter 6) considers the complex economies at work in knowledge transfer and their implications for the valuation, or revaluation, of the first-year composition course in light of its charge to produce writing skills with exchange value as commodities ostensibly transferable to sites outside that course (in the disciplines and the workplace). The chapters that follow explore recurring concerns in writing studies through the framework of the interplay of a range of economies of value. Yuching Jill Yang, Kacie Kiser, and Paul Kei Matsuda (chapter 7) consider the matter of teacher identity, especially as expressed and assessed in terms of intersecting linguistic as well as ethnic, regional, and gender markers, through contrasting case studies of teachers' and students' negotiation of status and authority in undergraduate writing courses. Kelly Ritter (chapter 8) uses the contradictory relations between assumptions of writing ability as a means of achieving economic capital and writing ability as a marker of cultural capital to better grasp the difficulties faced by those arguing for writing instruction at the graduate level. Samantha Looker (chapter 9) turns our attention to the economics of assigned handbooks in writing programs and the ways such handbooks' commodifications of knowledge about writing not only obscure the concrete labor at the heart of writing instruction but, by virtue of their economic cost, contradict pedagogies meant to engage that labor. Finally, in "Psychoanalysis, Writing Pedagogy, and the Public" (chapter 10), T. R. Johnson recuperates psychoanalytic theory—all but banished in recent years from mainstream work in writing studies—to reconfigure the field's modes of engaging with the wider communities that surround colleges and universities, to earn more support from those communities, and to counter the "therapeutic" economic models of writing instruction directed at maintaining a rationalist model of individual production, posing as an alternative an emancipatory model that allows for exploration of the contingency of use-value through attention to the particular and local.

The investigations that appear in Part 3, "Economies of Language and Medium," consider the economic implications and complications of linguistic and technological boundary crossing. Rebecca Lorimer Leonard's chapter (chapter 11) uses two case studies, both of multilingual women pursuing nursing degrees in the United States, to examine the shifting cultural and economic value that attaches to their literate resources as they move through a range of professional and social contexts. Scott Wible (chapter 12) looks at the economic and social costs and benefits of language policy—specifically, the requirement to provide linguistic access for individuals with limited English proficiency—within the United States' complex healthcare systems, arguing for the need to hold the economic costs of public translingual writing in tension with the need to protect and promote social, cultural, and political rights. In "Web 2.0 Writing as Engine of Information Capital" (chapter 13), Christian J. Pulver locates Web 2.0 writing in a late-capitalist mode of information production, arguing that the exchange values created by Web 2.0 technologies are always in dialectical relation to their use-values, creating tension among digital literacy practices, user-created content, and commodified data. Jay Jordan (chapter 14) continues these inquiries into the economies of digital writing production, using the emergence of international domain names (in nonroman script) to explore the continuing, if continually evolving, dominance of English-language features, and thereby the economic value of English, in the production and formulation of web pages and websites despite efforts at establishing and expanding non-English-medium means of digital site location, production, and circulation.

The three chapters that make up the collection's final section examine writing economies within and across a range of public domains. Donna LeCourt (chapter 15) offers a thematic bridge between previous chapters' digital considerations and an orientation toward the public sphere by reconfiguring Habermasian theories of public deliberation for use in an analysis of web-based communications. Against imagining digital public spheres purely in terms of the circulation of voices and texts, LeCourt argues for recognizing our immaterial labor not simply as grist for the web's information economy but also as a potential means of exercising civic agency through direct influence on markets. Jason Peters (chapter 16) examines the ways an economy of writing coheres out of patterns in the circulation and interplay of texts and scripts surrounding public debate over the cleanup of a Rhode Island brownfield, arguing that translation might serve as "a kind of currency exchange" within that economy to make environmental activism and intervention possible. Phyllis Ryder's "Democratic Rhetoric in the Era of Neoliberalism" (chapter 17) offers a broader meditation on the relation between the economic and civic spheres, presenting an optimistic, though hardly anodyne, inquiry into the ways in which participatory democracy might prevail despite the pressures exerted by what she terms "a market-infused attitude toward public decision making." Insofar as speaking and writing operate within—indeed, work to constitute—various overlapping economies, Ryder reminds us, we cannot afford to concede that their injustices and inequities are inevitable. In her afterword, Deborah Brandt brings the collection to a close by situating it in the larger context of Dell Hymes's (1974) concept of speech economy as well as Bourdieu's (1977) notion of the economy of linguistic exchanges, reminding us how these notions of the economic are at their root material and emphasizing the consequent need to recognize that language is both made from and integral to reworking the economic.

Taken together, these chapters are meant to extend and deepen broader debates concerning the teaching, administration, research, and public import of writing in a globalizing age. By expanding the range of points of departure for studying political economies of writing as course subject, pedagogy, technology, and social practice and by attending to local, or immediate, manifestations of such economies (e.g., a particular institution's writing program) in terms of larger economies and pressures, the arguments of individual chapters and the collection as a whole work to render the economic as a necessary point of departure and contention for the field. While rhetoric and composition scholarship includes longstanding traditions attentive to particular ways of inflecting the economic in addressing writing and its teaching, those traditions compete with, and are vulnerable to being dismissed as, subfields distinct from mainstream scholarship in the discipline—scholarship that sets aside matters of the economic, however understood, as at best secondary to what is thought to be the field's primary concern with rhetoric, stylistics, language, cognition, and teaching methods. *Economies of Writing* insists, instead, that these concerns are always and inevitably participants in, shaping and shaped by, political economies in their concern with forms of valuation, production, and circulation of knowledge; with labor; and with capital. In this insistence, and in the specific demonstrations individual chapters provide of its necessity, *Economies of Writing* seeks to contribute to the field's understanding of and ways to address the seemingly perdurable economic unease of its work.

Note

1. See for example Berlin 1988; Bousquet, Parascondola, and Scott 2004; Brandt 2005; Brodkey 1992; Downing, Hurlbert, and Mathieu 2002; Fox 1990; Haas 1996; Horner 2000; Schell 1998; Scott 2009; Selfe 1999; Shor 1997; Soliday 2002; and Stygall 1994.

PART I

Institutional/Disciplinary Economies

1

THE POLITICS OF VALUATION IN WRITING ASSESSMENT

Tony Scott

Two contrasting situations have become familiar tropes of writing program administration and writing assessment scholarship in our field. Chris Gallagher (2009, 29–30) opens an article about assessment in *Writing Program Administration* with the description of one scenario in which university administrators are seeking to impose standardized assessments on a first-year writing program. The administrators are tying assessment to efficiency, centralized quality control, and accountability. Looming ominously within the scene is the Spellings Commission Report, which uses crisis rhetoric to call for an overhaul of higher education that has efficiency and accountability (typically code for mandated large-scale assessment) as central elements; also looming is the testing/textbook/curriculum industry, which has become an important, politically active driver of state-imposed assessment mandates on higher education across the country. After presenting this daunting scenario, Gallagher offers a contrasting scenario in which the writing program administrator (WPA) is respected and placed in a position of agency. The empowered WPA in the more positive scenario is recognized by interdisciplinary colleagues and higher-level administrators for expertise in writing, and she is initiating informed, democratic assessment practices with teachers that have positive effects in classes across campus (30).

Cindy Moore, Peggy O'Neill, and Brian Huot open an influential article in *College Composition and Communication* with similarly contrasting situations. In the first, a dean initiates contact with a WPA to seek advice about assessment in a writing-across-the-curriculum initiative. Moore, O'Neill, and Huot (2009) see this as an important development for its "implied message about the potential role of the composition director in the broad-based assessment this dean is beginning to imagine" (108). As with Gallagher's more positive scenario, here the WPA is in a position of power that comes from institutionally recognized expertise in

DOI: 10.7330/9781607325239.c001

both assessment and writing. She is not only able to shape how writing is conceived and assessed in the writing program, she is also able to shape assessment policy across campus. The article then describes contrasting, negative scenarios, which, the authors acknowledge, are common enough to have become established lore in the field. Here, assessments are imposed from outside, and WPAs are forced to work within narrow parameters that offer little autonomy for the writing program and little control over how scores will be used (108–9).

The problem posed in both articles is, How we might do assessment constructively, responsibly, and in a way consistent with current scholarly understandings of writers and writing, under circumstances not *yet* of our making? The responses to the problem are nearly always individualistic and focus primarily on the actions, rhetorical acumen, and agentive scope of the WPA, who represents the seemingly unified interests of an entire writing program. A minimum requirement is that the WPA learn about assessment. Moore, O'Neill, and Huot (2009) advocate a fairly deep and rigorous knowledge that includes understanding of complex conversations in psychometrics and educational measurement. Gallagher (2009) advocates a perhaps more familiarly composition-situated expertise that combines a current understanding of writing pedagogy with a general understanding of technical concepts in assessment. Both envision responses to assessment challenges that involve a rhetorically adept WPA who, lacking institutionally conferred agency and expertise in writing education, must create the conditions for it through the power of persuasion.

The trope of the can-do, rhetorically savvy, resourceful WPA holds its own place in the WPA scholarship. In her award-winning monograph, *The Activist WPA*, Linda Adler-Kassner (2008) offers frameworks WPAs might use to build relationships and coalitions across campuses and beyond to secure resources. While the techniques are drawn from activism, the purposes to which they are put are hardly radical—to create the conditions for a responsible and effective writing program. Kelly Ritter (2006, 61) similarly advocates that WPAs go public, outside of institutional structures, to gain a "hard-fought" authority not conferred institutionally and to secure seemingly basic operational resources. She advocates negotiating and building consensus with a broad swath of people—upper-level university administrators, regional WPAs, trustees on the school board, feeder institutions, high schools, and state boards of higher education. All of this work is to happen, one imagines, in addition to the demanding day-to-day work of actually administering a writing program.

What are the conditions that have led WPAs to envision this superbly skilled, tireless, and self-sacrificing professional paragon whose primary goal is to overcome considerable institutional friction—only to responsibly do what the institution mandates? How does the function of WPAs as skilled negotiators and assessment experts relate to the agency and conditions of the TAs and contracted part- and full-time non-tenure-track instructors who teach most writing classes? Why, when so many first-year writing programs aren't regularly resourced at minimally responsible levels and in a time of austerity in higher education, is there such a strong push at state and federal levels to mandate writing assessments? In this chapter, drawing on my experiences with designing and implementing program assessments as a WPA, I further examine the political economic implications of large-scale writing assessment and how it relates to management/labor dynamics in composition. Though technical expertise in assessment is certainly important, so too is critical understanding of the persistent political economic ordering functions of assessment. I argue that a vital but largely missing element of the assessment scene in the scholarship involves labor struggle, or how assessment functions as a means of misrepresenting and ordering the labor of teachers and students through controlling the terms of its valuation. The push to make writing labor (teaching and composing) a commodity, an exchangeable unit divorced from material situations and laboring bodies, extends from a neoliberal political economic ideology that seeks economization of all human relations according to a singular model of efficiency, competition, and concentrated accumulation. I argue that large-scale writing assessment mandates function as a means of making the terms of labor invisible through shifting the focus from the qualitative to the quantitative, from multiplicity to singularity, and from the agentive exercise of professional expertise to the ordered achievement of symbolic outcomes.

DIFFERENT REPRESENTATIONS, DIFFERENT ORDERS

In *Testing Testing: Social Consequences of the Examined Life*, Allan Hanson (1993) argues that assessment is ubiquitous in contemporary Western life because it serves as a means of imposing order and discipline. Hanson describes practices as varied as medieval witch tests, drug tests, polygraph tests, and standardized achievement tests that help to maintain order through enforcing and clarifying culturally/politically sanctioned categories. Testing therefore serves to create boundaries, hierarchies, and representations according to the dominant assumptions of a time and place.

I offer another WPA assessment scenario drawn from my past experience, one I will describe with emphasis on how it represents and orders labor.[1] As an accreditation review approached at a large, public university in the Southeast, a dean was placed in charge of assessment across all colleges and units. The university had an assessment officer who, in coordination with the dean, developed an interpretation of the requirements of the accreditation body. Based on that interpretation, a set of assessment guidelines and a reporting process were developed. As WPA, I was told to design and implement my own assessment of the writing program. However, we were required to use formalized procedures designed to respond to accreditation reporting guidelines, and all assessing units were required to report using the same form.

This requirement was important because the form was not philosophically neutral. It framed assessment in terms of deficit location and diagnosis at the programmatic level and it reflected an objectivist perspective on measurement (a copy of the reporting form is included in Appendix 1.A). The ordering "story" the form is designed to create is that

- We have deficits in teaching in the program occurring across classrooms.
- Those deficits can be identified and quantified through the reliable evaluation of students' texts, where they will manifest in aggregate.
- Those deficits can be remedied programmatically, and the results of the remedy should show in the next round of assessment. The program structure is such that this instrumental action is possible.
- What we value in student writing and how we value it is necessarily constant over time. If we don't maintain the same stated outcomes, and the same means of measuring those outcomes, there is no means of comparison between assessment years, no way of tracking progress or regression. So the assessment mandate also requires stasis. We must close the discussion of what we value and how we assess: in this endless growth model, the premium is on comparison and directed change over years.
- Assessment is positivistic and objective. Through sound measurement and adjustment, we will be able to make verifiable progress toward a defined notion of perfection in student performance (and yet perfection remains outside of what the reporting form allows programs to claim).
- Language use can be extracted from the messy varieties of everyday utterances (*parole*) and seen and measured as it relates to a targeted, context-transcendent system (*langue*).
- The program is organized in a way that enables it to be honed by the administrator to address deficits effectively. So the assumption is also that there is a stable and professional teaching cadre with adequate administrative support for emphasis and focus.

My colleagues and I recognized in the approval and reporting process the "accountability" rhetoric that has become a central platform of national educational policy and instrumental in establishing the pervasiveness of testing in K–12 education. Objectivist assessments align with a labor model that technocratizes teaching and writing, seeking to convert it to measurable, manageable units. The assessment mandate compelled us toward methods of assessment that countered our constructivist understanding of all acts of reading, writing, and learning as socially situated and our understanding that standards are ideologically contended and socially produced.

Our requests for funding to develop a qualitative assessment were turned down (we were only given enough funding to pay scorers during scoring sessions). Fortunately, in a competitive process we secured a program-development grant to conduct a constructivist assessment with substantial qualitative elements that built on the dynamic criteria mapping (DCM) model developed by Bob Broad (2003). This model seeks to include teachers in every phase of the assessment, including the development of the assessment standards. While it generated aggregate numbers to satisfy the institutional requirement, the model was designed to be primarily descriptive rather than evaluative, a means of doing research on teaching and writing in our program and then using the findings to discuss the variety of practices and values that were present.

However, we still had to report out using the required form. The process we developed for the assessment had elements we could embrace: it helped us to foster deep, informed discussions among a portion of the writing faculty about what we value in writing, and it gave us the opportunity to collect, describe, and discuss the types of writing students were doing across the program. Nevertheless, the broader administrative process at the institution—how it solicited, circulated, and sought to use scores—remained unchanged and was philosophically incongruous with the view of writing education we sought to promote within the program. Regardless of how we performed the assessment, the administrative process converted the labor of teachers and students—which we qualitatively described and discussed in the local assessment—into flattened signifiers, a set of singular numbers that related to simply stated outcomes.

Below is the required set of numbers solicited within the process: an overall score accompanied by scores in five categories that aligned with the stated learning outcomes of the writing program. These numbers were obtained from a statistically significant sample of students' writing.

Overall Score	*Rhetorical Awareness*	*Development*	*Purpose/ Writerly Ethos*	*Content*	*Technical Accuracy*	*Overall Average*
2.95	2.9	2.75	3.5	2.9	3.2	2.95

This representation was produced by the reporting requirements and circulated as a true and objective portrait of student learning in the first-year writing program.[2] The representation, and the circumscribed method through which it was reported, depicts a program in which there is agreement on what good writing looks like; it has been measured competently, and the program is functioning adequately. Proficiency in this assessment was designated as 2.5, so we seemed to be doing better than the baseline. Administrators got an assessment that satisfied our accreditation body; there was no reason for concern and no obvious impetus for greater investment of resources.

Now I offer another set of numbers, another way of representing the writing program that originated from another set of values and another ideology of labor. As we conducted this assessment, we were also steadily arguing that the writing program was substantially underresourced. The table below presents a different portrait of the writing program at the time of the assessment.

Total number of sections of first-year writing for the year	*272*
Percentage of sections in the program taught by part-time teachers on one-semester contracts	58%
Amount part-time faculty were paid per course	$2,000
Amount of funding set aside annually for part-time benefits	$0
Average annual turnover of part-time faculty	31%
Average amount of experience of part-time faculty in the program	< 3 years
Percentage of all instructors teaching in the writing program in this assessment year who were teaching in the program during the prior assessment year	< 50%
Designated annual budget allotment to the first-year writing program for professional development	0
Number of tenure-line faculty who taught in the first-year writing program during the assessment year	0
Number of tenure-line faculty getting release time to administer the program	1

The second table portrays a program that is likely struggling, if not in disarray. Most of its teachers are working under exploitative terms; they are not very experienced, and they are turning over at a high rate. The administrative structure involves one tenure-line faculty member. Professional development is undersupported, with no guaranteed annual allotment. There is no ethical means of compelling most instructors to participate.

The first representation was generated in response to a mandate that carefully constrained what is reported and how. The second representation was not mandated by any reporting mechanism. Indeed, even outside of the assessment there was no established requirement to compile any of these numbers, and there was no established pathway to report them. Through focusing narrowly on the assessment of students' work (which was removed from the situations of its production) according to a handful of outcomes, the first representation created an order in which the onus of action was solely on the teachers and the WPA, carrying the underlying assumption that any deficits result from inadequate job performance rather than systematic institutional neglect; the second representation eroded the credibility of the assessment numbers as an indicator of the success and adequacy of the program structure and put the onus on the institution to create the professional conditions for success.

THE POLITICAL ECONOMICS OF ASSESSMENT

I want to turn now to explain some of the political economic logics at play in large-scale writing assessments like this one, and I will start with value. *Value is a noun.* In its noun form, a value is a property of something that can be expressed as an abstract signifier. The categories we use to assess writing are values but so also are the symbolic markers we produce. The noun form is the expression of *exchange value.* Some important characteristics of the noun form of value (*a* value) are its abstraction, its transferability, and its transcendence of the situations of production. We can assign an essay a 3 on a five-point scale, but the essay is not the 3. In terms of the assessment, the essay is a material object with rhetorical *use-value* that doesn't have any exchange value in circulation, but the generic value assigned to it, the 3, does.

When we assign values to students' writing work we enter it into a closed economy of exchangeable signifiers. The relationship between valuation of writing and valuation of material commodities is parallel.

A student text = 3
A pair of jeans = $50.00

A unique piece of writing with use-value produced under singular conditions is given a generic exchange value that exists within an ordered economy of values.[3] Likewise, a pair of jeans produced by real people under material terms is given an abstract exchange value for sale, represented in cost. This cost connects the commodity to an ordered system, an abstract economy of exchangeable values, and the terms of production are obscured.

When writing is produced for some purpose beyond a grade, but is also commodified through the assignation of a signifier within an established system of valuation, it becomes a contradictory unit of use-value and exchange value. Which brings me to the next point. *Value is also a verb*: it is material enactment. In assessment, valuation is a socially situated, ideologically shaped act performed by real people in specific circumstances. We value when we respond to work, when we grade work, and when we assess work on a large scale. The dual function of value as abstract signifier on one hand, and on the other as material labor performed by human beings, merits more focus. As assessments create economies of value, they create orders according to political economic ideologies that create tensions and contradictions between abstraction/ exchange value and materiality/use-value.

Much of Marx's (1990, 1993a) most important and influential work centers on his "labor theory of value," which describes the relationships among money, value, and commodities. The labor theory of value can help shed useful light on how large-scale assessments often function in academic institutions. In a classic, liberal theory of value, the basic formula for the relationship between money and commodities is expressed as M > C > M, where money (M) is exchanged for a commodity (C) in an act of purchase: M > C. Then that commodity is sold again for money: C > M.

Marx (1993a) points out that through M > C > M, something mysterious, seemingly even magical, happens to value: the value invested in the beginning of this process can increase or decrease by the end. So the M in the formula of exchange is not constant. In fact, an increase of value in this exchange, the creation of surplus value, is at the very heart of capitalist economics. This is a part of what is called *the magic of the marketplace,* and it looks no less miraculous than transubstantiation: as though it is invested with its own life and natural reproductive powers, money somehow creates more money. It defies elementary logic: from nothing comes something. This seems magical because at first glance market valuation seems to be based on equivalent exchanges. At the moment money is exchanged for a commodity, M1 > C, the money and the commodity, by market definition, have the same value: M1 = C. A chair costs $150: $150 purchases a chair. However, the chair can then be sold at a different value: C > M2; therefore C = M2. Someone can purchase chairs at $150 in one time and place, then sell them for $250 at another time and place.

Marx (1993a) uses this analysis of exchange as a cornerstone of much critique, but he was not just a quantitative researcher. Qualitative inquiry into terms of production and exchange enabled Marx to follow *values* through actual material processes of *valuation*, describing what is so often obscured in a liberal political economy. Marx didn't just work at the level of abstraction and representations of surplus (input and outcomes); he worked to describe the materiality of labor and *how* surplus is realized. This description is what makes Marx's theory of value a labor theory of value.

In capitalist economies, human beings sell their labor for money, and human time and energies become exchangeable commodities. Marx devised a labor theory of value to recognize that human labor power (LP) plus the material terms of production (MP) are included in the commodity.

M1 > C **[LP + MP]** > M2

In summary, the model of classic liberal economics seems to create the magic of increased value, of money somehow creating more money, because it emphasizes inputs and outputs, and its representations keep the terms of production and valuation (human labor) out of the equation. The focus is on the signifiers of values, the nouns, and not on valuation and the ongoing, ideologically driven and messy processes and terms of production. Our periodic individual retirement account (IRA) reports, for instance, may show steady long-term increases in symbolic indicators on tables, but nothing in the representations encourages us to understand how the surplus that leads to our investment gains is generated. Unless you believe in magic, though, capital does not increase in value on its own.

As a researcher of how labor relates to value, Marx painstakingly documented the terms of labor in nineteenth-century industry that are systematically ordered out of the liberal economic formula: the exploitation of children, working conditions that maimed and sometimes killed people and often took years off of their lives, conditions that kept people working long hours at wages that never enabled them to accumulate capital and sometimes didn't even enable them to acquire adequate nutrition or housing.

Valuation in assessment performs a similar function. Assessments create constrained representations of quality that render invisible many of the factors crucial to quality, such as the maintenance of a stable cadre of writing teachers who have professional status and benefits, are credentialed in the field in which they are teaching, and are supported within a professional-development structure that enables them to innovate and grow in relation to research. Through reducing valuation to the measurement of a handful of traits in students' work, large-scale writing assessments in higher education are used to create the deception of more for less.

DEMOCRATIC ASSESSMENT AND ORDER

Over the past decade, Bob Broad's (2003) innovative dynamic criteria mapping method has been very influential in writing assessment. Rightfully so: we drew heavily on the DCM model in the design of our assessment and were impressed with how it can make assessments meaningful for teachers and thus actually enhance pedagogy through the way it uses qualitative research methods. DCM assessments don't appeal to universal values through employing standard rubrics but rather conduct systematic qualitative research that surveys the faculty who work at the site of the assessment to ascertain their perceptions of what should be valued in writing. They then seek to foster a degree of local consensus at sites concerning what will be favored in the assessment of students' drafts. Students' work is assessed based on whatever consensus has been built using this qualitative-research and consensus-building process. There is an important egalitarian spirit in these models, and they do get at least partially down into the messy material labor of valuation as teachers and administrators perform it. Yet, for all of its promise, there are also significant problems in the ways these assessments are sometimes deployed.

In *What We Really Value: Beyond Rubrics in Teaching and Assessing Writing*, and in the introduction to *Organic Writing Assessment*, Broad (2003, 2009) variously characterizes DCM as "democratic," "communal," and "transformative" in addition to "organic." These characterizations create the familiar contrast mentioned above between an externally imposed assessment and system of order and one that is locally conceived and affords agency for the WPA. Summarizing the strengths of his organic model with the help of assessment participants' (teachers') quotations, Broad writes (2003, 21), "Participants in a recent DCM process wrote of their experiences: 'Helpful to hammer things out with colleagues' and 'this was the kind of conversation [writing faculty] needed to be doing all along.' . . . DCM also leads to a sense of ownership and belonging on the part of writing instructors—including teaching assistants and adjuncts—who see that they have a strong voice and a crucial role in articulating their program's values. Plus DCM is fun—an intellectual, rhetorical, and pedagogical party." DCM is cast as an empowering process of democratic consensus building, a tool for promoting ownership and buy-in, even a means of fostering a sense of belonging. The problem is the implication that there is a "natural" order in writing programs that has not been contaminated by externally imposed assessments that should be honored. In Broad's (2009) collection *Organic Writing Assessment*, most descriptions of democratically minded DCM-initiated assessments erase asymmetrical power relations among administrators, teachers, adjuncts, and teaching assistants. The result is that most of the assessments don't challenge how writing is perceived outside of programs, nor do they bring any attention to the professional status and terms of work of the largely part-time faculties who are tasked with doing their own assessments. The pervasive use of part-time teachers becomes an elephant in the room remarkable for its presence as a natural given and its absence as a point of focus. Indeed, it could be argued that assessments democratized in this way are unintentionally serving as palliative managerial measures that divert attention from deep issues in terms of work through providing innocuous opportunities for expressing a voice.

For instance, in a chapter in *Organic Writing Assessment*, Barry Alford (2009) describes an assessment that is democratic but also seamlessly aligns writing pedagogy with the Academic Quality Improvement Plan for general education undertaken at his institution, a state community college. Here the democratic process initiated by the assessment is used to better meet the mandates imposed by upper administration—mandates designed to monitor and order teaching. Noting that many of the faculty at his college teach a five-course-per-semester load, Alford lauds DCM for its efficiency: because DCM is "grounded in the work students were already doing" and it is "based on the values that faculty already had," DCM is "critical to making assessment work in an environment where resources and time are already at a premium" (37). Because it enabled his program to develop standard rubrics (aligned with the large-scale assessment), Alford contends that the assessment gave adjuncts a voice in the assessment of their work and gave them a "concrete" means of understanding values and outcomes (46). A concrete means of understanding values and outcomes that came "organically" from them? This seems to be democracy put to the purpose of a managerial accountability prerogative.

Jane Detweiler and Maureen McBride likewise describe an organic and democratic process of consensus building that also meets an institutional mandate to, as they put it, show upper administration "the precise ways that the program appeared to be succeeding 'by the numbers'"

(Detweiler and McBride 2009, 65). In this description, the democratic and organic assessment is used by the WPA to prove success to upper-level administration. Detweiler and McBride reveal that they were operating with limited funding when carrying out their organic assessment when they write, "We involved our instructors in revising teacher resources. For example, we asked for volunteers for a working group to look at examples of assignments from high-scoring (4.5 to 5.5 range overall) portfolios. We chose only high-scoring portfolios to ensure that the assessment did not become a critique of teaching. We had six volunteers meet for a Saturday with only a small bribe of homemade snacks and potential CV lines" (71). While qualitative, "local" models have the potential to describe the pervasive problems that result from the underresourcing of first-year writing education, in these descriptions of DCM there is no mention of problems with preparation, terms of work or oversight, and turnover among writing teachers. There is almost no acknowledgment of the differentiation of status among teaching faculty. One wonders why Detweiler and McBride were "bribing" first-year writing teachers with the proxy wage of snacks and CV lines? Is it because they were unable to pay the instructors a real wage for their extra work? Why is the administration requiring proof of success without even paying for the assessment? In her critique of gender and labor exploitation in writing programs, Eileen Schell (1998, 40) writes about "psychic income," another form of proxy capital. Psychic income is the alleged privilege and status of teaching at a postsecondary institution and the gain of some temporary sense of professional status—one that isn't actually recognized or rewarded by the institution (see Scott 2009, 62–64). Most first-year writing faculty are part time and female, and women have traditionally been expected to do low-status work for psychic income. In my experience, people are willing to give up their free time to do unpaid work like this in writing programs because they are otherwise institutionally disenfranchised and are only able to compete for the types of low-level opportunities that would make such a line on a CV worthwhile. Moreover, many part-time instructors feel compelled to "volunteer" for unpaid work, in part because they are on short-term contracts and feel they must do whatever they can to ensure they continue to get work.

The language of democratization and the fostering of buy-in becomes, at the very least, complicated when we acknowledge the stark power differentials and exploitative practices that characterize so much of the scene of first-year writing instruction. Notably absent in descriptions of progressive, democratic writing assessments is any significant presence of tenure-line faculty, who typically don't teach the courses subjected to large-scale assessment (like first-year composition) and who usually require more than snacks or a CV line to be compelled to go into work on a Saturday to read portfolios. In these descriptions, democratic processes are put to use to meet administratively imposed assessment mandates designed to ensure quality without addressing the terms of labor and professional status of those who teach and perform the assessments. The democratic processes and qualitative writing assessments might be put to more activist, agentive uses. How might the scope and function of writing assessments change if the terms of labor became an essential component in how labor is represented and how performance is evaluated?

TOWARD A LABOR THEORY OF WRITING ASSESSMENT

In his critique of the relationship between colonialism and modernity, Walter D. Mignolo (2011) describes a "matrix of power" with two interrelating sides, which he argues poststructuralist and postcolonial perspectives never escape. One side of modernity is "constantly named and celebrated (progress, development, growth)"; the other side is "silenced or named as problems to be solved by the former (poverty, inequality, etc.)" (xviii). Mignolo goes on to describe how technology is joined with "free markets" and Western European- and American-sanctioned models of democratic governance in narratives in which growth and progress overcome crises. The rub is that it is so often the means of progress, development, and growth that cause the problems they are alleged to address. It is a self-perpetuating cycle of crisis production. The current wave of state-level "reforms" and the Obama administration's Race to the Top initiative build on the work of the Bush-era Spellings Commission. Claiming there is a crisis in higher education, the Obama initiative seeks a substantial restructuring of higher education through employing a raft of neoliberal efficiency measures that include curricular control mechanisms, privatization schemes, and plans to offer transcript credits based on assessed competencies rather than credit hours from completed classes. Of course, the 30-year decline in state spending per full-time enrolled student and the increasing reliance on contingent labor in higher education are not mentioned as factors in this "crisis."

Gallagher (2011, 45) very usefully connects the dots among government reforms, accountability, and the current concerted political effort to bring higher education more into alignment with neoliberalism.

> Accountability is the lever that will force U.S. higher education to recognize itself for, and start behaving as, what it is: both a competitor in a global market and itself a market in which individual institutions compete. Yet the commissioners leave "accountability" undefined, perhaps because it seems self-evident—and self-evidently good—within a neoliberal agenda. However, they frequently link the term to "transparency," suggesting that accountability consists of institutions furnishing evidence that they are good investments to those who foot the bill—that they add value to their (student-) products. In the report . . . we find repeated calls for a systematic, comprehensive, outcomes-based, and, above all, consumer-friendly database.

Unfortunately, the ways in which the field envisions WPA responsibilities and does writing assessment may be helping to facilitate this project. We do now have sophisticated constructivist assessment models that include democratic elements. The problem is that you can arrive at numbers that measure outcomes using a constructivist and democratic approach, but the numbers then circulate as objective truths about students' writing and the performance of teachers and the program—absent the qualitative elements that tell so much of the real story of postsecondary writing education. The terms of labor of writing and teaching—even the terms of labor for those who did the work of the assessment—are erased. The outcomes focus ignores a model for excellence in higher education based on professional expertise, research, and innovation and aligns with one in which drafts written in classes taught by seemingly any teachers working under any conditions meet acceptable thresholds for measurable outcomes in aggregate. The former, qualitative model puts emphasis on investment in the maintenance and support of a professional, credentialed cadre of teachers; the measurable outcomes-driven model aligns with a technocratized neoliberal model in which underpaid, often variously credentialed teachers are plugged into static curricula that focus primarily on those aspects of writing that can be measured reliably. Innovations that make assessment more democratic and consistent with contemporary understandings of literacy and learning don't escape the fundamental modernist narrative of narrowly determined growth through a regularization process that involves circumscribed goals, the commodification of labor and outcomes, and increased managerial control over intellectual work. I question the value of consensus-building processes that pave over the messiness on which consensus is built and arrive at neat, familiar orders that don't represent the materiality of writing and teaching labor or the ideologies of values. When the drive for consensus overshadows critical analysis and struggles for more resources and better terms of work, democratic processes can actually serve to bolster professionally and socially irresponsible structures and practices. Democracy becomes amelioration when alternative values are procedurally discarded and the truth behind the magic of more for less remains safely hidden.

The field must continue to work on developing qualitative assessment models but ones that are based on a labor theory of value and that incorporate the terms of labor into their notions of validity. These assessments should

- leave the question of what and how to value open from one assessment to the next, emphasizing dialogue about pedagogy and what is valuable in writing over the need to compare; Broad's DCM provides a good model for this;
- qualify any reporting of aggregate numbers as representing a singular set of values among others that might be equally legitimate; we did this in the assessment we implemented, in part by reporting two different sets of numbers from two different value systems so that no single number could be taken as the one accurate representation of performance in the program;
- include reporting of the terms of labor in the writing program, taking the opportunity of mandated assessment reports to publicize those terms, which we did as an addendum in the reports we filed; highlighting program facts like percentages of part-time faculty, lengths of contracts, levels of turnover, and allotments for professional development can undermine the mirage that many programs have the resources and stability to respond to issues raised in assessments from one assessment period to the next;
- preserve teaching and writing as creative, intellectual, collectively imagined endeavors; an assessment based on a labor theory of value recognizes that creativity is a basic right of all workers, and assessment cannot be used as a means of overdetermining labor or making its terms invisible.

Assessment issues are inescapably labor issues. Greater critical understanding of the politics of valuation and the political economic functions of assessments is crucial to achieving the educational ends assessment mandates purport to support but are too often designed to undermine.

Appendix 1.A

Reflection on the Continuous Improvement of Student Learning

1. List the changes and improvements your program planned to implement as a result of last year's student learning outcomes assessment data.
2. Were all of the changes implemented? If not, please explain.
3. What impact did the changes have on student learning?

Student Learning Outcomes (Knowledge of Skill That Is to Be Assessed)

Changes to the Student Learning Outcomes Assessment Plan: If any changes were made to the assessment plan (which includes the Student Learning Outcome, Effectiveness Measure, Methodology and Performance Outcome) for this student learning outcome since your last report was submitted, briefly summarize the changes made and the rationale for the changes.

Effectiveness Measure: Identify the data collection instrument, e.g., exam, project, paper, etc. that will be used to gauge acquisition of this student learning outcome and explain how it assesses the desired knowledge, skill or ability. A copy of the data collection instrument and any scoring rubrics associated with this student learning outcome are to be submitted electronically to the designated folder on the designated shared drive and hyperlinked to the Effectiveness Measure.

Methodology: Describe when, where and how the assessment of this student learning outcome will be administered and evaluated. Describe the process the department will use to collect, analyze and disseminate the assessment data to program faculty and to decide the changes/improvements to make on the basis of the assessment data.

Performance Outcome: Identify the percentage of students assessed that should be able to demonstrate proficiency in this student learning outcome and the level of proficiency expected. *Example: 80% of the students assessed will achieve a score of "Proficient" or higher on the Oral Presentation Scoring Rubric.* (Note: a copy of the scoring rubric, complete with cell descriptors for each level of performance, is to be submitted electronically to the designated folder on the designated shared drive and hyperlinked to the Effectiveness Measure above for each student learning outcome.)

Notes

1. These events happened at an institution at which I am no longer employed.
2. We did subvert this somewhat in our reporting. Because we didn't want any singular standard to stand as a universal set of values, we evaluated the students' work using two different perspectives and reported two sets of numbers as equally valid.
3. I realize that the degree to which writing produced in school settings has use-value varies and depends on how students' writing is solicited and circulated. Much writing produced in school doesn't have any circulation beyond the teacher and isn't produced for any clear purpose beyond performance for a grade. It is produced purely for exchange value, making the writing alienated labor. Also, though I don't have the opportunity to develop the point in this essay, *parole/langue* certainly parallels use/exchange, as the latter requires stability and is undermined by variety.

2

(RE)WRITING ECONOMIES IN A COMMUNITY COLLEGE

Funding, Labor, and Basic Writing

Katie Malcolm

> *The point is that structures, from wherever they derive, can and do serve as vehicles for change. Such structures have to be corrupted—when they can be.*
>
> Keith Gilyard (2000, 38)

Keith Gilyard (2000) stakes an important third position here between the heated debates for and against the abolition of basic writing that ignited the pages of the *Journal of Basic Writing* from the mid-to-late 1990s. While acknowledging Ira Shor's (1997) argument that basic writing courses do indeed support oppressive economic structures (e.g., labor inequality and delayed or obstructed graduation for many working-class students of color), Gilyard (2000, 41) adds that basic writing classes can also be sites of "challenge and change" to these institutional structures, particularly because they have an explicit commitment to creating access to higher education. Today countless courses offered throughout the United States deemed "basic," "remedial," "precollege," "developmental," or simply "noncredit" fit all too neatly into Shor's (1997, 99) depiction of the "cash cow" in which overpaying students and underpaid instructors toil away in meager conditions while the administration reaps immense financial profits. As these classes continue to pervade the landscape of higher education across the United States, Gilyard's call to "corrupt" the common structures of our institutions that limit the availability of college credit, meaningful reading/writing instruction, fair compensation, and equitable working conditions remains salient (Gilyard 2000, 38).

In this chapter, I describe a series of structural corruptions in an unlikely place: an open-admissions community college where part-time instructors make up around two-thirds of the English faculty;

DOI: 10.7330/9781607325239.c002

where students test into a myriad of non-transfer-credit "reading" and/or "writing" courses based on their scores on a multiple-choice placement exam; and where skills-based textbooks permeate the English curriculum at all levels. At this urban, state-funded community college (henceforth referred to as UCC), located in one of the most racially, ethnically, linguistically, and socioeconomically diverse neighborhoods in the Pacific Northwest, the dominant writing economy is embedded in the commodification of abstract skills underpaid instructors are expected to provide students in exchange for limited wages and benefits. As the narrative goes, after students acquire these basic skills, they can then move on to read and write successfully in their credit-bearing college courses. However, the complicated reality of UCC students' reading and writing practices has clashed with this fiction, and as a result, this writing economy has become vulnerable, in spite of its deep roots in our institution. As public and private grants incentivize increased graduation rates among state-funded colleges, particularly community colleges, the low retention and pass rates of these courses no longer provide a satisfactory product. By leveraging the rhetoric and resources of one such grant, two part-time faculty members, working with various staff and administrators, were able to actively abrade the unstable structures of this economy to increase access and equity for our students and ourselves. As a result, we achieved (1) a mainstreaming model for students in the highest "developmental" writing course, English 098; (2) the institution of a five-credit supplemental class for these students with one of the lowest course caps on record; (3) an increase in student pass rates from 70 percent to 93 percent over the first year of study; and (4) a rupture in the pervasive skills-based economy historically endemic to UCC.

These are no small feats at a place that can require students to take up to five noncredit classes *before* entering the college-level composition course, English 101. The sequence of English courses at UCC is pictured in Figure 2.1, the "English Flow Chart," which has been posted on UCC's advising website.

To the right of the vertical line separating the "Professional-Technical" sequence, Figure 2.1 shows that students who enter UCC with a university transfer goal select (or are placed into) one of three separate tracks, which the chart lists from left to right as (1) IEP (intensive English program) for international students; (2) ESL, which is primarily for immigrants; and (3) writing/reading. The last track is where UCC's English department is housed, and it is where students from the IEP and ESL tracks who hope to complete an AA or AS degree eventually converge—if

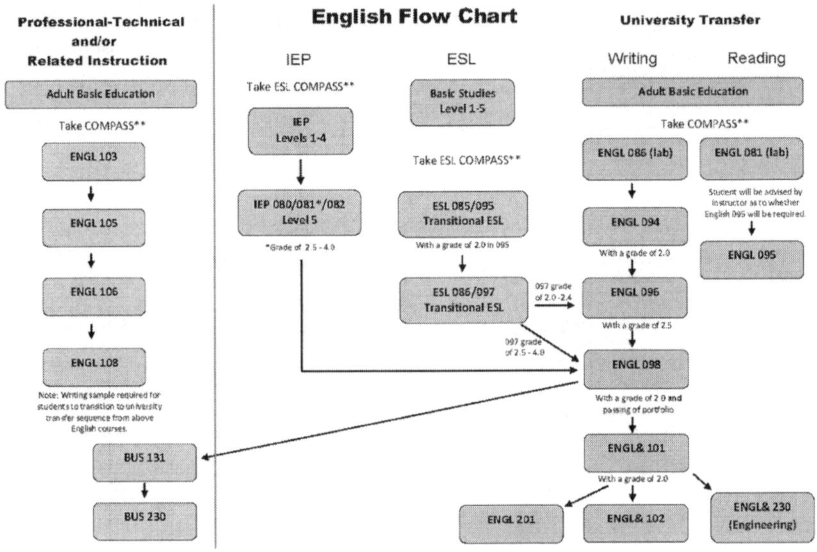

Figure 2.1. Urban Community College's "English Flow Chart" (2013).

they're lucky enough to make it that far—as the arrows pointing from their tracks into English 098 indicate. Within the writing/reading track, students place into separate writing or reading classes at various levels after completing any adult basic education (ABE) requirements, such as passing the GED. See Figure 2.2 for a focus on just this sequence.

This figure illuminates several of the structures upholding UCC's dominant writing economies. First, as the top of the chart shows, students are required to take the COMPASS test, a multiple-choice exam, to determine their placement in the academic-programs sequence after fulfilling any ABE prerequisites. COMPASS, like many computerized placement exams, has two divided English portions: a reading test that asks students to read a passage and then select a multiple-choice answer to a question about it, and a separate writing test, wherein students are given examples of supposedly effective topic sentences, incoherent ideas, and "errors" in a text and are asked to identify a correct answer about these. This instrument sends clear messages across the UCC campus about the dominant currency of college writing—for example, that finding the "right" answer to a text is more valuable than critical thinking. Scholars have invalidated these placement exams' measurements of students' actual abilities in a classroom (e.g., Royer and Gilles 2003); however, at UCC, instructors are often told that students' performance on the COMPASS trumps everything else.

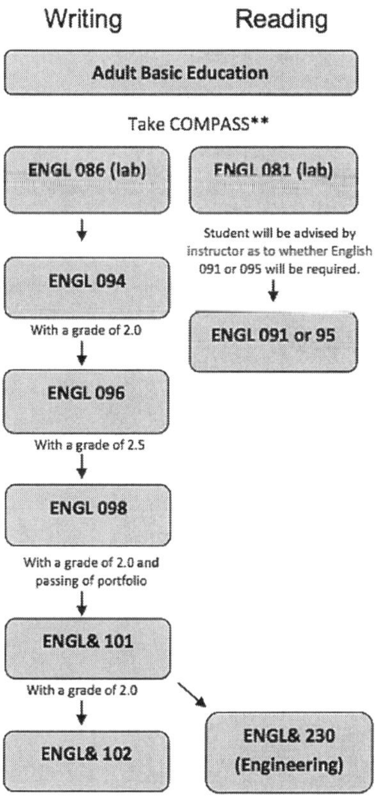

Figure 2.2. A close-up of UCC's classes in the writing/reading track.

Another problem Figure 2.2 highlights is the overwhelming number of sub-100-level classes students face if their COMPASS placement score is low. These are commonly referred to as *developmental* courses at UCC, and they carry the same tuition price as college-level classes but no transfer credits—a fact that is particularly unfortunate given that most of these students hope to advance to a four-year university. The classes are sequenced as small building blocks, historically with a focus on sentences and grammar skills in the English 086 lab and English 094, writing paragraphs in English 096, and writing five-paragraph essays in English 098. The separate reading courses focus on skills such as the survey, question, read, recite, review (often abbreviated as *SQ3R*) method.

Basic writing teacher-scholars (e.g., Bartholomae 1979; Rose 1981, 1985; Shor 1997) have long challenged the validity of skills-based classes for learning/practicing literacy successfully in academic contexts, but this curriculum has dominated UCC's developmental sequence since its inception. As outdated as the sequence may seem, these courses were designed—as were most during the growth spurt of open admissions—to help meet the perceived needs of students whose academic preparation differed from that of traditional college students. At the time of the last reported enrollment measure in 2012, available on UCC's website, 54 percent of UCC students were first-generation college students, 41 percent reported that their "family language" was not English, and 22 percent were working more than 40 hours a week while attending school. If we understand these students' needs in the terms the COMPASS placement test suggests, it makes sense that so many of them would need this breadth of skills courses. However, these classes have not proven to be helpful to our students. Data compiled for a Federal Title III grant (US Department of Education 2012), which I will discuss shortly, show that only 48 percent of students who tested into English 096, the paragraph class only two courses below English 101, made it into English 101 within *two years* at UCC. Here the cash-cow economics are undeniable; students pay tuition for a course that gives them no transfer credit and less than a 50 percent chance of helping them reach their goals for college-level enrollment within eight quarters.

Although alarming, this statistic would not surprise most basic writing teacher-scholars, particularly given Peter Dow Adams's (1993) now decades-old research shared in "Basic Writing Reconsidered." In listing the dangers of tracking students into remedial courses, Adams notes the "stigma" tracking imprints on the students' peers, teachers, and themselves; that students' demoralized feelings may result in poor writing; that they are denied the kinds of "role models" of "proficient" work and class behavior students in mainstream courses receive; and that "dumbed down" materials limit students' abilities to perform at a college level (23). In his study of students' placements and performance at Essex University, Adams found that students who somehow evaded their basic writing requirements passed the required mainstream course at Essex (English 101) at a higher percentage than their peers who followed their placement in the basic writing sequence (33). In addition, over half of the students who placed into the lower of the two basic writing courses at Essex never took any writing courses there at all (29). Although Adams's research shows remedial writing courses can do more harm than good, a number of community colleges, my own included, still require at least two "developmental" courses in their English sequence. At UCC, the idea that literacy "development" happens by first learning to write "correct" sentences, then paragraphs, then five-paragraph essays, has dominated for decades. However, the impetus of a Title III (US Department of Education 2012) grant motivated two part-time faculty members to disrupt this emphasis on abstract, skills-based instruction and instead funnel institutional resources into sponsoring the social and material practices of reading/writing at UCC.

FUNDING SHIFTS

In the fall of 2010, UCC received a federal Title III grant, awarded to nationally accredited schools that serve predominantly low-income students. The Title III grant is popular among community colleges; its web page on "Awards" (US Department of Education 2012) reports that 15 colleges from across the United States were rewarded hundreds of thousands of dollars each to design and implement new programs that would help "strengthen institutions." Like any funding, Title III comes with a barrage of political and bureaucratic hurdles, and one seemingly insurmountable obstacle at UCC was that our administrators applied for the grant without any faculty consultation, even on its required outcomes. Therefore, when faced with the grant's mandate to improve pass and retention rates, our overextended full-time faculty members, entrenched in teaching three classes and other duties, were not motivated to implement top-down-driven changes to courses they had spent decades developing and teaching.

In a shift from the typical labor dynamics at a community college, part-time faculty were therefore given an opportunity to develop and lead pilot projects under the grant's jurisdiction. With the opportunity to develop pilot courses, earn a $25 hourly stipend for all work related to the grant (including reading/reviewing scholarship, writing and reading e-mails, assembling course proposals, developing curriculum), and receive funding for professional development (including all expenses and meals paid for at 4Cs and other conferences), this project was appealing to my colleague Holly Gilman and me, and we became co-leads in facilitating the grant's projects related to English. Because we were the only two faculty members with graduate degrees in rhetoric and composition, the grant also gave us a chance to corrupt aspects of UCC's writing economy that devalued the work of our field; we now had funding to use scholarship historically overlooked or dismissed at UCC in curriculum and course development. Excited by the research we presented for possible pilot projects, our dean and grant-project directors told us we could "be creative" in how we designed and implemented any well-informed projects as long as they would potentially move students through our developmental sequence more quickly and with higher pass rates.

In addition to the troubling institutionalization of our "developmental" courses, Holly and I faced two other impediments to student success: first (as mentioned above), students in sub–100-level classes at UCC do not earn the college credits they need in order to receive an AA or AS degree and/or transfer to a four-year school. At least one study (Dryer 2007, 45) has shown that student performance in a class is largely determined by the attachment of graduation credit (or lack thereof). Second, the multiple-choice placement exam at UCC has been the sole assessor of students' needs. When Holly and I began working on the grant, several UCC faculty members were developing COMPASS prep courses, similar to ACT/SAT study classes, with the goal of helping students achieve higher test scores. Of course, these "prep" courses only increased the expenditure of valuable resources on an already costly and questionable instrument. Holly and I could not begin our work on the grant by challenging the institutionally embedded COMPASS outright, but we could begin with a small measure of directed self-placement by offering students in English 098, the highest developmental writing course at UCC, an optional mainstreaming alternative that would fulfill the Title III (US Department of Education 2012) grant's initiative to "improve student progression to college-level courses." Although it's only one course below English 101, institutional data show that English 098 generally has a 30 percent fail rate at UCC. One mainstreaming model we considered, immensely popular among community colleges today, is the accelerated learning program, ALP (2012), led by Peter Adams and fellow faculty members at the Community College of Baltimore County (CCBC). There, ALP allows students who receive a low score on their placement exam to volunteer to take English 101 *and* CCBC's highest basic writing course, English 052, in one semester. The same instructor teaches both English 101 and 052, and English 052 has a cap of only eight students to allow more individualized instruction, a sort of real-time experience of addressing difficulty in the context of their work in English 101.

Adams and his colleagues at CCBC have proven that this model is wildly successful for several reasons. First, students learn academic reading/writing practices while actually *practicing* academic reading/writing in English 101, so what they learn is situated in an immediate context (Adams et al. 2009, 60–61). Students are also earning college credit for their work in English 101, which helps them to move forward in their educational goals and take themselves seriously as college students (60). Finally, the small class size and curriculum allow teachers to spotlight the material conditions that can interfere with students' success, such as losing handouts, poor time management, or confusion about how to interpret an assignment (62–63). As Adams et al. contend, these challenges present greater obstacles to students' reading/writing success in English 101 than does their knowledge of writing conventions. Their research has disrupted the skills-based writing economy at CCBC, placing new value on understanding and meeting students' social and material needs in actual college writing courses.

With sensible theory, nationwide results, and seemingly easy importability (as the ALP does not require any new courses), ALP was a desirable model for us at UCC. One quality ALP lacks, however, is the complicated "thirdspace" component that underpins another model for mainstreaming: the Writing Studio alternative (cf. Grego and Thompson 1996, 2008; Tassoni and Lewiecki-Wilson 2005). While the Studio model *also* allows students who test into precollege courses to take English 101 and a small "support" class (also typically with a cap of eight students), the Studio course is not institutionally recognized as a "basic" or "developmental" course, and it is not hard linked to any particular English 101 class. The eight students in Rhonda Grego and Nancy Thompson's Studio course are typically enrolled in different sections of English 101, and their Studio teacher is usually not the English 101 teacher. This thirdspace configuration gives the Studio instructor an important opportunity to help students recognize and navigate the inevitable conflicts they experience as writers, which can be particularly important for students who feel that what they are learning about academic reading/writing (and/or their English 101 instructor) clashes with perceptions of their experiences or themselves. Because many of our students at UCC report experiencing this dissonance in English 101, offering a space separate from their English 101 classrooms seemed key to helping them voice and traverse these conflicts effectively.

The Studio course would also allow us to corrupt disturbing historical trends in the institutionalization of "developmental" reading/writing at UCC. According to Adams et al. (2009), CCBC's English 052 curriculum in the ALP model does resist skills-based instruction, but at UCC, nearly all of our institutional forces position English 098 as a writing-skills class. Although developing a brand-new course at UCC would mean extra work, starting from scratch seemed to be the most effective way to disrupt the dominant writing economies funding the inequities within our developmental sequence.

(RE)WRITING "NEEDS" AT UCC

Because we knew providing college-level credits would be one key to the success of our pilot, Holly and I began the design of our Studio as a 100-level, transfer-credit-bearing course. English 100 was an available college-level course number at UCC, so our dean began the process of claiming English 100 in the catalog. Our next steps were to determine how many credits English 100 would carry and to secure its small class size. I had two fears about making English 100 the one-credit Studio course typical in other schools. The first was in the long term sustainability of a single-credit class; one-credit classes can be all too easy to eliminate during times of budget crises and cutbacks (Malcolm 2011, 167–68). The second concern was about time, particularly in the already condensed, 10-week quarter system common in the Pacific Northwest. Most quarter-system classes carry five credits in place of the three-credit courses at schools on semesters. An additional complication was that any course carrying *fewer* than five credits is virtually unteachable for part-time faculty who don't want to take a pay cut because our contract prohibits us from teaching more than 10 credits in a given quarter. With only six out of our 18 English instructors employed full time, we couldn't design a course that less than a third of the faculty could teach. Holly and I proposed a five-credit class with a cap of 12 students to our administrators.

Even with research to prove that the small class size would make English 100 more profitable (ALP 2012), this issue became the toughest to negotiate with our dean and vice president. Until this point, the smallest class size in UCC's university transfer division belonged to our "developmental" writing courses, with 25 students. Our college-level composition courses have a cap of 28, and overwhelming class sizes have been a central issue in an ongoing battle between UCC faculty and administration. In this climate, our VP was simply unwilling to "set a precedent" by creating a new class with a cap lower than any other on the books; by his logic, this change would lead to an insurmountable disruption in the labor economy at UCC, which has maintained unwieldy class sizes for decades in the name of a never-ending budgetary crisis. English 100 would become a five-credit, college-level course with a class cap of 25. This outcome was not what Holly and I had hoped for, but it gave us a place to start.

Now that we had an institutional framework, we had to figure out what a five-credit Studio class with 25 students might look like. Because English 100 would carry the same number of college-transfer credits as English 101, we needed a curriculum with assignments and grades—again, unlike most Studio courses. However, this need provided us with an opportunity to develop an entire college-level course dedicated to highlighting what Grego and Thompson call the "invisible" aspects of composition instruction: establishing trust, attending to interpersonal relationships, and negotiating emotional/intellectual resources (Grego and Thompson 1996, 71–74). As Grego and Thompson argue, these invisible components consume just as much, if not more, of composition instructors' time and energy than correcting "errors" on student papers, but the structures of our institutions keep these aspects of our work hidden where they cannot be recognized or compensated (63). Holly and I hoped English 100 would help us redirect the writing economies at UCC to spotlight and respond to these historically concealed needs in our students. In doing so, we also hoped to shift an institutional understanding of writing instructors' labor from one of inculcating skills toward one that attends to the complex social and material aspects of reading/writing in academic settings.

The first 25 students who volunteered for English 100 were enrolled in the class for the first time in the winter 2012 quarter. In order to help these students articulate, reflect on, and successfully complete their work in English 101, Holly and I designed one-page weekly reflective essays, asking students to respond to prompts such as "What are you learning this week?" "What are you having difficulty with? How are you attempting to work through these difficulties, and where are you getting stuck?" and "What have been some of your successes so far in English 101 and/or English 100, and why do you think you have been successful?" We also used the reflective essays as an opportunity for students to investigate questions that arose throughout the quarter, such as "How do I use a quote?" "What makes a good thesis?" and "How do I stop writing so many run-on sentences?" To answer their questions, students consulted materials from their English 101 or 100 instructors and/or they searched online for reasonable answers, wrote about what they learned, and shared it with the entire class the next day. The latter helped us call attention to—and, as a class, negotiate—the inevitable conflicts between competing sources of information. The reflective essays were not graded based on "correctness" but on depth and thoroughness in response to the questions or prompts. Most importantly, they helped English 100 instructors to address students' invisible needs each week—which had more to do with time management, interpreting an essay assignment, or approaching their English 101 teacher than with understanding subject-verb agreement.

Although the reflective essays provided us with an opportunity to make attending to the social/material conditions of writing a college-level enterprise, our class size still set English 100 apart from the Studio with its cap of eight. To narrow this gap, Holly and I decided to make small-group work the second hallmark of English 100's curriculum. Usually, for two to three of our five hours a week, students worked in small groups in order to share, receive feedback, and collaborate on their work in English 101. To keep this time productive, another component of the English 100 course grade was devoted to group work. To achieve full points, students had to provide their group members with a readable copy of something they were working on in English 101 and a cover letter offering a detailed explanation of what they were sharing, what the purpose/goal of the assignment was, how it was being graded, and what, specifically, they wanted their group members to offer feedback on. Because the students were in mostly different sections of English 101 (and therefore unfamiliar with their group members' assignments), the cover letter was necessary for productive feedback. However, it also gave students a chance to engage with an assignment and its purpose beyond an English 101 teacher's in-class lectures/instructions and to reflect upon what each of them needed for success, given their current conditions as they worked on that assignment.

At the beginning of the quarter, students' cover letters usually requested "grammar help" (echoing their institutionally designated needs), but after practice and feedback from their group members, students began to articulate their writing needs in terms that constructed their work more productively. For example, the student who asked for "grammar help" on a one-page draft that had only two days to become a five-page essay quickly learned that "grammar help" did not assist him in completing the essay on time. For his next session of group work, the student asked for feedback on specific examples, details, and arguments he could add into his essay to meet the required page length. Consequentially, this student disrupted the dominant writing economies at UCC in two ways: (1) by resisting the idea that his primary literate needs were based solely on identifying grammar deficiencies, and (2) by deriving this shift from his own reading/writing experiences rather than explicit directions from an instructor or administrator.

Understanding the best questions to ask for feedback on their own writing also helped students offer productive guidance on their group members' work, another component of the English 100 course grade. When grading each other's feedback, English 100 students assessed how effectively their group members answered their own and their group members' questions and stated needs in the cover letter. Holly and I were nervous about not being able to participate actively in all of the small groups (as Studio teachers typically do), but we found that once we created a graded structure for effective group work, students did not need a teacher involved—we could usually stand back and listen from a distance as students discussed their work, then jump in when a group was lagging or the students had a question they were unable to answer themselves.

Although our first two quarters of the English 101+100 pilot were successful, with a 91 percent student pass rate in English 101 (compared to 70 percent in English 098), Holly and I feared the course would not be sustainable, for even with our curricular compromises to meet class-size demands, collaborating with 25 different students five days a week still became exhausting for all of us. When Holly and I expressed these concerns to our dean, to our astonishment he responded that we would have to lower English 100s cap—as he put it, "We don't want you to burn out from teaching this important class." Starting in its third quarter, the course cap in English 100 was lowered to 20 students. Twenty may still seem like a large size for a Studio-inspired course, but it is the smallest cap currently in existence within the university-transfer division at UCC, and two non-tenure-track faculty members were given the resources to create it. With 20 percent fewer students, we noticed a significant improvement in our energy when teaching English 100 during the following quarters.

Attending to both students' *and* instructors' social and material needs at UCC has paid off: after four quarters, 93 percent of the UCC students who enrolled in English 101+100 passed English 101, and more than half of those with a 3.0 (B) or higher. English 100 is now offered every quarter (with additional sections budgeted for the 2013–2014 year) and is taught by a variety of UCC instructors. The course has created ripples on the entire campus; excited advisors, students, and instructors of the pre-English 098 classes (including teachers in the ESL and IEL tracks) have reached out to Holly and me to learn more about this new opportunity for students to begin their college coursework more quickly. The students themselves also report being grateful—98 percent of them have reported feeling confident at the end of the quarter about their decision to take English 101+100 instead of English 098.

Although English 101+100 borrows extensively from ALP and Studio mainstreaming models, instituting English 100 with five college-level credits and a class size more comfortable for an anxious administration has allowed for a widespread corruption of the cash-cow and skills-based writing economies maintained by English 098 and other developmental reading/writing courses at UCC. I have never heard of a class like our English 100 at any other school—probably because it was created under very specific institutional circumstances that required acceleration, provided funding for research (giving Holly and me ample time to review different models of mainstreaming), and required design by part-time instructors compelled to resist institutional labels (such as *developmental*) to which we felt no allegiance. The future of the English 101+100 pilot is uncertain, of course, but new language and concepts have now been woven into the institution—in some cases replacing *developmental skills* with *foundational practices*; *universal* with *context based*; and *COMPASS placement* with *student agency*. This experience highlights that even (or perhaps especially) in the most despairing situations, the most insidious economic structures of our institutions can become conduits for their own change.

3

DWELLING WORK AND THE TEACHING OF WRITING

Responding to the Pressures of For-Profit Instruction

Steve Lamos

For-profit educational institutions have captured a large proportion of the undergraduate population in the United States, as much as 12 percent by some counts (Tierney 2011, 29), enrolling large numbers of diverse learners that include first-generation college students, students of color, and students with low incomes (Bennett, Lucchesi, and Vedder 2010). Proponents of for-profit institutions routinely attribute this rapid growth to an educational model rooted in the twin premises of standardization and outcomes assessment. For-profits routinely develop standardized curricula designed by a few "experts," deliver these curricula at scale using almost exclusively part-time teachers and tutors, and measure the outcomes of students' exposure to these curricula through various standardized measurements (Breneman, Pusser, and Turner 2006; Tierney 2011). Further, many for-profits cite standardization and assessment as the basis for claims that the undergraduate education they offer is not only different from but better than that offered by traditional not-for-profits. For instance, Andrew Rosen (2011), current chairman and CEO of Kaplan University, argues that "private-sector colleges may be better equipped to enhance learning outcomes" (138–39) than are traditional not-for-profit educational institutions simply because for-profits are prepared to offer "more standardization and more accountability" (133). At the same time, for-profits are offering increasing numbers of writing courses that seem to be shaping what not-for-profit writing teachers do: as Luana Uluave (2005, 121–22) points out, for-profits are "influenc[ing] the ways writing is conceived of as an academic subject for increasingly significant numbers of students, faculty in and out of the discipline of composition studies, and administrators."

DOI: 10.7330/9781607325239.c003

The rapid growth and increasing influence of for-profit institutions may make those of us teaching writing within traditional not-for-profit contexts feel a bit nervous. We certainly do teach writing in ways that serve a diverse student body, especially through our work with "basic writing" programs, ESL programs, writing centers, and the like. We also certainly do try to provide holistic and meaningful assessments of student writing, both in terms of product and process. But we might not always be documenting or publicizing the value of these activities in the same seemingly straightforward ways that for-profits are.

At the same time, we might also feel increasing pressures to revise our pedagogies to reflect for-profit values more fully. For instance, rather than tailoring writing instruction to the needs of diverse students or to the exigencies of linguistic and cultural difference within the classroom, we might feel strong pressures to standardize what we do while assuming concerns with diversity can be "outsourced" entirely to some external entity (e.g., a fix-it-shop-style writing center). Or perhaps, rather than providing significant and detailed feedback to individual students on their writing in the context of small classes, we might feel strong pressures to offer writing courses at scale—perhaps even as part of MOOC-based partnerships with Coursera, edX, or other for-profit companies—in ways ensuring that feedback and grading are left entirely to paraprofessionals or to students themselves. And we might also feel increasing pressures to conduct our classes in keeping with the tenets of "customer satisfaction" rather than critical literacy or engagement, especially as so many of us are increasingly employed as contingent faculty perceived to be wholly interchangeable with other (purportedly) semi-skilled teaching laborers.

Important to note, however, is that while for-profits may be growing rapidly, and while they may be offering increasing numbers of writing courses that challenge what we do as not-for-profit writing teachers, their claims regarding the superiority of for-profit educational offerings are increasingly being questioned. For instance, recent work by educational researchers David Deming, Claudia Goldin, and Lawrence Katz (2012), cited by the US Government Accountability Office during a recent investigation of for-profit educational efficacy, finds that the for-profit sector as a whole is failing to retain, graduate, satisfy, or employ its students at the same rate as not-for-profit institutions, even when student preparation levels and demographic factors are accounted for directly (Deming, Goldin, and Katz 2012). Specifically, this research demonstrates that for-profits graduate anywhere between 12 percent and 19 percent fewer BA students than do not-for-profits overall (158–59) while graduating

5 percent fewer students than not-for-profits enrolling identical student demographics (e.g., colleges serving large numbers of first-generation students) (159); that students in for-profit institutions are less satisfied with their educational experiences than not-for-profit students are (159); and that students from for-profits have lower rates of both post-graduation employment and loan repayment than do their peers from not-for-profit institutions, accounting for as much as 47 percent of all undergraduate loan defaults in the United States (153).

Given these troubling statistics, and given Pegeen Reichert-Powell's (2009, 669) recent assertion that we in not-for-profit composition are especially well positioned to consider issues such as retention, graduation, satisfaction, and employment in light of the "unique context of the writing classroom as an interface between students' past and future educational experiences," I want to offer a hopeful assessment here of the ways in which we in not-for-profit writing instruction can respond to the pressures being placed on us by for-profit institutions. Specifically, I argue that we in not-for-profit composition perform a good deal of important work foundational to effective and far-reaching undergraduate education in ways worth explicitly identifying and publicizing in the face of for-profit pressures.

THE PROMISE OF DWELLING WORK IN NOT-FOR-PROFIT COMPOSITION

To make my case, I turn first to Nedra Reynolds's (2004) notion of "dwelling" to theorize the pedagogical work—what I term here *dwelling work*—we commonly perform within not-for-profit writing courses. Reynolds defines "dwelling" as the process whereby diverse individuals (i.e., individuals whose bodies are marked by differences such as race, gender, sexuality, class, and so on) make choices about where, how, and how long to remain in and engage with particular material and discursive spaces (143). Reynolds further argues that, during the course of actively dwelling within particular spaces, diversely embodied individuals create "thirdspaces" from which to explicitly question hegemonic power structures (141). In an important sense, then, Reynolds insists dwelling requires creating and recreating social spaces in ways that seek justice for all those living, working, and learning within them. Furthermore, she implies strongly that dwelling is fundamental to educational effectiveness: if individuals' learning is to prove worthwhile, they must both dwell within educational spaces and seek to effect critical thirdspace-oriented change within and across these spaces.

The importance of Reynolds's conception of dwelling is further underscored by recent scholarship regarding the issue of transfer of writing and literacy skills and abilities from one setting to another. Admittedly, a good deal of recent scholarship concludes that transfer may not be occurring as often as we might hope: as David Slomp (2012, 83) suggests, many well-known composition scholars interested in transfer (e.g., Beaufort 2007; Smit 2004) conclude that "little evidence exists to support the idea that students are able to transfer knowledge about writing across diverse contexts." Recent work by Doug Brent (2012, 562), however, suggests that this contemporary transfer research may not yet have asked the right kinds of questions. He contends that much transfer research to this point has tended to provide its focal learners with "a surprisingly short time in which to learn relatively complex concepts" and then has quickly "expected [learners] to reproduce them in a situation and according to standards that are often extremely narrow and prescriptive." He finds that, as a result, this work has tended to conceptualize writing activities and skills as "modular entities that can simply be picked up from one situation and dropped down in another" (562) rather than as complex activities that can manifest across situations in a variety of ways. Or, to put things more simply, Brent finds that much contemporary work may not be finding evidence of transfer because it is not yet looking for the concept in the proper places or using the proper methodologies.

Brent (2012, 562) concludes that we need a view of transfer that can account for the ways in which "learners re-create new skills in new contexts by building on foundations laid down in earlier contexts." He therefore advocates that researchers investigate carefully how those interested in teaching writing and literacy attempt to foster particular mindsets within particular spaces—what he refers to as "transfer dispositions or 'habits of mind'" (563) that encourage students to think long term about themselves, their futures, and the work they need to do in order to be successful. He further advocates that researchers study "long-term immersion" within particular learning spaces as well as the creation of "microcultures that nurture particular learning dispositions" (563). Finally, he recommends that we conduct more research into the ways in which not-for-profit writing teachers effectively teach for transfer within specific spaces, particularly through the "explicit teaching of rhetorical principles" within a larger "complex rhetorical environment in which [students] must rapidly adapt to competing rhetorical exigencies" (590).

Brent's ideas about "dispositions," "long-term immersion," and "microcultures," as well as his insistence that teachers engage in "explicit teaching" of various sorts, relate directly to Reynolds's (2004) notion of dwelling. Brent insists, in effect, that transfer occurs when diverse learners are invited to dwell: that is, when they are invited to spend significant time within significant spaces while engaged in significant and challenging work (often without a clearly measurable endpoint in sight). He insists further that it is our responsibility as professional writing teachers to promote transfer through precisely such dwelling: to ensure, in other words, that diverse learners are simultaneously supported and challenged within the spaces where they are engaged in writing and literacy learning.

Brent's work also begins to suggest reasons why a standardized and outcomes-assessed curriculum of the sort routinely championed by for-profit institutions may be less likely to promote things like retention, graduation, satisfaction, and employment than does a more dwelling-focused one. To return again to Brent's (2012, 562–63) terminology, a curriculum focused primarily on standardization and outcomes is premised on the ideas that writing and literacy can and should be measured in "a short time," be reproduced quickly "according to standards that are . . . narrow and prescriptive," and operate as "modular entities that can simply be picked up from one situation and dropped down in another." A dwelling-focused education, by contrast, is aimed at building spaces designed to foster critical "habits of mind" and to promote "long-term immersion" in learning spaces with less regard for immediate or simplistic outcomes. It is these latter habits of mind that seem especially likely to help students persist and graduate, to view such persistence as worthwhile, and to demonstrate similar persistence in the pursuit of a career after college.

On the basis of this work from Reynolds and Brent, I contend that dwelling helps us to theorize what not-for-profit writing instruction can provide to our students that for-profit instruction does not. Specifically, it helps us to demonstrate that we provide a kind of supportive, diverse, and thirdspace-oriented critical immersion within dedicated learning spaces where students can grapple with complex problems over time and that we help to improve retention, graduation, satisfaction, and employment metrics in the process. Both of these points will be illustrated in the two brief examples that follow.

EXAMPLE #1: DWELLING WORK THROUGH STUDIO PROGRAMS

An example of dwelling work we teachers of writing in not-for-profit contexts routinely perform can be found in Studio programs of the sort imagined by Rhonda Grego and Nancy Thompson in the context of basic writing instruction (Grego and Thompson 2008) but since adopted in other contexts as well (e.g., Webb-Sunderhaus 2010). Studio programs are premised on the notion that all students, but especially those deemed "basic," "remedial," "at-risk," or simply "diverse," can and will succeed within "regular" curricula if provided with additional pedagogical and institutional support. Accordingly, Studio programs provide one-on-one and small-group support to students as they take nonremedial writing classes. At the same time, studio programs explicitly aim to function as critical thirdspaces from which students are required to analyze the writing and writing instruction they receive through critical attention to unequal power relationships—or what Grego and Thompson (2008, 5) define as a "heightened awareness of the institutional power relations that define not only 'basic writing' but also 'student writing.'" Studio programs thus require diverse students to complete assignments while simultaneously examining and interrogating the power dynamics inherent in those assignments, fostering students' critical meta-awareness of audience, context, and purpose in the process. And, in these ways, Studio programs promote two crucially important dimensions of dwelling: first, they provide diverse students with a supportive environment within the writing classroom that provides a level of comfort as these students learn and grow; second, they challenge diverse students to move beyond merely feeling comfortable and toward effecting substantive change in the world.

A growing body of preliminary research suggests that Studio and other similar dwelling-oriented writing-focused programs also help to increase retention, graduation, and satisfaction rates among undergraduates who might otherwise be perceived as "at risk." For instance, Peter Dow Adams, Sarah Gearhart, Robert Miller, and Anne Roberts have been tracking the course completion and overall retention rates of students involved in the accelerated learning program (ALP), a Studio-type basic writing program at their home institution, the Community College of Baltimore County. They find that ALP "doubles the success rate [for course completion], halves the attrition rate [from the first-year course], does it in half the time . . . and costs slightly less per successful student [than the traditional model]" (Adams et al. 2009, 64). Along similar lines, Michelle Cleary (2011, 47), writing about a study of the Studio writing program at DePaul University in Chicago, concludes that her program improved next-term retention by 8 percent and one-year retention rates by 25 percent. Still further, Matthew Kilian McCurrie (2009, 44) finds important retention gains for students enrolled in a Studio-type summer bridge program at Columbia College in Chicago: its freshman fall-to-spring retention rate improved from 61 percent in 2004 to 68 percent in 2008 (although he notes this rate still lags behind the 84 percent retention rate for regularly admitted students). McCurrie concludes that this program improves students' overall satisfaction with the college experience by helping to "draw in students who felt alienated or silenced in high school or in their lives generally and give them a space to re-position themselves as successful students. Students felt successful [in Bridge] . . . when they were able to use their own language, select their own texts, and pursue their own interests. . . . These students see [programs like Bridge] as a resource to help them build fulfilling lives" (44–45). Of course, this fledgling body of research does not prove unequivocally that not-for-profit Studio programs are superior to standardized for-profit writing programs or the types of support the for-profits offer. Nor does this work yet touch on issues of postgraduation employment directly. But it does begin to demonstrate that Studio instruction positively affects the sorts of retention, graduation, and student satisfaction metrics researchers (and pundits) typically use to measure institutional success—thereby helping students who, in McCurrie's words, might otherwise feel "alienated or silenced" within higher education to dwell long enough to create a space within which to "build fulfilling lives."

It is also worth pointing out that Studio programs do not seem particularly likely to take root within for-profit institutional contexts. Whereas Studio programs are premised on helping students to identify and critique the particularities of their educational, social, and political contexts in decidedly nonstandardizable ways, for-profit institutions' work requires, by definition, that institutions try to standardize their experiences and outcomes. Furthermore, whereas Studio work actively seeks to foster a kind of thirdspace political consciousness rooted in critical attention to difference, for-profit institutions aim first and foremost at providing an apolitical "customer-satisfaction" experience—or what for-profit DeVry University characterizes as a "world class customer service" experience and a "product buy-in" orientation (Miller, Smith, and Nichols 2011, 28). While we should not simply dismiss for-profit efforts to retain and graduate diverse populations, we can and should recognize that the customer-service orientation upon which these institutions rely, as well as the standardization and outcomes-assessment ethos that ultimately undergirds such a customer-service orientation, is not aimed at thirdspace interrogation but rather at the sale of educational products.

In these ways, we can begin to see how Studio programs help us to perform a fundamentally important type of dwelling work on behalf of our not-for-profit students that is not only different from but potentially better than that offered by for-profit institutions. Indeed, through programs like the Studio, we simultaneously help students to succeed in the short term while preparing them to understand how this success is intimately related to a critical mindset necessary for making long-term changes in the world.

EXAMPLE #2: DWELLING WORK THROUGH COMMUNITY ENGAGEMENT AND SERVICE-LEARNING WRITING PROGRAMS

A second important example of dwelling work routinely conducted within the not-for-profit composition classroom can be found in community engagement and service-learning writing courses that require students to write across a variety of experiences, both within and alongside local communities. These courses routinely send students out into the community, requiring them to write individually and in groups (often with community members themselves) about these experiences, and, ultimately, to generate literate thirdspaces in which students' writing and learning are integrated with those of the individuals and groups with whom they work. Tom Deans (2000, 9) characterizes these courses as taking "the next logical step of widening the audience for student writing to include those beyond the classroom" while simultaneously straddling "both disciplinary and wider nonacademic communities." Carmen Kynard and Robert Eddy echo this claim as they characterize exemplary courses operating on historically black college and university (HBCU) campuses: such courses aim to promote "collaborative-community teaching and learning" as well as to cultivate a "political stance for pedagogy where shared fate with neighboring communities allows for a transgression of the physical-ideological walls of university spaces" (Kynard and Eddy 2009, W38). Community engagement and service-learning writing courses thereby aim to create thirdspaces in which students learn to write at the same time they dwell within and alongside diverse communities beyond the academy, a form of what Deans (2000, 10) calls "pragmatic civic action." Or, to put things differently, community engagement and service-learning writing programs actively use dwelling as a means to integrate "town" and "gown" into a new town-and-gown thirdspace.

There also exists a small but growing body of research suggesting that community engagement and service-learning writing courses help to improve student retention, graduation, satisfaction, and employment metrics. For instance, in a study of more than eight hundred students across 22 service-learning courses on 11 campuses, Robert Bringle, Julie Hatcher, and Richard Muthiah find that these types of courses were moderately related to students' intentions to reenroll in courses from semester to semester and year to year (Bringle, Hatcher, and Muthiah 2010, 43–45). They also find that students' impressions of their experiences in these courses were highly positive, improving the "extent of peer interaction, extent of faculty interaction, course satisfaction, perceived learning, degree of active learning, and personal relevance" (45). Regarding service-learning writing courses more specifically, Mary Prentice (2009) finds that focal students at Miami-Dade Community College (more than 95 percent of whom were students of color) achieved statistically significant improvements in terms of retention (280) along with increased scores on various tests of "college learning skills," "interpersonal skills," and "postcourse civic responsibility" (279). She also determines that, among members of a small focus group she interviewed extensively, students perceived clear benefits from these courses in terms of their future employability, stressing that these courses "reinforced [students'] desire to persevere toward their career goals" (279).

This growing body of research on community engagement and service-learning writing courses indicates an important connection between the dwelling work of not-for-profit writing instruction and measures of retention, graduation, satisfaction, and employability. Students do appear to leave courses like these with an increased sense of dwelling—of both their place within an increasingly diverse world and of their responsibility to improve that place—in ways that seem worth publicizing. Equally worth publicizing is the fact that for-profits seem largely uninterested in offering community engagement or service-learning writing courses, perhaps because, as Shawna Shapiro (2011, 29) stresses, such courses "ask more from the institution" while at the same time making "fewer guarantees" regarding easily measurable outcomes. This lack of interest is perhaps best illustrated by the fact that, of the 1,289 for-profit institutions currently recognized by the Carnegie Foundation (Carnegie Classification of Institutions 2016, 7), not one—*not a single one*—currently stands among the 361 institutions possessing Carnegie's Community Engagement classification (New England Resource Center for Higher Education 2016), a designation reserved for institutions demonstrating a significant commitment to community engagement and service-learning activity. This striking statistic indicates that the for-profit higher education sector does not generally wish to pursue the kind of dwelling work increasingly pervasive within the not-for-profit writing classroom.

It seems clear that we not-for-profit writing teachers are performing important dwelling work in the context of community engagement and service-learning programs of the sort that for-profits either will not or cannot typically perform. We should both recognize and publicize this difference: through community engagement and service-learning writing courses, we prepare students to function as writers, readers, and literate persons who can both thrive and promote change within an increasingly diverse world, both in the short term and the long term.

FUTURE POSSIBILITIES FOR DWELLING WORK

I began this chapter with a quick overview of the pressures I think for-profit writing instruction is placing on those of us who teach writing within not-for-profit contexts. These pressures, as well as the dual emphases on standardization and assessment that undergird them, remain very real. Nonetheless, I believe strongly that we not-for-profit teachers (and researchers and administrators) of writing are well positioned to respond to these pressures by identifying and championing the kinds of dwelling work we routinely perform—work that helps to distinguish our educational enterprise as different from, and indeed better than, that of our for-profit counterparts. To this end, I think we should focus on at least two things as we move forward.

First, we must consider ways to expand our use of dwelling-centered pedagogies and practices within the not-for-profit writing classroom. This can and should mean, of course, that we continue offering Studio-type and community-engagement/service-learning writing courses that explicitly aim to foster thirdspace-oriented engagement on the part of students. But it might also mean that we continue to seek ways to infuse these and other courses with new sorts of explicitly dwelling-focused strategies that eschew facile attempts at large-scale standardization in favor of small-scale engagement with diverse students' needs and interests. Toward these ends, pedagogies rooted in translanguaging seem to hold particular promise. Such pedagogies are premised on the basic notion that, as Suresh Canagarajah (2006, 593) contends,

> multilingual people always make adjustments to each other as they modify their accent or syntax to facilitate communication with those who are not proficient in their language. Furthermore, they come with psychological and attitudinal resources, such as patience, tolerance, and humility, to negotiate the differences of interlocutors.

Translanguaging pedagogies ultimately require that we not-for-profit writing teachers continue to offer our diverse students effective one-on-one and small-group instruction designed to recognize and cultivate their strengths—indeed, to help "facilitate communication" through virtues including "patience, tolerance, and humility" in the classroom. They also require that we resist "outsourcing" our work with diversity or otherwise acquiescing to the idea that effective writing instruction can be delivered by semiskilled paraprofessionals. Given these requirements, we should try to expand our use of translanguaging pedagogies to help us ensure that diverse students can and will dwell effectively, both within our classrooms and in the world beyond them.

Second, we must imagine new ways to showcase the fundamental importance of our dwelling work to writing instruction and undergraduate education more generally. One way to do so would be to continue studying and documenting the work of various kinds of dwelling pedagogies and their effects on students. Indeed, by producing more research demonstrating the value of dwelling work to retention, graduation, satisfaction, and (especially) employment, we can further establish that dwelling can and does have measurably positive effects in terms of students' lives after and outside of college. Another way to do this would be to implement new sorts of research-supported advertising campaigns designed to promote dwelling. For instance, during the course of performing preliminary research for this chapter, I did some quick Internet searching for the terms *Studio*, *community engagement*, and *writing instruction*. One of the websites that emerged repeatedly during my searching was that of the liberal arts school Hobart and William Smith Colleges (HWS) (2013a, 2013b, 2013c). Although I had no prior knowledge of HWS or its activities, I was struck by the ways in which it seemed to promote a dwelling-type focus across its site. This focus is evident within the HWS official slogan, "Worlds of Experience; Lives of Consequence," which immediately evokes a dwelling orientation stressing spaces, places, and responsibilities (Hobart and William Smith Colleges 2013a). This focus is further evident in the specific ways HWS champions its focus on community engagement and service learning: it repeatedly mentions its status as one of the 115 institutions to earn Carnegie's Community Engagement classification (Hobart and William Smith Colleges 2013b); it provides detailed discussion of its involvement with the local Geneva, New York, community, including specific efforts to help local K–12 students with literacy learning (Hobart and William Smith Colleges 2013a, 2013b); and it even describes in detail what appears to be a thoughtful undergraduate writing and rhetoric major and minor that stresses the primacy of rhetorical analysis, revision, and student choice rather than a one-size-fits-all standardized curriculum (Hobart and William Smith Colleges 2013a).

I am not suggesting that those of us who teach writing in not-for-profit institutions should simply copy HWS's strategies as we imagine ways to publicize our dwelling work. But we ought to try understanding the ways in which we might adopt a similar dwelling-oriented focus within our own work with groups such as CCCC, WPA, and other professional organizations. By actively researching, documenting, and promoting dwelling work as a central benefit of our professional activity, we seem more likely to distinguish ourselves from for-profits in favorable ways—thereby pushing back more forcefully against the pressures we increasingly face within a for-profit world.

4

OCCUPYING RESEARCH—AGAIN/STILL

Joan Mullin and Jenn Fishman[1]

Historically, writing studies (under a variety of names) has generated policies and publications that recognize the worth of teachers of all ranks, administrators of all kinds, staff members, and independent scholars. Likewise, research in writing studies reflects the usefulness and importance of projects set in classrooms, writing centers, and other campus locations as well as diverse workplaces and community sites. A field that is currently flourishing, writing studies can measure its prosperity in terms of proliferating journals, conferences, departments, programs, graduates, and jobs. However, these familiar markers of disciplinary success also signal a fundamental paradox: namely, a conflict between the principles and practices espoused within the writing studies microeconomy on one hand and, on the other, the ideology and related valuation of academic labor determined by the macroeconomy of academe. Thus, while writing studies educators seek employment, advancement, and professional rewards regulated by the academy, their day-to-day activities and long-term pedagogical and scholarly work more closely align with field-specific ideas and values. For writing researchers, this situation results in a state of contradiction, especially when researchers occupy marginal positions, such as undergraduates and graduate students completing thesis research; teachers and administrators leading classroom and program inquiries; or researchers conducting studies in languages other than English. In these situations, writing research may have high stakes (e.g., degree requirement, program funding, job retention) and high impacts (e.g., on individual researchers' subsequent work, local teaching practices, institutional policies) but only limited credibility, such that the individuals who do the work seldom receive the credit they deserve.

The Research Exchange Index (REx) offers the writing studies community a means of negotiating—and ultimately even changing—these conditions. As an open-access database of writing research, REx differs

DOI: 10.7330/9781607325239.c004

from resources such as ERIC and CompPile, which collect mainly bibliographic citations for published scholarship. By contrast, REx focuses on research activity and collects information about individual projects regardless of their publication status. Adopting a census-like model of crowd sourcing, REx gathers information periodically and directly from individual researchers, who fill out brief online forms for each study they have conducted between 2000 and the present. Just as REx editors review the contents of each form after it has been submitted, REx itself is peer reviewed by the digital academic press that publishes the database. At the time this essay was published, the first edition of REx was in process, and plans for updating the database after its initial publication were already underway.

As a database, and a form of peer-reviewed scholarship, REx is more than a practical resource designed to increase the accessibility of knowledge about writing research. REx is also a collective action planned to promote equity and access within the writing studies community while challenging the efficacy and fairness of the academic macroeconomy. In particular, by privileging the activity of research over one of its products, scholarship, REx confronts the powerful market bias in favor of traditional scholars and scholarship. This bias not only marginalizes the labor, desires, and value of many writing researchers, it also distorts the field of writing studies, skewing our sense of who conducts research and how, why, and to what ends it is conducted. Although neither REx nor this essay is a site for interrogating the evolution or intentionality of such inequities, the former invites active collective participation in redress, while this essay explains the rationale for change.

SHIFTING THE ECONOMIC BALANCE

Part protest, part takeover, part tactic for transforming academic currency, REx calls on the writing studies community to occupy research. For the Occupy Wall Street protesters who camped in Zuccotti Park and other public locations throughout the United States, occupation meant an actual invasion of physical as well as cultural and psychic space. In New York's Financial District and elsewhere, occupation was also a demonstration of civil disobedience: an action performed both to broadcast social critique and to cultivate the solidarity required for collective action against injustice and toward systemic, democratizing change. Notably, Occupy Wall Street engaged in a distinctly contemporary kind of occupying. As in the Arab Spring uprisings, not only did new, mass, and social media radically extend the reach of Occupiers' site-specific protests, but the movement's messages also clearly connected redress with access to technology. According to the NYC General Assembly's (2013) "Principles of Solidarity," Occupy Wall Street's "points of unity" included transparency, responsibility, and "redefining how labor is valued" as well as "making technologies, knowledge, and culture open to all to freely access, create, modify, and distribute." Similarly, since 2008 when our pilot for REx went live, we have been calling on colleagues to democratize the field. Using everything from postcards and listservs to conference presentations, digital academic publications, and the database itself, we have been rallying active writing researchers to unite behind a resource designed to make their work freely available to anyone who wishes to access, reference, aggregate, or replicate it.

"Make your research count!" is the call we repeated most frequently while we collected data for the first edition of REx, although it would have been just as accurate to have advertised "No project is too _______ or too _______ to be included." Both overtures call for active participation: filling in blanks, that is, filling out short reports about individual research projects and, as a result, working against the culture of exclusion that has been naturalized in mainstream forms of scholarly exchange. In this way, REx is an antidote to the assumptions that shape our expectations when we skim the index of a new journal issue or click a conference link to read the list of plenary speakers. When we engage in these activities, as when we discuss academic exclusions, we usually think categorically, grouping those present and absent from different professional rosters according not only to names but also job titles (e.g., adjunct, assistant director), workloads (e.g., part time, four/four), and locations (e.g., regional faith-based college, non-US university). REx protests these practices and related habits of mind procedurally by changing the terms of inclusion. By inviting everyone who has conducted writing research since 2000 to register their work, REx turns the focus from researchers to research. Thus, even while contributors must begin the registration process by establishing a personal account, REx is more than a Who's Who of the field. As an index of contemporary writing research, REx collects and makes accessible information about the who, what, where, when, how, and why of writing studies.

The radicalness of REx's inclusivity should not be underestimated. So deeply ingrained are the values of the academic macroeconomy that it has been difficult to convey the idea that REx is not only open access but also open to all researchers and all kinds of research projects—published and unpublished, completed and in process, large and small, quantitative and qualitative, and so on. While, on one hand, we receive continuous positive feedback on the idea of a comprehensive writing-research database, on the other hand, we continually field questions that indicate the gestalt shift REx represents. Colleagues repeatedly ask us if REx is for only one kind of research (i.e., published or unpublished). More than once colleagues have asked for advice about starting something like REx for research in their writing subfields or geographical locations. We receive messages from colleagues who work with data they cannot share publicly (e.g., registrar records) and who therefore apologize because they believe that prevents them from reporting their research. We also receive enthusiastic participation from prolific researchers who register only a single study, usually their most recent or best-known work, but do not report their programmatic research (e.g., program self-studies). And we receive promises from researchers who tell us they would like to participate but only have one pilot study or thesis project and believe they need more (e.g., published and/or funded research) before they can contribute. As editors, when we respond to these comments, we become teachers and activists, and we find ourselves teaching not only the basic functionality of REx but also the critique of academic values REx contributors and users perform when they report their research and search the database.

As a mode of protest and a tactic for takeover and transformation, REx pairs inclusivity with efforts to increase REx contributors' access to academic currency. These efforts are concentrated in the REx editorial cycle, which begins with a set acquisitions period (as opposed to rolling acquisitions) and is followed by a two-part editorial process. During part one, as we lead editorial reviewers in reading and commenting on individual reports, our criteria for review are calibrated to clarity, correctness, and the usability of reports as searchable text. In part two, we submit the database along with supporting text to a digital academic press, much as one would send a manuscript to a traditional scholarly publisher for peer review. This editorial process eschews the speed and communal nature of wiki-style publication, but it offers the writing studies community something that is, at least at present, arguably more valuable: the academic currency contributors gain when their reports become both accessible and citable as part of a peer-reviewed scholarly publication. Serving as a new kind of literacy brokerage, REx shifts the editorial paradigm from one of evaluation geared toward gatekeeping to a system of valuation that promotes visibility.

Critiquing the current performance-based economy, our own field tends to draw on the work of public intellectuals, philosophers, and cultural critics such as Pierre Bourdieu (1986, 1991a) or Bruno Latour

(2005), who articulate critiques of not only evolving labor and valuation practices but also of the nitty-gritty of language and writing instruction. The special issue on economies of writing Bruce Horner (2012) edited for *JAC* is a case in point. Contributors to that volume, all plenary speakers at the 2012 Thomas R. Watson Conference at the University of Louisville, questioned our reification of particular alphabetic systems (Cushman 2012; Lillis 2012), the actual public consequences of engaging language beyond academe (Brandt 2012; Gilyard 2012), and the contexts that led to the valuation of certain forms of writing to the exclusion of others (Gunner 2012; Milson-Whyte 2012). As Horner (2012, 460) writes, such examinations of the "political economies of writing remind us not only of the materiality, and the effect of limited material working conditions to, academic work (that the academy often denies); they also remind us that the material working conditions of particular academic settings 'affords' the possibility of just such challenges to dominant economies of writing." The Research Exchange allows us to challenge the dominant economies by asking that current forms of already publicly valued production occupy space alongside writing and research practices less visible, recognized, and, therefore, valued.

On one hand, the actual REx site provides users with a genuine way to help create an "oppositional culture," an academic counterculture that resists the "competitive, market-based, high-performance habitus designed for [academics] by management" (Bousquet 2008, 13). On the other hand, the process of designing a scholarly resource that challenges how work has traditionally been conceptualized and valued has shown us how difficult enacting political desires can be. Even while colleagues' responses to REx have been encouraging, our own revisions and rearticulations of the project serve as regular reminders of how difficult it is, first, to think differently about doing academic work and, second, to go ahead and do work differently. Certainly we have been continually challenged to question our own position in the normative academic culture from which we benefit. Likewise, we have had to ask ourselves and each other if it is worth expending our own academic capital on REx and, more broadly, if it is realistic to promote and expect others to join an oppositional economy based on the networked distribution of both labor and wealth instead of trafficking in individual reputation and capitalistic chains of supply and demand.

We continue to believe the time is right for REx, and creating ways for writing researchers to participate in our profession differently is one more necessary step toward rethinking the profession itself. To that end, REx recognizes a range of materials with which scholars engage;

offers visible alternatives to market definitions of writing by including a wider representation of studies; makes known the value of writing researchers' work processes to expand corporatized definitions of work; highlights research processes that can serve as mentoring models; and enacts equity, diversity, and access by challenging global inclinations to mechanize language and elide difference. REx answers Theresa Lillis's (2012, 718) call to rethink access by giving the writing studies community another way to look at "what scholars are doing, why and under what conditions." Further, the development of REx has led us to think deeply about why we need to resist a system that has excluded so many of those whose labor ought to count.

ACCESS AND LABOR

Since the publication of *Research in Written Composition* in 1963, writing scholars have focused a great deal of attention on assessing and improving the quality of writing research. However, when we go back to this field-shaping text, we notice additional, equally important issues of access and labor. The well-known and oft-cited 142-page assessment of the state of knowledge about composition offers a comprehensive review of writing research published before 1961. Commissioned by the National Council of Teachers of English, sponsored by the United States Office of Education and the University of Iowa, compiled by an ad hoc, 10-person committee, and written by Richard Braddock, Richard Lloyd-Jones, and Lowell Schoer, *Research in Written Composition* reports:

> Today's research in composition, taken as a whole, may be compared to chemical research as it emerged from the period of alchemy: some terms are being defined usefully, a number of procedures are being refined, but the field as a whole is laced with dreams, prejudices, and makeshift operations. Not enough investigators are really informing themselves about the procedures and results of previous research before embarking on their own. Too few of them conduct pilot experiments and validate their measuring instruments before undertaking an investigation. Too many seem to be bent more on obtaining an advanced degree or another publication than on making a genuine contribution to knowledge, and a fair measure of the blame goes to the faculty adviser or journal editor who permits or publishes such irresponsible work. And far too few of those who have conducted an initial piece of research follow it with further exploration or replicate the investigations of others. Composition research, then, is not highly developed. If researchers wish to give it strength and depth, they must reexamine critically the structure and techniques of their studies. (Braddock, Lloyd-Jones, and Schoer 1963, 5–6)

This pointed critique helped set the field's agenda for years to come. It informed surges of research activity in the 1960s, again in the 1980s, and at the turn of the twenty-first century; it echoes in debates about the place and importance of replicable, aggregable, data-driven (RAD) research in writing studies; and it resonates through recent calls to combat anti-education rhetoric with quantitative data (Anson 2008; Haswell 2005).

We recognize the contribution these conversations have made to writing studies' currently robust research culture, and we appreciate their influence on current writing theories and pedagogies, including our own. At the same time, we recognize ongoing conversations about the conduct and quality of writing research as artifacts of the circumstances in which they emerged. This is not simply the product of reflective human dialogue, which we might track with Michael Oakeshott (1962) and Kenneth Bruffee (1984) from primeval forests to the vigorous, sometimes heated exchanges of the Burkean parlor. Instead, the shaping conversations about writing research present as formal, scholarly, and public in a traditional sense. As such, they are marked by researchers' ongoing efforts and obligations to credential their work in terms set and continually reset by the dominant academic research economy. Accordingly, we can read in the writing research that has accrued a metastory about researchers' responses as well as their responsiveness to the system that establishes widely adopted standards for what constitutes knowledge, who can and should produce it, and how and in what formats it should be produced.

Perhaps it goes without saying that all of us have a relationship to this system, and many, if not most of us—if we have earned advanced degrees, if we hold academic or alt-ac (i.e., nontraditional) academic jobs, if we strive to be retained or tenured or promoted—profit by it. Yet our relationship does not preclude us from scrutinizing and critiquing this system, nor does it prevent us from working to advocate for and attempt to create change. In fact, having benefited from the system should obligate us, given our discipline, to see it, not be blinded by it. REx represents one platform for cooperatively engaging this challenge, providing a database that includes information about not only completed and published research but also about unpublished projects and work in progress. With this inclusion, REx offers writing studies a means of changing how research is represented and circulated as well as published. In turn, it stands to change the horizon of possibility for how we value and evaluate knowledge making in our field.

When the labor of writing research goes un- or underrepresented and when projects disseminated exclusively through informal and/or alternative means remain largely invisible, many inquiries and inquiry practices that inform the field cannot be valued, and the actual labor of writing research is erased. This problem is everywhere in evidence, although one must look for it because it is often hidden in plain sight. Take *Research in Written Composition* as an example. Although the report and its general conclusions are often cited, its methods are not, nor are the studies selected as exemplars. Indeed, only the most conscientious readers, readers with superlative memories, and readers quick to open a browser window are likely to recall the Buxton, Harris, Kincaid, Smith, or Becker studies, which emerged as "the most soundly based" among the hundreds Braddock and his colleagues evaluated (Braddock, Lloyd-Jones, and Schoer 1963, 55). Instead, we read that the *Research* authors' evaluative methods were rigorous. They started by scanning "some [twenty] summaries and bibliographies" in search of studies based "at least in part on the direct observation of writing." The committee also sought research that involved "a generous number of students," clearly described data collection procedures, featured appropriate quantitative data analysis, and was "as objective an investigation as possible" (2, 55–56). The ad hoc committee whittled an initial list of 1,000 titles to 485 potentially relevant published and unpublished studies, which they procured and read before selecting 100 for the close analysis the first sections of the report summarize.

Today, were a group of scholars to undertake a similar study, they would be able to marshal a greater range of resources, starting with available bibliographic tools. As of June 2013, CompPile (Rendleman 2013) includes 104,865 records focusing on postsecondary writing alone, from "journal articles, review-essays, [published] notes and comments, books, dissertations, *ERIC* items, and edited collections." As a complementary resource, ERIC contains not only citations for presecondary writing research but also references to materials CompPile does not currently include (e.g., conference papers, technical reports). In addition, contemporary scholars might turn to DAI, the electronic counterpart to the printed volumes of Dissertation Abstracts that Braddock and his colleagues consulted, and to the growing number of prepublication papers stored in repositories and included in their online catalogs. Given these and other related resources, today's Braddock-style researchers would certainly have incredible reach. But they would still be missing some of the kinds of research REx reports contain.

In contrast, REx calls for wider public deliberations about what constitutes the production of knowledge about writing by collecting, in one space, information about a broader range of work than Braddock and his colleagues were able to consider. Defining writing research as systematic inquiry into some aspect(s) of writing that involves one or more human subjects, REx welcomes a diversity of research subjects and methods from ethnographic to experimental studies. Designed both to reflect and invite reflection on the full breadth of contemporary research activity, REx also collects information in a way fundamentally different from bibliographies and other resources that feature records of scholarship or publications of different kinds: REx's online form invites, directly from researchers, brief, census-like information about their projects. This tactic enables principal investigators to report on the rationales for and designs of their projects, their plans for execution, and their earliest findings separate from articles they may or may not write, conference presentations they may or may not deliver, white papers they may or may not circulate publicly, and so on. To be sure, REx also collects information about extant results, findings, and publications related to each study in the database. However, by design, REx places priority on indexing research activity in the protean field of writing studies. In doing so, REx invites access to information about research motives and practices that would otherwise remain largely undocumented, unknown and unknowable beyond the comparatively small scope of interpersonal exchange or listserv inquiries.

REx also solves another problem: the impulse driving a great deal of writing research not readily available is urgency—a persistent classroom problem, a time-sensitive need to defend course caps in first-year composition, a public demand for evidence of student achievement. However, the logic of much writing research is longitudinal, and even short-term studies are grounded in previous cyclical questions and take a long time from start to finish. With Julie Lindquist (2012, 645), then, we are "interested in thinking about how we might enable and come to value the products of research that is, by most standards of disciplinary knowledge-production, emergent or slow-growing." We also want to value explicitly the often slow processes of research, including work like Lindquist's own, which she describes as methodologically "emergent, abductive, unpredictable, time- and equipment-intensive, and entirely inefficient" and thus not quick or productive in any conventional sense (651). By making this kind of research more visible (through citable database listings), REx not only changes the accessibility of such work, it also challenges existing citation practices and, at the same time, requires database users to think about what constitutes knowledge, its production, and its value. Whether the academic macroeconomy chooses to recognize the newly exposed forms of common labor REx makes visible, whether and how the availability of such new data promotes new motives and measures for assessment, remains to be seen.

EQUITY

Thanks to the proliferation of both print and online publications, scholarly production and communication are more widely available, enabling searches across (sub)disciplinary and national boundaries. This development should be an advantage for a field like writing studies, which draws from multiple perspectives and sites (e.g., linguistics, cognitive science, geography, design, IT, rhetoric, sociology, gender studies); however, many have pointed to the inequities advanced technologies have also produced (Gorski 2009; Selfe and Hawisher 2006). Such inequities exist not only between first- and third-world universities, but across US institutions where colleagues can be handicapped by site-limited search engines, budget-limited library resources, and currency-limited travel funds; limited knowledge of or participation in professional organizations; limited mentoring and time to mentor or be mentored. Tracing historical contexts that contribute to current publishing practices, Cynthia Selfe and Gail Hawisher call for a reconsideration of our often exclusionary peer-review processes, noting that increased publication and specialization have created "a hierarchy of prestige that has continued to exert pressure on scholars and departments" (Selfe and Hawisher 2006, 677). They point to alternative models emerging in open-access digital resources such as *Kairos, CCC Online, Computers and Composition Online,* and *Across the Disciplines,* "convinced that only through such exploration and experimentation will we, as a large and complex profession, develop better, more productive, and more humane ways of dealing with the peer review of scholarship" (693).

As can be seen recently in scientific and historical research, alternative models are worth pursuing since even peer-reviewed studies can be found wanting or fraudulent (Steen 2011). That there needs to be some method of reviewing work is not being argued, but at issue is at what point and how that review takes place. One of the more questionable practices emerged in a recent WPA listserv exchange about predatory online journals that feature slick websites and require a hefty publication fee. Addressing the need to be cautious about such digital-born journals, Charles Bazerman (2013) also points out that publication limitations have always been in place: "The print world is equally full of predatory practices, though not necessarily so visible in upfront costs to the authors, only in downstream costs to libraries, restricted access to relevant audiences, pressures on editors to make choices based on profit-directed metrics, etc. The predation is also hidden under the cover of long-standing institutional practices and the brand-name recognition of traditional publishers." Given the pressures Bazerman points to and the limits of access, time, and technology for many, how representative is our current scholarship? As Richard Haswell (2005) and others have pointed out, the lack of broadly representative findings in our field calls into question the scope of our knowledge, and, we believe, invites us to investigate whether current constructions of writing, research, and methods are representative of the whole or equally limited.

It may be easier to understand how such publication practices exclude a range of important writing research by looking at their effect on international scholars who have limited access to Anglophone privileges and publication traditions but are increasingly being required to publish in English-medium journals (Horner, Donahue, and NeCamp 2011; Lillis and Curry 2010). Diane Belcher (2009, 221) notes that articles in three primary Anglophone journals still demonstrate "less rhetorical diversity in their contributions than expected." That scholarship must resemble mainstream expectations makes sense (genres demand certain rhetorical moves), but in this case, the consequences should make us pause to think about whose logic such genre arguments employ. Theresa Lillis and Mary Jane Curry address these questions in their seven-year study of multilingual scholars seeking to publish in English-medium journals (Lillis and Curry 2010). Among other findings, their examination of scholars' drafts, editorial feedback, revisions, and editors' responses to those showed how the peer-review process could serve as exclusionary gatekeeping, even when performed by those in the profession dedicated to international knowledge building. Research questions, methods not valued in some Western traditions, or bibliographic citations unfamiliar to reviewers could result in a publication's rejection. Authors were asked to reshape research questions, to do more "recognizable" research, to include familiar canonical scholars, and exclude those deemed "too regional." Lillis and Curry's study corroborates Selfe and Hawisher's (2006, 680) claim that "peer review can be a conservative force across the disciplines with prominent gatekeepers often participating as reviewers." To be fair, Selfe and Hawisher note that finding those qualified to review new areas of study can be difficult, and any editor knows that when they must choose among the many manuscripts they receive, those working differently can and do get marginalized and rejected.

Openness must come from within the writing studies community, understood as an international community that embraces fully both the conceptual and practical risks equity demands, for equity brings with it both opportunities and requirements. As Sedef Uzuner (2008, 251) writes in his review of multilingual scholarship, peripheral scholars "enrich the knowledge base of core academic communities in two important ways: (1) they write about things that mainstream disciplinary communities do not know of; and (2) through accessing works that mainstream academic communities had not heard of, they draw attention to untapped or unknown resources." Anticipating that providing research equity and inclusion will not for the first time raise fears of quality control, Suresh Canagarajah (1996, 469) notes that the inclusion he—and Uzuner—call for is

> not just another [call] by the materially underprivileged seeking set-asides, neither is it a plea to overlook excellence to provide greater representation for periphery scholars in center publications. Rather [it] is an attempt to deconstruct the bases of "excellence" in published scholarship and knowledge construction. It is an argument for reconfiguring the relationship in academic publication networks so that we can construct knowledge—and presumably conduct international relations—in more egalitarian and enriching terms.

Canagarajah asks that we consider how language abilities and rhetorical conventions work together to limit participation by peripherals (436), a challenge REx addresses. Contributors only provide summaries and short responses, making language and the rhetorical conventions demanded by academic journals less of a problem. While researchers are asked to enter the title of their studies in English, they are welcome to enter other details in their home language(s). As a literacy brokerage, REx encourages its users to become multilingual literacy brokers themselves and to work together to increase cross-border research along with cross-border access to research partnerships.

Whether international or local, the information researchers enter into REx makes explicit the labor that produces it and creates equity among researchers and research traditions. Such affordances speak especially to those for whom our national organizations have been strong advocates and whose research is often missing from our histories: writing program administrators, classroom teachers, and student researchers. Currently, robust writing studies resulting from PhD, MA, and (mentored) undergraduate courses and tutorials are available, at best, through college and university library catalogs and/or institutional repositories. By including these studies in a visible, searchable database, REx provides a space where the field places traditionally validated forms of capital alongside those studies equally valuable in terms of their expended labor and knowledge. As a result, REx provides not only agency (in the Burkean sense) for present and future research action/activism but also a mechanism for creating new histories of writing by engaging in the history of writing (research) in a new way.

Serving as a collection point for information about the broadest possible range of labor and production, REx makes research, its processes, and its range more visible. As a result, our institutions, policies, and committees—within which each of us holds power—can choose to define and allocate differently our tightly held academic currency. Instead of working from a model of scarcity and limited resources, REx hopes to demonstrate that there is more than enough to go around and that the distribution of capital rests on a willingness to share a different orientation toward wealth, need, and community with respect for the labor from which we all benefit.

Note

1. As long-time collaborators, we follow the feminist coauthoring best practice of alternating the order of our names from publication to publication.

5

THE POLITICAL ECONOMY OF ENGLISH

The "Capital" of Literature, Creative Writing, and Composition

James T. Zebroski

I didn't get a Ph.D. in rhetoric and composition to teach freshman composition.

Recent graduate of PhD program
in rhetoric and composition

You don't need a PhD in rhetoric and composition to teach freshman composition.

Rhetoric and composition faculty person and
WPA at Another University

It's not personal; it's business.

Michael Corleone in *The Godfather*

Since 1970 or so, the United States has experienced one long, drawn-out economic crisis with occasional short spurts of growth. Incomes of middle-class families basically plateaued in the early 1970s and since 1973 have declined. In fact, incomes as a proportion of GDP have reached pre–Great Depression lows while corporate profits have skyrocketed.[1] A *New York Times* article by Samantha Lowrie, published on September 11, 2013, calls our time a new Gilded Age as far as the gap between the haves and have-nots is concerned.[2] It reports that the top 10 percent of earners took home 50 percent of all the income made in the United States. Put another way, as Christopher Newfield says, "People don't seem to realize the U.S. has the first generation that has attained less than its parents. This correlates with the era of privatization, which has been going on for 30 years" (DePaul 2010). There have been very few long stretches of economic prosperity and security in any of our lifetimes, young or old. As

DOI: 10.7330/9781607325239.c005

Paul Krugman argued in a *New York Times* article published on September 18, 2013, "The evidence suggests that we have become an economy whose normal state is one of mild depression, whose brief episodes of prosperity occur only thanks to bubbles and unsustainable borrowing."

This macroeconomic crisis has obviously affected college English, starting with the job-market crash in literature around 1970, chronicled by Richard Ohmann (1996) and others, and the emergence of other specialties including creative writing and rhetoric and composition thereafter. In addition to a crisis in the job market in English, there have been enormous cuts to state higher education, a decline of state support of universities from perhaps 50 percent of the university budget to 5 percent. Newfield (2008, 146) tracks both the state cuts and the ideology that prepared for and accompanied them in his book *Unmaking the Public University*, noting that "rather than putting the development of cultural understanding ahead of market logic, LCS [literary and cultural studies] leaders criticized the impact of markets on academic labor while continuing to adapt to them." The leaders of literary and cultural studies, he emphasizes, cooperated in downsizing and self-imposed austerity (150). In an interview with Amy DePaul (2010), Newfield argued that "'conservative elites have long targeted higher education because of its role in creating a more empowered, democratic, and multicultural middle class.'" As DePaul points out, "[Newfield's] view is that decades of slash-and-burn-budgets, culture wars, affirmative action attacks and pressure to run universities as a business are part of concerted effort."

Given these trends, how have college English departments managed to survive? Why do college English departments at least manage to get by? Why have English departments not—so far at least—gone the way of classics departments?

This essay argues that it is in the political economy of English where we find some answers to these questions. The way each subfield of English makes sense of itself varies. These views are important and are certainly worth exploring, but that is not my primary focus, though there will be occasional allusions to these views when relevant to the larger argument. What the cultural anthropologist would call an *emic* or *insider's view* is no doubt crucial, but this essay stays within the bounds of the political economy of English—how labor and resources are generated, circulated, sustained over decades, and become a part of what we call *the field of English* and *English departments*, which embody that field. My claim in this chapter is that in very specific ways, the aggregate labor literature, creative writing, and rhetoric faculty contribute to English makes us dependent on one another and constructs what we take to be the problems—but also the potentials—of our field.

Within that thesis, my first claim is that English, like any good corporate entity in a capitalist economy, has responded to this prolonged crisis by expanding its product line—the products it offers to students, to the university, and to its subdisciplines—and by cutting labor costs, the most obvious but by no means the only way being the reduction of tenure-track faculty positions and the increased use of adjunct and part-time labor. Further, I argue that academic capital has formed in English since about 1970, when the crisis in literature hit. Academic capital might be defined as aggregate labor (value and specifically surplus value) that has been extracted from its workers, accumulated over time, and reinvested into English. At least three sorts of what might be called *academic capital* circulate in English locally and nationally: (1) leadership capital associated with literature, (2) artisan capital associated with creative writing, and (3) professional capital associated with rhetoric and composition. Each of these will be further defined as I take them up. My next claim is that these capital formations do the work of these subdisciplines and tie one another together through economic networks in English. The main device by which this transaction occurs is composition (especially TA lines and adjunct labor), which all fragments of "English" "teach" and which provides a kind of common currency—a coin of the realm, a vehicle for the circulation of value, for English as a whole. Before launching this analysis, I ground it in the tradition within which this work has been done.

The work of this chapter follows certain precedents. Perhaps the earliest and most influential is Ohmann's 1976 *English in America* (republished in 1996), in which he tries to understand from a Marxist point of view the institutions of college English. He notes:

> I look at the folkways of teachers, at English departments, at freshman composition textbooks, at the Modern Language Association of America, at the Advanced Placement system. The point is to understand some of the institutions that are most responsible for the transmission of literacy and culture. Their forms often reveal more about culture than do public pronouncements. (Ohmann 1996, 3–4)

Ohmann's study remains a model of clear writing and deeply critical analysis of our own work that questions our institutional culture and tries to place it in a larger political economy.

While probably no one would see his work as dealing with the political economy of English, David Bartholomae (2005), by focusing on a close reading of student writing, tangentially does often make professional claims. His essays are often critical not only of the commonplaces of English but also of composition. For example, he argues that composition but also the university are institutions "designed to produce and reward mastery, not to call it into question" (2005, 330). This orientation leads us "to give awards to papers we do not believe in and to turn away from papers we do, papers most often clumsy and awkward but . . . ambitious, interesting, a sign of a student for whom something is happening" (331). We are trapped in our own discourse. Matched with his extensive experience not only teaching freshman composition but also as an English chair and as a national consultant, Bartholomae sees patterns of practice that feed into a political economic analysis.

Finally, John Trimbur's (2000) essay "Composition and the Circulation of Writing" lays the groundwork for my analysis. Trimbur argues for a focus on the circulation of writing that goes beyond attending to the individual writer or the individual text in the intimate, bourgeois familial space of the classroom (a focus he says Elbow and Bartholomae, for all of their differences, share) (193–95). Rather, when we look at the circulation of writing in the tradition of the Marx of the *Grundrisse*, we see much more than a product, much more than a commodity. When we look closely and deeply at a commodity (even writing), we see the social relations it embodies. Trimbur says, "The human productive activity (the labor power) 'congealed' in the commodity form not only produces worldly goods but also reproduces the prevailing and contradictory social and economic relations of capitalism, where socialized production, with its promise of overcoming material scarcity, is at odds with the goal of private profit" (Trimbur 2000, 208). Although Trimbur, rightfully, looks at the whole process when attending to the circulation of writing, I will focus on only one part of that process—production—where "profit" ultimately is produced, though, of course, without circulation and consumption there clearly is no production—or profit. Although Trimbur moves toward focusing on writing as commodity, my chapter attends to curriculum as commodity or, perhaps, as a vast assemblage of commodities. If by curriculum we mean the courses we offer, the knowledge we produce and circulate, and the end products—educated students and graduates—we produce, then curriculum is, among many other things, a commodity, and English is a political economy through which and in which these commodities are made and shared.

So this essay takes up not composition but English as a political economy because with some exceptions that is where we find composition and because we are dramatically influenced by—in fact tied to—the others in our departments in terms of how our work and theirs proceeds and is valued.[3] Most historical accounts since Ohmann (1996) have stayed inside their professional territories.[4] Because most of us work in English departments, this account returns to English.[5] The chapter, then, is divided into three parts:

1. A theoretical analysis of English as a political economy
2. A brief analysis of the place of composition in this political economy—as an oddity and a commodity[6]
3. English in the year 2026—tendencies in the political economy of English over the next decade

I: THEORETICAL ANALYSIS OF ENGLISH AS A POLITICAL ECONOMY

Labor, Capital, and the Crisis of English

Labor, dynamically understood, is the source of all value and of all culture. Labor, then, must be where any materialist analysis begins. In a capitalist mode of production, the regulation of labor occurs both in the marketplace and, invisibly, in the production process in the extraction of value. Capitalism is necessarily about the extraction of labor: capitalists get profit not simply because they are crafty or cagey in the marketplace but by taking a share of workers' regulated labor in the production process and by keeping it for themselves. All workers give up a part of their worth to provide this surplus, which fuels expansion. This surplus value goes to the capitalist in seemingly natural and invisible ways in the production process—in what is agreed to when a worker is hired and what the employer can get out of the worker once they are on the job. Still, the capitalist is not necessarily appropriating this surplus only to live well. A business must expand to compete; to expand profit, this surplus the capitalist gets from the labor of the worker must be reinvested, or the capitalist enterprise fails. The tendency in the political economy then is for competition to increase, which means profits must increase. That inevitably means at some point in the longer run, workers' wages and benefits must go down or, the same thing, the worker must produce more for the same wage and in the same span of time. The tendency in any enterprise over the longer run, then, is (1) crisis, (2) expansion, and (3) deeper crisis. The labor that makes possible an expansion is increasingly exploited, and the distribution of wealth, all else being equal, increasingly favors those at the top.

Behind curricular practices in English are labor, labor power, and these deepening market crises. We—understandably—concern ourselves with matters that on first inspection do not seem to be related.

For example, we concern ourselves with the numbers of undergraduates admitted each fall; with class-size numbers, the number of English majors, whether a course "goes" or not, the amount of the coursework a student completes in an acceptable fashion, and the amount of work reasonable in a course; with time to degree, whether we are graduating students fast enough; with admissions to graduate programs (especially to PhD programs); and with whether our PhDs are finishing quickly enough and getting jobs. Yet all of these are markers of regulated labor in English. So while the process of deepening crisis and the ever-expanding extraction of surplus value is *difficult* to see on the factory floor, it is nearly *impossible* to see in the rarefied forms it takes in our everyday professional academic practice.

We—all of us—students, graduate students, TAs, instructors, faculty, even administrators, are workers. We are wage labor. We do a particular job over a specified time for set wages and benefits, including grades and degrees for undergraduates and graduate tuition for TAs. All of these incomes come about because we are in the system in which labor power is regulated. We inhabit a system in which the surplus of our labor is taken off the top by the university. The university survives on the aggregate surplus value it extracts from us. And universities, especially state schools, for a variety of reasons find themselves in an economic crisis, no less than the wider culture. What is striking given cuts is that so-called state universities have responded as well and as imaginatively as they have. We are booming despite these deep contradictions. We are the only sector of the economy it would seem where we are more and more successful by any business criterion and yet, for that success, get cuts. So we are—and are not—being held to a business model.

Responding to the Crisis

English perhaps has been even more imaginative in response to this economic crisis than the university as a whole. Beginning around 1970 with the sudden and unexpected collapse of the market for PhDs in literature, English responded as any good corporation would—it expanded the product line and cut labor costs. Let me take each of these strategies in turn.

Expand the Product Line

First, English expanded the product line, the commodities we sell. For example, it is not by chance that basic writing and composition become major new areas in English during the 1970s, right after the literature

PhD market crashed, or that they were largely staffed by English graduates with PhDs in literature. James Berlin came over from Victorian literature, for example, as did David Bartholomae. Basic writing and composition were among the first product lines expanded in English. The expansion of creative writing programs traced by the founding of the Association of Writing Programs in 1967 (McGurl 2009) is also a marker of expanding the product line in English. The recent interest in creative nonfiction or literary journalism shows creative writing (and composition) still expanding. Theory in both literature and rhetoric and composition developed as one way to expand the product line by reconstructing the categories and subject matter of our work. And the founding of the Council of Writing Program Administrators (CWPA) in 1977 has been noted as a significant date for the expansion of rhetoric and composition into writing program administration. In rhetoric and composition, the expansion of the product through writing program administration was a move in both new and improved subject matter and techniques: one learned the subject matter of rhetoric and composition and then applied it as administrator rather than simply as teacher.

Cutting Labor

Labor in English was cut in a variety of imaginative ways as well. While the superstructure of the field of English and institution of English departments has remained remarkably stable since 1970, the infrastructure of English has been quietly and invisibly revolutionized. Despite utopian rhetorics, we cannot go back to the supposed Edenic days of the 1960s when there were all those jobs for fresh PhDs in literature because the very capital, the very political economy of English, that opens a space for people advocating utopian rhetorics to do their work is based on the thing they are critiquing—expansion of the product line and cuts in labor. A whole new infrastructure has been erected in the hollowed-out structure of English, the most obvious element of which is adjunct or part-time labor. But while adjunct labor and the abuse of part-time instructors is despicable, it is just the tip of the iceberg, the most visible symptom of a deeper transformation.

English did the usual things capitalist enterprises in crisis do—(1) outsource labor (in the case of the University of Houston Business College, writing instruction was sent electronically to Bangalore, India); (2) lengthen the working day (especially through technology—how many added hours a day do we spend on e-mail alone?); (3) add more work to each of our jobs (increased expectations for teaching—via the institution in the 1970s and subsequent mandatory use of student evaluations in faculty tenure and promotion decisions, but also in increased publication expectations and a myriad of new service obligations often involving ever-intensifying assessment of students and faculty); (4) privatize public labor (secretaries once did faculty typing and made travel arrangements for professional conferences); (5) intensify self-policing of work through annual reports (what at the University of Houston is so appropriately called the FARF—Faculty Academic Report Form); (6) automatize that policing by using online programs like Sedona that assess the value of publication venues (peer reviewed, on official lists); and (7) keep salaries basically flat regardless of merit pay.

But more important, English has also transformed how its subdisciplines work together to produce and support English. Now what I am suggesting here is that we must see English as this political economy in which the fates of literature, creative writing, and composition are now inextricably joined. I further claim that attempts of writing programs to go independent and form departments replicate the same basic structures in the new environment though filling these structures with a different set of personnel (see Zebroski 2002). I would go yet further: any political or economic analysis that remains inside the subdisciplines—that is, that focuses only on literature or creative writing or rhetoric and composition—will miss the central point, which is the way in which these enterprises form what I am calling *academic capital in English.*

Academic Capital in English—Leadership Capital, Artisan Capital, and Professional Capital

Why do literature, creative writing, and rhetoric and composition subdisciplines continue to inhabit the same house of English? Obviously there are many reasons. The areas of literature, creative writing, and rhetoric and composition have stayed in English because of (1) tradition, (2) ideology, (3) disciplinary practices, and (4) material reasons. In the material realm, all parties stay in the political economy of English because their separate academic capital is intricately interdependent. In short, all parties, whatever the disadvantages, gain more than they lose by remaining in this political economy. English departments survive because they produce, reinvest in, and expand these three conjoined forms of academic capital. English, then, is a system of labor extraction, a machine that extracts surplus value, making it into academic capital, which it circulates and trades. As I have said, there are at least three interrelated forms of academic capital circulating in English locally and nationally: (1) leadership capital associated with literature, (2) artisan capital associated with creative writing, and (3) professional capital associated with rhetoric and composition.

We often wonder why British literature scholars and often Shakespeareans tend to chair English departments when rhetoric and composition seems to make such an important contribution. Why, when we have all the students, does the literature faculty seem to control English—still? Why does the *New York Times* go to Stanley Fish, a Milton scholar, and not a rhetoric and composition faculty person when it wants an academic columnist? Why does popular culture including film tend to represent the English professor as a literature specialist?

Most research university English departments have a much larger number of literature faculty than rhetoric and composition faculty if we discount, as often happens, contingent faculty. Rhetoric and composition faculty (or staff) tend to take up lower-level administrative positions within English, while higher-level administrative positions tend to go to literature faculty. A different valuation is assigned to English majors pursuing literature and creative writing versus the number of actual students enrolled in courses.

Obviously, literature can claim to speak for tradition and high culture in ways neither creative writing nor rhetoric and composition can easily claim. But it seems that one of the reasons for going into and surviving in literature in English as a PhD student is that one receives, if successful, leadership capital, this added value by which one receives the authority to become a spokesperson for English to the external culture, whether spokesperson for what Murray Krieger (1994) calls the ideological tradition (high culture and elite values) or the counterideological (the political critique of such values). We have always known certain areas of specialization carry more value, more prestige. But beyond the analysis of binaries, there is the issue of aggregate accumulated labor. At the local and national levels, leadership capital ties into national discussions of English and academe and culture. The public sphere in English belongs to the leadership capital of literature; there is little evidence or reason to believe that is going to change soon.

If literature capital is leadership capital, then creative writing capital is artisan capital. Literature provides an objective tradition for our work, and creative writing provides everyone—students and faculty and the community—with the subjective, with the claim for uniqueness and specialness. Creative writing provides an artisan or crafted product that balances the more objective product of literature. If literature provides access to the Tradition, creative writing provides access to the Self, to that which makes each of us uniquely ourselves. At the local and national level, artisan capital ties into networks of the arts and arts funding. Obviously, this is not how our literary and creative writing colleagues view their work, but it tends to be how the wider culture—and our students—understand it, a fact that directly influences the decisions of provosts and deans.

Perhaps the most extensive analysis of creative writing as a national academic culture so far published, Mark McGurl's (2009) *The Program Era,* looks at the ways the increasing popularity of creative writing programs in university English departments has shaped post–World War II American literature. McGurl notes that creative writing programs at the graduate level went from a handful in the 1940s, to 52 in 1975, to 150 in 1984, to 350 in 2004. Nearly all have been housed in English departments. Citing David W. Fenza, McGurl notes that creative writing programs are "the largest system of literary patronage for living writers that the world has ever seen," running to at least $200 million annually (24). Further, McGurl argues that creative writing curricula produce two values for the student—first, the opportunity to reflect and write about personal experience in an otherwise objective curriculum (12), and second, what might be called *creative writer ideology* but that he names "the charisma of authorship": "An elective element of the undergraduate curriculum, creative writing issues an invitation to the student consumers to develop an intensely personal relationship to literary value . . . in favor of a more immediate identification with the charisma of authorship" (15–16). Such work allows the student to, in McGurl's words, "take a vacation from the usual grind" (16). All of these values, embodied in the word *craft,* are included in my term *artisan academic capital.*

Finally, rhetoric and composition provides English with professional capital—ways to service the English department and the graduate students but also service the university through first-year composition, writing across the curriculum, and writing in the disciplines. But materially, rhetoric and composition provides the TA lines English graduate students from literature and creative writing inhabit.

Rhetoric and composition also appears to provide a growing proportion of tenure-track jobs for the English department's PhD graduates. A 2012 *Report on the MLA Job Information List* notes that since 2000–2001, about 30 percent of the positions advertised have been in rhetoric and composition, close to the number of lines advertised in British literature. The third largest number of advertisements is for positions in American literature, ranging from 20 percent to 28 percent (Modern Language Association 2013, 17). However, what the MLA numbers support, but also obscure, is that the growth over the last 30 years has been in rhetoric and composition at the expense of literature. Sharon O'Dair (2000, 47–50) cites three dimensions of the market we must consider—(1) the number of positions, (2) the number of PhDs awarded, and (3) the kinds of positions, that is, whether literature, creative writing, or rhetoric and composition. When O'Dair includes these factors in her analysis, she discovers that the total number of positions has stayed the same or has slightly decreased and the number of graduates of doctoral programs in English has declined, but the number of rhetoric and composition tenure-line positions has exploded from 21.8 percent in 1982 to 26.5 percent in 1993 to 29.1 percent in 1996 (50). O'Dair concludes that rhetoric and composition has taken over the lines that before 1982 had gone to literature. And as we know, the competition for literature lines is usually more intense if one measures only by the number of applicants.

Rhetoric and composition provides the coin of the realm in first-year composition. While it is unlikely that chairs would hire rhetoric and composition graduates to teach literature—though many of them have master's degrees in the subfield—it is common to hire a literature scholar or creative writer to teach first-year composition, at least for contingent positions, and at small colleges often for regular tenure lines, too. Teaching first-year composition is the foundational job that the actions of chairs and hiring committees imply anyone can do for a time—especially if there are no jobs in one's area. This power asymmetry is further analyzed in the next section.

In sum, from a political economic point of view that includes English and extends to the public culture, literature provides the spokesperson for the public sphere, creative writing provides a place for "personal experience" (McGurl 2009), and rhetoric and composition provides those TA lines for all English graduate students and the jobs—first, tenure-track jobs for rhetoric and composition PhD graduates and, second, first-year composition work for the folks in literature and creative writing who do not immediately get jobs in those specialties. It's not personal; it's business.

II. FIRST-YEAR COMPOSITION AS AN ODDITY AND A COMMODITY

Let me move to first-year composition, which is central to the circulation of value in English. My goal here is to try to defamiliarize something so normal, so natural, so automatic for most of us.

The people who teach first-year composition are always already provided, and at the Tier 1 research university, they are mostly not rhetoric and composition faculty or graduate students in rhetoric and composition. In fact, quite the contrary. But then, faculty in rhetoric and composition are often not encouraged to teach first-year composition either, often being saddled with administrative work. Bartholomae (2005, 338) sees the trend, too, and is concerned about "the career of the composition specialist who never teaches composition."[7] And a surprising number of graduates of rhetoric and composition doctoral programs do not want to teach it. One of the epigraphs for this chapter is from a newly minted PhD in rhetoric and composition who informed me that they did not get that PhD in order to teach first-year composition. And as Bartholomae notes, it is hardly ever the case that English hires graduate students with an eye to their participation in the undergraduate curriculum. Rather, first-year composition is the term used "to front the widespread support of graduate study in English" (337–38).

The biggest problem of first-year composition in English departments is that it provides the TA lines that float the literature and creative writing PhD programs, and no matter how goodwilled these TAs may be, they aren't brought in to teach composition. And sometimes, the graduate student—or faculty person—acknowledges a distaste for teaching composition. While admitting that "we are not listening to what the market is saying, and neither are our graduate students. For if we were, more of our graduate students would be doing dissertations in rhetoric and composition," O'Dair (2000, 47) nevertheless captures the sense of many colleagues in areas other than rhetoric and composition in that she would prefer to take the chance on a literature position, and if that doesn't happen, leave academe altogether rather than teach composition. She says:

> But if our graduate students responded to that pressure by doing dissertations in composition—the only logical market response—then it follows that we literary and cultural critics would have fewer graduate students to work with and to supervise, or even to take our classes. We might find ourselves, occasionally, teaching composition. Instead of accepting that horrifying situation . . . [we] would rather take the risk of grabbing the gold ring of getting a tenure-track position teaching literature. (50)

The horror, the horror—teaching first-year composition!

Anyhow, as another epigraph for this chapter from an established faculty member and WPA notes, one does not need a PhD to teach first-year composition. How does this compare with other disciplines? Who teaches the introductory courses? Is it a regular faculty member or a teaching fellow?

Here, then, are some of the ways first-year composition is an oddity and a commodity:

1. Most people who teach first-year composition have little academic or professional interest in it (see Gadzinski 1997; Jones 1997; O'Dair 2000).
2. Most people who teach first-year composition are literature or creative writing students.
3. Few rhetoric and composition faculty teach first-year composition; if they do, it does not happen very often.
4. Reading and discussion of essays plays the central role in most actual classes of first-year composition. Texts like *Ways of Reading* are bestsellers for this reason and because the readings are related to what the graduate-student teacher is studying—literature or creative writing.
5. First-year composition is the only core course that is "small" (about 25 students) and has one of the smallest class sizes of any course on campus until one reaches graduate seminars.
6. Adjunct and part-time labor trades mostly in first-year composition. First-year composition for our graduates who do not get jobs is what is available when everything else has fallen through.
7. Most adjunct and part-time instructors who have the doctoral degree are PhDs in literature or creative writing. Hardly any have PhDs in rhetoric and composition.
8. The move in the last decade to "argument" in first-year composition is partly about "expanding the line." Textbook publishers need a "new and improved" product to sell. WPAs need a new set of simplistic, enforceable "deliverables."
9. What is crucial in the political economy of English is not first-year composition as subject matter per se but (1) the TA lines embedded in first-year composition that support the PhD programs in literature and creative writing, and (2) the flexibility and fluidity of exchange that labor facilitates (i.e., anyone in English is believed to be able to teach it at any university or college or community college or high school at any time. No specific credentials in rhetoric and composition are needed).

No one seems to want first-year composition—except if there are no other courses to teach or no other jobs to be had. It's not personal; it's business.

III: TENDENCIES (ENGLISH 2026)

If we follow out the consequences of this analysis, what can we expect? Given the tendencies we have seen over the last 40 years in the political economy of English, in the next several years several things will happen:

- English departments will still exist at large universities.
- Rhetoric and composition will still mostly exist in English departments.
- Few writing departments will go independent.
- Rhetoric and composition PhD programs will mostly be located in English. English provides security or "cover" in existing budgets in the largest department on campus but also prestige and the site of the most secure tenure-track faculty jobs for rhetoric and composition. Rhetoric and composition provides enrollments and TA lines through freshman composition. Rhetoric and composition also provides for the "feeding" and care of all English graduate students and jobs for its graduates. Rhetoric and composition job numbers, aggregated into the department numbers, float lower numbers in literature and creative writing PhD programs.
- Publication of research will remain the coin of the realm. "Excellence" in English departments will increasingly be determined by publication. The threat if one does not publish will be, ironically, heavier teaching loads; teaching "functions" as punishment despite what administrators say.
- A focus on publication does not mean teaching will disappear or that it will not in some way be valued. But it means that at large state universities, we are moving to a two-tier faculty system, predicted by Michael Murphy (2000), that will value teaching differently. Research faculty will teach larger numbers of graduate courses and will largely be assessed by publication and national reputation; clinical faculty, which will probably increase in numbers, will be constituted out of existing tenure-track lines that open with retirements. Clinical faculty will be the site of teaching at the undergraduate level. Clinical faculty will teach heavier loads and will be assessed on the quality of their teaching.
- English departments will lose support if time to degree (TTD) at both the undergraduate and graduate levels is not soon improved. This means literature PhDs with a TTD of seven-plus years will especially be on the chopping block. With the cut of programs in literature, literature PhDs may be doing their work in literature within the structure, under the guise, of rhetoric and composition PhD programs in the next decade.[8]
- Creative writing futures will peak and begin to decline if all other things remain equal. To offset a worsening job market in creative writing, we should expect a countertrend in expansion in new offerings in creative writing. If poetry and fiction were the mainstays of the past, creative writing programs of the future will also offer creative nonfic tion and playwriting courses (Galef 2000, 161).[9]
- Rhetoric and composition futures in writing program administration

will peak and begin to decline.

- Rhetoric and composition futures in electronic curricula will increase exponentially. Online undergraduate curricula from start to degree will be the growth area in rhetoric and composition.
- Intense pressure will be applied to cut labor by outsourcing first-year composition, especially through dual-credit programs in the high schools or via community colleges and University of Phoenix-like online courses.
- As first-year composition is outsourced, there will be huge struggle—the mother of all battles—between provosts and English chairs about keeping existing TA lines and keeping them in English.
- First-year composition will be evenly split among traditional face-to-face classes, hybrid classes, and online courses. Soon all first-year composition courses will use digital textbooks. The day of university bookstores is nearly over. In the short run, this means there will be opportunities to not use textbooks; in the longer run, textbook use will be even more closely policed and required. Curriculum in the long run will be shaped even more than currently by textbook publishers. Textbook company profits are huge; the corporate hold over first-year writing will increase, only with severe digital monitoring, which will increase the panopticon effect. For digital policing that is on the way, see the April 8, 2013, article in the *New York Times*, "Teacher Knows if You Have Done the E-Reading."

Looking at the political economy of English should help us to see that regardless of the tendencies, we have agency, individually and collectively. This chapter does not argue what Christopher Newfield (2008, 168) calls "market determinism"; rather it begins with Jeffrey Williams's (2013, 6) observation that "the market, after all, is not a natural force but a human arrangement, based on social contract, protected and encouraged by law as well as regulated by it." This analysis, I hope, helps us to see what is the essential part of the system. In that respect, it helps us to pick our battles. As Maxine Hairston (1982) long ago pointed out, the first charge of rhetoric is to discover whether the issue in question is worth arguing about.[10]

But an analysis of the political economy of English also begins to point to the contradictions, fissures, and unintended consequences that can open up new spaces of agency and sites of innovation in curriculum. There clearly will be a lot of opportunities for rethinking the teaching of writing. Given online and hybrid and MOOC instruction, we will also need to revisit the last 40 years of research on the teaching and learning of writing. For example, we have good evidence that small groups in face-to-face instruction when carefully designed and implemented in a class seem to improve student writing. But this research has all come from classes with face-to-face instruction. Is this principle still true for online instruction? We do not know yet, though recent work suggests the old research holds true for online education as well (see Miley 2013). So the point of this analysis is not that things are hopeless but rather that things are changing and that we and our students must change, too. We must remember that rhetoric and composition as a discipline emerged from the catastrophic failure in the job market for English PhDs in the 1970s. The analysis of the political economy of English helps us to imagine a better collective and individual future.

Notes

1. The research on this matter is voluminous, but see Paul Krugman's (2007) *The Conscience of a Liberal.* Both in his books and in his regular columns in the *New York Times*, we have a record and a call to action based on such evidence.
2. See the *New York Times* article by Floyd Norris, August 10, 2013. According to figures collected by the US Department of Commerce's Bureau of Economic Analysis and known as National Income and Product Accounts (NIPA), income in 2012 amounted to 42.6 percent of GDP while corporate profits, after taxes, amounted to 9.7 percent of GDP, a record. To give some sense of what this signifies, the earlier record high, if we go back before the last three years, was 9.1 percent in 1929, just before the Great Depression.
3. This essay focuses on the "typical" large Tier 1 research university despite the fact that half of my professional life has been spent either at small liberal arts colleges or medium-sized state colleges. This focus should in no way be seen as assuming the priority of large state schools; it is simply a convenience. As Jeffrey Williams (2013, 5) notes, "We take research universities as the standard, but they are not really typical of most people's experience." While I do think that some of what I delineate here also fits with smaller schools and departments, there can be no doubt that these private and so-called teaching universities have their own histories and values. Over thirty years of teaching in my professional life, the only places where teaching was truly valued were at two small liberal arts universities whose English faculties were miniscule—one was five and the other eight faculty. The work these colleges do is extremely important and of high quality.
4. See Gerald Graff 1987, D. G. Myers 1996, and Mark McGurl 2009. Even Thomas Miller (1997) does not fully focus on contemporary English departments and the value of the work they do. What is critical is to not simply add parallel accounts or make some general claims about X in lit influencing Z in composition but rather to analyze how doing X and doing Y creates value in English.
5. I want to make it clear that by using the term *English*—or *creative writing faculty* or *rhetoric composition faculty*—I do not intend to personify social forces as agents. The whole point of this essay is to recognize the human-made nature of the market and political economy and to argue for transformation. When I, quoting McGurl (2009), say something like the "creative writing curriculum creates an experience of subjectivity and a 'charismatic model of creative being,'" this is shorthand. There is no monstrous single force out there labeled the *creative writing curriculum.* Certainly there is no such force in any English department. Such an effect comes from many individuals joined in a collective enterprise locally, nationally, and globally, and there

are fissures and divisions and fragments within any of these communities that are themselves crucial to examine. So each time I use such a representation, it is with this awareness and is an attempt to make the reading of this chapter a little easier.

6. For the phrase *the commodity as oddity*, see the excellent analysis of David Smith and Phil Evans in *Marx's "Kapital" for Beginners* (Smith and Evans 1982, 31). Ultimately, the idea is embedded in Marx's analysis in the first volume of *Capital: A Critique of Political Economy* I (Marx 1990, 163–77). Further, see Bertoll Ollman (1976) and Terry Eagleton (2011).
7. My home institution is unusual in that all of our rhetoric and composition tenure-track research faculty teach first-year composition regularly. According to my data, our three active faculty members have over the last three academic years taught seven sections of FYW during the year and an added five during the summers. This averages to about one or two sections of FYW each year per faculty person, though the specifics depend on other rotating administrative and graduate commitments.
8. At the University of Houston, we are already seeing students who have primarily literary interests applying for admission to the rhetoric, composition, and pedagogy doctoral program, even though it was created only in 2010. The RCP faculty have recently taken up the issue of establishing a process and criteria for "internal transfer" from the literature PhD program into the RCP program.
9. David Galef (2000, 168) says, "Concomitant with comp/rhet's ascent as a discipline is the rise of creative writing programs to the point where most colleges in the United States now have at least some form of fiction and poetry workshops." He adds, "As with comp/rhet the trend is economically driven—creative writing is a cash cow, a popular offering with low overhead. . . . As one professor with a foot in literary criticism and creative writing cynically commented: 'All you need to start is a copy machine and an instructor with a few poetry publications under his belt'" (171).
10. Maxine Hairston (1982), unlike many current rhetoricians, does not argue that everything is argument. She, in fact, radically constrains rhetoric by asserting that there are plenty of times when argument is "pointless," a "waste of time." In *A Contemporary Rhetoric* (3rd ed.), Hairston has an entire chapter (chapter 6) about when rhetoric and argument is helpful and when it is not, entitled "Where Rhetoric Starts—and Stops."

PART II

Economies of Writing Pedagogy and Curriculum

6

ECONOMIES OF KNOWLEDGE TRANSFER AND THE USE-VALUE OF FIRST-YEAR COMPOSITION

Anis Bawarshi

One does not have to look far to recognize the economics inherent in the concept of knowledge transfer, a concept that has garnered a great deal of attention in composition studies in the last few years because of its relevance to writing development, especially the ability to adapt writing knowledge and skills across contexts. The term itself is inflected with economic associations: the transfer of assets and funds, bank and account transfers, and so on. And indeed, traditional approaches to knowledge transfer have tended to treat the phenomenon in this more obvious economic way: as the carrying over of knowledge and skills from one context to another. However, in the last three decades and within the fields of cognitive psychology, education, and more recently composition studies, there has been an effort to understand knowledge transfer in more nuanced ways that account not just for the cognitive but also for the sociocultural factors involved in transferability. These contributions encourage us to consider the more complex economies at work in knowledge transfer, a project that has implications not only for the study and teaching of writing but also, as I argue in this chapter, for how we imagine the possible value of first-year composition courses.

Questions regarding knowledge transfer have become increasingly common within composition studies, engaging some of the core issues involved in the study and teaching of writing and in the development of writing ability. In particular, they get to the heart of fundamental debates about the place, purpose, and use/exchange value of first-year composition (FYC) courses: whether (and what kinds of) knowledge and skills developed in FYC courses are useful to other contexts within and beyond the academy; whether there are generalizable writing skills that traverse contexts or whether writing skills are so situated in epistemological, material contexts that they can only be acquired

DOI: 10.7330/9781607325239.c006

and deployed within those contexts. These questions have animated debates between writing in the disciplines and FYC approaches to writing instruction. David Russell (1995, 1999), for example, has likened the teaching of generalized writing skills in FYC to teaching a course in general ball handling, under the assumption that such a course can prepare students to play any sport that involves a ball. Russell's analogy challenges us as a field to examine our operating assumptions about writing development and its transferability across contexts. As Elizabeth Wardle (2007, 66) puts it, we "would be irresponsible not to engage issues of transfer," a point that follows from David Smit's (2004) identification of "transferability" as a primary consideration for writing instruction in his book *The End of Composition Studies.*

In particular, Smit (2004) questions composition's faith in the generalizability of writing skills and knowledge. Although he is certainly not the first to raise these questions (see, for example, Petraglia 1995), the timing of his book and the provocation implied in its title posed a considerable challenge for the field, as the number of writing-transfer studies that have appeared since its publication attest, most recently in the form of a special issue of *Composition Forum* devoted to transfer (see also Artemeva 2005; Beaufort 2007; Bergmann and Zepernick 2007; Brendt 2011; Dias and Paré 2000; Driscoll and Wells 2012; Ford 2004; Fraizer 2010; Jarratt et al. 2009; Nelms and Dively 2007; Nowacek 2011; Reiff and Bawarshi 2011; Roozen 2010; Wardle 2007). In brief, Smit (2004) argues that there is no such thing as a generic writing ability (beyond syntactic fluency), that writing is task-and-domain specific, that genre conventions are too complex to be learned through explicit instruction, and that there is no such thing as an "academic discourse community" for which FYC prepares students. Instead, he proposes that writing instruction must take place within task-specific contexts and that writing is most effectively acquired through critical, reflective immersion. Although he describes an ideal curriculum that proceeds from a more general Introduction to Writing as a Social Practice course, which introduces students to the idea of genre, discourse communities, and the critique of discourse communities, the main focus of writing instruction in his proposed curriculum would take place within disciplinary contexts and through apprenticeship.

My aim is not to get into the specifics of Smit's arguments and recommendations, important as these are. Rather, I want to focus on the assumptions about transferability that underlie his critique of FYC courses. Smit's definition of transfer reflects a long-held understanding of the concept: "In what sense can various kinds of knowledge and skill be transferred from one situation to another, or learned in one context and applied in another?" (Smit 2004, 119). As Smit goes on to explain, "Overwhelmingly, the evidence suggests that learners do not necessarily transfer the kinds of knowledge and skills they have learned previously to new tasks" (119). In making this observation, Smit echoes many studies that have challenged what Perkins and Salomon (1988) have called the "bo-peep" theory of transfer—the idea that once initial learning takes place, transfer takes care of itself. Instead, transfer research, since E. L. Thorndike's (1999) work in the early twentieth century, has revealed the extent to which learning is a highly situated activity, and that once acquired, specific content will not necessarily transfer to new situations (Bransford and Schwartz 1999, 62).

Space does not permit a fuller discussion of transfer research, but a couple of distinctions are worth making. First, all learning involves transfer in some sense, although transfer researchers distinguish between immediate demonstrations of initial learning and the transfer of learning across some gap: the learner doing something with what has been learned, under a different set of conditions, with a different appearance (Perkins and Salomon 2012, 249). Second, transfer is a more complex phenomenon than it initially appears to be. As Bransford and Schwartz (1999) have argued, evidence of failed transfer is often the result of perspectives on transfer that obscure its presence. Prevailing theories and methods of measuring transfer, they claim, "represent too blunt an instrument for studying the smaller changes in learning that lead" to transfer of knowledge (66–67). They describe these prevailing perspectives as based in direct application theory: the ability to directly apply one's previous learning to a new setting or problem. This direct-application view has pervaded transfer research and reflects, I argue, the more traditional economic view of transfer I mentioned earlier. It also underwrites Smit's and others' critique that FYC courses do not have transfer value because skills learned in FYC do not appear to directly transfer to new contexts.

Direct-application views of transfer are often based on what Bransford and Schwartz (1999) describe as "knowing that" and "knowing how." *Knowing that* refers to replicative knowledge we carry with us from one context to another. *Knowing how* refers to applicative knowledge we can apply to new contexts and tasks. Generally speaking, learners can directly apply *knowing that* and *knowing how* to new contexts and tasks as long as the contexts and tasks are *perceptually similar*. This is a crucial point. As research has demonstrated, while evidence of direct application of knowledge and skills can be found across similar contexts (known as *near transfer*), rarely can we find evidence of direct application across dissimilar contexts (known as *far transfer*)—the very kinds of dissimilar contexts student writers often encounter after FYC.

Far transfer is much harder to notice using traditional "economic" measures. As Perkins and Salomon (1988) explain, far transferability "depends on deliberate mindful abstraction of skill and knowledge from one context for application in another" (25) and "involves reflective thought in abstracting from one context and seeking connections with others" (26). Bransford and Schwartz (1999) describe the metacognitive processes (the ability to inventory, monitor, and assess one's thinking and problem solving) involved in far transfer as based in individuals' "Preparation for Future Learning." A PFL perspective on transfer looks for evidence of learning a later task as a "*function of*" learners' previous experiences (69, emphasis added)—that is, not a direct application of prior experiences but a *function of* prior experiences. Citing H. S. Broudy (1977), they describe "function of" as a form of "knowing with," a special kind of knowing that involves associating, interpreting, adapting, and translating prior knowledge to help us perform new tasks in new contexts. *Knowing with* means we think about new tasks in light of what we already know or have learned to do, asking questions like these: In what ways is this task similar to and/or different from others I have performed in the past? How can I adapt what I already know to help me figure out this new task? What prior skills, knowledge, and experiences do I have that can help me figure out what to do in this less familiar task? What problem-solving strategies learned through previous tasks can I use to help me figure out a new task? How can I translate writing experiences, genre knowledge, and discursive resources from one context to another? *Knowing with* requires that we maintain a productive relationship with what we already know, including knowing when to let go of prior knowledge. Relying too much on what we already know or rejecting too much of what we already know can limit how we engage with new tasks. In short, a *knowing-with* perspective on transfer involves taking the knowledge, skills, or thinking strategies learned in one context and translating/transforming that learned knowledge, skill, or thinking strategy to accomplish a task in another context.

In terms of writing, the difference between *knowing how* and *knowing with* can be seen in what students do with their prior writing knowledge. For example, students who *know how* to write a five-paragraph essay (and who initially learn it as a universal, fixed formula) may try to reproduce that formula when they encounter a more complex writing task in FYC. Students who *know with* a five-paragraph essay (and who initially learn it as a problem-solving tool rather than a formula) may be more inclined to abstract and adapt parts of it when they encounter a more complex task. We observed this phenomenon in a study of students' use of prior genre knowledge, in which some students persisted in using such genres wholesale while others repurposed parts of their prior genre knowledge for use in new writing tasks (see Reiff and Bawarshi 2011). We see examples of *knowing with* whenever writers translate prior genre knowledge or work to extract principles and strategies from prior writing experiences for use in new writing situations.

A *knowing with* approach to transfer shifts our attention away from direct application, a traditional economic perspective that measures the carry-over of knowledge and skills, and focuses instead on the metacognitive, problem-solving dispositions involved in transfer. And indeed, a dispositional view of transfer (see Bereiter 1995) has become more prominent in transfer scholarship, with Wardle, Dana Lynn Driscoll and Jennifer Wells, Linda Bergman and Janet Zepernick, Rebecca Nowacek, and others arguing that we must cultivate students' dispositions for transfer rather than (or in addition to) teaching them directly transferable skills—in other words, teaching students how to *know with* what they are learning in our courses. Such a dispositional approach, however, involves more than metacognitive abilities. As transfer scholars have begun to demonstrate, dispositions are not only cognitively framed, they are also situated within and shaped by sociocultural conditions that challenge us to consider more complex economies of transfer.

Tuomi-Gröhn and Engeström (2003) as well as others, for example, have described the complex educational, socioeconomic, cultural, material, and political economies that inform how, why, and when students transfer knowledge, including factors such as motivation, task recognition, stakes, engagement, and teacher and peer feedback as well as assignment prompting and other affordances that can cue or limit transfer. For example, in one study of FYC and transfer, Wardle (2007) found that one reason students did not transfer knowledge and skills from FYC is because they rarely reported the need to do so. They were not given transfer-inviting tasks. Wardle found that, in addition to the nature of the task and its degree of difficulty and authenticity, teacher expectations and feedback played a role in transfer, along with time constraints, students' investment and engagement in the task, and their sense of the stakes involved. All these affordances reveal the interconnected elements of an activity system (subjectivity, mediational means, object-motives, affiliations, and divisions of labor) that affect transferability and that call on us to consider wider economies of transfer.

King Beach (2003) has also identified the sociocultural conditions involved in transfer, challenging the stabilities assumed in the very term itself. Traditional views of transfer, according to Beach, assume a stable set of contexts between which knowledge and skills are transferred, a stable understanding of knowledge and skills that remain unchanged in the process of transfer, and a stable self that transfers knowledge. In Beach's view, all these components are, in fact, in dynamic play and are subject to transformations during transfer (see Wardle's [2007] memorable example of looking for apples when they have been transformed into apple pie). As a result, Beach (2003, 42) proposes the concept of "consequential transitions" to describe the shifts involved in transfer have consequences for the individuals, the contexts, and, indeed, the transferred knowledge itself. As a result, measuring transfer becomes a great deal more complex because the elements involved are transforming in the process. Marilyn Sternglass's (1997) study of student writing development, documented in *Time to Know Them*, provides insight into these consequential transitions. For one case-study student, Linda, we see how transfer of knowledge among a basic writing course, a psychology course, a world civilization course, a women's studies course, and nursing courses was tied up with Linda's changing relationship to her mother, herself, and her place within the university, which allowed her to transfer knowledge via a changing understanding of women's role in society. Sternglass's research calls on us to consider the wider economies involved in transfer—how transfer needs to be thought of in terms of changing relations to oneself and others, one's context, and one's prior knowledge and experiences. It also challenges us to take a long-term, multidimensional view of transfer in order to account for the subtle but consequential transitions that take time to unfold before transfer can appear. Such a perspective is not accounted for in traditional, economic views of transfer.

More recently, Jarratt et al. (2009) have described the influence of students' pedagogical memories on how they transfer knowledge. As their research shows, pedagogical memory informs how students encounter FYC courses and make long-term use (or not) of what they learn there. In one memorable case, Jarratt et al. describe a student who recalls her disappointment about the location of her composition course more than anything she learned about writing: "Wow, I'm sorry. I don't really remember a lot about first-year writing. That was my first class ever at UCI. It was in a trailer [laughter]. I was like, I'm going to university and I'm in a trailer? That's a little disheartening" (63–64). Here we see how material conditions and affects (what Jarratt et al. [2009, 48] call "emotional dispositions") inform this student's relation to her writing course and its transfer value, an issue Angela Rounsaville (2012) has recently taken up in her examination of the complex memory uptakes involved in transfer. Dan Fraizer (2010) has likewise described how location impacts transfer, exploring how third spaces like studios and writing centers can help students make connections across disciplinary courses by virtue of their interstitial positioning.

Other studies provide greater insights into the complex economies of transfer. Bergmann and Zepernick's (2007) research reveals how the institutional status of FYC (including the status of those hired to teach it, its relation to English, etc.) affects how students perceive its long-term value. They observe that "the primary obstacle to such transfer is not that students are *unable* to recognize situations outside FYC in which those skills can be used, but that students *do not look for* such situations because they believe that skills learned in FYC have no value in any other setting" (139). Again, we see how transfer is subject to a larger set of economies and ideas of value that affect how learners see and make connections.

Along these lines, Rebecca Nowacek's (2011) research reveals how transferability is a rhetorical act, one that involves not only seeing connections but also selling them within material conditions as well as institutional systems of value. In this way, transfer involves brokering and is subject to power dynamics. It is not enough for students to transfer knowledge across disciplinary contexts; they must be able to "sell" it *and* it must be validated, which is where power comes into play in terms of what knowledge transfer is sanctioned, who is granted authority to see and sell it, the institutional affordances that enable or prevent the seeing and selling, and so on. For instance, Nowacek examined an interdisciplinary learning community in which a cohort of students was enrolled in a team-taught cluster of history, literature, and religious studies courses. In some cases, because the connections among courses were institutionally made visible (or "seen") by the very nature of the cluster, there was not a need for students to sell these connections to the faculty teaching each course, as when one student recognized connections between and brought historical knowledge about the Reformation to bear on his literary analysis of *Doctor Faustus* (44–45). There was no need to sell these connections because the institutional arrangement and coordination among the coteaching faculty had already authorized them. Even within such an institutional arrangement, however, Nowacek identified several instances in which students needed to or were not able to sell the connections they had seen. One student, for example, needed to sell the connection she was making between the religious studies and literature courses. For a literature paper asking students to compare *The Merchant of Venice* and *Paradise Lost*, the student chose to compare the versions of marriage represented in each text, using Thomas Hobbes's *Leviathan* (which she had read in her religious studies course) as a framework for analyzing marriage. To sell the connection to her literature professor, the student employed a series of rhetorical strategies and attributions that enabled successful transfer, as validated by the professor's positive responses (52–53). In some cases, though, students were not able to sell connections across powerful institutional and epistemological boundaries, as in the case of one student who struggled to apply ways of knowing from history to an analysis of a literary text. In this case, the history course's collectivizing perspective came into conflict with the literature course's individualizing perspective on the nature of experience (60–62). As a result, while the student was able to see connections between disciplinary ways of knowing, she was not able to sell them in ways her literature professor would find persuasive, as indicated by the professor's skeptical reactions to the paper. Institutional and epistemological contexts, as well as the complex economies, systems of value, and power dynamics inherent in them, all play a role in how transferability is performed, recognized, and validated.

Nowacek (2011) also demonstrates how genres are powerful exigencies for transfer, which become another affordance within its complex economies. Genres are not simply buckets in which students can transfer knowledge across contexts. As epistemological formations, involved phenomenologically in how we recognize, encounter, and engage with situations, genres play an important role in transferability. For instance, Nowacek describes a history assignment that asks students to write a medieval diary entry in which they chronicle the material reality of someone living in medieval times. However, one student wrote a psychological portrait instead, in part because for us today, a diary's use-value is largely measured by its introspective function. In this case, genre becomes a significant variable within complex economies of transfer, exerting its own epistemological and sociological use-value in ways unaccounted for by traditional economic views of transfer.

Artemeva and Fox (2010) recently studied the transfer of genre awareness into performance in a first-year engineering communications course. Students in the study demonstrated genre awareness of technical reports, but when asked shortly after as part of a diagnostic exercise to write a technical report, the majority defaulted to producing traditional high-school English essays instead. What I find interesting, though, is that we learn later in the study that the technical reports written for the diagnostic were graded, which raises a question about the role the economies of grades played in leading students to default to producing English essays rather than risk taking up their still-tentative awareness of technical reports. In addition, Natasha Artemeva's (2005) research on engineering students' transitions from academic to workplace genres further illuminates the complex economies involved in transfer. For one case-study student, Sami, the ability to challenge workplace genres and transfer prior knowledge early in his professional career is tied to his sense of cultural capital, which allows him to redefine a kairotic moment at work (394). Sami's cultural capital is an inheritance of sorts, willed to him by his father and grandfather, also engineers, and by this sense of belonging. As Sami tells Artemeva, "[My dad] passes that information to me, so . . . I have the feeling I've been there before" (401–2).

So what does all this mean? In her afterword to the recent special issue of *JAC* devoted to "Economies of Writing," Deborah Brandt (2012) explains that economies of language are not stable: "Rather they constantly must absorb and adjust to the dynamic, changing conditions of local pressures, and they can be highly susceptible to the influences of distant locations, especially politically and economically powerful ones" (772). Considering the *economies* of writing, Bruce Horner (2012) explains, means accounting for the political systems of production, circulation, ideology, and engagement that "left unchallenged, set terms for debate and exchange that define in advance the value and meaning ascribed to the work of writing and its teaching and study, and all those involved in that work" (459). The same can be said about the complex economies of knowledge transfer, which are subject to the dynamics of local and distant pressures as well as to the political conditions that define in advance what counts as evidence of transfer. In Horner's (2012, 459) terms, we must reset the "terms for debate and exchange that define in advance the value and meaning ascribed" to knowledge transfer, especially as these play out in debates about FYC.

Economic views of transfer as direct application tend to measure the value of FYC courses in terms of what might be called (or what I am loosely calling) their *exchange value*, the extent to which they provide something directly transferable to other contexts. But given how complex a phenomenon knowledge transfer is, I would like to propose that, rather than measuring FYC courses in terms of their exchange value, we instead see them as having a use-value in and of themselves as sites not only of *knowing that* and *knowing how*, but also of *knowing with.* That is, I want to propose an FYC course whose goal, at least in part, involves teaching *about* transfer—a course in which knowledge and skills such as learning how to develop complex claims, how to write in academic genres, how to deploy evidence, how to read critically, and how to conduct research in support of inquiry are not the ends but the means or occasions for practicing and developing metacognition. In such a course, students examine the economies of transfer; read research on transfer; reflect on themselves as learners and on the predispositions that shape their encounters; negotiate and repurpose prior knowledge and experiences in relation to new tasks and contexts; develop problem-solving strategies; hone their abilities to see similarities in differences and differences in similarities; learn how to see and sell connections across contexts; practice the adaptive skills that can come from engaging in cross-language and cross-genre performances; engage in what Wardle (2012) has recently called "problem-exploring" dispositions, which can incline students toward curiosity, reflection, and a willingness to engage in trial and error; and so on. In short, I want to propose that the use-value of FYC should be defined not by the extent to which students can directly transfer skills and knowledge from it to other contexts (*knowing how*) but by the extent to which it prepares students for future learning (*knowing with*).

Such an FYC course would focus students' attention on the transitional spaces, the interstices, the in-betweens where transfer takes place. We know from transfer research that near transfer (the transfer of knowledge and skills across perceptually similar contexts) is fairly unconscious and automatic, as in the case of transferring driving skills from a sedan to an SUV. Near transfer involves what Daniel Kahneman (2011) has called "thinking fast," a form of routinized thinking that enables us to negotiate daily life without cognitive overload. Within activity systems, for instance, most genres enable fast thinking. I have taken to calling fast thinking *once-upon-a-time* thinking because of the way it ritualizes our behaviors and quickly tells us what to expect. Far transfer, however, requires "thinking slow," what Perkins and Salomon (1988, 25) describe as "deliberate mindful abstraction" of skills and knowledge across dissimilar contexts. When a student writes a five-paragraph essay in response to an assignment asking for a technical report, that student is likely engaging in fast once-upon-a-time thinking when the rhetorical situation requires slow thinking—thinking that involves taking stock, figuring out what the student already knows and does not know, abstracting from, adapting, and translating prior genre knowledge. Positioned as it is on the edges of the university, a liminal space, FYC can be a productive site for students to think critically (and slowly) about the nature of transitions, the negotiation between prior and new knowledge, how to know with the discursive resources they bring with them as well as their prior knowledge. In my FYC program, for instance, we begin by asking students to write on one of three prompts:

- Describe a previous writing experience you had (in or out of school) and reflect on what you learned from that experience (not just skills but also habits and ways of thinking about writing) that you can draw on when writing at the college level. As you imagine what college-level writing will be like, what can you *know with* that prior writing experience?
- Of the reading and writing skills you bring with you, which ones do you think will serve you most and which ones do you think will serve you least? And why? In what ways, if any, do you imagine you might need to adapt these skills?
- What have you done when you have encountered new ideas, especially ideas that challenge your certainties or strongly held beliefs? Describe a time when you encountered ideas that challenged you and reflect on how you learned with the knowledge you gained from this challenging encounter. What did you learn *with* that experience that you might want to emulate and/or avoid?

If fast thinking involves once-upon-a-time thinking, then slow thinking involves what I have taken to calling, courtesy of a line from Dylan Thomas's poem "Fern Hill," *once-below-a-time* thinking. When we encounter a phrase like *once below a time*, we are forced to slow down, invited to linger and to consider what it means to think about time in this way. It also changes our relationship to the familiar *once-upon-a-time* phrase. Inviting students, similarly, to engage in acts of translation, in which they recontextualize familiar genres or other discursive resources and then reflect on these performances, not only teaches students valuable rhetorical skills, it also creates a reflective space for students to examine the affordances made possible through different genres, languages, and forms of expression. At key points of transition, we can ask students to think critically about their encounters and performances: to consider what a particular task is asking them to do, to think about what it reminds them of and how it might be similar to and different from other tasks they have done, to monitor the ways they went about solving a problem and performing a task, to consider what they want to remember from the experience and how they can *know with* it in the future. By asking students to spend time in these in-between spaces, we provide them with opportunities to develop their metacognitive skills—to sharpen their abilities to *know with* that can then prepare them to encounter later transitions more deliberately and productively.

Likewise, by giving students opportunities to write across genres, languages, and media, we also can help them develop their abilities to "sell" connections, especially those that are not obvious or are politically fraught or are subject to power imbalances. Often, as Nowacek (2011) has described, students' attempts at making far-transfer connections are ignored, misunderstood, or rejected. A significant use-value for FYC can be its role in teaching students how to see and sell connections to various audiences, including audiences that may be predisposed to reject the connections. Such an assignment could be especially valuable to translingual and transcultural students seeking ways to work and make meanings across boundaries.

Too often we think of activities in FYC as having failed because their transfer value is not obvious. For example, students and teachers may complain that peer review of student writing is useless because the feedback is not helpful or because there is little student uptake of the feedback. However, another way to approach the use-value of peer review is by framing it as an exercise in feedback selection. Its transfer value in this case is not measured by its direct application but by the opportunity it provides students to assess the feedback they get against their writing goals. *Knowing with* how to assess, select from, and make use of peer (and instructor, for that matter) feedback can prepare students for far transfer whether or not there is evidence of direct application of feedback in a student's revised paper. The point is that we still can and should ask students to write papers, practice and demonstrate academic writing conventions, work across media, genres, and languages, do peer review, and perform other typical FYC tasks. But rather than defining FYC's exchange value by the extent to which such skills and knowledge directly transfer to other contexts—an economic view of transfer that if "left unchallenged, set[s] terms for debate and exchange that define in advance the value and meaning ascribed to the work of writing and its teaching and study, and all those involved in that work" (Horner 2012, 459)—we should define FYC's use-value by the extent to which it prepares students for future learning by providing them with opportunities to inhabit transitional spaces and consider the more complex economies involved in knowledge transfer in ways that can serve them well, well beyond FYC.

7

SYMBOLIC CAPITAL IN THE FIRST-YEAR COMPOSITION CLASSROOM

Yuching Jill Yang, Kacie Kiser, and Paul Kei Matsuda

In the first-year composition (FYC) classroom, teachers' identities play an important role in shaping interactions and learning. The implications are even more significant in classrooms where teachers represent social attributes (e.g., age, gender, ethnicity, education, nationality, and language) often associated with having less power than those sanctioned by the dominant ideology. Over the years, scholars such as Min-Zhan Lu (1994), Cheryl L. Johnson (1994), Jeanne Gunner (1993), and Terry Dean (1989) have examined how students construct their writing teachers as "racialized, gendered, and political subjects" (Royster and Taylor 1997, 27). Adding another dimension to the discussion of writing-teacher identity, Jacqueline Jones Royster and Rebecca Greenberg Taylor argued for the need to consider how teachers' subjectivities are constructed and negotiated not only by students but by teachers themselves (Royster and Taylor 1997). While it is important to understand how and to what extent the teacher's subjectivity is constructed by both parties, it is also necessary to consider how larger social forces assign value to various identity traits.

The goal of this chapter is to explore, from a Bourdieuian perspective, how teachers' symbolic capital is affected by the force of a particular market and how those values might be negotiated through agentive rhetorical actions. To this end, we present narrative case studies of two writing teachers—Kacie and Yuching—who negotiated their symbolic capital as they moved from one linguistic market to another. Our exploration is preliminary, based largely on the two teachers' perceptions and self-assessments. Still, we hope to illustrate how market forces affect the values of various types of symbolic capital. We also hope to show that, although teachers' ability to negotiate individual traits may be limited, it is still possible to negotiate the net worth of their symbolic capital by rhetorically constructing various types of identity traits.

DOI: 10.7330/9781607325239.c007

Based on the narratives of two teachers, we argue for the importance of seeing symbolic capital as a portfolio rather than focusing on a limited number of traits.

IDENTITY TRAITS AS SYMBOLIC CAPITAL

Pierre Bourdieu's (1986) notion of symbolic capital provides a useful lens for explaining how various social attributes affect a teacher's standing in the classroom. Bourdieu defines capital as "accumulated labor . . . which, when appropriated on a private, i.e., exclusive, basis by agents or a group of agents, enables them to appropriate social energy in the form of reified or living labor" (46). The accumulation and distribution of capital can influence how a person is positioned within a certain social space. Capital can be manifested in three different "guises," including economic, cultural, and social. Economic capital is "immediately and directly convertible into money." Cultural capital is "convertible, on certain conditions, into economic capital [that] may be institutionalized in the form of educational qualifications." Social capital, "made up of social obligations ('connections') . . . is convertible, in certain conditions, into economic capital and may be institutionalized in the form of a title of nobility" (47).

Among these three forms of capital, cultural capital is the most complex, as it can appear in three different states: the embodied state, the objectified state, and the institutionalized state. Cultural capital in the embodied state involves "long-lasting dispositions of the mind and body" (Bourdieu 1986, 47). One type of embodied cultural capital is linguistic capital, which can be either consciously acquired or passively inherited. Linguistic capital represents a means of communication and self-presentation, which is acquired and learned from a person's surrounding culture. The value of one's linguistic capital is determined by the linguistic market, but, as Bourdieu (1991a, 18) explains, "The more linguistic capital that speakers possess, the more they are able to exploit the system of differences to their advantage and thereby secure a *profit of distinction*" (italics in original). Cultural capital in the objectified state consists of "cultural goods (pictures, books, dictionaries, instruments, machines, etc.), which are the trace or realization of theories or critiques of these theories, problematics, etc." (Bourdieu 1986, 47). One form of cultural capital in the objectified state is the institutionalized state, which is "a form of objectification which must be set apart because . . . it confers entirely original properties on the cultural capital which it is presumed to guarantee" (47).

Bourdieu has been critiqued by some scholars, such as Judith Butler (1997, 147), who see his work as deterministic, not allowing for individual agency or for social change. The view that Bourdieu's notion of capital is overdetermined, however, ignores not only possibilities for individual negotiation but also for long-term fluctuations in the values that attach to various forms of symbolic capital. As some scholars, such as George Steinmetz (2011, 46), have recently argued, Bourdieu's ideas embody historical dimensions, making them far from deterministic. Another important factor often overlooked is the shifts in contexts; as individuals move from one market to another, the value of their capital may also be affected. Equally important is the possibility for agency in negotiating the values attached to various social traits. In the context of short-term teacher-student relationships, a more pressing question is whether and how the relative values of various forms of symbolic capital can be negotiated in the immediate context of the classroom.

TWO CASE STUDIES: KACIE AND YUCHING

The two teachers whose cases we examine in this chapter—Kacie and Yuching—are doctoral students specializing in rhetoric, composition, and linguistics as well as teaching associates (TAs) with a two-one teaching load in the writing programs housed in the English department at Arizona State University (ASU). In the ASU Writing Programs, all first-year TAs teach English 101 and English 102, a mainstream FYC sequence. These courses consist primarily of native English users, although many sections include a few L2 writers, mostly resident students (Matsuda, Saenkhum, and Accardi 2013). The dominant presence of privileged varieties of US English creates a particular kind of market, which largely privileges linguistic homogeneity (Matsuda 2006). This market condition affected the perceived value of Kacie's and Yuching's symbolic capital, requiring them to negotiate their net worth in various ways.

During the second year of teaching, after having taught the two-semester sequence of mainstream composition courses, Yuching and Kacie chose to teach sections of FYC courses designed specifically for nonnative English users. The students were mostly international visa students from outside the United States. The new teaching situation placed these instructors in a different linguistic market, requiring adjustments in how they negotiated their linguistic capital as well as other types of symbolic capital. Paradoxically, the L2 sections, despite their inherent linguistic diversity, tend to embody an even stronger inclination toward linguistic homogeneity because students and teachers often see it as a language class as much as a writing class (Racelis and Matsuda 2015). In this analysis, we explore how differing linguistic markets affected the perceived value of the instructors' symbolic capital and how they negotiated their net worth.

Negotiating Symbolic Capital in Shifting Markets: Kacie's Case

I am a native English speaker, born and raised in southeastern Virginia, and I speak a variety of southern American English, often referred to as a *southern accent.* I am a 26-year-old female, a fact that seems to make some of my students question my authority. However, I am both an experienced teacher (having taught high school) and an L2 writing specialist. This background gives me confidence in my teaching abilities despite the feeling of self-consciousness my gender and age can sometimes bring. However, when I became a TA at ASU, I found that my teaching experience and L2 knowledge did not prepare me for the work of negotiating my symbolic capital in the composition classroom. These were skills I had to learn on my own as I taught.

Kacie's Linguistic Capital

In the context of the mainstream composition classroom, my linguistic capital as a native English speaker was not challenged, as I shared the same language with my students, all of whom were native English users. Yet, I did make a conscious effort to monitor my speech, something I have done since my first year of college, because I was aware of the stigmas often associated with a southern dialect. People with a southern accent are perceived as "slow" or uneducated, labels college instructors want to avoid, especially when teaching English. It isn't that I am ashamed of my background; rather, I do not want to have to deal with the stigmas associated with speaking a southern dialect. Because my authority is already somewhat challenged in the classroom because I am young, female, and a graduate student, I do not need my linguistic capital to be challenged as well.

In the L2 composition classroom, I was surprised by how much my linguistic capital seemed to increase in comparison to the mainstream composition classroom. The diagnostic writing I assigned my students during the first class revealed their reliance on me to help them improve their writing and speaking skills in English. One student wrote in a note to me on his paper, "Help me, Professor Kiser. I need you," emphasizing how important it was to him that he improve his English writing skills in my class. My students assumed that, as a native English speaker, I had the linguistic as well as metalinguistic knowledge required to help them improve their writing in English. The sudden increase in my linguistic capital in the L2 composition classroom also made me feel uncomfortable. I was concerned that my students would feel that their language backgrounds were not valuable and that they did not have anything to contribute. I learned to handle this discomfort by engaging my students and asking questions about their own languages and cultures to help them understand that I valued their backgrounds. For instance, I occasionally asked my students how to pronounce a word from their language that they had used in their writing. When we discussed pop culture, I asked them to talk about pop culture in their own countries. I find that engaging my students in this way helps them feel more comfortable in class, encouraging active engagement.

Kacie's Cultural Capital

Much like my linguistic capital, my cultural capital was unchallenged for the most part in the mainstream composition classroom. Yet, there are aspects of my cultural capital that I felt my students pushed against occasionally (for instance, the fact that I am a young female TA). In these cases I played up the cultural capital I brought to the classroom by emphasizing the similarities I shared with my students (beyond our language). Despite the decade or so between us, we shared similar backgrounds, values, and knowledge of US culture, so I was able to put myself in the position of their "ally." Because I usually had a pretty good understanding of what they were interested in, I was able to use this knowledge to foster their interest and ask questions to motivate them to perform inquiry and analysis in their own research and writing. In addition, placing myself in the position of "ally" allowed me to build better rapport with my students and opened up lines of communication, which I believe contributed to their success in the course.

In the L2 composition classroom, I found myself having to do more negotiating in regard to my cultural capital than I did in the mainstream classroom because I had very little in common with my L2 students. For instance, unlike my experience in the mainstream composition classroom, it was challenging to find commonalities in terms of background, as the majority of my students had just arrived in the United States from their home countries, and some were just beginning to learn English. I knew that the topics we discussed and the prompts I gave in class would have to be more culturally sensitive and accessible to L2 students, but I had not anticipated the gap between my students and me in terms of cultural knowledge. I had to put more time into thinking about topics that would engage them. I learned to avoid examples that were specific to US culture, which seemed unfamiliar to them. I also learned to be more open to the cultural values and assumptions my L2 students brought with them to the classroom.

I was also afraid my L2 students would be skeptical of my ability to relate to them and their experiences as international students. I had not had the experience of leaving my home country, traveling abroad to a new place, trying to adapt to vastly different cultural values and practices, and learning a new language all at the same time. I feared that my students would not open up to me or trust me to understand them and that our cultural differences would inhibit communication between us. To address this issue, I sought to negotiate what I perceived to be my lack of cultural capital right from the beginning, changing my usual self-introduction to include the fact that I am an L2 writing specialist with significant knowledge and training in working with nonnative speakers. This information would not be important in a mainstream composition course, but I felt it mattered in the L2 class. I hoped it would show my students that, despite not sharing a common background with them, I was capable of meeting their needs.

Kacie's Institutional Capital

In the mainstream composition classroom, I tried to compensate for what I lacked in institutional capital because I could tell my young appearance was quite surprising to them. On the first day of class, I established what institutional capital I *did* have by giving my students a brief self-introduction and explaining my background and experience both in my own education and in teaching. This included listing my credentials (i.e., a master's in English and my status as a doctoral student in rhetoric, composition, and linguistics) and letting them know I had experience teaching at the high-school level, the college level, and also in the writing center. I felt that, by playing up these parts of my institutional capital, I could assure my students that I was qualified and capable of teaching their composition course.

In the L2 composition classroom I also felt the need to compensate for what I lacked in institutional capital, but the feeling was not the same. While I had no idea what my L2 students' previous educational experiences had been like, I was certain they were probably used to having instructors who were older and more established in their positions, and I was concerned they might see me as unqualified and inexperienced. To establish my credibility as a competent writing instructor, I described my background in education and experience in teaching on the first day of class, much as I did with my mainstream composition class, and when I talked to them about my background and experience, I added that I was an L2 writing specialist, which I hoped would show them I was knowledgeable about L2 writing and capable of teaching them.

Constructing Symbolic Capital in Response to Student Perceptions: Yuching's Case

I am a native Mandarin speaker, born and raised in Taiwan, where I obtained a BA in foreign languages and literature, a secondary English teacher certification, and an MA in teaching English as a foreign language. After graduation, I worked as an instructor at two prestigious Taiwanese universities for three years. As a nonnative English speaker who held only a master's degree, I had strived to develop different strategies to establish my credibility when teaching students at various ages and levels and offering courses on diverse topics. With all the challenges, training, and teaching practice, I saw myself as an experienced teacher informed with expertise in second-language writing. My confidence, however, was challenged in the FYC classroom in the United States as an international TA. The sharp contrast between the United States and Taiwanese contexts has forced me to seek other strategies to position myself professionally.

Yuching's Linguistic Capital

The first day I stepped into my mainstream composition classroom, I looked into my students' eyes and there was silence. There was no way to hide my skin color or my "Asian look." I directed their attention to my name, Yuching Yang, and its Chinese representation, "楊雨芹," on the screen. I explained that "*Yang* should be pronounced as *young*." They laughed. I then said, "but you can just call me *Jill* because, for many people, that's much easier to pronounce and remember." While attempting to build the connection with my native English-speaking (NES) students, I was still constantly reminded of my "real" identity. Thus, I tried to create the image of me not as a nonnative English speaker (NNES) but as a bilingual teacher. To emphasize additional linguistic capital I possessed, I mentioned my training in linguistics as well as my ability to speak German and Japanese.

The possibility of negotiating linguistic capital became clearer to me during one of the peer-editing activities. I noticed that one of the students had confused *a while* with *awhile*. I thought that was only a slip, so I just casually asked them the difference between the two terms. To my surprise, the conversation turned into a heated discussion of grammar. I then decided to offer a more formal explanation of the usage. After class, one student told me he was frustrated by his partner, who "grew up speaking English" but made so many grammatical errors. He also mentioned that I, as an NNES, knew more about English writing. This student's comment helped me realize that linguistic capital can be viewed from multiple perspectives, at least in terms of metalinguistic knowledge, not necessarily proficiency.

In the L2 classroom, I felt much more comfortable and confident positioning myself as a writing teacher because of my own educational background and teaching experience. On the first day, I bluntly spoke to their possible doubt by saying, "You must have asked yourselves why you should take an English writing class with this nonnative English-speaking teacher, didn't you?" I smiled, and they smiled back. In order to preempt the stereotypical image of an NES instructor in an English composition classroom, I decided to bring in another language, Chinese, as a tool to negotiate my linguistic capital: "I'm a native speaker of Chinese, which, as you might know, is a language that is becoming more significant in the world nowadays." I made eye contact with my Chinese students, the majority in the classroom. I continued to make the connection for them: "This is a composition classroom, but what you'll be learning is not limited to English. What's more important is the knowledge and experience of the process and difficulties in learning a second language I can share with you." To boost their confidence, I added, "Can you imagine how many years it would take for a native English speaker to learn your language to the level of your English proficiency?" Most of them shook their heads while laughing. Highlighting the process of enhancing linguistic capital called attention to the value of their linguistic capital while also enhancing mine.

Yuching's Cultural Capital

Unlike Kacie, I do not have the kind of linguistic capital my NES students value, which may weaken my credibility. In the mainstream FYC classroom, I had to generate my cultural capital by mentioning how the differences I brought would contribute to their learning. The fact that I did not share a common background with those students was the niche I was able to take advantage of. When we discussed controversial issues, I did not take any stance in the beginning. I encouraged them to express their own ideas. Building upon what seemed to be shared knowledge, I pinpointed the divergence of thought among them. I then questioned their assumptions, asked for further clarifications, and offered alternative perspectives and explanations both in classroom discussion and writing. The intended message was that, with their richer understanding of how "differences" benefit their thinking and writing, the heritage of my cultural background could be viewed not as a "lack of" shared knowledge with them but as a source of new insights that complement their knowledge. ASU students are known as *Sun Devils*, so I told my students I would be "the Sun Devil's advocate in this classroom."

In the L2 writing classroom, my background as an NNES international student helped create a common ground with my students, thus enhancing the value of my cultural capital. In contrast to the mainstream sections, where I was their "devil's advocate," I positioned myself more as an ally in the L2 classroom. Like them, I learned English as a foreign language. Every so often, I shared with them my personal encounters with the challenges in a new environment and with academic tasks, and I shared some of the strategies I adopted. I saw myself not only as a writing teacher but also as a mentor.

"Silence is also a form of classroom participation." I repeated the words of Dr. Matsuda, who said this in a graduate class I had taken. Until I first heard this phrase, I had been frustrated by not being able to participate fully in the discussion. I was struggling with a new type of academic discourse in this new environment. Dr. Matsuda's words did not entitle me to remain silent; instead, I became more comfortable with the uncertainty, which allowed me to accept the possibilities of making mistakes. "I've been there," I told my students. I continued: "I still want to see your active participation, but participation is not limited to class discussion. Your posting questions on Blackboard, sharing ideas in groups, and e-mailing me any thoughts are all evidence of your effort." While some students remained relatively silent, others tried different ways of communicating with me. Addressing the concerns mentioned by most of the students at the beginning of class by sharing my struggles and strategies for dealing with them, I felt I was able to direct their attention to the course content. The constant and comfortable interaction among us further opened a window for me to know their lives from various perspectives, and the valuable information helped me adjust pedagogies or materials to cater to individual students' needs.

Yuching's Institutional Capital

While teaching the mainstream FYC course affected the value of various forms of my symbolic capital, not all of them were significantly affected. I saw myself as an experienced teacher, and being a female was not a major concern for me. Aside from my language background,

I was most concerned about my youthful appearance. I emphasized my experiences in teaching college students and adult learners and being a full-time instructor for three years. However, one student jokingly asked, "So, you started to teach at like the age of eighteen?" At that point, I only laughed with them, not saying anything further. I knew I needed to seek different opportunities to establish my credibility and authority in that classroom in addition to the title of teaching associate in the Department of English. I wanted to emphasize how my achievements elsewhere brought me here. The universities where I have worked are well known in Taiwan (National Taiwan University and National Tsing Hua University are ranked first and second in Taiwan, respectively) but not to my American students. In one class discussion of our decision-making and sense-making processes, I asked them why they chose ASU. I then shared my reasons by mentioning the other universities I was accepted into: PhD programs at the University of California at Santa Barbara and the University of Texas at Austin. I explained how I evaluated each program and why ASU emerged as the best choice. While each student might have still interpreted my credibility differently, highlighting my institutional capital did seem to contribute to my students' interpretation of my qualifications as their composition teacher.

In the L2 classroom, I did mostly the same self-introduction as I did in the mainstream classroom, emphasizing my educational and teaching experience. Yet, I did not see the need to mention the graduate programs I had been accepted into because being a TA at a US university seemed to give me enough institutional capital. In the fourth week when both the students and I had become more familiar with each other, one Chinese student told me after class about his first impression of me as an international TA. He said in Chinese, "You must be outstanding so that you can teach at the university. You are not an American but you teach English writing." To that student, an NNES teacher is not necessarily inferior to NES TAs; on the contrary, to be entitled to this position as an NNES, they must possess some other traits to be competitive enough, if not exceptional. The writing program at ASU gave me my institutional capital, yet its value was negotiated or even increased by my L2 students, who had their own perceptions, impressions, and interpretations of my international TA status.

NEGOTIATION OF SYMBOLIC CAPITAL AS RHETORICAL ACTION

The narratives constructed above represent how different linguistic markets contributed to the fluctuation of values ascribed to various forms of symbolic capital—as they were perceived by Kacie and Yuching. They also show how Kacie and Yuching negotiated different types of symbolic capital in two different linguistic markets. Their experiences show that different linguistic markets *do* influence their sense of (1) the relative value of different forms of symbolic capital, (2) what is negotiable, (3) how it can be negotiated, and (4) to what extent it can be negotiated. In some cases, cultural capital was derived from visible assets, such as the teachers' appearance and language features as well as information about their credentials; in other cases, their assets—such as knowledge and experience—were invisible.

Visible assets are more susceptible to the forces of the market because students are more likely to perceive those features, to value them according to prevailing sociocultural expectations, and to respond to them directly and indirectly—through comments they make to the teacher and through more subtle forms of communication, such as facial expressions and even silence. Invisible assets, on the other hand, are not readily accessible by students, and they must be brought to students' attention in order for them to contribute to the teacher's symbolic capital—like cards still held in the teachers' hands, awaiting opportunities to be played. In fact, invisible capital can create more possibilities for negotiation through rhetorical action; teachers can foreground these assets by discussing them in a positive light or keep them invisible by not calling attention to them. To Kacie and Yuching, their previous teaching experience as well as their expertise in second-language writing constituted an important part of their overall symbolic capital. From time to time, Kacie and Yuching brought them onto the table to play up or down those assets or even to divert the students' attention away from visible assets that might hurt Kacie's or Yuching's credibility. When and how they played these cards, however, was also shaped by the force of the linguistic market and the particular strengths of each teacher.

It is important to note that the distinction between visible and invisible assets is not always clear cut. Language background, for example, is visible in some cases—when the teacher has what students perceive as a "nonnative" or "foreign" accent, which was what Yuching had to contend with—while for others, it is something that can be concealed with some effort, as was the case for Kacie's southern dialect. Some types of invisible assets are made visible institutionally. For example, some aspects of a teacher's credentials—and labels that "usually accompany credentialing rites" (Casanave 2002, 24)—become visible as institutions list teachers' ranks through registration systems and directories, while other credentials, such as master's degrees, may need to be made visible by the teacher. The symbolic value attached to credentials seemed to play an important role as students gauged their teachers' qualifications and, by implication, their authority in classrooms. Yet, the symbolic value of credentials does not always work against the teacher. In Yuching's L2 writing classroom, for example, her ability to hold a TA position at a US institution while being an NNES enhanced her credibility. By being aware of the symbolic value of different credentials and labels, teachers can choose to make visible assets more valuable or divert students' attention from negative stereotypes attached to them.

It is important to point out that Kacie and Yuching did not simply bring different forms of capital to be evaluated in different markets; rather, they negotiated the overall value of their symbolic capital by rhetorically constructing different forms of symbolic capital. The process of interaction and discussion helped the teachers to know what capital was worthy in the students' minds. Understanding students' current ideological positions may not immediately diminish the force of the prevailing ideology; yet, such an understanding may have helped these teachers expose dominant assumptions through the process of negotiating their various forms of capital. The exchange of the encounters, interpretations, and strategies also provided the two teachers with insights into their net worth as composition teachers.

TOWARD THE SYMBOLIC CAPITAL PORTFOLIO

As we have tried to demonstrate, writing teachers' symbolic capital is not entirely overdetermined in the context of first-year composition classrooms. The values of various identity traits fluctuate in different markets, as Kacie's and Yuching's transitions from the mainstream section to the L2 section illustrate. It is also important to note that the rhetorical negotiation of symbolic capital does not happen only within each form of capital. Rather, various forms of capital are negotiated systemically, each contributing to net worth. To fully understand the implications of various identity traits, it is important to think of symbolic capital from a broader perspective—as a kind of portfolio—rather than focusing on a specific type of symbolic capital or a limited range of identity traits, such as ethnicity or native-language status, no matter how salient they may seem.

Finally, we acknowledge that this exploration is based on the two teachers' own perceptions and assessments of the market forces and their symbolic capital. As such, we did not attempt to assess the actual shifts in the market forces or the results of the negotiation efforts. To continue this line of inquiry, future studies might explore the valuation and negotiation of symbolic capital portfolios by also exploring how students' perceptions shift over time in conjunction with the teachers' efforts to understand and negotiate their symbolic capital.

8

A QUESTION OF MIMETICS

Graduate-Student Writing Courses and the New "Basic"

Kelly Ritter

It is common for universities to sell writing instruction to first-year students as edifying drudgery—we faculty (and administrators) say, "These courses are *good for you.*" The "good" there is both intellectual (learn to write well, do better in school, have a sharper mind) and socioeconomic (learn to write well, get a better job, contribute to the community). Such inherent goodness is tied to a political notion of ultimate worth in a knowledge-based economy. Students should have a proper education in writing, the logic goes, to prepare them for the kinds of work they will do both in college and beyond it. Such preparation will make them not only smarter people but better and more economically viable people. As Deborah Brandt (2012, 770) notes, "The fake economy of language runs closely in synch with other faked up economies of scarcity, like the economies of respect or rights . . . [thus] language crises are always political." In making this point, Brandt highlights the power of literacy acquisition as an economic good; those with less political, socioeconomic, or cultural capital possess less ability to gain traction through language, always competing with those higher in the social order and always being made to feel inferior through language (769).

We see this microeconomy at work in the systems that control and define our first-year writing programs. WPAs always are faced with an incoming class of students who are, by university-level sorting mechanisms, labeled as *ready* or *not ready*, even sometimes before or in counterstatement to other mechanisms by which writing programs themselves seek to place students. Many of our institutions offer a range of courses designed to meet these labels, but increasingly, the decision as to who is "ready" and who is not (and for what, and with what kind of credit toward graduation) is made not by the writing programs themselves.

DOI: 10.7330/9781607325239.c008

More prevalent are the widespread proficiency measurements (in the form of timed tests offered by conglomerates external to the institution itself) that are transferable across various campuses and institutional types, that privilege white middle- to upper-class students, and that are provided only at an additional cost, outside the curriculum. Chief among these are Advanced Placement, the ACT, and the SAT. More and more, students come to university writing programs such as my own less defined by what *we* see in their *writing* and more defined by what national *testing* companies that subscribe to the power of *language* see in the students' more abstracted uses of it. As an industry, those who measure language skill and language facility make a significant number of judgments about what our students can and will do *with* that language, despite being divorced from any local rhetorical conditions under which that writing may be produced.

Brandt's (2012) notion of "fake" economies is thus not about actual falsehoods but about "the political production of suffering and want" (770), which certainly plays a primary role in students' approach to their increasingly expensive college educations, and the promise of getting "out of the way" general education courses—like first-year writing—that our culture mistakenly believes these students should have been finished with by high-school graduation, if these students were at all worthy of admittance into the postsecondary population. Given this national imperative, there is a real sense in which writing instruction itself only *means* as much as it signifies in various economies—which for undergraduates are those specific to the metrics of the university (tuition, course requirements, certification upon graduation for a profession or a job) and which outside that system may be variably inflated in order to put more pressure on the value of measuring proficiency through language testing. It is also true, Brandt observes, that "writing . . . participates in real economies because writing takes time and uses up mental energies, both really valuable yet finite commodities. Writing also obviously requires tools and material that must be acquired or supplied beforehand" (770). There is a larger system of writing that involves people, products, production, and of course, labor.

This combination of real and false economies of writing, even at a very abstract level, makes it all the more striking—but completely logical, also—that we rarely talk about writing instruction "goodness" in the same imperative register at the *graduate* level in the humanities, including English graduate programs, where such instruction may be not celebrated but instead scorned, and where the stakes of language use and political capital obtained via literacy acquisition are arguably even higher. Even as we frantically work to secure tenure-track jobs for our doctoral candidates in this scarce market, and recognize that "good" writing is part of that economic equation, we routinely save the instructional component of that preparation for comments and responses to the dissertation near the end of the educational process, if we attend to it significantly at all. Even as we recognize that writing courses can help students to grow intellectually in a community of like learners, with a psychic and systematic economic power both inside and outside the classroom, we do not seem uniformly to see the power of that instructional setting for graduate students—who theoretically have a much higher intellectual bar to clear than do their first-year counterparts. We are, I argue, still tied to cultural fears of inadequacy—of demonstrating the "language of those in charge" (Brandt 2012, 769) without ever admitting some of our students don't really know what that *is*, how it comes to be acquired, or how it matters to their own prose, both inside and outside the courses in our programs. Further still, we are loath to admit that the needs of our first-year students may, in fact, not completely dissipate as they move through the curriculum. Some of those students meet us later, in graduate school, and despite our field's recent research on transfer theory and now threshold concepts, we stubbornly refuse to believe such difficulties would ever also apply to graduate-student writers.

I contend that English studies graduate programs frequently pay scant curricular attention to students' own intellectual and professional development *as* writers, even as these students are also teachers *of* writing, assuming instead that writing need not be explicitly taught to graduate students and that the benefits undergraduate writing students receive are either not aligned with those of graduate students or are not reproducible on a scale. We require that graduate students write seminar papers, presentations, and so on, but in terms of separate instruction in the writing of that seminar paper or presentation, we typically are without outlets or curricular mechanisms that even approach our careful attention to first-year writers on the other "end" of the curriculum. Our "instruction" in writing at the graduate (read: professional) level is usually embedded, at best, in the content-based seminars themselves rather than in a separate, freestanding course that mimics, but at a higher rhetorical register, the kind of instruction we see as so valuable at the first-year level. In other words, we like the idea of first-year writing very much—as a site of instruction that crosses students' intellectual interests and academic specialties—but we do not like to see this system replicated at the graduate level, even within the much smaller range of specialties typically found in an English department. We might find ourselves saying, "Isn't that *remedial* work? Aren't these *graduate* students?"

From where does this reluctance emerge, and how does it inform the ways in which we guide these students through the profession? And further, how does our reluctance to help graduate students develop as writers both mirror and contradict the kind of careful attention rhetoric and composition studies, in particular, has given to so-called basic writers in the last two decades? One initial way to map the answers to these questions is again through economics. As faculty, we are reluctant to admit that writing at the graduate level (and beyond) takes a significant amount of work—work that will undoubtedly impact these candidates' time once they do secure faculty positions postgraduation. We know the time commitment good writing requires; as faculty, we are often overworked already with committees and dissertation directions, let alone our own scholarship and teaching (and service, which on many campuses, including mine, is how dissertation direction is framed—not as a separately compensated activity). We further know that one more course—one more commitment within the graduate curriculum—takes time away from what we call *content* courses, or those that focus on the analysis of texts and theories central to English studies. This notion of a "content" course is regularly contrasted, imbued with markers of intellectual superiority and field-specific knowledge, with both writing and pedagogy-focused seminars in graduate programs, which focus on the analysis and practice of methods or strategies for navigating aspects of the profession itself. As a consequence, writing and pedagogy courses for graduate students are positioned in an identical manner to first-year composition courses (especially basic writing courses) within the larger undergraduate curriculum—as courses that students should not actually need, and that distract from "real" coursework in other academic subjects.

And so to go deeply into writing instruction for graduate students, as we do with our undergraduates, is an explosion and exploitation of economic resources many faculty feel they do not have, or do not want to commit to, for the greater intellectual and labor good. But the longer view beyond our programmatic conditions—that of the new assistant professor who struggles to rewrite her dissertation into publishable articles and/or a book—is even more dire economically. Faculty must, by and large, publish to gain tenure in our economy; there no longer exists a kind of institution in which scholarship matters not at all (community college campuses, perhaps, excepted—though note the rise of PhDs taking those positions and their attendant research agendas that will at some point make scholarship a perceived natural component of the job, on some smaller scale). Worse still are the significant numbers of graduate students who will work in non-tenure-track positions with much higher course loads and much less job security while either revising or finishing their dissertations; these students struggle to gain those precious publications without even having the resources of a tenure-track position and a campus that fully supports research and scholarship. In short, as faculty who eschew graduate writing courses outside the dissertation-writing process, we push forward the problem of helping graduate students to become better and more confident writers, on a systematic level, and this can be devastating in economic terms.

My aim in this chapter is to recall the ways in which graduate students[1] seeking explicit writing instruction—whether in the form of market-related and thus what I would call *just-in-time* genres (job letters, curriculum vitae, teaching statements) or other more long-term professional writing (articles, book chapters, book manuscripts)—have become, for the above national/cultural reasons as well as other specific local ones, the new "basic" writers in our academic hierarchies and in our departmental conversations. I contend that even though our institutional response to and regard for basic writing students has dramatically improved since the curricula discussed in the work of Mike Rose (1985), David Bartholomae (1993), and Mina Shaughnessy (1977), among many others, we now have transferred our fear of development *as* remediation onto our graduate-student writers, who seek and find some of the same learning pathways in their road to postdoctoral work as do our first-year underprepared writers.

Both sets of writers—graduate and undergraduate—are entering a new and strange intellectual world in which skills, knowledge, and the ability to deftly shift voices and registers and purposes at will is always already assumed. While we are willing to help one set, we are still often unwilling to help the other. This reluctance is because—unlike when we look at the first-year writer, from whom we have some social and intellectual distance (and who we may never have been, given that many English faculty never were first-year composition students)—we are afraid that if we look too deeply into the graduate-student writer asking for help, we may see ourselves reflected. Worse yet, we will *not* see our reflection, and thus the mimetic chain that links us to our graduate charges, that which is tethered by emulation and the result of which might uncharitably be called a "mini-me" creation, is broken.

To admit that graduate students in one's program need writerly help, for one thing, is to imply that the prestige of the program (and perhaps its faculty) itself is "less than," a particular fear in this unsteady job market and one that extends beyond any particular writer or future faculty member. While I embrace Laura Micciche's (2009, W47) vision of the graduate writing course as a study of "how writers make meaning, forward and test new ideas, contribute to ongoing conversations, and interrupt or disrupt knowledge practices and paradigms," some faculty's view of graduate writing instruction mirroring sentiments about undergraduate basic writing—is that it is "remedial," a corrective measure we should be ashamed to offer. As we know, the fight against basic writing curricula nationwide is lodged in many versions of sheep's clothing: dual credit, early college, and now curricular-based exit exams of the Common Core curricula, such as those in PARCC consortium states. In economic terms, basic writing is expensive, reductive, time consuming, and thus inefficient; students should either gain traction in high school—ideally through coursework that counts for both secondary and postsecondary requirements—or their instruction should be relegated to sites where inefficiency in curricula is less expensive (i.e., community college campuses). Few faculty outside rhetoric and composition programs would equate "basic" writing instruction with a disruption of practices and paradigms or with knowledge making—even as, theoretically, it can offer both of those things.

Indeed, even the ways in which Micciche (2009) describes her own course are telling in terms of the relationship between first-year writing and graduate writing instruction. I should note that I do not believe Micciche herself embraces these parallels, but the rhetoric surrounding her course—itself an extended exercise in rhetorical strategies in various genres—is nonetheless relevant, so I want to momentarily explore it, as my work here is in many ways a direct extension of and expansion upon her thesis. Specifically, in as nonpejorative a manner as possible, I'd like to resituate graduate students as not just a community of developing writers with common intellectual needs and interests, as Micciche does, but go further and consider their stance as potentially "basic" in terms of actually offering very fundamental and necessary instruction and inculcation into a particular discourse community (for graduate students, that of faculty scholars). I do so in order to complicate exactly how we approach explicit and intentional graduate-student writing instruction in our English studies programs and to question how differently it should be regarded from first-year writing *if* we affirm that first-year writing is, in fact, a positive and necessary space for learning for all students. In offering this extension of Micciche's work, and of similar scholarship on graduate professional development, I thus challenge those of us in rhetoric and composition studies to consider whether we have, in fact, worked as hard as we believe we have to liberate first-year—and particularly basic—writing students and courses from pejorative historical and cultural associations and remedial stigma. If we want graduate students to develop their professional writing voices, perhaps in alignment with the enlightened curricular and institutional frameworks we have produced and sustained for first-year writers, we should make sure those frameworks are, in fact, themselves enlightened.

As is often the case, stigma in part arises from intellectual location within a department; such is the case for Micciche's (2011, 479) course, as she notes it is unofficially known in her department as "comp for grad students." She is, however, careful to situate the course as multidisciplinary in nature, much in the way first-year writing can and often must behave within the larger undergraduate/general education curriculum:

> I especially like the fact that the course is not viewed as a "rhet comp" course, but as a *writing* course relevant to all English graduate students—this seems to me a promising indicator that students view critical writing as rigorous intellectual and rhetorical work that does not belong exclusively to specialists in rhetoric and composition. At the same time, I realize that the very aspect of the course that I view as a success might, for others, raise formidable problems in some departments, especially where tensions around turf and specialization are prominent. One might counter, for instance, that what improves student writing is more study of content knowledge in a given area rather than rhetorical study. (495)

It is first interesting that the association with rhet-comp *itself* might be seen as a stigma, at least within a multifaceted English department, and in line with the stigma of first-year writing or basic writing within the college curriculum nationwide. Indeed, by framing the course as a study in rhetoric, Micciche does classify its work to a great extent in terms of subdisciplinarity but also runs the risk of moving it further to the margins in terms of typical English-department hierarchies (even as, economically, rhetoric and composition at the current moment holds far more real market value than does literary studies in terms of jobs advertised yearly and placement rates for rhet-comp graduate students within larger English departments, including my own). Such is also the case, of course, in departments that possess a strong writing track in their major or have on the faculty a number of writing and rhetoric specialists. These are attractive structural strengths for some stakeholders, while less so for others.

But I find more noteworthy here that even Micciche's (2011) course—which sounds quite successful and is clearly seen as valuable within her department's curriculum—is grounded in the same kinds of practices we might *teach* in a first-year or a basic writing course: rhetorical strategies, genre awareness, audience considerations. It is not, as I read it, a course in the very specific "market" considerations that graduate students face (journal-submission practices, comparative readings of publishers and publications, etc.). This choice, of course, is deliberate on Micciche's part, designed to cater to the multiple specializations present in her seminar—including, it's important to note, creative writers, who are the hallmark of her institution's PhD program. But I call attention to the structure of her seminar because it is *so much* like a first-year course in its aims and because it differs from how I have taught such a seminar, as I will explain momentarily.

Moreover, Micciche's course mimics the way we *approach* first-year and basic writers in our curriculum. And as such, the *comp for graduate students* moniker is an apt and not necessarily negative one. Micciche seems to be replicating the structure that has worked so well for students and instructors in the graduate classroom. As she notes,

> Although writing has principally denoted *first-year required composition* throughout composition's history, this association is currently undergoing considerable revision. Writing instruction at the graduate level presents exciting possibilities for reimagining where and how writing can be taught. More ambitiously, it asserts a shift in the mission of English graduate programs by admitting that critical writing is not a mere extension of undergraduate writing practices, and is not best learned by tacit immersion. (Micciche 2011, 497, emphasis in original)

So Micciche's class—one that *works* for her students and curriculum and is often referenced in current field discussions of whether or how to offer writing courses to graduate students—makes that alliance between first-year writing and graduate writing very clear. But despite this prominent (if not completely conscious) call for such an alliance, there are still myriad negative connotations where graduate writing coursework is concerned, particularly if we consider English departments as a whole, beyond rhetoric and composition programs per se.

Basic writing instruction has been thoroughly interrogated in our field as a fruitful site for these disruptions of meaning and of staid practices, even as our discussions of professional development for graduate students often elide in-depth discussions of writing development. And while basic writing is not equivalent to standard first-year writing, the impetus for points of discussion such as *preparedness, development,* and the more negative *gatekeeping* still apply. In fact, very few articles on the subject of graduate writing per se, beyond Micciche's (2011), have even been published, with Mike Rose and Karen McClafferty's piece—which appeared in a non–English studies journal (Rose and McClafferty 2001)—following a handful of relevant others (most notably Patricia Sullivan's 1991 *JAC* piece and several others focused on the importance of helping students to publish).[2] This scarcity indicates that we have far to go before such curricula can be offered without the associative stigma of compulsory remediation and without the assumption that enrolled students are those who don't "fit" in our erstwhile prestigious degree programs or with our own conceptions of ourselves as mentors and progenitors of future scholars.[3]

Micciche (2011) presumes that the students who seek such help *belong* in the program and that they have come together in a community atmosphere, much like the workshop structure common to creative writing graduate programs. Indeed, she asserts that her "push here is for a graduate writing course—required or not, depending on local circumstances—the aim of which is to create space, community, and rhetorical awareness/flexibility necessary to brainstorm, create, and sustain a wide variety of critical writing projects" (478). She further observes that "it's no secret that graduate students (much like faculty) regularly encounter academic writing as an emotionally fraught, privately experienced hardship" (479). So, while this piece recognizes that such a writing course might constitute a *community*, there is still what I would call an *upward* alliance and even solidarity between her graduate students and *faculty*, rather than downward to first-year or basic writing students.

Herein, I think, lies the tension we face in teaching graduate students to write: we want them to be like us and want to teach them to master genres in which *we* write because soon enough, they will *be* us. But we also need to make connections between their stance as burgeoning community members (à la David Bartholomae) and their current political space and economic fragility in the academic hierarchy. They are "basic" in terms of their knowledge of community conventions and discourse requirements. But they are also *us*. How can that paradox ever be reconciled unless we acknowledge that we faculty, too, were once "basic"? In fact, it further elides the real conditions under which we faculty are *still* "basic"—in that most writing theorists would agree that our development as writers never stops and that when we enter new rhetorical situations (writing for a different journal audience, writing a grant, giving a talk to a group outside our discipline), we return, in many ways, to the position that many of our graduate students now occupy: entering, for the first time, that proverbial conversation.

The discourses about basic writing and graduate writing thus—by design—must and do uncomfortably overlap and intersect. A reification of how faculty see graduate writing instruction—not as absolute professional emulation but as professional and intellectual development toward beneficial alliance(s)—may allow faculty clearer avenues for supporting and guiding our students toward becoming academic professionals. I next move away from a dialogue with Micciche's (2011) piece to offer two of my own experiences teaching graduate student writing on two very different campuses, each with its own local impetuses for what that writing course was to achieve. In doing so, I illustrate how our own class- and community-based assumptions about graduate school may be behind our unwillingness to offer, support, and/or teach graduate writing courses that necessarily must include some recognition—whether it be explicit, as in Micciche's course, or implicit, as might be the case with my own instructional design—of the resemblances between basic writers and graduate-student writers. Basic (first-year) writers and graduate-student writers share a trajectory toward their eventual linguistic and intellectual goals that is often nonlinear, frequently messy, yet incredibly important in their growth as writers and scholars. They both seek a linguistic position that enables their desires toward the top of the socioeconomic hierarchy—one in the postsecondary academic and nonacademic world and the other in the postgraduate job market and larger profession. What makes us uncomfortable, perhaps, as a discipline is the recognition of that very alliance as we puzzle over how to support graduate students as we do support (or as we aim to support) undergraduate basic writers.

* * * *

When we talk about graduate writing courses, we must engage in a careful and perhaps uncomfortable reexamination of what further happens to terms like *good* (or *good for you*) versus *too good* in this new setting. As noted previously, while graduate writing courses are (in most settings) not compulsory, unlike their first-year course counterparts, they are frequently unfairly stigmatized, set in terms of remediation, often pointing to the poor socioeconomic, ergo poor intellectual, preparation of the students enrolled. *Why don't you already know how to do* this stuff? Alternatively, we have Rose's myth of transience—here, that while we may have one "bad" class of graduate-student writers on a campus or in a program, it's an anomaly we can eradicate and then move on (perhaps by not mentoring them well enough so that they drop out or by discouraging them sufficiently such that they fail). We also see the familiar argument raised regarding knowledge versus style/language conventions that also arises in basic writing discourse. Well, graduate students should be *smart enough* to know those genre conventions. Issues of knowledge transfer—which we know now is critical in undergraduate-student writing development—are completely elided here, as Patricia Sullivan first noted in 1991.

Do we give graduate students sufficient opportunity to learn the conventions of scholarly writing as compared to the consideration we give our undergraduates? Or do we withhold that opportunity due to the stigma with which we typically associate basic writers? In addition, at what point do we draw the line between *compulsory* writing instruction for graduate students (i.e., the framework of much basic writing curricula) and *elective* writing instruction (aligned with other electives in a masters or doctoral program)? Perhaps my own two narratives can illustrate these rhetorical and paradigmatic quandaries, complete with noted flaws in execution, in local contexts.

STORY #1: A MASTER'S COMPREHENSIVE REGIONAL INSTITUTION

In January 2008, as I transitioned from being a tenured associate professor serving as the first-year writing program administrator to being interim writing-across-the-curriculum director at Southern Connecticut State University, I was asked to teach (off the books, interestingly enough, in terms of economies of labor) a writing workshop for graduate students in the master's program in public health. The class was held once a week in seminar format (three hours per week) for eight weeks and was pass/fail—a noncredit, compulsory enrollment based on the results of a holistic essay exam given in the previous term. I thought this sounded like a great set-up for working with motivated adult students, especially because it would be graduate-level WAC in action, an initiative supported by the provost as well as the dean. As such, I eagerly helped to design this course in consultation with the director of the public health graduate program.

That graduate director had, in past conversations, vociferously lamented the grammar, usage, and style problems found in these students' work. He groaned at the thought of their butchering of APA style-sheet principles. He could barely stand to talk about their (in) ability to summarize work or analyze source material, let alone write a coherent, compelling master's thesis. Oh, and he said they plagiarized, too, probably because they didn't understand how to properly cite their sources, as many of them were encountering APA style for the first time. In doing so, he enacted the paradigm of lack I heard English (and other departments') faculty also do, on occasion, but without offering any viable solutions for what they perceived as systemic writing problems among their students.

This director was a thoughtful, long-time faculty member whom I respected, despite his vitriol, so I was calm instead of launching into my own practiced lament of the one-size-fits-all myth of undergraduate writing education. We discussed, at some length, how these students' difficulties could be at least addressed if they were to take a writing course of some kind. I mentioned that in researching this possibility, I had found that a number of institutions around the country—including at the University of Chicago, the University of Michigan, and the University of Alabama at Birmingham—had extensive writing and research courses in place, some even with professional centers for graduate education in writing the thesis and/or dissertation. In fact, as of this writing (2015), there are no fewer than 30 of these kinds of courses offered nationwide, located in English departments with doctoral programs. So, I emphasized, it would not be out of turn for our institution to offer a course like this also. It would not be perceived as "remedial" work in this national context, I thought, but it could be compulsory in nature. After all, using my WPA training up to that point, I reasoned that such a course would be good for the students, so it would make sense to require that they take it. *Right?*

We struck a bargain, after some discussion and subsequent planning, that only those students who demonstrated *true need,* based on the results of a two-hour timed essay exam, would be required to take the course. We found a brief but seminal article in the field of public health, distributed it to all the students, and announced that the exam would be held in about three weeks' time. We said the exam would be based on the article and that they could bring the article as well as any reading or writing notes they wished to the exam. I hammered out a four-pronged, three-level rubric with which to score the essays. Student essays would be coded and read blind, with my assessments sent to the graduate director with the codes attached.

In sum, about half of those tested showed "need," and of those, almost all enrolled in the course after advisement. These 12 students and I spent our class time going over conventions of academic arguments in their field, and I read copious amounts of PCH literature on the side, trying to familiarize myself with the field's discourse conventions and commonplace arguments. We did in-class and out-of-class writing, worked in groups, unpacked scholarly documents. By the third week, half of the students had dropped out. By the fourth week, the remaining students began to falter with the work, claiming it was "too much," especially because it was not a credit-bearing course—a sentiment with which many readers may be intimately familiar from their own experiences teaching basic writing and an issue I had already tackled in our own basic writing course in English at SCSU. After some difficult discussions with the class, we decided to discontinue the course altogether around week five—it just didn't work for any of us. As far as I know—though I have been away for many years now—the course has not been offered since.

STORY #2: A RESEARCH II DOCTORAL INSTITUTION

Fast forward to 2010. I am now a tenured associate professor serving as the WPA at the University of North Carolina at Greensboro. I have created, in consultation with several English-department colleagues, a graduate writing course called Writing for the Profession. We created this course for our department's doctoral students based on their observed difficulty with final papers in our seminars and their difficulty outside our courses with article drafts as well as other professional or job-related materials—what I earlier in this chapter termed *just-in-time* writing. The course is an elective, is credit bearing, and is graded, aimed at those who are ideally in their second or third year of doctoral study within a five-year program.

In its first offering, we enrolled about 12 students, and the course was team taught, with my colleagues giving guest lectures on subjects such as writing and submitting articles, developing dissertation abstracts, and preparing job letters. In spring 2011, considering the positives and negatives of the previous year's offering, we made some revisions (increasing the time spent on individual student writing within class meetings) and offered the course again, this time to seven students. In summer 2012, we offered the course a third time, with some further amendments, to 10 more students. Throughout this process, the faculty with whom I had collaborated—all junior literature faculty save for one in rhetoric and composition—talked frequently about student evaluations, individual components of the seminar, and our desire to make the seminar a permanent course offering (which, as I noted above, did eventually happen). Other senior literature faculty in the department were aware of the course, and we brought a few who were positive about the offering into the mix of presentations for its second and third iterations.

In all three semesters of the course pilot, no one dropped out. No one complained of the work or the time spent (well, not *in* class, anyway—I cannot account for hallway conversations or social media exchanges outside my hearing). Students did the work and, by all accounts, did it well. Student course evaluations were very positive. Students who did not take the class asked when it would be offered again.

Then one day in 2012, we proposed the course as a permanent offering. The course passed the faculty vote and remains on the books. But it has also not been offered as a regular semester course since. What was notable about that process were the sentiments expressed in a faculty meeting to vote upon that proposal—sentiments that have, I submit, influenced the health and welfare of the course as something more than just a listing in our catalog that never is taught. Maybe readers will recognize some of these sentiments, all of which come from statements made aloud during the time I stood at the front of the room filled with English faculty with the course proposal before me, defending the rationale. I have bolded the words and phrases I heard that are most relevant to this chapter's argument:

> Don't we already teach this material in our **regular** graduate courses?
>
> Why do students **need** this kind of help? They are PhD students!
>
> Isn't this a remedial course? **Why** are we teaching remedial writing to grad students?
>
> Isn't this going to take away from their **REAL** courses?
>
> Our students need more **literature** or **subject** courses. They don't need this.
>
> **Who** is going to teach this course? How can we **afford** to have a faculty member do this?
>
> I don't understand—**what do you mean by** a "graduate writing course"?
>
> You want to make this a **graduation requirement**, don't you? I know what you're up to.

These two courses, across two very different campuses and student populations, offered students fundamentally the same instruction but with entirely different approaches—one was required, the other is elective; one was for entry-level students, to teach them to get "caught up," whereas the other is for continuing students, to teach them better strategies for what they are already doing. But the first course, for the MPH students, was framed, I fully admit, as remedial in a stereotypical and pre-Shaughnessy-era way. It did not bear credit; it was not even a real course offering—making me now think of the Yale basic writing courses I would later discover in my own archival research, those that did not "exist," either, and are susceptible to being lost to history. Like the Awkward Squad, there will be little—if any—trace of my MPH experimental course. The course at UNCG, in contrast, is officially in the catalog, albeit after a political struggle, but it will likely never be offered again. It bears credit, is graded similarly to a "regular" graduate seminar, and offers what I and the original proposers aimed to be a truly preprofessional experience for a specific population. But still, we see embedded in the faculty outcry regarding the second course typical fears of instruction in "skills" versus "content"; fears of time to degree and students' progress toward the doctorate having obtained *correct and necessary* field knowledge (insofar as this can be separated out from writing through that knowledge in scholarly genres); and fears of economic viability, that is, how can a faculty member be paid to teach such a class, and how will it impact the economics of our salary and course allocations (in other words, our OE, or operating expenditure)? These fears—despite the best intentions with course design and other faculty buy-in—still negatively impacted its long-term success.

* * * *

What I hope readers hear in these local comparisons are two possible paradigms for basic writing on campuses nationwide—the former being a bad one and the latter a better one but with its own systematic limitations and shortcomings. In reality, neither of these courses worked because the larger political and economic system within both universities misunderstood the imperative behind the courses. And this misunderstanding—this fear and confusion over what "basic" writing instruction means to a graduate-student population—is not a fear that will subside without concentrated efforts to address the *system* as well as the pedagogy itself. While I hold up neither course as a perfect model, certainly I want to emphasize beyond these paradigms the perhaps more pressing issues as we consider how or whether graduate writing instruction should be a point of study for students in our English programs. What seems most critical is how we *talk* about graduate-writing pedagogy and how our notions of class, commodities, and academic systems, including economic models, shape that talk. We must confront our fears about the relative costs of different educational initiatives as well as different pedagogies. Are we committed to not only a social but also a financial investment in writing instruction from the first year through graduate studies? If so, what other accommodations will we need to make in order to make this instruction a reality? Will we need to restructure graduate programs such that we reconsider "content" versus "noncontent (skill)" paradigms and reallocate our resources to merge these concepts in our courses? Further, will we need to more explicitly talk with graduate students about the economic realities of their own writing—the viability of their ideas *as* marketable in a field, the reception of their writing *as* writing as well as a marker of their own professional identities?

One may argue that part of the reason some members of my department at UNCG opposed this course is because, as a field, we still resist writing as part of an English studies curriculum that does what I describe above: helps students work toward or grow a skill or ability as opposed to certifying or verifying existing abilities as if prior models are infinitely valid in the postgraduate world. But one can also argue that when faculty members begin to admit that students need "help" with their writing (and I put that in quotation marks to emphasize that some faculty see this concept as actual, while others see it as imaginary), the mimetic transfer from faculty to graduate student is broken, and this break is where many ideals about economic value (and resistance to efficiency models in instructional paradigms) begin to fall apart. Of course, mimesis continues as one of the vexing foundations of graduate study—whether it be in literary analysis, creative writing, or even rhetoric and composition. We are to absorb, imitate, and repeat. Explicit instruction in writing, language facility, literacy acquisition, and genre identification should have already happened in our undergraduate studies, so by all means, don't *ask* for it now.

What one may just as forcefully argue about my students at Southern Connecticut is that they pushed against the course for reasons akin to what my fellow UNCG faculty felt about graduate-writing instruction as a freestanding course. These students felt the stigma of remediation foisted upon them, and they were, in a sense, correct. Indeed, I should have railed against teaching this course without pay; I should have also protested the idea of a "secret" course that required students' time and labor for no tangible academic credit. Even though our weekly writing and reading activities were centered on public health scholarship (in which I tried to become conversant and largely failed—myself a "basic" reader and writer in this context, an irony not lost on me), they were there because they were told, *you don't yet qualify. You are not ready.* We gave them a timed test—like we give first-year writers—and many "failed," like our basic writers do. This course certainly didn't even meet the bar for successful basic writing courses, which, as Mike Rose (2010, 5) notes, "set high standards, are focused on inquiry and problem solving in a substantial curriculum, utilize a pedagogy that is supportive and interactive, draw on a variety of techniques and approaches, and are in-line with student goals and provide credit for coursework."

Embedded in the comments of my UNCG English department colleagues, as well as in the valid fears and anxieties of my Southern Connecticut MPH students, is not just a striking and occasionally explicit parallel to the discourse of basic writing but also a real anxiety about the future of English graduate studies, from both faculty and students' points of view. I argue that many graduate programs unwisely continue to view their mission and their general composition from an elite perspective—in other words, that students who are admitted are simply being certified to exhibit what they already know and that the knowledge graduate students exhibit will be a recitation of that which is already formed. This perspective makes labor discussions about teaching content versus skill far simpler: there is only content; there is no skill.

This model, however, is particularly striking in terms of social class. Just as basic writers are typically framed as socioeconomically disadvantaged and/or persons from underrepresented minority groups—a myth I've tried to debunk in my own scholarship—graduate students who come from working-class backgrounds often struggle to be seen as "equal" to their more privileged colleagues and even their faculty.[4] Even as we very generously welcome—indeed, on my own campus actively, at some level, recruit—basic writers who *are* from underprepared communities and/or working- or lower-class families, we do not seem to translate this generosity into our graduate curricula—even though, theoretically, these students are *one and the same.* We see this paradox invoked in publications in the field and in trade-centered outlets, such as the *Chronicle,* as well as in our private department conversations about tenure and promotion. We want to support, for example, our junior colleagues in their quest for tenure, but we hire them based on their ability to "jump-start" their careers and to *do* the work we need them to do. We don't really care if they have been amply supported in these writing endeavors along the way; that stops now. And this does not even begin to address the idea of "investing" in a future colleague, from a departmental perspective. We generally agree that we hire in order to tenure—we don't, as a rule, want to hire someone we feel we cannot keep. So why, in terms of that hire's scholarship, are we so unwilling to invest in success at the graduate level? Why do we persist in thinking that the economics of graduate education and the economics of the tenure-stream labor market are divorced from one another, at this level?

When we *are* willing to say graduate students are in need of *more,* we frame that as subject specific. What we are far less willing to do is to say that these are also *growing and developing writers.* We instead revert to the "lack" paradigm, backed by the "good" exemption, deeply afraid of what other possibilities it entails, economic or otherwise. As we do with basic writers, we want our graduate students to be "already done" with that which is the entrance to their educational path. We want them to be *able* to write, but we are not sure we really want to teach it. Graduate students (and many faculty) grapple with the same sets of new language (terminology) and content (theories, paradigms, materials) undergraduates do, just on a higher scale. Graduate writing courses are not, however, remedial—students cannot have already been taught what they have not needed to know before (how to write an article, how to compose an abstract, how to craft a job letter). Such also holds true, I argue, for basic or mainstream/standard first-year writers. My mantra, well known to my own graduate students, is that writing for college happens *in* college, or, college instruction happens on college campuses.[5] But we could learn quite a bit about how we frame "remediation" and basic writing at the undergraduate level by looking to our better undergraduate writing programs.[6]

I encourage faculty, in their design and implementation of graduate writing curricula, to draw upon a distinction Paul Kameen (1995, 449–50) made 20 years prior to this writing:

> The discourses available to use for thinking and writing about the undergraduate classroom . . . are not directly transferable to the venues—seminar rooms, staff meetings, departmental committees—that predominate at the graduate level. In the graduate arena our roles as masters and mentors, as gate-keepers and door-openers, are more intensely driven by contradictory combinations of . . . power and humility, authority and deference, knowledge and reputation. And students come to us driven by their own contradictory desires for emulation and mastery, originality and conformity, rebellion and compliance.

Kameen's point is crucial as we recognize the intricacies of teaching graduate students to work successfully in the complex writing genres we have long since taken for granted in our own work. I urge faculty to see both the positive and negative parallels in our socioeconomic discourse on graduate-student writing and our discourse on basic writing and to work to make the enterprise of writing as important to our future colleagues—our graduate students—as it is to the first-year students we also teach.

Notes

1. I use this term to encompass both MA and PhD students—and to illustrate the effects of graduate writing on these two populations in my own brief narratives later in this chapter—but as someone who advocates for explicit and deliberate (and separate) writing instruction in graduate programs, I specifically call

attention to doctoral students, as it is these students who are most likely to be called upon to mimic the kinds of writing faculty do in their own (potential) future faculty positions.

2. For example, see Duane Roen et al. (1995), Paul Kei Matsuda (2003), and Richard McNabb (2001).
3. On this point of mentoring, it does seem that in the absence of adequate writing support from faculty in various English programs, students are well equipped, in some cases, to form that support themselves through writing groups. For an example of this in the specific context of mentoring, see Lisa Cahill et al. (2008).
4. For example, see collections such as William DeGenaro (2007), Dews and Law (1995), and Gabriella Gutiérrez y Muhs et al. 2012. Also see Shepherd, McMillan, and Tate (1998). For a broader take on the importance of social class in literacy instruction, see Irvin Peckham (2010).
5. And thus I take an explicit stand against dual-credit, dual-enrollment, and early-college programs as a whole. But that is an argument, while certainly germane to this conversation surrounding where writing instruction "lives" and in what register, for another day.
6. I put *remediation* in quotes here because while I respect Rose's (2010) use of the term in his scholarship, I do not believe all basic writing is remedial, so I resist the term as a general rule when discussing writing studies.

9

COMMODIFYING WRITING

Handbook Simplicity versus Scholarly Complexity

Samantha Looker

In "Activity Theory and Process Approaches," David Russell (1999) reports the experience of seeing four bright yellow one-word posters on his daughter's elementary-school classroom wall: PREWRITE. WRITE. REVISE. EDIT. Reflecting on how something so complex as writing processes became so effectively distilled down to four words, Russell contends that "the discipline of composition studies, like other disciplines, *commodifies* the products of its research and theory to make them useful to practitioners, clients, customers, students" (85, emphasis in original). Such commodification, he argues, is a necessary process, for otherwise many teachers and students would not have access to or understanding of theoretical scholarship. Russell cautions, though, that commodification can carry a risk of overgeneralizing, too much of which can render our scholarly products "useless or counterproductive" (86).

An obvious form of commodification in writing studies is textbooks—those literal commodities we write and ask our students to buy. I worry that, particularly in the specific genre of the first-year writing handbook, we have become insufficiently vigilant with regard to the sort of harmful overgeneralization Russell cautions against. If, as Debra Hawhee (1999, 504) says, composition handbooks both "write the discipline" and "discipline the writer," we must consider carefully what our handbooks are saying to students, teachers, and our wider scholarly communities.

In fall of 2011, I was hired to direct a first-year writing program that I am, at the time of this writing, leading through changes in its textbook policy. The policy I inherited with the program stated that instructors could choose any textbooks and materials they wanted for their classes, except that everyone was required to adopt a handbook from a select list of approved titles. From my own discussions with fellow writing program

DOI: 10.7330/9781607325239.c009

administrators and from other scholars' surveys (e.g., Rendleman 2013; Thompkins 2007), I know many other writing programs also have handbooks as their only required textbooks. Why this circumstance worries me, and why I worked to change it in my own program, is that it says misleading things about the priorities of a writing program.

As we know, first-year writing programs have a wealth of goals, including critical thinking, process, working with sources, and rhetorical awareness. I fear, though, that we frequently demonstrate to students and faculty through our choice of textbooks that our priorities are grammar, style, and documentation format. Granted, programs that decide to require only handbooks do so for a variety of reasons, many of which have nothing to do with making surface issues a priority. For instance, program administrators may make blanket handbook decisions for the program in an effort to free up instructors for what they believe is the more important work of choosing other texts and materials. Regardless of intent, however, when faculty across the university observe the dominance of handbooks on the bookstore shelves and students pay 75 dollars for a handbook but only 15 dollars for a coursepack of readings, the handbook, and its content, can easily come to look like a programmatic priority.

To complicate matters, regardless of their internal priorities, writing programs may wish to demonstrate exactly this priority on surface issues to their wider university, and even public, communities. As Robert Connors (1985, 67) points out, demonstrating attention to mechanical issues can be an understandable defense against a "furor over 'illiteracy,'" and popular and scholarly discourse has reached such a furor relatively regularly throughout the history of higher education in the United States. To borrow Karen Spear's (1997, 331–32) words, "Expressions of alarm about student illiteracy have become one of those discourse conventions through which members of the academic community validate themselves in the eyes of their peers." Composition teachers, then, have a history of being faulted for their inattention to grammar, both by their extradisciplinary peers and by published books and articles (e.g., Gross 1999; Lyons 1976; Mulroy 2003; Sheils 1975). One option for responding to such criticism is publishing in defense of the field's pedagogical priorities (examples of this practice abound throughout the past five to six decades—e.g., Agee 1977; Hourigan 1994; Memering 1978; Spear 1997; Tighe 1963; J. Ward 1981); another is demonstrating through observable pedagogical decisions (such as textbook adoption) that surface correctness is indeed a programmatic priority, a move that may present an acceptable compromise on a number of campuses.

Ultimately, by adopting a textbook, regardless of what we do with it in our classrooms, one of the things we also do is demonstrate to outside audiences some level of commitment to that text's priorities (Bleich 1999; Hawhee 1999), and the first-year composition handbook's priorities are surface issues like grammar, style, and documentation. These priorities are not in themselves a problem; in fact, one of the points I wish to argue here is that these *should* be the priorities of a handbook. Many handbooks, especially the large comprehensive ones, include sections on topics like disciplinary genres, rhetorical concerns, or writing process, but this is rarely something to applaud. The format of a handbook can only accurately convey absolute rules, and we should not mistake what a handbook can do for true instruction in complex rhetorical and writing issues.

In 1999, Peter Mortensen summed up the views of "a good many critics of composition textbooks" by stating that "there is a serious gap between what research and textbooks say about the teaching of writing" (Mortensen 1999, 219). My goal here is not to replicate that criticism, which is both abundant and insightful (see, e.g., Gale and Gale 1999; Meyers 1971; Miles 2000; Rendleman 2009; Rose 1981; Segal 1995), but rather to situate within it a specific argument related to first-year composition handbooks: handbooks should not attempt to be rhetorics, and writing teachers and writing program administrators should not rely on them as such. The format and language of handbooks are well suited to rules but poorly suited to any facet of writing involving interpretation, contingency, or complexity. When academic writing is commodified in a handbook format, it is too often distilled into something more likely to mislead students than assist them.

THE HANDBOOK FORMAT

Given my own scholarly interest in how academic writing and language are defined for undergraduate students, I have examined many of the longest-running and most frequently updated first-year writing handbooks for the definitions, explanations, and restrictions they offer (see also Looker 2011). In this process, I have found consistent contradictions between complex information and commodified presentation.

Commodification and oversimplification are common to most textbooks, which, according to David Bleich (1999, 34), are written in the "language of simplification":

> The language of simplification, of boiling down, of giving summary sections and "bullets," is present in every textbook. . . . While it is true

> that more people will likely buy a book if its language seems simple, or if there are both complex discussions and "boil-downs," it is also true that pedagogical and mercantile purposes conflict on this score. Teachers who write and use the textbooks are forced by the language of the text to teach the erroneous thought—for example, [in the case of one text Bleich examines,] that there "are" four categories [of writing purposes]—and they are forced unconsciously to present the text's language as exemplary.

This language of simplification, and its accompanying distortion of material, seems especially characteristic of the first-year-writing-handbook genre, with its wealth of bulleted points, checklists, and dos and don'ts. Handbooks' layout and language lend an air of authority and objectivity inappropriate to the complex, context-dependent nature of academic writing. Although students and instructors retain the option of reading textbooks against the grain, when rhetorical possibilities and stylistic preferences are presented in the same definitive statements and succinct lists as punctuation rules, it becomes much more difficult to examine standards critically. Because, as Bleich contends, students generally are conditioned to read textbooks for facts and instructions, they would be unlikely, without strong and deliberate scaffolding from an instructor (an act that in turn requires the instructor to be very well trained in the nuances of academic discourse), to read their texts in a way that allows them to imagine the wide range of options and alternatives available to them.

Presenting all material as a rule may not truly be the goal of most handbooks; *The St. Martin's Handbook*, for instance, advises students that there is a difference between "conventions," which can be flexible and varying, and "hard-and-fast rules" (Lunsford 2011, 15). However, even when the message is more nuanced, the format of handbooks makes it difficult to distinguish between what is a rule or fact and what is not. Thus, even though *The Scott, Foresman Handbook for Writers*, for example, has text encouraging students to view distinctions among formal, informal, and casual styles as "points on a continuum rather than hard and fast categories" (Ruszkiewicz et al. 2011, 210), its accompanying chart on "Levels of Formality" does not reflect that flexibility. Instead, we see three columns labeled "**FORMAL**," "**INFORMAL**," and "**CASUAL**," showing students and teachers three distinct registers with different expectations for tone, word choice, format, and other factors. Here are several lines from the chart (211):[1]

Formal	*Informal*	*Casual*
Abstract and technical language; precise vocabulary: *the diminution of nationalistic sentiment*	Mix of abstract and concrete terms; direct language: *the weakening of patriotic feeling*	Concrete language; slang and colloquial terms: *nixing the flag waving*
Impersonal tone; infrequent use of *I* and *you*	Occasionally and comfortably personal; some use of *I* and *you*	Unapologetically personal; frequent use of *I* and *you*
Serious and consistent tone and subject matter	Moderate variations of tone and subject	Wide variations in tone and unexpected shifts in topic—sometimes light and satirical

Similarly, *The Writer's Brief Handbook* gives students a somewhat nuanced explanation of Standard English: "American Standard English (see pages 129–132) is the customary level of formality used in academic writing, but even within the fairly narrow confines of that standard there is room for individual differences of expression so that your writing can retain its personality and appeal" (Rosa and Eschholz 2011, 48). However, upon seeing pages 129–132 as directed, one observes that the only large, full-color heading on page 130 presents a much less nuanced picture of the issue: "3b Use Standard English." I am reminded here of Mike Rose's (1981, 67) point that textbooks' "overall structure stands as a more potent statement than scattered caveats." Chapter subheadings phrased as imperatives and neatly divided charts send a far stronger message than any qualifying that might happen within a handbook's text.

COMMODIFYING THE ACADEMIC COMMUNITY

Composition handbooks discuss a great deal more than mechanical rules. Like most texts directed at first-year writers and their instructors, they often include among their goals introducing students to college-level writing and to the standards to which they will be expected to conform. Almost invariably, these books paint a picture of a cohesive academic community with shared standards and expectations. This cohesion is implied throughout handbooks by statements that tell students what to do in college writing or what an academic audience will expect. Most handbooks have a chapter titled something like "Expectations for College Writing" (Fowler and Aaron 2010; Lunsford 2011; Ruszkiewicz et al. 2011).

Many handbooks also make more explicit statements about a unified academic community. *The Longman Handbook for Readers and Writers,* for example, identifies academia as a single discourse community, explaining that "a discourse community consists of people with shared goals and knowledge, a common setting or context, and similar preferences and uses for verbal and visual texts" (Anson and Schwegler 2011, 2). The academic community, this handbook says, is one of "three major communities of readers, writers, and speakers," the other two being public and work communities (4). A chart describing these communities lists idealized roles, goals, forms, and characteristics for each. The forms and characteristics, for instance, are as follows (4):[2]

Academic	*Public*	*Work*
FORMS	FORMS	FORMS
Analytical report; interpretation of text or event; research proposal or report; lab report; scholarly article; annotated bibliography; grant proposal; policy study	Guidelines; position paper; informative report; letter or email to agency or group flyer or brochure; action proposal; grant proposal; charter or mission statement; letter to editor; Web announcement	Informative memo; factual or descriptive report; proposal; executive summary; letter or memo; guidelines or instruction; promotional material; minutes and notes; formal reports; internal and public Websites
CHARACTERISTICS	CHARACTERISTICS	CHARACTERISTICS
Clear reasoning; critical analysis; fresh insight; extensive evidence; accurate detail; balanced treatment; acknowledgment of competing viewpoints; thorough exploration of topic	Focus on shared values; advocacy of cause or policy; fairness and ethical argument; relevant supporting evidence; action- or solution-oriented; accessible presentation	Focus on tasks and goals; accurate, efficient presentation; promotion of products and services; attention to organizational image and corporate design standards; concise, direct style

By contrasting features like an academic focus on "clear reasoning" against a public focus on "shared values" and a work focus on "tasks and goals," *The Longman Handbook* ignores the enormous variation within scholarly and other communities in favor of presenting the three communities as internally cohesive and distinct from one another.

As they claim a cohesive academic community, handbooks also frame themselves and the classes in which they are used as representative of this community. *The Little, Brown Handbook* advises students to disregard individual variation among teachers in favor of viewing teachers as representatives of academia in general: "Like everyone else, instructors have preferences and peeves, but you'll waste time and energy trying to anticipate them. Do attend to written and spoken directions for assignments, of course. But otherwise view your instructors as representatives of the community you are writing for. Their responses will be guided by the community's aims and expectations and by a desire to teach you about them" (Fowler and Aaron 2010, 166). With statements like these, composition handbooks support efforts to make their writing standards, and those of the teacher and class, appear to be universal. This is a dangerous illusion to present to students, given that there is no universal academic standard for quality writing and that much of being a savvy college writer is being able to adapt to different instructors' standards. In the words of Mike Rose (1981, 72), "Every student knows exactly who his or her audience is—Mr. Jones, Ms. Smith, Professor Simpson. What the student needs to know is that Mr. Jones, Ms. Smith, and Professor Simpson might have very different tastes and standards. . . . Texts should offer sound advice on variation in academic audiences and further advice on how, purely and simply, to determine those audiences' demands." By painting academia as a cohesive community with shared standards, and by denying the need for students to adapt to individual instructors, handbooks can thus discourage the rhetorical development of college writers.

COMMODIFYING ACADEMIC LANGUAGE

While the directive format of handbooks is problematic for the more complex aspects of writing, it works fine for some messages. In addition to "Use Standard English," *The Writer's Brief Handbook* also includes subheadings stating "Make an appositive fragment part of a sentence" (Rosa and Eschholz 2011, 178) and "Be sure a pronoun's antecedent is clear" (167). Because there are no genres in which one customarily puts a period after an appositive, nor are there any circumstances under which an *unclear* pronoun/antecedent relationship might be preferable, these statements are just the sorts of rules to which handbooks are well suited.

Single-sentence handbook directives can also work for rules that are clear issues of appropriateness in an academic setting. The *Simon & Schuster Handbook*, for instance, lists "Never use sexist language or stereotypes" among the items in its "Language to avoid in academic writing" Quick Reference box (Troyka and Hesse 2009, 261–62). This is an excellent suggestion for life, never mind academic writing. What is unfortunate here, though, is that other items in the same box include far more negotiable stylistic preferences like "Never use colloquial language," "Never use nonstandard English," and "Never use regional language" (261–62).

Simon & Schuster is far from alone in this juxtaposition; in nearly all of the handbooks I have examined, issues of formality and dialect are addressed together with issues of offensive language and incorrect word choice. Here is the series of directives provided in the chapter subheadings of *The Bedford Handbook*'s "Choose Appropriate Language" chapter:

- Stay away from jargon.
- Avoid pretentious language, most euphemisms, and "doublespeak."

- Avoid obsolete and invented words.
- In most contexts, avoid slang, regional expressions, and nonstandard English.
- Choose an appropriate level of formality.
- Avoid sexist language.
- Revise language that may offend groups of people. (Hacker and Sommers 2010)

At least this nonstandard English directive is qualified a little in that we are to avoid it "in most contexts" rather than all, but the conflation of nonstandard language and sexist and offensive language as equally "inappropriate" is still troubling. We see a similar series of directives in the subheadings of the "Choose the Best Words" chapter in *Keys for Writers* (I have included a few sub-subheadings here to better show where nonstandardized English is):

- Use a dictionary and a thesaurus.
- Use exact words and connotations.
- Monitor the language of speech, region, and workplace.
  - the language of speech
  - regional and ethnic language
  - the jargon of the workplace
- Use figurative language for effect, but don't overuse it.
- Avoid sexist, biased, and exclusionary language.
- Avoid tired expressions (clichés) and pretentious language. (Raimes and Jerskey 2011)

As the evaluative language of the chapter titles tells us, the tips in these lists are intended to foster "*appropriate* language" and use of "the *best* words" (emphasis added). Apparently, the "best" words are the standardized ones, not those characteristic of ethnic or regional dialects.

Again, as in some of the earlier examples, some of the material communicated in these word-choice chapters is suited to quick directives. In the "Use a dictionary and a thesaurus" section, *Keys for Writers* points out that students must be careful of words that are commonly confused but have different meanings: "Use a dictionary to learn or confirm the *denotation*—the basic meaning—of a word. Some words that appear similar are not interchangeable. For example, *respectable* has a meaning very different from *respectful*; *emigrant* and *immigrant* have different meanings; and so do *defuse* and *diffuse, uninterested* and *disinterested,* and *principal* and *principle*" (Raimes and Jerskey 2011, 368; italics in original). This works because there is no need for context-based negotiation; there are no communities or genres in which *principle* is considered the correct spelling for the person who is in charge of a school.

In contrast to "should I use *respectable* or *respectful*?" or "does this pronoun have an antecedent?" though, "what constitutes academic language?" is a complex question. Yet most handbooks answer it with little hesitation, through seemingly simple bulleted points and headings. This simplicity may result in part from the fact that, historically, one of the most common and least questioned assumptions about academic writing has been that it must be written in standardized English. As Paul Kei Matsuda (2006, 640) contends, "Implicit in most teachers' definitions of 'writing well' is the ability to produce English that is unmarked in the eyes of teachers who are custodians of privileged varieties of English." With this in mind, it is not surprising that we see handbooks issuing blanket directives like "Never use nonstandard English" (Troyka and Hesse 2009, 262).

Though unsurprising, this practice is based on a faulty assumption that remains deeply objectionable because it does not reflect the reality of scholarly writing. Language-focused work by composition scholars in recent decades has worn away at many of the assumptions made about nonstandardized language varieties in relation to academic work (see, e.g., Buell 2004; Canagarajah 2006; Horner and Trimbur 2002; Lu 2004; Matsuda 2006; Young 2009). Such scholarship has illuminated how present nonstandardized language already is in published academic writing and has challenged traditional assumptions that nonstandardized language varieties are less effective for clear communication or formal, complex messages. Such discussions of nonstandardized language in academic writing fit into an ongoing expansion of our definitions of the academic: as we now know, what qualifies as "academic writing" is shot through with a multiplicity of genres, voices, and textual histories that make the category far more blurry than traditional representations would suggest (as discussed in, e.g., Biber 2006; Cope and Kalantzis 2000; Duff 2005; Prior 1998; Thaiss and Zawacki 2006).

If we continue to assume that all academic language is standardized, we reinforce harmful and exclusionary language ideologies. Biber and Finegan (1994) note that registers perceived as literate and academic are similar to the speech and writing of more empowered social groups, both because these groups were able to create the standards and because their power sustains access to these privileged registers for learning and maintenance. The inherent power imbalance here, then, means traditional academic language standards both undermine efforts at inclusivity and fail to reflect the evolving diversity of the academy. As

Suresh Canagarajah (2006, 587) points out, "every time teachers insist on a uniform variety of language or discourse, we are helping reproduce monolingualist ideologies and linguistic hierarchies."[3] This is problematic enough when done by an individual teacher, so why do we quietly tolerate it when it is done by millions of copies of central course texts?

I understand that material must be somewhat simplified, that we cannot all assign Canagarajah articles to our composition students (although I and many other instructors do, and I applaud the ability of readers like Wardle and Downs's [2011] *Writing about Writing* to bring students into the complex theoretical discussions of our field). However, going back to Russell's (1999) point, we must ask what types of simplification make our knowledge useful and what types make it so oversimplified as to be use*less*. A complex question like What constitutes academic language? is more appropriately addressed outside of the handbook genre.

COMPARISONS: HANDBOOKS AND RHETORICS, TEXTBOOKS AND PROFESSIONAL PUBLICATIONS

To illustrate the benefits of addressing these complex questions in other textbook genres, I offer a few brief examples from first-year composition rhetorics, whose format allows for a much more nuanced treatment of academic language issues. The minirhetoric *They Say/I Say*, for instance, includes the chapter "'Ain't So/Is Not': Academic Writing Doesn't Always Mean Setting Aside Your Own Voice," which talks to students about mixing styles and language varieties, using examples including nonstandardized English phrases from Geneva Smitherman and non-English ones from Gloria Anzaldúa. It tells students outright that "what counts as 'standard' English changes over time and the range of possibilities open to academic writers continues to grow" (Graff and Birkenstein 2010, 128). It also encourages students to try out less traditionally academic forms of language for rhetorical benefit, as in this end-of-chapter exercise: "Find something you've written for a course, and study it to see whether you've used . . . any words or structures that are not 'academic.' If by chance you don't find any, see if there's a place or two where shifting into more casual or unexpected language would help you make a point, get your reader's attention, or just add liveliness to your text" (Graff and Birkenstein 2010, 128). Granted, I still take issue with *They Say/I Say*'s reinforcement of a school/home language dichotomy through statements like "It is surprising how often such [academic] writing draws on the languages of the street, popular culture, our ethnic communities, and home" (128). Also, its frequent use of templates does little to move the book away from the directive tone of handbooks. Nonetheless, a chapter like this is definitely a step in the right direction, closer to simplifying than it is to oversimplifying and distorting.

In another rhetoric, Lisa Ede's (2008) *The Academic Writer*, discussions of the "best" or most "appropriate" language are replaced by a more nuanced discussion called "Analyzing Textual Conventions." The only bullet-pointed graphic in this section, titled "An effective academic essay is . . ." addresses academic language by saying that an academic essay "uses words, sentences, and paragraphs that are *carefully crafted, appropriate* for the writer's purpose and subject, and *free of errors* of usage, grammar, and punctuation" (58, emphasis added). This graphic is the closest the book comes to defining what counts as academic in language, and what I appreciate about it is the use of "appropriate *for*," not simply appropriate—it acknowledges that there are no intrinsically appropriate words, that appropriateness depends on context and aims.

What I appreciate even more about this section on textual conventions is that it encourages students to draw their own conclusions about general characteristics of academic language, to uncover trends rather than having rules handed down on a stone tablet. Within the textual conventions section is a subsection called "Observing a Professional Writer at Work: Comparing and Contrasting Textual Conventions," which presents excerpts from several articles by Deborah Tannen—all about her topic of agonism, but published in three different contexts: the *Washington Post*, the *Chronicle of Higher Education*, and the *Journal of Pragmatics* (Ede 2008, 65–67). By looking at the excerpts, printed much as they looked in the original sources, students can see at a glance the differences in format, use of visuals, and textual density. Students are also encouraged to examine details of the articles, such as the use of sources (anecdotal versus heavily documented) and the word choice ("attack" in the *Washington Post* is "oppositional argumentation" in the *Journal of Pragmatics*). What is especially invigorating about these examples is that we can also see commonalities between academic and popular writing that handbook definitions would not anticipate. For instance, the *Journal of Pragmatics* text is peppered with first person: in just the first paragraph, "we" use discourse analysis, Tannen claims her topic as "my" topic, and she ends the paragraph with "Here I turn my attention to . . ." (quoted in Ede 2008, 65).

Compare this to the earlier noted *Scott, Foresman Handbook* chart in which formal writing contains "infrequent use of the first person" (Ruszkiewicz et al. 2011, 211). Or to the statement in *The Prentice Hall Guide* that "first person is appropriate for a narrative about your own actions and for essays that explore your personal feelings and emotions. Some teachers encourage writers to use first person to develop a sense of their own voice in writing" (M. Harris (2005, 129). These sorts of statements give first person a role outside of most of the textual varieties privileged in academia and also serve to reinforce the exclusion of personal forms from academic writing.

In published academic writing, though, first person is regularly used, even in disciplines such as hard sciences where traditional wisdom has held that first person and personal opinions are inappropriate. In a study of scientific journal articles, Chi-Hua Kuo (1999, 131) found frequent use of *we* for purposes ranging from outlining methods and goals—such as, "In this section, *we* consider a number of spatial/spatial frequency representations"—to identifying disciplinary knowledge—such as, "Realize the further objective of what *we* call knowledge refinement" (126; emphasis in original). In a similar study, Iliana Martínez (2005, 186) found especially frequent use of *we* by scientists for the function of "stating results/claims," as in "*Xtrp* may function as an SOC in *Xenopus* oocytes. In support of this, **we** found that *Xtrp* was exclusively localized at the plasma membrane in *Xenopus* oocytes" (emphasis in original).

While the simple existence of first person in published academic scholarship already destabilizes claims about its absence, the ways in which first person is used also frequently blur related distinctions between the academic and the personal. When David Bartholomae (1985, 146), for example, says his students' essays "are evidence of a discourse that lies between what *I* might call the students' primary discourse . . . and standard, official literary criticism" (emphasis added), or Mike Rose (1985, 342) contends, "The more *I* think about this language . . . the more *I* realize how caught up *we* all are in a political-semantic web that restricts the way *we* think about writing in the academy" (italics added), they are undoubtedly explaining important theoretical concepts. However, we might also call these concepts their personal opinions, which are arguably vital to the nature of theoretical academic discourse, even (or perhaps especially) when expressed in the first person. As Ken Hyland (2002, 1091, 1093–94) asserts, "Writers gain credibility by projecting an identity invested with individual authority, displaying confidence in their evaluations and commitment to their ideas. . . . First person then, is a powerful means by which writers express an identity by asserting their claim to speak as an authority, and this is a key element of successful academic writing." From this perspective, first person, and its accompanying visibility of personal identity and perspective, serves an important role in establishing a scholarly ethos. When students are discouraged from use of the first person for anything but storytelling, they are denied that opportunity for authority. First person, then, is a useful representative example of how the discrepancy between textbook representations and academic practices restricts students' ability to fully develop as academic writers.

CONCLUSION

My goal here is not to engage in a blanket vilification of handbooks; some are better than others at avoiding stylistic and rhetorical choices as what Mike Rose (1980) memorably called "Rigid Rules." I also cannot blame handbooks for including stylistic and rhetorical issues, however oversimplified they become as a result, because their inclusion makes significant sense from a sales perspective. Our field's emphasis on process pedagogy in recent decades has meant a danger, at least widely perceived if not actual, of teachers "tossing out their handbooks and grammar exercises to focus on process-oriented teaching" (Clark 2003, 5); by emphasizing issues beyond surface ones, publishers respond to a perceived demand from the composition community. Also, it is important to note that nearly all handbooks do some things quite well. For example, when we have citation practice day in my class during which teams of students test their MLA understanding by selecting from a pile of resources and creating works-cited entries, I appreciate that they can use their handbooks to locate instructions for citing a work with multiple authors or an edited collection.

I also understand it is simply not possible to fit a lengthy, nuanced discussion of certain stylistic or rhetorical issues into the limited space possible in a handbook. I argue, then, that any issue for which this is the case would be better left out altogether rather than pared down until we can no longer recognize it as anything resembling reality. Is there anything to be gained from an oversimplified representation that conveys to students little or no truthful or useful information?

In making pedagogical and programmatic decisions, let us encourage handbooks to do what they do well and think twice about adopting handbooks that oversimplify complex issues better addressed elsewhere. We should remain aware that it is difficult for students to negotiate with textbooks' authority through questions or discussion. One of the selling points of handbooks, in fact, is that students can grab them at any time so that they do not need a teacher around to answer their basic questions. If my students have a quick question about anything other than a basic rule, I sincerely hope they *will* ask me rather than consulting the book I want them to use solely as a punctuation and documentation resource. As Michael Kleine (1999, 139) contends, writing textbooks "posture as authoritative and mysterious texts, prescribing writing behaviors and establishing standards of good writing without revealing how and why the values underlying the advice that they give were constructed historically." If it is true, as Kleine asserts, that students tend to "internalize" their composition textbooks' content and priorities, I do not want my students, or any students, internalizing rules about language that are questionably accurate at best and linguistically exclusionary at worst.

Notes

1. Because the visual cues in handbook charts carry significant messages, I have endeavored to reproduce their boldface type, capital letters, and other visual elements in addition to their content.
2. I have reproduced the use of full caps and bold type from the original chart; the chart also uses different colors to shade in each column.
3. These monolingualist attitudes, incidentally, are why more recent efforts to include sections for ELL writers in first-year composition handbooks are admirable but insufficient. By singling out ELL writers as the primary group whose language differs from the standard expected in academia, handbooks neglect to acknowledge that diversity is everywhere in academic writing and thus that linguistic difference in the classroom is the norm for everyone, not the exception for a few international students or students from immigrant families.

10

PSYCHOANALYSIS, WRITING PEDAGOGY, AND THE PUBLIC

Toward a New Economy of Desire in the Classroom and in Composition Studies

T. R. Johnson

"I must mention it," said Sigmund Freud (1964, 146), near the end of his life, "because it's so exceedingly rich in hopes for the future, perhaps the most important of all the activities of analysis. What I am thinking of is the application of psychoanalysis to education." And Jacques Lacan (Schneiderman 1983, 169), also fairly late in his career, said he understood his work to be, finally, a contribution to the centuries-old discipline of rhetoric. Given the interest in pedagogy and rhetoric voiced by Freud and Lacan, respectively, one would assume teachers of writing would have a lot to say about—and through—various concepts derived from psychoanalysis. They haven't.

"*So exceedingly rich . . .*" said Freud, in the remark quoted above, and perhaps an unintended echo in these words reveals part of the rub: psychoanalysis has long been seen as the province of the leisure class, at least in the United States, of those rich to such an excess they can presumably afford to indulge in seemingly endless and relatively private introspection about miseries far removed from the material conditions of whatever work they might do. In contrast, those who teach writing tend to identify with a rather more hardscrabble ethos: brutally overworked, underpaid, often with no job security, but devoted to empowering—on a very tight schedule—significant numbers of people through grueling practice in principles of rhetoric. Thus, psychoanalysis and writing instruction would seem affiliated with quite distant registers in the United States class hierarchy and seem therefore the strangest of bedfellows.

But maybe not.

DOI: 10.7330/9781607325239.c010

As Lad Tobin (1991) noted, a number of scholars in composition have pointed out the considerable parallels between writing pedagogy and psychoanalysis only to disavow the connection as ludicrous: James Moffett (1988), Donald Murray (1968), Thomas Carnicelli (1980), Stephen Zelnick (1983), and Louise Rosenblatt (1938), among others, have all cautioned teachers away from a framework that in their view can only lead to trouble. Such a framework, they warn, seeks to replace the rightful focus on student prose with volatile intimacies entirely inappropriate to the classroom. Taking a new tack, Tobin (1991) set forth a psychoanalytic approach to the teaching of writing that did not seek to engage the unconscious of the student writer but instead to instill in teachers the habit of reflection on how their own work is shaped by the unconscious. But Tobin's essay may only have added to the difficulty psychoanalysis has had in finding acceptance among teachers of writing because, as Tobin frames it, psychoanalysis seems to compromise quite radically the teacher's authority: even if everyone knows that teachers are not repositories of objective knowledge and ideal standards (i.e., in popular parlance, that they *are*, in fact, "only human" and "just like the rest of us"), the institutional setting requires everyone to pretend otherwise. Besides, if unconscious desires and biases loom too far into the foreground of classroom activity—as, presumably, they inevitably would in any psychoanalytically inflected undertaking—then, rest assured, lawyers are soon to follow.

But what if Tobin and others are foreclosing too soon the potentials of psychoanalytic concepts to help teachers understand their work? What if, more specifically, our field has thought of psychoanalysis in a too-limited way as focused on intensely *private* issues? I'll argue over the coming pages that psychoanalysis is an invaluable resource for organizing the public dimensions of our work and that, as such, it can shift our relationship with the public in ways that could improve the material conditions of our work.

Specifically, when we modify our courses by linking them to projects of public service and publicly circulated student writing, repositioning the economies of student and teacher around a third term—the *public*—we reopen the possibility of a rich relationship between pedagogy and psychoanalysis. More precisely, as I'll argue here, in our efforts to engage effectively with a public, we can find no better tools with which to do so than those we borrow from psychoanalysis. Why? Because, too often, the university's relation to the wider community defaults to a highly problematic parent-child dynamic—a dynamic psychoanalysis is singularly prepared to dismantle. In other words, when our efforts to engage the public fail, they often do so because the academic side of the dynamic sees itself as a knowledgeable sort of parent bringing charity and economic development to an ignorant child or, perhaps less frequently, to an ignorant child venturing (usually through some sort of internship) into the real world to reap knowledge and another résumé line from the experts, who supervise, much the way a parent would, the child's vaguely entrepreneurial gambits there. Either way, the binary of classroom and "real world" is entrenched rather than dissolved, and much is lost, especially when either side begins to revolt against the woefully inadequate parent-child model in ways not guided by the conceptual repertoire of psychoanalysis. That is, if too many on the nonacademic side, for example, come to resent our condescension, they'll likely start to mock us and support politicians who promise to slash our budgets, turning the tables so we become the impudent children who need to learn a hard—that is, punishing—lesson. And conversely, if we send students into these nonacademic settings too ill prepared to contribute much and in overmuch need of supervision, the nonacademic side of this dynamic will increasingly turn away from us and stoke further the flames of the crisis of relevance already burning brightly in the academic humanities. Clearly, a more nuanced dialogue between the university and the surrounding community is essential to our long-term vitality. Through the concepts of psychoanalysis, we stand a better chance of building one.

I will elaborate this position, first in the context of the recent history of composition studies by showing how an emphasis on the public takes us beyond the outworn binary that pits a pedagogy of self-expression against its ostensible opposite, and more specifically how psychoanalytic concepts can provide terms that foreground the link between an individual's experience and broader social forces, thereby muting the potentials for melodrama that inhere in the illusion of their opposition. These psychoanalytic concepts, moreover, give us a healthier framework for navigating what we used to call *the dynamics of town and gown* and, in turn, perhaps, a less hardscrabble future as we gain credibility and in turn more resources.

I will then elaborate this possibility more broadly and define key terms in greater depth by situating it in two longer histories: one that led to a relative dead end among writing teachers in the United States after the 1960s, the other that led in roughly the same period to much the opposite in the streets of Paris. From here, I invite writing instructors to imagine through these terms and these histories new ways of defining and locating and articulating their own work.

BEYOND PERSONAL NARRATIVE AND ACADEMIC CRITIQUE

The psychoanalytic pedagogy I have in mind, rather than plunging both teacher and student into the domain of the intensely personal in ways that are messy, even dangerous, can provide us with powerful conceptual tools for navigating and articulating the dynamic between our classrooms and a wider public. Specifically, following Alan France (1993), John Trimbur (2000), and others, I'll suggest here that our classroom should move not only beyond the expressivist rhetoric that awards increasing value to increasingly honest and authentic personal narratives (which is probably what many assume a psychoanalytic pedagogy would become in actual practice), it must move beyond, as well, the approach that has presented itself as a corrective to expressivism, the pedagogy associated with David Bartholomae and Anthony Petrosky (1986) that would emphasize the project of bringing students into increasing mastery over a cluster of texts (synthesizing or contrasting them, delineating their strategies, implications, and assumptions) (Bartholomae and Petrosky 1986). Instead, we must link our courses to the public through service-learning projects and by enabling our students to experiment with giving their writing a public meaning, a public life. Our classrooms, in short, must become staging areas, as it were, for journeys outside the confines of campus, an ongoing inquiry into highly particularized, local contexts and communities in which we don't erase the authority of the teacher—as Tobin's psychoanalytic pedagogy threatens to do—but rather cast the teacher's authority as one more force in an overdetermined blend of others.

Though I'm addressing here, specifically, the pedagogy of service learning, those researchers interested in discussions of ethnographic method will instantly recognize these concerns as central to the complex ethical dynamics of doing academic work in, among, and upon nonacademic communities (see Brown and Dobrin 2004; Cushman 1999; Kirsch and Ritchie 1995; Mortensen and Kirsch 1996). To draw our service-learning students into the same kind of reflection, and to help them by giving them the conceptual tools of psychoanalysis, could, I think, go a long way to building a better relationship with the wider communities of which we're always, even if only unwittingly, a part.

Most simply, as Linda Adler-Kassner (2008, 4) has insisted, we can, through service learning, "re-articulate the college or university as part of rather than opposed to the local community" in ways that go well beyond the obvious: not just an economic engine that supports nearby pizza joints and bookstores and laundromats, not just as a provider of a variety of low-paying jobs for secretaries, professors, and groundskeepers, not even as a place that "incubates" economically valuable new information and ideas that might stimulate the larger economy but, beyond all of these, as part of the same fabric of ideological and cultural themes in which a thread pulled at one end can create tensions at what is wrongly seen as a very different area. To see the connection, says Adler-Kassner, requires "a crucial and difficult rearticulation." I claim that psychoanalysis can help a great deal with this rearticulation because such rearticulation is precisely the purpose of psychoanalysis: it provides a language for discovering the ways the other and the self are always imbricated in each other and, ideally, for realigning them as equals who together transcend, as I'll explain later, generalized exchange value to root in the particulars of use-value.

To say it another way, as our courses become sustained, explicit engagements with some wider public, some Other—that is, with what we don't and can't fully know—psychoanalysis can give us an essential set of tools for doing so. Psychoanalysis can help us delineate what Raymond Williams (1977, 132–33) calls "structures of feeling": the hybrid of fixed social codes inherited from the past and mixed with the spontaneous realm of immediate, personal experience, the "meanings and values . . . actively lived" in a continuously evolving dynamic with "formal or systematic beliefs"; the specific, always unique, and ever changeful internal relations of thought and feeling that seem to be private but that in a properly psychoanalytic pedagogy are revealed to be thoroughly social formations. I hasten to emphasize that, in order to analyze and modify these structures of feeling, I do not recommend that a teacher function as a psychoanalyst; rather, I suggest that we adopt psychoanalytic terms in our conversations with each other and with students for these terms' power to help us articulate what unfolds as our work winds its way through public space.

An example: consider the interpretation Adler-Kassner, Crooks, and Watters (2006) offer of Bruce Herzberg's detailed account of a service-learning student who developed a "sharp disjunction between [her] attitude toward the individual she worked with and her attitude toward a social group that this individual represented." Adler-Kassner, Crooks, and Watters borrow the Freudian concept of "isolation" to identify how a person can "hold contradictory ideas or attitudes, provided the ideas never come to consciousness simultaneously" (9). This uneasy suppression of contradiction, this particular structure of feeling, is illuminated by the psychoanalytic concept of isolation—that is, the concept functions as a set of tongs for grasping and examining items that could otherwise be too heated, too polarizing to engage. What Adler-Kassner,

Crooks, and Watters do with Herzberg's anecdote is what all of us can do more and more in reflecting on our teaching and thereby gain greater chances of intervening in various sorts of impasses between ourselves and the wider community more effectively.

A brief survey of the partial precedents for the move I'm suggesting will elaborate the point Adler-Kassner, Crooks, and Watters's example illustrates and clarify what I'm after.

TWO SHORT HISTORIES OF PSYCHOANALYSIS SINCE THE SIXTIES: IN COMPOSITION STUDIES AND IN THE STREETS OF PARIS

In 1964, Janet Emig published an article in *CCC* called "On the Uses of the Unconscious in Composing" that offers a fully sophisticated notion of the unconscious and does so in language perfectly accessible and practical (Emig 1964). She describes the unconscious as the other-within, what literary traditions often call the Muse, a sort of psycholinguistic lover who has an overwhelming power to generate and shape a writer's greatest work. Soon thereafter, however, when Peter Elbow (1973) began to advocate for freewriting in what was perhaps the quintessential and defining breakthrough of that period in our field, no one ever made much of this invention strategy's obvious link to the psychoanalytic technique of free association, much less explored the wide array of implications this link might imply. Why didn't anyone say more about the obvious link between Elbow's famous freewriting technique and Freud's talking cure?

Because, I argue, writing teachers in the decades that followed were increasingly consumed with the project of establishing their professional and disciplinary status, which meant minimizing dialogue with that which is distinctly Other: an other field (psychoanalysis), an other-within (Emig's account of the unconscious), and, most broadly, the other that is the wider, nonacademic public. The last we almost entirely ceded to our colleagues in creative writing, who were happy to accrue the vast cultural capital associated with the production of "Literature," while we, trapped in a different class affiliation, focused more or less scientifically on determining how best to transmit a narrowly cast set of writing skills we deemed essential to landing a job and joining the adult middle class, thereby enabling a sort of access for our students that, in turn, they would pass along to us, as our grim march toward disciplinary status inched along, one wave of relatively error-free student prose at a time.

Thus, the tradition of psychoanalytic writing pedagogy that seems to have begun in the mid-1960s with Emig and to have bounded forward with Elbow never really got off the ground. Some 20 years later, in 1987, *College English* broke the silence by devoting a special double issue, guest edited by Robert Con Davis, to the dynamic of psychoanalysis and teaching. As Davis (1987) asserted, all the articles in these two issues argued the point set forth in Shoshana Felman's classic essay that our work as teachers is paradoxically suffused with the very resistances it seeks to overcome; that is, that insights are not opposed to but imbued with certain blindnesses; that knowledge doesn't vanquish ignorance but proceeds only and always in a structural dynamic with ignorance; and how particular personalities are constituted shapes directly their capacity for navigating these dynamics of knowledge and ignorance—that is, knowing how to know and how *not* to know in order to hold open the potential for more learning.

Of course, the particular sorts of powers that inhere in the psychoanalytic way of knowing have an uneasy relation, at best, to the more commodified sorts prized in the academic institution, as manifest, that is, in more and more lines on the CV for one's annual review and, in turn, the possible prospect of ever greater salary increases. Perhaps this explains why another 10 years passed with no more work on the subject among a generation of writing teachers who were eager to establish further, even fully professionalize, their growing discipline.

In 1997, however, Nancy Welch devoted a book to the psychoanalytic study of how writers resist the work of revision and also how they "get restless" and push to unsettle, in turn, their texts and their ways of thinking. Most broadly, she showed how psychoanalytic terms could enable a much more sophisticated and ambitious approach to teaching revision (Welch 1997). Around the same time, Mark Bracher (1999) published a book on how unconscious forces inevitably shape the struggle to write and the dynamics of writing instruction. And a few years later, Marshall Alcorn (2002) used Lacanian psychoanalysis to describe the project of enabling students to move away from the binding force of the ego's identifications with authorities (which so mitigate students' capacity for political engagement, to say nothing of their processes of revision) toward a more egalitarian social field and, moreover, for mobilizing, even radicalizing, their desire for social justice. These excellent books constitute a minor tradition in our field; and yet, despite them, psychoanalysis has never played much role in our conversations.

The challenge this tradition faces, as Peter Taubman (2012) explains in *Disavowed Knowledge: Psychoanalysis, Education, and Teaching*, is that the academic institution is organized by an intolerance of ambiguity, a yearning to be perfectly straightforward, at one with itself, transparent, devoid of ignorance, ready for accreditors, eager to measure up to various objective standards and "learning outcomes," wholly obedient to the authorities who preside over the dominant economy of knowledge production, for whom concrete results are always the key to more money: more publications on the CV mean a better salary next year; higher performances on standardized tests mean a school is succeeding and is worthy of more and better resources.

This entrepreneurial logic and unthinking submission to the values of established authorities is the opposite of psychoanalysis. The latter frames the economy of knowledge production in terms of an ineradicable excess: like those in our field most enthusiastic about the idea that writing is a process (of revision ad infinitum), the psychoanalyst knows there will always be yet a few more loose ends to tie up, and then a few more, always a few other implications to trace, and then a few others still; there can never be complete self-accountability, for the unconscious guarantees there is always some dimension of one's self one cannot anticipate or recall or know. This is the logic of unconscious desire—the constant unveiling of an Other in which one is wholly imbricated and by which one is utterly divided. In fact, for psychoanalysis, this distinction between what one can know and what one cannot know is the grounds for a dialogue between them, as it were, and this dialogue is the stuff, the activity, the work and the play, of psychoanalytic knowing. This way of knowing never seeks to be devoid of ignorance but pulls ignorance to the center of its processes, an insistent other in a structural dynamic that propels what William Covino (1988) called the "art of wondering"—an art of wondering, most specifically, about *values* rather than an unthinking devotion to and perpetuation of the values foisted upon one by the dominant culture, the values, still more precisely, of distinct particulars rather than those available to generalized exchange, about which I'll say more later.

Taubman (2012, 5) reminds us that Freud referred to both pedagogy and psychoanalysis as "impossible professions" because they both act on and with the unconscious, and this "intimate alterity" always resists and disrupts the sorts of simple, causal narratives people, especially in institutional settings, are pushed to pursue. Taubman and others suggest that, in essence, the conflict between psychoanalysis and schools can be distilled into the distinction between two approaches, which are sometimes called *the therapeutic project* and *the emancipatory project*, a difference in essence between the individual and the subject. The therapeutic project seeks to *cure*, to restore the individual as a sovereign unit to some sort of optimal level of functioning, productivity, and free-market agency;

the emancipatory project is more attuned to the pure form of Freud's discovery of the unconscious, the aspect of the subject that links to otherness and disconnects from or overrides the ego, the self, or individual. The emancipatory project eschews the naïve notion of a cure and aims instead toward ever-greater understanding, which is to say the constant renewal of dialogue with what the subject cannot know. Clearly, in an era obsessed with accountability, with concrete outcomes, the emancipation of the subject becomes a radically undervalued project, and the cure of the individual even becomes our sole mission, a mission defined, most darkly, around the impossible dream of removing the unconscious from the realm of human interaction altogether.

The best illustration of this distinction comes from Paul Verhaege (2004), who casts it as the difference between medical and psychoanalytic approaches to knowing: when a child exhibits certain symptoms such as a rash and fever, the parents take the child to a doctor who looks at the child and links the symptoms together and, in turn, to a generalized syndrome on an objective continuum of health and illness, then sets forth a treatment that will return the child to a prior optimal state. However, in contrast, suppose a teenage boy has developed the habit of stealing cars and joyriding down the highway in them: his parents insist that he speak to a different kind of doctor, one who will listen to him and develop an interpretation of the roots of the behavior that extend well beyond the boy himself; the doctor explores how the teenager has unwittingly inherited certain conflicts from his parents and their relationship and how he is perhaps unconsciously striving to reconcile these conflicts, to regain something these conflicts, he feels, are costing him by producing the symptom that is the problematic behavior. The more the doctor listens to the boy, the less he links the symptoms to a generalized syndrome and the more he connects them to increasingly particularized roots that are not simply unique to the boy but extend into the particulars of the intersubjective web in which the boy is, as humans always are, unconsciously imbricated—and that dominant, free-market ideology would deny and erase, thereby likely exacerbating the boy's symptoms.

In Verhaeghe's example of the teenage car thief, it turns out that the boy only steals Mercedes, that his mother comes from a well-to-do family in a nearby town named Mercedes, that the boy always ditches the cars there after an evening of joyriding, that the father is a working-class striver who has prospered and whose wife (the boy's mother) is betraying him with a secret lover. What exactly does all of this mean? Whatever it means, it means only in this case, making it very different from the fever and rash in that other case to which the doctor appended the generalization *chickenpox.* In sum, the analyst's goal is to extend an interpretation as far as possible into the particular, renewing the always unique act of overturning what was hidden, to accept the surprising discovery of what one didn't realize was a part of one's self. In contrast, academic life in our time follows the medical model: we academics exchange highly conventionalized and generalized representations as commodities, mostly to bolster our authority, boost our lagging salaries, and buttress us against surprises.

I'll say more in the final section of this essay about the distinction between exchange value and the always particularized use-value; first, though, I'd like to trace an alternative to the history I've just sketched, one that shows how well psychoanalysis can serve in the work of engaging public life. We can see this alternative in bold, graffiti-like terms if we consider what transpired in Paris in the aftermath of the student uprising of 1968. As Sherry Turkle (1979) writes, while a great many people were moved in an intensely personal way, even transformed by this far-reaching shutdown of the major institutions of the country, the revolt was not a political success. One outcome, however, was the complete reversal of the place of psychoanalysis in French life—it went from a very minor, marginal, fairly maligned enterprise to one of overwhelming centrality and popular enthusiasm. Describing Paris some 10 years after the events of 1968, Turkle says psychoanalysis had been embraced as a fully emancipatory rhetoric as opposed to a therapeutic science.

In short, as people grew disillusioned with the forms of political struggle that held their attention in the period that climaxed in May of 1968, they turned inward. At the same time, much the same turn was made in the United States, and for the same reasons, but in the latter setting, this turn carried a spiritual rather than intellectual emphasis, leading not to psychoanalysis but to religious retreats, meditation seminars, encounter groups, and what we now call the *New Age movement.* Moreover, in France, this inward turn did not mean a complete disconnection from politics; rather, the French continued to engage politically, but they did so psychoanalytically—that is, through a devotion to psychoanalytic theory and training and by undergoing analysis itself—as if psychoanalysis, like war, were simply politics by other means, a different form of political struggle, a bridge between an inward politics of the person and a politics of social activism. Thus, after May 1968, psychoanalysis became thoroughly intertwined with analogous projects of Marxism, feminism, and antipsychiatry, suffusing the language of social criticism as activists devoted themselves, through psychoanalytic concepts, to transforming interpersonal relationships, a spirit expressed in the well-known slogan

"The personal is political." They devoted themselves in particular to dismantling the binary of parent versus child to which interpersonal dynamics too often default and by placing supreme value on equality.

They felt they could use psychoanalysis to critique the rigid, impersonal, abstract, overly structured order that keeps people so alienated—so alienated, that is, from each other, from the world, from themselves, from knowledge, from meaning, from life, all of which are expressions of their alienation from the language of unconscious desire. And thus, says Turkle (1979), in the aftermath of the May 1968 uprising, vast numbers of Parisians were discovering *that* language—feeling, that is, that they were speaking to each other through the language of psychoanalysis as they had never spoken to each other before, with what they felt to be a new depth and directness, a new excitement and pleasure, a new wit, profundity, and warmth. In short, after the uprising of May 68 collapsed, psychoanalysis became the key to renewing—with all the intensity of the deeply personal—a public life.

To many observers, May of 68 seemed to be an instance of surrealism in action, a celebration of the unconscious not as a deeply personal, private reserve of secret passions, as commonly misunderstood, nor as a milieu merely influenced by or reacting to social and historical forces; rather, as Fredric Jameson (1981) would argue in *The Political Unconscious*, the unconscious *is made of* social and historical forces, overdetermined by them, the milieu in which they do their work and articulate themselves, a river of purest and most profound meaning, an overwhelming excess of meaning. Thus, the unconscious speaks the language of poetry and serves as the staging ground of revolution. The title of a key book to emerge from that era—Julia Kristeva's (1984) *Revolution in Poetic Language*—captures well the zeitgeist, as the book delineates what Kristeva calls "the semiotic chora," the roots of language's capacity to be musical, playful, poetic, charged with desire, and hence revolutionary in relation to the ego's bureaucratic fantasies of control and pervasive alienation from and constant misrecognition and disavowal of the others that constitute it (25–30).

The legacies of these postsixties psychoanalytic radicals have, in fact, *already* shaped the practices of writing teachers in the United States: as Taubman (2012) notes, the simple act of asking your students to put their desks in a circle, rather than in orderly rows, largely derives from the psychoanalytic radicals' moment; as does the use of small groups to get students to relate their feelings about a topic and to confront issues of bias; as does the inclusion of self-reflection, freewriting, and journal writing in the writing process. Moreover, whenever we try to make the curriculum relevant to student interest and/or more socially relevant, we are continuing the work of the radicals of that time. By bringing psychoanalytic language into reflections and conversations about our engagement with the public, we can carry that tradition further forward.

A qualification: I am, of course, *not* suggesting we simply revert to the wild, even anarchic realities of the streets of Paris in that era. In that situation, as Taubman (2012) notes, there followed a kind of revolutionary zeal in linking the radical edge of psychoanalysis to schooling, to abolishing all disciplinary and institutional mechanisms, even the nuclear family itself, for all of these were understood as merely the fountains of the neuroses that give rise to racism, sexism, and imperialist war; in this view, schools only exist to create well-adjusted cogs in the social machinery, and thus teachers should instead seek to nurture rebel-artists, whose mission would be to free up erotic energy across the rest of the population. Obviously, all of that is long gone, and, many would add, *thank god.*

Rather, what I mean, at the risk of redundancy, is that when I link my course assignments to the public, my students no longer experience the university as a vertically organized mechanism of exclusion. In parallel, the ego too partially melts away to the point that it can enter into dialogue with the unconscious, or what has heretofore been unconscious—the powerful, overdetermined energies of the wider public. In a sense, this isn't so far from the aftermath of May 68 if we understand that period's "erotic energy" as an interpersonal economy that refused all parent-child dynamics in favor of radical egalitarianism. And, again, our best tool for doing this is the conceptual repertoire we inherit from psychoanalysis.

CONCLUSION: USE-VALUE

In the context of projects of service learning, where strictly academic ways of knowing are explicitly pushed past their limits by the off-campus engagement in nonscholarly settings, my students become intensely conscious of who they are; more precisely, they can't help but wonder quite pointedly about the various social positions coming into play around the project quite concretely; they become immersed in rhetoric as what Verhaege (2004) casts as a journey into the particular, a poetically charged language that can be richly supported by key terms drawn from psychoanalysis.

And when they must produce something that will exist outside the immediate confines of the class and the semester—say, a short video or a training manual for future students who enroll in the course and for the people in the community with whom they've worked—this link to the public, to a dimension that exceeds them, radicalizes their self-awareness still further. In other words, when a student creates a paper purely as an academic assignment, it has only exchange value—that is, it equals a certain amount of academic credit; as Evan Watkins (1989) argues in *Work Time*, that paper, much as it might enrich in subtle, personal ways the student's understanding of some aspect of her life, never travels outside the university except as a unit within the larger unit that is her course grade, which in turn constitutes a unit within the larger unit of value that is her diploma and which, in turn, circulates only in very abstract and increasingly unreliable ways in larger, more vague systems of economic exchange. However, when a student creates something that has use-value—when it is broadcast through the Internet or some other medium to serve a purpose in some specific community—it becomes particularized in the way that psychoanalysis so prizes and that so energizes one's relation to the unconscious. And the students themselves often come to particularize these experiences, to set them apart from the stream of generalized exchanges that otherwise blur together as "the college years."

An appeal for precisely such a move was mounted by John Trimbur (2000) in "Composition and the Circulation of Writing." He asked that we teach the old rhetorical canon of delivery in a fundamentally new way. No longer a question of how speakers gesture or modulate the sound of their voice, as in classical rhetoric, nor even the more recent way of thinking about delivery in terms of the physical design of one's written document (typography, and what's sometimes called *visual rhetoric*), Trimbur asks us instead to "devise delivery systems that circulate ideas, information, opinions, and knowledge [more widely] and thereby expand the public forum in which people can deliberate the issues of the day" (190). Rather than narrowly code the scene of writing instruction as a sort of middle-class family drama in which the teacher, as authoritative parent, demands that the students make an account of themselves (either by narrating an experience as in expressivism or by demonstrating a command of assigned readings, as in Bartholomae and Petrosky's [1986] well-known corrective to expressivism), Trimbur would instead link student work to worlds outside of the academy, to the public "circulation of cultural forms and products" (190), to lay bare certain volatile contradictions between, for example, the exchange value that organizes the economy of authoritative experts (what, a moment ago, I characterized as *medical knowledge*, as the therapeutic project) and the use-value that organizes the particulars of the economy of lay people (what, a moment ago, I called *emancipatory* or *psychoanalytic knowledge* that is the basis of more robust and resilient subjects).

Again, Trimbur (2000) insists that simply "doing service learning" is not enough, for it can entrench what he sees as a false dichotomy between the real world and the academic world, especially when representatives of the latter are merely doing charitable works upon representatives of the former and, especially, when motivated solely by the goal of accumulating various forms of academic credit or professional credential. Rather the key is to open economies that allow knowledge from both sides of this dyad to flow back and forth, economies in which neither side imagines itself to be answering to a parent or helping out a child. For Trimbur, the primary direction of pedagogy must be into greater and greater historical specificity, which he casts as Marxist, and that I, a moment ago, cast as psychoanalytic and emancipatory as distinct from medical or therapeutic ways of knowing.

In such a pedagogy, we seek knowledge that is neither purely personal nor merely academic but rather is articulated within a broader economy of desire, of self-other dynamics, that is always localized and particularized and rooted in public use-value. Such moves can only strengthen our bonds to the wider public, which in turn can only help to improve our working conditions and muffle those political factions that seem most bent on shutting us down altogether. The key, for Trimbur, is to set aside the powerful, parent-like figure of the teacher, which both expressivists and their detractors place at the center the pedagogic enterprise, and instead bring the students into a dialogue with a public, drawing knowledge from and testing their ideas against an audience that, again, is not a form of parent or of child but ideally becomes increasingly an equal. As academic and nonacademic forms of working and knowing grow more equal with respect to each other, perhaps the broader and more brutal inequities of the US class hierarchy can be mitigated, one local community and one semester at a time. Such radically egalitarian immersions in the particular, in use-value, is the stuff of the unconscious, an economy of desire always, by definition, new and surprising. Its older name is *love.*

Acknowledgment

Portions of the argument advanced in this essay appear in my book *The Other Side of Pedagogy: Lacan's Four Discourses and the Development of the Student Writer* (Johnson 2014) and also in my essay in *JAC,* "How Student Writers Develop: Rhetoric, Psychoanalysis, Ethics, Erotics" (Johnson 2011).

PART III

Economies of Language and Medium

11

LITERATE RESOURCES AND THE CONTINGENT VALUE OF LANGUAGE

Rebecca Lorimer Leonard

Literacies and languages have long been understood to have social or economic worth. But in the context of a globalizing economy, literate resources have "gained salience and value" and are understood now to be commodities with a direct exchange value in shifting global markets (Heller 2010, 107; see also Park and Wee 2012; Rubdy and Tan 2008). The literate resources that power this economy differ from primary (metals, food) or industrialized (electronics, processed food) resources in that they trade in information and services (Heller and Duchene 2012, 9). Linguistic instrumentalism (Wee 2003), the idea that languages are useful tools for economic goals, frames an economy in which language workers are central to processes that move information, people, and materials around the world. For Park and Wee (2012), this commodification of language represents a marked shift. They argue that in the past, language was a "marker of one's social identity and therefore not something subject to exchange," but once commodified, language "loses that association, which opens up the possibility of treating language as an economic resource to be cultivated for material profit" (125) and, as Monica Heller (2010, 108) has noted, as a "resource to be produced, controlled, distributed, valued, and constrained." Heller asserts that identity, too, is for sale, suggesting that both language-as-skill and language-as-identity (i.e., "authentic" experiences for tourism) are commodities on a literate market. In this context, the discourse of literacy and language as "resources" takes on symbolic and volatile meanings.

At the same time, those who study and teach writing increasingly call for writers' literate resources to be recognized. Evoked often in calls for change, the word *resource* challenges deficit models of literacy, foregrounding amplitude rather than lack, the varieties that exist rather than the standard varieties that are missing. For example, Horner, Lu, Royster, and Trimbur (2011, 299) suggest that linguistic difference

DOI: 10.7330/9781607325239.c011

is "a resource for producing meaning in writing, speaking, reading, and listening." A. Suresh Canagarajah, in an undated post to *CCCC Conversations on Diversity*, has promoted a "resource discourse" over a "rights discourse," saying that a rights-based discourse "simply affirms the existence or preservation" of different codes and languages; a resource-based discourse, by contrast, views "language differences and fluidities as resources to be preserved, developed, and utilized" (Horner et al. 2011, 304; also see Bawarshi 2010). Scholars studying multilingualism in educational contexts similarly suggest that "there is a need for teachers to draw on the considerable language resources that such students bring with them to class" (Block 2007, 80) because multilingual students use "the languages at their disposal as a resource in communication" (Cenoz and Gorter 2011, 358). Canagarajah (2011, 407), for example, describes a student writer who "considers her background as a resource" and "draws actively" from her "multimodal resources for expression." In other words, writing researchers and teachers recognize the value of literate resources in changing cultural contexts, asking that teachers draw them out in instruction and encourage their manipulation in writing. An understanding of difference-as-resource—difference as locus of meaning—is distinct from and more precise than language-as-resource or background-as-resource. But resource talk often slips among these frames, and by evoking a discourse of resources, scholars and teachers deem literate practices marketable and take on roles in the literate markets described above.

This essay explores the use of *resource* to describe literate abundance. What are these resources made of—what are their raw materials? And how do these resources become re- or devalued in specific communicative contexts? By approaching literate resources in this way, this chapter acknowledges a paradox—some writers benefit from their valuable literate resources while others do not—and attempts to show how and why resources are differently valued in the everyday experiences of two immigrant multilingual writers.

THE VALUE OF LANGUAGE

As resources move across the world with their writers, they move through markets that value literacy and language differently. Following Michel Foucault and Pierre Bourdieu, Allan Luke (1996, 329) argues that literate capital "acquired in school and fully credentialed through grades or degrees" has no "intrinsic power of the skill, text, competence . . . acquired" but instead depends on (1) any given market's valuing of that resource and (2) the will of institutions or powerful individuals to convert those resources into further social purchase. The realization of further capital is "contingent on institutional pre-conditions which delimit and authorize what one is 'entitled' to do" (329). Thus, no matter the extent of one's literacy and language resources, literate capital cannot bring about further social or cultural capital without access to specific institutional sites. If writers cannot access a graduate program, workplace, or community center because of their accent, lack of documentation, or financial status, they cannot put their existing resources to use, and these resources may remain inaccessible or invisible. In other words, whether existing literate resources can be converted into further material or symbolic gain is contingent upon the relations of power that grant or withhold value. If one is already at risk of discrimination within certain institutions like schools, as oftentimes immigrants, refugees, or dialect speakers are, the value of one's literate resources can be volatile indeed.

Further, this revaluing occurs within what Jan Blommaert (2010, 3) has called globalization's "new and complex markets for linguistic and communicative resources." Park and Wee (2012, 143) argue that globalization has created a "diversity of [market] conditions" such that "there can virtually be no . . . process in which there is no loss or distortion in the value of linguistic capital." As markets have formed and reformed under a globalizing economy, they create competition among linguistic "winners and losers" (Blommaert 2010, 3). The language repertoires of multilingual immigrants are subject to these competitive markets before, after, and along their paths of migration. As migrating writers encounter shifting global conditions, so too do their resources experience shifting value. In fact, the travel of language resources, the movement from one place and language to another, makes writers both socially mobile and socially marginal because their resources are always in flux. The accounts below show that it is in fact the mobility of the resources—a fact often celebrated—that causes the resources' value to shift.

Thus the discourse of resources is fraught, not only because language and literacy resources can be highly valued, bringing about important material gain, but also because these resources are not automatically valuable in the constantly shifting linguistic markets across which migrating writers move. For example, Marco Jacquemet (2005, 267) claims that learning English, Chinese, or French is "the best—and sometimes the only—opportunity currently available to many bright people . . . for social and geographical mobility," while Ilene Crawford (2010, 82) notes that developing such language resources can "secure a job with a foreign company that pays significantly more." For many, the acquisition of economically viable languages does, indeed, make life easier. But for others, "no amount of English fluency" can "completely transcend" the stereotypical designations the global economy assigns them, especially when that English fluency carries an accent (Prendergast 2008, 4).

In fact, scholars have long noted that literacy and language resources do not guarantee economic betterment (G. Graff 1987; Heller 1999, 2003; Hernandez-Zamora 2010; Luke and Carrington 2004). For example, Deborah Brandt (2001, 179–80) finds uneven literacy sponsorship—family support but not more economically profitable institutional recognition—behind the "unstable currency" of Spanish-English bilingualism. This instability is why some resources "allow mobility while others will not"; such resources "follow the predicament of their users: when [they] are socially mobile, their resources will follow this trajectory; when they are socially marginal, their resources will also be disqualified" (Blommaert 2010, 24, 47). In other words, literate resources are bound up in the social positions in which writers find themselves as well as the economic forces through which they write.

TWO WRITERS' RESOURCES

The accounts of Khadroma and Tashi, multilingual nurses from China and India, respectively, illustrate the constantly shifting conditions that assign value to literate resources. These accounts are drawn from ongoing qualitative research that traces how literacy practices travel among languages and locations in the world. In initial and follow-up interviews, Khadroma and Tashi were asked to describe their literacy memories, current literacy practices, and opinions about communicating as multilingual individuals. Khadroma is a registered nurse from China who grew up speaking Tibetan at home and Mandarin in school. Tashi is a registered nurse from India who grew up communicating among English, Hindi, Tibetan, and Kannada students in an English-medium boarding school for Tibetan refugees. Both Khadroma and Tashi communicate with highly developed literate resources, but their similar resources have been valued differently since their immigration to the United States.

Khadroma

In China, after completing her early schooling, Khadroma attended a teaching college where her classes were conducted in English, Mandarin, and Tibetan, a multilingual setting that Khadroma explains was noteworthy for its inclusion of Tibetan language in the curriculum. This wasn't "just for the sake of language" or the learning of the languages themselves, says Khadroma, but for the sake of understanding sociology, anthropology, and world literature through the frames of these languages. After college, she entered an English training program funded by "a couple of American foundations" in which she was trained in interpretation and translation. At this time, Khadroma also was employed as a civil servant, writing eulogies for a newspaper and essays on health information for politically important retirees. Through connections from her American teachers, Khadroma also wrote translations and interpreted for American NGOs doing work in China. Though this was weekend work, she was happy to travel and work in her multiple languages.

Upon immigrating to the United States, none of Khadroma's school credit or credentials transferred, but her interpretation practices became important resources. She decided to "start all over" and become a nurse, attending a local community college and then transferring to a nursing program at a four-year university. While in the nursing program, she was employed by the county public health department as an on-call and on-site interpreter for Mandarin- or Tibetan-speaking patients. Khadroma's nursing program also asked her to serve in a position called *a Chinese officer*, translating policy documents for the program and offering interpretation support. Later she was asked to help translate documents in preparation for the university chancellor's trip to China. In other words, Khadroma's multilingual resources were deemed highly valuable, not only in her program but also by local government and the university's administration.

In the hospital where Khadroma is currently employed as an RN, multilingual patient support is regulated through a handful of policies and institutions. She says, "This is something that they are pushing forward now . . . we have materials printed in Spanish . . . [and] we do provide on-site interpretation through a different company. We are required to ask people if they speak English as a different, second, or third language." Khadroma identifies these policies as different from those in her nursing program in that they are regulated by "Jayco, a committee that assesses the quality of care at different hospitals."[1] According to Khadroma, "Jayco"—shorthand for Joint Commission on Accreditation of Health Care Organizations (JAHCO)—requires that nurses "ask people if they need language help in terms of their care" but then also read a script before starting service as an interpreter, as Khadroma explains:

> We do have something that, prior to dropping in as interpreter, you have to read saying, "This is my name, I'm going to be the interpreter, I'm going to interpret from this side and from that side, no matter what you gonna say." So that kind of lay a general rule for people. . . . whatever you said gonna be delivered to the other person. I kind of like that because, as interpreter myself, people tell me, "Oh don't interpret what I said," but it's not fair. Whoever is in the room, I'm here to facilitate the communication. I'm supposed to deliver the message.

Khadroma's literate resources are clearly vast and also viable in the United States. Across multiple professional and geographic settings, her facility in Tibetan, English, and Mandarin is valued highly, causing Khadroma to decide she is "fortunate to know more than one language" as her economic prospects multiply in turn. Though Khadroma characterizes her resources as uneven, saying her English is not as proficient as her Mandarin and Tibetan, her facility in moving among these language proficiencies is itself a resource that proves valuable. But Khadroma's experiences are noteworthy both for the presence of outside organizations and for the specific ways these organizations, and Khadroma in turn, value Tibetan, English, and Mandarin.

Three different organizations seem to manage the language work in the description above: one company provides bilingual health pamphlets, another provides on-site interpretation, and an accrediting organization regulates both. While Khadroma is certainly agentive in how she leverages her resources, corporations and organizations also play a role in the process of valuation in both China and the United States. As Luke, Luke, and Graham (2007, 5) and others have suggested, in the globalized new economy, supranational corporations and organizations assign value to language goods and language workers more than do nation-states, which have been left simply to regulate their flows across borders. This is certainly the case throughout Khadroma's literate history, as Western-language teachers, traveling business people, and government and university organizations deemed her Tibetan, Mandarin, and English each to be economically valuable.

Further, this high value is assigned especially when Khadroma treats her literate resources as straight language work, as standardizable skills. The script she is required to read reveals the influence of what Heller calls "Taylorist" management techniques that synchronize language work, like that done in call centers, into a "standardized sequence of steps" (Heller and Duchene 2012, 12; also see Cameron 2000). As Khadroma says, no matter the content of the translation, she is going to follow the protocol, translating "from this side and from that side." From this point of view, the value of her literate resources resides in their status as language-as-skill. Khadroma presents herself as a conduit through which languages move, as present to "facilitate the communication" and "deliver the message." That Khadroma treats her multilingualism as a tool to be manipulated, as a skill rather than an identity, seems to have kept her languages viable.

Tashi

Tashi's literate history, however, includes institutions and powerful agents that value her literate resources differently. She grew up attending an English-medium boarding school for Tibetan refugees. The colonial legacy of the school included instruction only in English from the first standard (kindergarten) on: "Only thing I was doing was English. I learned math in English. I learned science in English. I learned social studies in English." Tashi believes that having had to "comprehend into English" and then write in English the "main core values or the main theme" of this content shaped her proficiency. She considers herself able to "express what [she wants] to write . . . 100 percent in English," while she feels she can write about 70 percent of what she wants to express in Tibetan and about 10 to 20 percent in Hindi. So, while in practice Tashi's school was multilingual ("The teacher teaches in English, but students answer in Tibetan."), and she spoke Tibetan and Kannada at home before moving to school, Tashi identifies as an English-dominant communicator.

Though she immigrated to the United States with a master's degree in science education, Tashi's credentials, like Khadroma's, did not transfer. Tashi entered the same prenursing community college program as Khadroma and transferred into the same research university, writing a successful scholarship application along the way that fully funded her nursing degree. Tashi found much of the coursework in the university nursing program to be repetitive but was interested to discover that nursing's "main language" was the communication of being "compassionate, ready to help." As a Tibetan-trained teacher, she felt she was already fluent in this language as well. Tashi found it "really easy to study psychology, sociology, and all because [she] can express especially easy when it's writing." Given her English education in India, which Tashi says was very focused on grammatical "rules, policies . . . similar to languages in the books," she was surprised to see that English speakers in the United States "just write . . . put it down as they speak." She says when writing summaries of readings with her nursing study group, "actually it doesn't make sense, doesn't look really good or grammatically right." In other words, Tashi not only feels proud of her literate resources in multiple languages, especially her English writing, she also often feels more proficient than her US counterparts.

However, in the high-stakes context of a hospital, Tashi feels her literate resources are devalued, each in a slightly different way. Tashi has experienced discrimination against her spoken and written English accent, explaining that if you don't use English "as a native, like American people do, then people try to rough you, overlook you, or make you repeat it, like 'what did you say?'" In interactions that "happen quite often in day-to-day life," Tashi feels "not accepted if you don't know that language" by people who "think in the world there's only one language." For Tashi, these experiences are particularly frustrating in light of her English fluency and the fact that she has come to "know that language" through a lifetime of schooling and well-honed academic literacy practices.

Further, Tashi's Tibetan, the language with which she identifies culturally, speaks at home with her family, and is proud to be passing on to her two children, is not valued at all:

> I had the experience in my class, when I see my partner I speak in Tibetan and the patient felt kind of offended. So my clinical instructor, she called me aside and she was like "[Tashi,] you are not allowed to speak in your language when patient is there. She was offended." I was sorry, it was so unconscious, like when I see her face, just comes out. . . . I thought, it can be true because patient like, all patient might not be feeling bad, but still, like some patient do have concern. And in her case like she has a right to feel offended because I didn't ask for permission, so she might have felt hurt and she might have felt isolated or excluded? I told [my partner] sorry, but after that she chose another partner.

In this moment—in which she was communicating in a high-stakes clinical setting—Tashi's literate resources were revalued into a liability. She saw her partner's face and Tibetan just "came out." Tashi's full literate repertoire is rendered invisible in a context in which she becomes an othered, transgressive student. Instead, her use of Tibetan violates an implicit English-only policy seemingly created to avoid the potential "offense" to a real clinical patient. Tashi says, "I tend to speak to [my partner] in Tibetan as soon as I see her face. And if do this mistake, at the bedside of the patient, that's breaking the policy."

Tashi is doubly devalued in the American hospitals in which she learned to be a nurse and currently works. English, the language in which she feels most literate, is valuable in her classroom writing assignments but marks her as an outsider in spoken hospital interactions or on written charts. Tibetan, the language with which she identifies, is not treated as an asset for interpretation or translation but instead as something dangerous. So though she speaks the national language, she does not "speak it properly," in the opinion of those she describes, which, according to Heller and Duchene (2012, 5), requires that "you still need to constantly prove yourself against the measures developed by the dominant group." Her facility in Hindi, Kannada, or what she calls "nursing's main language" remains invisible, while Tashi uses neither her English nor Tibetan resources in sanctioned ways.

LITERATE RESOURCES IN A GLOBALIZING ECONOMY

This parallel presentation of Tashi's and Khadroma's accounts isn't meant to polarize their literate histories. Though their resources were valued differently in these specific incidents, both writers are content with and proud of their work and family life in the United States. However, the accounts reveal the complex underpinnings of multilingual literate resources. Khadroma's and Tashi's literate histories are different, but their lives in the United States are similar: they attended the same community college and university nursing programs; both participate in the local Tibetan community and are married with young children; both found full-time RN jobs in hospitals in the same city; and both write among multiple languages including fluent English. But while Khadroma's multilingual resources are highly valued both in China and in the United States, many of Tashi's resources have been devalued in the United States after immigration.

The accounts above suggest three possibilities for this difference. First, while both writers treat Tibetan as a language of identity—the one with which they identify culturally, celebrate during community gatherings, and pass on to their children—only Khadroma converts her Tibetan into a marketable interpretation skill valued by government and corporate organizations. (She treats her Mandarin simply as a skill, neither identifying with the language culturally nor hoping to pass it on to her daughter.) Tashi explains that she speaks Tibetan exclusively at home or among friends at community events. As is evident above, her negative experiences with Tibetan at work reinforce this separation of language contexts. So Khadroma's Tibetan is valuable both as a language of identity and a language of skill, while Tashi's Tibetan is a language of identity but not one deemed economically valuable by the very hospital that hired Khadroma to interpret for Tibetan-speaking patients.

Second, while Tashi's literate repertoire is arguably more abundant than Khadroma's—Tashi speaks, reads, and writes among more languages and has studied academic English for many more years—it is still a repertoire with more variability than standards. In a globalizing and increasingly saturated English-language market, organizations and corporations—NGOs, language schools, interpretation/translation companies, accreditation agencies—attempt to "manage the movement of resources across linguistically diverse spaces" where linguistic variability encounters the strict standards important for "Taylorist" efficiency models (Heller 2010, 107). Tashi's accented English is not standard in a US context. In other words, in a saturated English-language market, powerful agents feel more pressure to discipline the language. So no matter the extent of Tashi's literate repertoire or the deft wielding of her language resources, these become less valuable in a language economy of standardized needs. Khadroma, on the other hand, believes the accreditation agency's standard policies to be fair and transparent and benefits from these rules.

Finally, while both writers employ a range of linguistic resources, Khadroma "navigates them expertly," an appealing skill in a global work context that demands movement and flexibility (Heller 2010, 106). While Tashi tends to separate her languages according to space, Khadroma blurs the lines among work, home, and community. In Khadroma's case, this navigational skill has a history: she was shown during her years at the American-run language school in China how her languages might be valued by travelers, tourists, and business people in a global economy. Her teachers modeled this navigation by employing her to interpret for their friends early on, and Khadroma traveled with this skill to the United States. Global organizations and corporations sit quietly in the background of both Khadroma's and Tashi's experiences, valuing and revaluing the rising language work of an information-dependent economy. This influence was already present in the late 1990s in China and prepared Khadroma to leverage her multilingual resources after immigration to the United States.

Therefore, in a context of commodification, the value assigned to literate resources fluctuates according to economic, organizational, or political conditions and the powerful agents that determine them. Heller notes that "we cannot abstract away" from the values "attached to linguistic forms and practices" (Heller 2010, 102), and Khadroma's and Tashi's accounts show that, indeed, language valuation is firmly tied to specific contexts, moments, and interactions. These lived experiences resist an abstract discourse of "resources." But the repetition of *resource* in the introduction above indicates its abstract use in writing scholarship, particularly in perspectives that treat separate, individual languages as distinct resources. While usually used in nuanced ways to describe varying phenomena, the frequent appeal to resources can open up a terminological vacuum into which expectations and beliefs are loaded. One of these expectations is that literate resources are durable—unchanging, always on call, reliably valuable—as writers carry them into new writing or communicative contexts. But, as the accounts above show, because the value of literate resources is always in flux, this discourse of resources might leave multilingual writers feeling less rather than more empowered. For these reasons, the term and the claims implied in its use merit further consideration.

But as Khadroma's and Tashi's accounts show, the potential of recognizing an abundance of literate resources is great: when multilingual writers are allowed or asked to call on their existing language and literacy resources, they often are able to put into play a heightened awareness of audience and language, to compose from a spectrum of lived literacy experiences, and sometimes to leverage their practices for economic gain. A nuanced understanding of what lies behind resources, and what in fact these resources are, might support more critical conversations among teachers, students, and scholars about who values which registers, accents, dialects, and languages in what situations and why. This understanding might also help researchers to broaden or complicate the practices they aim to trace when searching for the resources writers carry from one context to another. Teachers and scholars ought not avoid a discourse of resources but could instead reconsider how the word's existing prefix—*re*source as a continual return to a literate font—might point back to the sources of writers' literate practices.

Note

1. JAHCO seems to have recently evolved, but Khadroma described the organization in the manner above. Read more at http://www.jointcommission.org/.

12

THE RHETORIC OF ECONOMIC COSTS AND SOCIAL BENEFITS IN US HEALTHCARE LANGUAGE POLICY

Scott Wible

While English-only policies and other restrictive language policies are, at their core, grounded in nativist and racist ideologies (Davis 1990; Fishman 1992; Hill 2001; Sledd 1993), their supporters often promote them via explicit arguments about the economics of public bilingualism and multilingualism (US English 2013a, 2–3; US English 2013b). As Bruce Horner and John Trimbur explain, "English Only advocates often portray immigrants as a drain on the economy—demanding health and social services, schooling, jobs, translations, housing" (Horner and Trimbur 2002, 618). Interestingly, Horner and Trimbur criticize the *opponents* of English-only policies because they too often "shy from confronting the material and cultural costs" of these policies, even going so far as to "[deny] any costs associated with the presence of non-English speakers" (618). Instead, Horner and Trimbur suggest, supporters of translingual policies emphasize "that immigrants pay far more in taxes and contribute far more to the economy than they receive in benefits, and they point to the insignificance of the costs of providing translations of government documents and the like" (618). While this particular "cost-benefit assessment" may be true, Horner and Trimbur argue, "it sidesteps the more significant costs and even more significant benefits, both economic and cultural" that would emerge in the pursuit of a translingual, English-plus policy, one that provides language accommodations for people who do not understand English and promotes English monolinguals learning a second language (618).

Over the past decade, one significant language policy has been advanced by the federal government (Holder 2011; OMB 2002) that openly acknowledges the costs of accommodating non-English speakers but subordinates these economic costs to the legal rights and social benefits that language accommodations support. Executive Order (EO) 13166

DOI: 10.7330/9781607325239.c012

(2000), signed by President Bill Clinton, renews the federal government's commitment and obligation to provide language accommodations so that all federal programs and activities can be accessed by limited-English-proficient (LEP) persons.[1] Several important government documents related to EO 13166, both those that accompanied its signing and those that examined its subsequent implementation, address the economics of this translingual policy and the significant costs of providing these accommodations for non-English users; however, they also apply pressure to common-sense notions about the cost of English-plus policies as they identify not only the cultural and social benefits but also the economic gains that could result from their implementation. Ultimately, the language-policy texts that give shape to EO 13166 show the need to address directly the economic costs of public translingual writing but to do so in a way that holds fiscal responsibility in productive tension with the protection and promotion of social, cultural, and political rights.[2]

To advance this argument, this chapter analyzes how EO 13166: Improving Access to Services for Persons with Limited English Proficiency has influenced research practices and written communication strategies within the healthcare sector, as the critical nature of medical services has put most hospitals and clinics into direct contact with linguistic minority communities in the United States. I begin by discussing the legal rights underlying EO 13166 and describing how these language issues manifest in relation to the ethical practice of health care. The chapter then takes up the Office of Management and Budget's economic analysis of implementing EO 13166, focusing on how the OMB balances its financial analysis with considerations of societal benefits and legal rights. Finally, I analyze the textual tactics deployed by healthcare agencies to create language accommodations for LEP persons. Here I attend to specific strategies that medical professionals have deployed to mitigate the costs of providing language accommodations while promoting the social and cultural inclusion of linguistic minorities in healthcare settings.

FEDERAL POLICY AND LANGUAGE-MINORITY ACCESS TO HEALTH CARE

Since the passage of Title VI of the Civil Rights Act of 1964, US law has required that federal and federally funded programs and services be accessible to all people who have a right to them. Title VI emphasizes an economic dimension to political and social justice when it highlights the financial contributions all taxpayers make to support these programs and services:

> Simple justice requires that public funds, to which all taxpayers of all races, colors, and national origins contribute, not be spent in any fashion which encourages, entrenches, subsidizes or results in racial, color, or national origin discrimination.

Significantly, since the 1974 Supreme Court case *Lau v. Nichols*, the "national origin" component of Title VI has been defined in part in terms of language use and linguistic identity[3] (US Department of Health and Human Services 2003; US Department of Justice 2002). That is, when federally funded programs and activities cannot be accessed by a group of people simply because they do not understand English, national-origin discrimination exists. Ostensibly, Title VI suggests that some public funds, acquired from citizens as taxes, be used to make these services and programs accessible to LEP persons. Since 1964 and 1974, then, US language policy has been grounded in the economic rationale that all taxpayers have the right to have at least some portion of those funds used to facilitate communication in non-English languages.

By August 2000, President Clinton saw the need to renew the executive branch's commitment to enforcing this law. In one sense, EO 13166 simply reaffirms the value of Title VI, but it also underscores the fact that many agencies were either unaware of or unclear about their obligation to ensure that LEP persons can access federally funded programs and activities. EO 13166 calls for each federal agency to examine the language accommodations they already provide and to "develop and implement a system by which LEP persons can meaningfully access those services consistent with, and without unduly burdening, the fundamental mission of the agency" (Executive Order No. 13166, 2000). EO 13166 also requires each federal agency to provide guidance to organizations that receive federal funding from it, clarifying their legal obligations to provide "meaningful access to their LEP applicants and beneficiaries" (Executive Order No. 13166, 2000). Significantly, given the interests of this present volume on economies of writing, the design and implementation of systems for complying with EO 13166 occur through texts, including each agency's written LEP plan. President Clinton's office created the Federal Interagency Working Group on LEP to disseminate information to all federal agencies about how best to comply with EO 13166 and to catalog each agency's LEP plan, which the working group continues to do via the website LEP.gov.[4]

The US Department of Health and Human Services (DHHS) has been a leader among federal agencies in designing and implementing strategies to accommodate the language needs and preferences of people who speak languages other than English. In many respects, DHHS led the way for federal agencies in anticipating Executive Order 13166, addressing language diversity concerns and crafting an organizational and disciplinary language policy. In March 2001, just seven months after President Clinton signed the executive order, the DHHS Office of Minority Health issued a report entitled *National Standards for Culturally and Linguistically Appropriate Services in Health Care* that aimed to create cohesion where there had been a "patchwork of independently developed definitions, practices, and requirements concerning [culturally and linguistically appropriate services]," or CLAS (US Department of Health and Human Services 2001b, vii). This patchwork, the Office of Minority Health explains, had contributed to "inequities . . . in the provision of health services" (1). With these standards, the DHHS Office of Minority Health aimed to make CLAS "more responsive to the individual needs of all patients/consumers" and "to ensure that all people entering the healthcare system receive equitable and effective treatment in a culturally and linguistically appropriate manner" (1).[5]

The DHHS's efforts to improve cultural and linguistic accommodation in healthcare settings have also been carried out through the department's Health Resources and Services Administration (HRSA), an office tasked with improving access to healthcare services for people who are "uninsured, isolated, or medically vulnerable" (US Department of Health and Human Services 2013a). Cultural and linguistic minority communities, of course, are disproportionately represented among the uninsured, isolated, and medically vulnerable, so the local healthcare organizations HRSA funds have long worked to identify and meet the particular needs, accommodate the linguistic preferences, and acknowledge the healthcare-related cultural beliefs of these communities. With this understanding in mind, the HRSA published a 2001 report entitled *Cultural Competence Works: Using Cultural Competence to Improve the Quality of Health Care for Diverse Populations and Add Value to Managed Care Arrangements*, which highlights HRSA-funded programs that employ innovative and effective strategies "to provide culturally competent care for diverse populations" (US Department of Health and Human Services 2001a, 1). These strategies include valuing clients' cultural beliefs, dialoguing with community members to identify their needs and preferences, acknowledging the complexity of language interpretation, and integrating cultural and linguistic competence into the mission and day-to-day practices of healthcare organizations.

The DHHS's investment in and leadership on the issue speaks to how cultural beliefs and linguistic frames shape people's understandings and enactments of health-related behaviors. Indeed, an increasing number of medical professionals believe language and culture are absolutely central to the work of achieving positive health outcomes. In healthcare settings, failures to communicate effectively across language and cultural differences can lead to financial difficulties, to be sure, but more importantly they can bring dire consequences for individual, familial, communal, and societal health. Gail Price-Wise, president of the Florida Center for Cultural Competence, articulates in precise detail how communication across language and cultural differences helps professionals to deliver effective health care:

> [For healthcare providers,] cultural [and linguistic] competence is as important to the outcomes of their patients, is as important to their mortality and their morbidity rates as anything that they're going to do in terms of pharmacology or surgical procedures. In order for a patient to be healed, several things have to happen. They have to come to the medical facility, they have to give a complete and accurate medical history, the provider has to order the correct diagnostic tests, and then the provider has to make the correct diagnosis and develop the best treatment plan for the patient. And the treatment plan has to be one that the patient understands and is motivated to follow. All of those steps require a good relationship between the provider and the patient. It requires trust, and that is completely dependent on the cultural [and linguistic] competence of the provider. (US Department of Health and Human Services 2010)

Price-Wise here speaks most directly to matters of oral communication and translation of the sort involved in patient-doctor consultations. Nevertheless, her insight underscores the importance of linguistic and cultural accommodation in written medical communication as well. Healthcare agencies cannot simply run written materials (such as medical history forms, treatment plans, or patient educational materials) through a machine translation program and consider their obligations for linguistic accommodation to be met, as such texts more often than not would fail to address differences in cultural beliefs about medicine and health. Healthcare facilities could hire localization firms to oversee this translation and cultural accommodation work, but even that approach falls short as a strategy for creating meaningful cultural and linguistic access to healthcare services and programs. Instead, as technical communication scholar Nicole St. Germain-McDaniel (2010) explains, the DHHS, the Office of Minority Health, and the HRSA urge healthcare agencies to take on this work themselves. The HRSA, in its *Cultural Competence Works* report, in fact, contends that local healthcare agencies can and should develop "practical, experience-based knowledge" about the communities they serve (US Department of Health and Human Services 2001a, 13) through the same types of qualitative research methods familiar to rhetoric and composition scholars, such as focus groups and interviews. The HRSA report also highlights how some healthcare agencies have composed organizational policies that channel resources and direct employees' practices toward accommodating language and cultural minorities (25), while others have created multi-institution networks to meet their respective communities' language needs (21).

While these strategies for community-based research, organizational policy writing, and networked language accommodation present a vision of how an English-plus US language policy can be integrated into the guiding mission and daily activities of healthcare organizations that serve LEP persons, these practices also bring the economic demands of language accommodations into view. In short, they cost time, they cost money, and they cost human resources. What emerges from the federal government's analysis of EO 13166 implementation, however, is a more nuanced statement about the financial costs of a multilingual language policy, one that highlights the significant costs, to be sure, but also attends to the cultural, social, and even financial value created through the widespread adoption of language accommodation practices in federal and federally supported agencies.

BALANCING THE ECONOMIC COSTS AND SOCIAL BENEFITS OF LANGUAGE ACCOMMODATION

In a March 2002 report to Congress about EO 13166, the US Office of Management and Budget (OMB) declared that the costs of providing language accommodations to LEP persons across all government and government-funded services would be "substantial" (OMB, 3). The OMB's conclusions were grounded in a quantitative economic analysis based on surveys of federal and state agencies, public comments, rough numerical estimates of national costs extrapolated from regional examples, and case studies of four sectors of US public life, including health care. The OMB (2002) estimated that the portion of federal, state, and local government services provided to LEP persons is about $46.7 billion, but it also noted that most of these costs would already be incurred in providing services to these same individuals, no matter whether they spoke English or another language. The OMB instead calculated a 1–2 percent "premium" for LEP services; that is, an estimated 1–2 percent could be added to the total cost of any service or program in order to make that service or program linguistically accessible. The OMB suggested, however, that the premium for healthcare services would be lower, at 0.5 percent. The OMB stopped short of "endors[ing] as accurate any single summation of LEP-associated costs across all government or government-funded services" (57), but it did estimate that the aggregate cost of providing language accommodation—not just the cost of implementing EO 13166—would be less than $2 billion, and perhaps even as low as $1 billion.[6] (The OMB conceded, though, that its analysis did not include private agencies or nonprofit organizations that receive federal funds, including those in health care.) That said, the OMB's analysis, particularly its case studies, focused exclusively on oral interpretation services; it did not calculate the costs of translating written documents such as medical forms into multiple languages. Ultimately, then, the overall cost to the nation of providing these language accommodations would most certainly be higher than the $1–2 billion estimate.

Notably, the OMB (2002) punctuated its quantitative economic analysis of language accommodation costs with qualitative and quantitative assessments in support of them. Specifically, the OMB identified two benefits that "eligible LEP individuals experience when they receive meaningful access to federally-conducted programs or activities": "First, LEP individuals may experience the intangible but very important benefit connected with the fulfillment of a legal right. Second, LEP individuals may benefit from an increase in access to federally-conducted programs or activities or to the programs or activities of recipients of federal financial assistance" (16). The first benefit speaks to the issue of social justice in the form of public recognition of one's right to government service. Equally important, in the second benefit the OMB highlights the economics of language barriers that prevent LEP individuals from accessing necessary services. In the specific case of the medical field, of course, these economic concerns are the financial consequences of healthcare disparities. A recent study estimated that between 2003 and 2006, the costs related to healthcare disparities, including the costs of inadequate or inequitable care leading to premature death, were $1.24 trillion (LaVeist, Gaskin, and Richard 2009, 1). Although this specific study appeared after the OMB report, this type of finding about the costs related to healthcare disparities led the OMB to declare that the US government and American society also stand to benefit from EO 13166. The OMB (2002, 16) suggests, "Increasing access to government programs may lead to cheaper, more targeted early intervention, avoiding long-term and more costly services to government and society"; the OMB here alludes to activities such as primary healthcare services focused on prevention, early detection, and treatment of disease as compared to the costs of late-stage disease treatment and emergency-room visits. Providing services to LEP patients in their own languages can be a means to increase healthcare utilization and, by extension, to provide more appropriate preventative and curative medical care, with appropriate care in most instances also being more cost effective. Assessing the economics of language accommodations in health care, then, in part requires weighing significant short- and long-term investments for government agencies and other medical organizations alongside potentially lower long-term expenses.

Given medical professionals' ethical obligation to "do no harm," the OMB (2002) complements its quantitative economic analysis with discussion of the social and political value created through language accommodations. The OMB notes that within the healthcare field, the benefits of implementing EO 13166 include not just decreased medical costs and improved health but also "increased patient satisfaction . . . ; sufficient patient confidentiality in medical procedures; and true 'informed consent' and understanding of other legal issues" (20). Indeed, the OMB here suggests that even potentially substantial economic pressures do not trump the legal rights or the personal and communal health benefits that result from providing language accommodations to linguistic minority patients. The medical profession faces substantial costs in providing language accommodations, but these must be paid in order to meet healthcare professionals' ethical obligation to provide the highest quality care possible to each individual.

The OMB's report, then, suggests that the costs of language accommodation must be considered but ultimately do not trump professional obligations and legal requirements. It's important to note that these relationships among economic, social, and political criteria have since been written into federal guidelines for implementing EO 13166. As part of its response to EO 13166, the DHHS (US Department of Health and Human Services 2003), like all federal agencies, created such guidelines for its own offices as well as for those agencies it funds in order to clarify why and how it can make language accommodations for its clients. Specifically, the DHHS sets out four factors that agencies should use to guide decisions about how to provide meaningful access for LEP persons to its programs and activities:

1. The nature and importance of the program, activity, or service provided by the program
2. The frequency with which LEP individuals come in contact with the program

3. The number or proportion of LEP persons served or encountered in the eligible service population
4. The resources available to the recipients and costs (US Department of Health and Human Services 2003, 7)

Significantly, with this fourth factor, the DHHS guidelines allow agencies to consider economic costs when designing their LEP accommodation strategies. Later in this same document, the DHHS explains why an organization's financial concerns must be taken into consideration when assessing its obligations to accommodate LEP persons. As the DHHS suggests, "'Reasonable steps' [to provide language accommodations] may cease to be reasonable where the costs imposed substantially exceed the benefits" (US Department of Health and Human Services 2003,10). In its own guidance document, the US Department of Justice (DOJ) explains that this particular economic factor—the resources available to the agency—carries significant implications for the services made available to all eligible persons, whether LEP or not (US Department of Justice 2002). In effect, these guidelines allow an agency to ask itself this question: would providing a specific type of language accommodation put a financial burden on our organization that significantly hinders our ability to carry out our mission?

A key consideration related to EO 13166 stems from the fact that while federal agencies such as DHHS and DOJ have an obligation under Title VI to provide language accommodations, nongovernment agencies that receive federal funding only face financial, not legal, consequences if they do not take steps to ensure LEP access. In short, if they fail to or decide not to comply with Title VI and EO 13166, they lose federal funding. The executive branch here anticipates that ignoring the economic pressures LEP accommodations can put on an organization could lead that agency to decline federal funding, which could in turn lead it to stop providing valuable services and programs to citizens who have the right and the need to access them. For these reasons, this economic criterion for determining how and when to create meaningful access for language minorities acknowledges the fact that language accommodations can and do have significant costs.

These economic concerns, however, do not override the other three factors, particularly the first, that speak directly to the legal and social obligations to provide language accommodations. If the program or service is extremely important to an LEP person's health and well-being, or if the agency frequently serves a large number of LEP persons from a particular language group, the organization receiving federal funds must find ways to enable LEP persons to access the service or program and, equally important, must find ways to advertise these critical services or programs to LEP persons who might not already know about them or might think they cannot meaningfully access them because of language barriers.

Indeed, even when organizations claim that costs prohibit them from providing a particular language accommodation, the DHHS nevertheless expects them to "carefully explore the most cost-effective means of delivering competent and accurate language services before limiting services due to resource concerns" (US Department of Health and Human Services 2003, 10). When agencies face economic constraints in the face of these language realities, they are required to document their financial circumstances and explain how implementing EO 13166 in a robust way would significantly hinder the agency's ability to do its work for the broader, English-speaking public. At the same time, the DHHS guidelines demand that these organizations document their efforts to identify and explore all alternative accommodations—cheaper yet no less effective—before it intervenes to assist the agency in implementing a plan to enable LEP access.

RESEARCH AND POLICY WRITING IN THE SERVICE OF LANGUAGE ACCOMMODATION

This section examines three specific linguistic accommodation and language policy-writing practices in the healthcare field, each of which illustrates concerns central to the DHHS guidelines, the Office of Minority Health's CLAS standards, and the HRSA's recommended practices for delivering culturally competent health care. While more attention has been paid to oral interpretation services in healthcare settings, the practices highlighted here speak more directly to writing-related concerns, both in terms of cultural accommodation and linguistic translation as well as in terms of organizational policy writing that informs an agency's practices in meeting a language minority community's health needs and communicative preferences. These three examples underscore the economic costs of translingual communication practices even as they complicate any analysis focused solely on financial considerations. Indeed, these organizational strategies for facilitating translingual communication highlight the range of benefits that follow from pursuing language accommodations in the name of the medical profession's ethical obligation to provide meaningful health care for all people.

Networked Translingual Writing and Communication Practices

Healthcare organizations have devised different strategies to marshal the economic and human resources needed to carry out the types of translingual writing and interpretation demanded by Title VI and EO 13166. The HRSA recommends that healthcare agencies "ma[k]e concerted efforts to create and sustain a 'learning loop'" between themselves and the communities in which their patients live (US Department of Health and Human Services 2013b, 17). According to both the CLAS standards (US Department of Health and Human Services 2013b) and the HRSA's (US Department of Health and Human Services 2001a) list of culturally competent healthcare practices, this learning loop means organizations invest in identifying and developing the language resources that already exist in their workforce. The CLAS standards in particular, though, encourage organizations to do more than simply identify bi- or multilingual employees and assign them to translation and interpretation tasks. Instead, these healthcare agencies must do as organizations such as Adventist Health Care, the parent of Washington Adventist Hospital in Takoma Park, Maryland, has done: create opportunities for its bilingual staff to develop higher levels of proficiency in a second language, to acquire medical literacy in a language, to learn and refine translation and interpretation techniques, or to receive other forms of cultural-competency training (Barclay, *Washington Post,* April 21, 2009).[7] Such training costs time and money, of course, but the OMB (2002, 44) determined through its economic analysis that the costs in hiring and training bilingual employees results in a significant reduction in resources needed to provide language accommodations—both in terms of money and the time employees end up spending in dialogue with LEP patients—compared to hiring and working through outside interpreters. In particular, the OMB suggests that if providers recruit, train, and retain bilingual staff, they will "not incur additional costs based on the interactions of LEP individuals with trained medical staff that are (at least functionally) bilingual, except in those cases where the staff are paid a premium for their bilingual skills" (47). The lower costs would result because personnel would already be interacting with these individuals no matter what language they spoke, whereas professional interpreters force medical facilities to pay costs they would not otherwise incur in the course of their normal practice.

While many organizations have made language expertise a key criterion in hiring decisions, others have established hiring or volunteer-recruitment networks within the local communities themselves to meet these needs (US Department of Health and Human Services 2001a, 19;

2013b). This practice has the added benefits, of course, of folding community knowledge into the organization's activities and approaches to health care as well as signaling that the organization trusts and is committed to serving that community. The costs associated with such professional development and language training, however, have led other healthcare organizations to create networks to meet their translingual and transcultural writing and interpretation needs. The OMB has highlighted one such practice now taking place in some metropolitan areas where nonprofit organizations have started "language banks" that recruit, train, and schedule interpreters in a variety of languages for doctors, hospitals, and clinics (OMB 2002, 44–45). Meanwhile, other healthcare agencies have created technological networks to meet the language needs of medical professionals spread across wide geographic areas. Eastern North Carolina's Tri-County Community Health Center, for example, serves an area that experiences the ebb and flow of migrant farm labor. Because of the area's relative isolation, hospitals and clinics found it difficult to hire translators and interpreters, so the Tri-County Community Health Center established an over-the-phone interpretation service to better support health professionals and their patients (US Department of Health and Human Services 2001a, 21; 2013b).

These linked language practices highlight the potential for broad-based EO 13166 compliance to help reduce the financial costs of providing language accommodations. The OMB suggests that if all federal agencies and all recipients of federal funding work to implement EO 13166, the increased demand for services that support language accommodations could drive down per-unit costs, especially in terms of telephone-based interpretation and translation services. The OMB (Office of Management and Budget 2002, 59) explains, "The Executive Order, by stimulating increased demand for language services, may increase the size and efficiency of the language service industry, and agencies might consider steps to facilitate bulk discounted purchasing of such services by federal programs and recipients of federal funds." Agencies would still be footing the bill for providing these language-accommodation services, but the cost burden could be lessened with a more broad-based effort to provide meaningful access to LEP persons.

All healthcare organizations have been prompted by EO 13166 to reflect on the limits of a monolingual communication strategy in practicing medicine and public health (Executive Order No. 13166, 2000). These collective strategies for meeting language obligations challenge the notion that translingual writing situations always demand that a single person must necessarily possess some sort of cosmopolitan ideal of fluent multilingualism in a host of languages. Organizations such as Adventist Health Care, the Tri-County Community Health Center, and the medical "language banks" have invested financial and human resources in building a multilingual network through which to create knowledge and design strategies for enacting more positive health outcomes.

Community-Based Research and Translingual Writing Practices

While geographically isolated medical facilities such as the Tri-County Community Health Center have networked with telephone-based interpreters to accommodate LEP persons, other community-based health organizations have directly dialogued with the linguistic and cultural minority communities they serve in order to tailor healthcare texts for these groups. Some agencies have used focus groups and interviews toward these ends (St. Germain-McDaniel 2010), while others have created advisory boards comprising community members or hosted regular public forums in which non-English-speaking individuals are able and encouraged to participate (US Department of Health and Human Services 2001a, 17; 2013b). Of course, healthcare agencies undertake these activities in order to gain valuable insights into local communities' cultural expectations and linguistic preferences for medical care as well as the cultural beliefs that shape their health behaviors. At the same time, as the HRSA notes, this dialogue also often exposes other aspects of life experience besides language and ethnic or national culture that affect people's ability to integrate medical treatments and preventive behaviors into their daily lives (US Department of Health and Human Services 2013a, 11). These factors might range from literacy levels and familial and communal gender dynamics to financial pressures and housing conditions. By engaging in community dialogue, local healthcare agencies are able to, in HRSA's words, "define culture broadly" (11), enabling healthcare practitioners to understand how different communal and group beliefs and experiences intersect to inform an individual patient's world-view and health-related behaviors.

Generating knowledge through these dialogues helps healthcare organizations to tailor written materials and medical services to specific community needs rather than adopting the cheaper translation strategy we might characterize as a one-size-fits-all-Spanish-speakers-everywhere-in-the-United States type of approach. Even more significant, this direct engagement with local linguistic minorities attributes greater value to their languages, which are too often politically and economically devalued within the United States. In the dialogues between healthcare organizations and community members, these traditionally marginalized languages become a legitimate means to define community health problems, identify existing community resources, and design strategies to create positive health outcomes.

One example of such engagement with language-minority communities, one that comes from HRSA's 2001 *Cultural Competence Works* report (US Department of Health and Human Services 2001a), highlights how healthcare organizations have drawn on the language and cultural resources of community members in order to localize their written materials and, in turn, to effect positive health outcomes. The Massachusetts Department of Public Health's Community Health Education Center, or CHEC, facilitated the client-centered production of a brochure on domestic violence. The research and writing process began with a focus group that included three Latinas, two Haitians, and three African American women. Initial conversations among this group revealed a wide range of cultural and personal perspectives—indeed, much disagreement—about what is and is not domestic violence. What emerged through continued dialogue and analysis, however, was the fact that these culturally distinct definitions of domestic violence were connected by a common thread, namely, fear of the man in one's domestic life. CHEC director Lisette Blondet explained how this communally constructed definition enabled the writing project to progress: "There was resistance to a homogenous definition of domestic violence, but we were able to come up with a core ingredient that's applied differently in different cultures. Once we were able to identify the root itself, we were also able to pick the different trees that can come from that root" (14). Specifically, the CHEC produced a brochure that reflected three dimensions of domestic violence: physical and sexual abuse, mental abuse, and emotional abuse.

This example illustrates the translingual research and writing practices demanded by EO 13166. From an economic perspective, these practices are resource intensive, particularly in terms of time and opportunity cost, but through dialogue and analysis, the CHEC and focus-group members reached stasis at the point of definition. Only after identifying this common definitional core of domestic violence could the CHEC compose its educational materials, texts that acknowledged the different cultural definitions of domestic violence and began to teach people how to integrate positive health practices into their lives. This nuanced cross-cultural writing practice, despite requiring more time and carrying a greater opportunity cost, best enabled the CHEC to create "meaningful access" for LEP persons to the healthcare services it delivers.

Organizational Policy Writing

In its policy guidance accompanying EO 13166 (US Department of Justice 2002), the DOJ recommends that all agencies that receive federal funding create formal language-assistance plans outlining the specific language accommodations they will provide (41455). This process calls on agencies regularly to identify the language communities they frequently serve as well as their needs and communication preferences; to ascertain the specific accommodations that enable these LEP persons to access services and programs in ways both effective and meaningful; and to educate relevant personnel about these procedures and train them to carry out the necessary accommodations. Drafting these written language-assistance plans is not required by law. Nevertheless, the DOJ emphasizes the many benefits agencies would likely realize in creating them: they would simplify their process of documenting Title VI compliance, but more important, they would supplement training, operations, and planning procedures by ensuring that "when the need arises, staff have a written plan to turn to—even if it is only how to access telephonic or community-based interpretation services—when determining what language services to provide and when to provide them" (41455).

Even as they draft these language-assistance plans, some agencies have engaged in an additional form of organizational policy writing that makes linguistic and cultural accommodation a central part of their missions and day-to-day operations.[8] These organizations have revised their mission statements and strategic plans to address the linguistic diversity of their patients. This organizational policy writing responds to CLAS Standard 9, which recommends that agencies "establish culturally and linguistically appropriate goals, policies, and management accountability, and infuse them through the organization's planning and operations" (US Department of Health and Human Services 2001b, 13). The following explanation, from Joseph Wahl of the Multnomah County Health Department in Oregon, illustrates how agencies can use policy writing to integrate cultural competence into their processes and decision making:

> One of the things that was the greatest step for us as an agency was the strategic planning process. We incorporated values on diversity, cultural competence, and quality into the strategic plan. . . . All staff can see the department is committed to achieving certain levels of quality improvement and cultural competence for everyone. We have cultural performance objective plans . . . for managers to help increase [their] own cultural competence, then they're able to work on that with their teams. The strategic plan states that all managers will go through an orientation . . .

> and will select objectives for their annual performance evaluations having to do with diversity and cultural competence that they will be evaluated on, so it becomes part of their performance evaluation. That's a way of building accountability into it, and because managers are now focused on that, [they make it] part of the team's focus. (US Department of Health and Human Services 2001b, 25)

It makes great sense, of course, that local health agencies and organizations would write cultural competence into their mission statements and strategic plans. Their ultimate goal is to effect positive health outcomes for individuals and communities, and linguistic and cultural accommodations are central to the very practice of delivering effective health care.

Significantly, Wahl's insights show that these changes in organizational culture can be created in part through writing practices, or more specifically, organizational policy-writing practices. Indeed, for writing scholars committed to promoting language diversity and supporting translingual writing, significant political and economic effects follow from textually weaving these values into an organization's mission and strategic plan. These policy documents guide key economic decisions about what positions, what services, what outreach activities, and what training programs to fund. When these organizational texts are written in ways that emphasize cross-language and cross-cultural communication, they prompt the healthcare agency to fund new hires, training, and writing activities that meet linguistic minority communities' health needs. In turn, these policies also create greater symbolic value for traditionally marginalized languages in the United States, as they show that financial pressures do not trump the necessity of enabling eligible people to access services and programs they have a legal right to enjoy.

CONCLUSION

The 2002 OMB report clearly confirms English-only supporters' common argument that public and private organizations—and by extension, taxpayers—incur significant financial costs when they create the type of linguistic and cultural accommodations required by Title VI of the Civil Rights Act of 1964 and EO 13166. While the OMB report calculated a 0.5 percent language-related "premium" for healthcare services delivered by federal agencies to LEP persons, several smaller community-based health clinics have estimated that these services account for anywhere from 30 to 60 percent of their overall costs of caring for patients from linguistic minority communities (US Department of Health and

Human Services 2001a, 30).[9] As one might imagine, then, community-based healthcare organizations that routinely serve linguistic and cultural minorities have made themselves into active grant seekers. Paradoxically, however, these agencies have found more grant support for implementing new programs than for sustaining proven language-accommodation activities (31). Moreover, there is vigorous debate within the healthcare field about how organizations' existing, effective practices for working with these communities would be enhanced or hindered by moving into relationships with managed-care organizations, the larger healthcare networks that provide insurance reimbursements to hospitals and clinics.

This debate about managed-care organizations gets to the heart of policy writing, economies, and the value of languages, particularly non-English languages. These managed-care organizations craft and carry out their own language policies when they decide whether to fund important practices related to linguistic and cultural accommodation such as translated and localized written texts; interpretation services; and the convening of community forums and focus groups. These activities improve a healthcare organization's ability to work with traditionally underserved groups, but they typically are not financially reimbursed. Community health agencies must make—and in several cases, have already made—both quantitative and qualitative arguments that their culturally centered practices improve the quality of service, the quality of patient care, the quality of employees' working lives, and the organization's overall cost and efficiency.

Of course, healthcare organizations that receive federal funding are required to enable LEP persons to meaningfully access their programs and services. LEP persons' economic contributions through taxes become, in theory, the financial source of the costs necessary to provide this access. Ultimately, though, private-sector policy created and implemented by managed-care organizations has the potential to greatly enhance or severely hinder EO 13166's aim of ensuring that medical professionals meet the healthcare needs of linguistic minority communities in the United States.

Notes

1. According to LEP.gov, a federal interagency website that provides information on EO 13166 and related language-accommodation concerns, limited-English-proficient (LEP) individuals are people "who do not speak English as their primary language *and* who have a limited ability to read, speak, write, or understand English" (Limited English Proficiency n.d.; italics added).

2. Following current thinking in sociolinguistics, political science, law, modern languages, and related disciplines, I define *language policy* expansively, considering not only government-related documents such as EO 13166 but also texts that emerge from a wide variety of public and private spheres of activity and either overtly or covertly attempt to influence peoples' or organizations' language practices. For an extended discussion of these definitional issues, see Thom Huebner (1999), Bernard Spolsky (2004), and Scott Wible (2013, 6–9).
3. The Supreme Court concluded in *Lau v. Nichols* (1974) that Title VI's prohibition on national-origin discrimination extends to "conduct that has a disproportionate effect" on people who do not read, speak, write, or understand English.
4. President Barack Obama's administration reaffirmed EO 13166 in the form of a February 17, 2011, memorandum from US Attorney General Eric Holder (2011).
5. The CLAS standards apply most directly to healthcare organizations, although the DHHS and Office of Minority Health encourage individual providers to use them as well in order to prompt them to examine their strategies and practices for making health services more culturally and linguistically accessible. The Office of Minority Health published enhanced National CLAS Standards in 2011 that build on the DHHS's 2011 *Action Plan to Reduce Racial and Ethnic Health Disparities* and that "reflect the past decade's advancements, expand their scope, and improve their clarity to ensure understanding and implementation" (US Department of Health and Human Services 2013b).

   There are 14 CLAS standards organized by three different themes: culturally competent care, language-access services, and organizational supports for cultural competence. The 14 standards are also arranged in terms of mandates, which the federal government absolutely requires of all agencies receiving federal funds; guidelines, which the Office of Minority Health recommends that federal, state, and national accrediting agencies adopt as mandates; and recommendations, which the Office of Minority Health suggests that healthcare organizations integrate into their agencies' practice on a voluntary basis. Of particular interest to rhetoric and writing scholars is the fact that all three mandates specifically concern language assistance, whereas cultural accommodations have been labeled as recommendations.

   Specifically, these CLAS standards require healthcare organizations to "offer and provide language services, including bilingual staff and interpreter services, at no cost" to each LEP patient (standard 4); to provide written notices to patients in their preferred language, informing them of their right to receive language assistance (standard 5); and to assure that the language-assistance services are provided by professionally and linguistically competent interpreters and bilingual staff (standard 6).
6. This estimate, the OMB (2002) noted, reflected the total cost of providing language accommodations rather than just the cost of implementing EO 13166. The OMB explained that it could not accurately calculate the cost of implementing EO 13166 because it could not establish a clear economic baseline for comparing pre- and postimplementation spending, as many government agencies already provided some types of language accommodations even before President Clinton signed EO 13166.
7. In its 2002 report entitled *Unequal Treatment: Confronting Racial and Ethnic Disparities in Health Care*, the Institute of Medicine of the National Academies recommended that all healthcare professionals, including clinicians, receive training in cross-cultural communication (Institute of Medicine of the National Academies 2002).
8. My argument here draws on the notion of "institutional critique" advanced by James Porter et al. (2000).

9. For example, in some parts of the country such as Washington, DC, hospitals and doctors report that contracting with interpreters to comply with Title VI costs up to $190 per hour (Barclay, *Washington Post*, April 21, 2009).

13

WEB 2.0 WRITING AS ENGINE OF INFORMATION CAPITAL

Christian J. Pulver

Toward the end of "Writing after Print Capitalism," John Trimbur (2012, 729) makes a particularly compelling observation:

> To my mind, the fuss about digital rhetorics, new media and composition 2.0 amounts in a certain sense to the invention of a past we are supposedly leaving behind in order to make the present knowable . . . an attempt to resolve the blurriness of the current situation we find ourselves in, to get some traction on our uneasy state of in-betweenness by coming to terms with the sentence imposed on us by the persistence of late capitalism and the human desire to break out of this prison of suspended animation.

Trimbur has, I think, articulated well the strangeness of the digital moment—one of those liminal historical junctures in which, as Raymond Williams (1977) puts it, *dominant* forms of cultural production are being overtaken by *emergent* forms. Emergent forms, more often than not, arise during periods of radical technological change. This is nowhere more evident than in the emergence of new digital writing technologies and the literacy practices they foster. Thus, as researchers and teachers of writing, we become both witness to and adopters of the newly networked, digital frontier—a frontier that, as Trimbur reminds us, emerges out of a long historical process of capital accumulation.

My chapter explores this uneasy sense of "suspended animation" by looking at the problematic phenomenon of Web 2.0 and a particular kind of writing theory it has inspired. Drawing on Marxian notions of *value* and the industrial circuit of capital as laid out in *Capital*, volume 2 (Marx 1993a), I explore how we can expand our analyses of Web 2.0 writing to better account for the growing tensions among user-created content, commodified digital data, and the changing literacy practices that invariably emerge with contemporary digital media. I argue that to more fully theorize writing in Web 2.0 we must keep it embedded in a late-capitalist mode of *informational* production in which the more

DOI: 10.7330/9781607325239.c013

conspicuous *use-value* of Web 2.0 technologies is always in dialectical relation with the less obvious *exchange value* they create.

WEB 2.0 WRITING THEORY

In "What is Web 2.0?" publisher and open-source evangelist Tim O'Reilly (2005) invokes the term as a way to describe the state of the web after the dot.com crash of the late 1990s. O'Reilly noticed that those companies that had survived—Google, Napster, Amazon, Yahoo—possessed certain traits that distinguished them from the failures. The successful companies were built on a more flexible web-as-platform model that effectively leveraged open-source technology. What emerged, according to O'Reilly, was a slicker web, built on a more transparent and cooperative ethos and propelled by social practices of networking, collaboration, participation, and sharing.

As would be expected, many writing scholars have found inspiration in these trends and have accepted Web 2.0 as a paradigmatic shift in the nature of literacy, leading to what I label here *Web 2.0 writing theory*. One of its tenets is that, in the shift from print to digitization, there's an expansion of textuality. That is, a lot more writing is taking place now than at any point in history. Drawing on research from the Stanford Study of Writing (2001–2006), Andrea Lunsford claims in a *Wired* interview that "we're in the midst of a literacy revolution the likes of which we haven't seen since Greek civilization" (Thompson 2009). As Lunsford emphasizes, Web 2.0 writing technologies aren't "killing our ability to write"; rather, they're "reviving it—and pushing our literacy in bold new directions" (Thompson 2009; see also Haven 2009). Kathleen Blake Yancey (2008) expresses a similar sentiment, calling Web 2.0 the "Age of Composition"—a blossoming of rhetorical activity brought on by the development of the personal computer, the web, and online social media. This is a qualitatively different public sphere from that of the print-driven twentieth century, a deinstitutionalized space where people engage more than ever in "self-sponsored writing" (Brandt 2001) that falls beyond the purview of formal schooling. As Yancey (2004, 301) notes,

> Today, we are witnessing a parallel creation, that of a *writing* public made plural, and as in the case of the development of a reading public, it's taking place largely outside of school. . . . Whatever the exchange value may be for these writers . . . it's certainly not grades. Rather, the writing seems to operate in an economy driven by use value.

Like Lunsford, Yancey sees the growth of a writing public as inherently positive and even "operat[ing] in an economy driven by use value." James Porter (2010, 176) concurs, arguing that this changing sense of value in self-sponsored writing is "the secret of the Web 2.0 dynamic." He insists that we cannot understand Web 2.0 writing practices from a purely economic model of monetary exchange. Rather, we need to imagine the web as more like a "gift-sharing economy" (188) in which writers engage in social, literate activity in exchange for a multitude of values (participation, connection, expression, collaboration) beyond the exchange of money.

Thus, in Web 2.0 writing theory, it's assumed that the growing textuality of the digital age is driven by the use-value writers find in digitized communication more so than its exchange value.[1] That is, for Web 2.0 writing theory, emerging digital literacy practices appear to be just beyond the imperatives of capitalism, circulating in a noncommodified realm. In Marxian terms, we might say Web 2.0 writing theory *inverts* the exchange/use relation. For Marx, value gets expressed in the shape of a *commodity*—the material expression of the contradiction between how useful a commodity is and how much profit it can make in exchange. In capitalist societies, use-value is often locked in an asymmetrical relation with exchange value—that is, subordinate to the imperatives of profit. Web 2.0 writing theory problematizes this assumption. In contrast to the "darker side" (Porter 2010, 174) of the exchange/use asymmetry, Web 2.0 writing theory prioritizes the use-value(s) of digitized, networked writing over its less assured, more ambiguous character as exchange value.

Web 2.0 is clearly an expansion of textuality that is reshaping public discourse, a phenomenon that Web 2.0 writing theory acknowledges while maintaining a broad sense of the value(s) we might attach to these changing literacy practices. At the same time, however, we must be careful not to disembed the growth of this user-created, use-value driven writing economy from the logics of capitalist accumulation. Web 2.0 writing theory falls into this trap. In light of recent trends in data collecting, mining, and selling, there's a need to extend Web 2.0 writing theory to account for the exchange value in digital writing practices and address how the expansion of use-value in Web 2.0 also (always) entails an expansion of commodification.

THE USE/EXCHANGE CONTRADICTION

As Porter (2010) argues, we must expand our notion of Web 2.0 writing and the kinds of value it produces. But this expansion shouldn't come by overemphasizing the use-value of digital writing. Rather, in following Marx's dialectics, we should also be exploring the material social relations that shape the use/exchange contradiction and inquire into the tensions that manifest as a product of this relation. At the same time, we should recognize that Marx's analysis of the use- and exchange value of industrially produced commodities doesn't always translate seamlessly into digital, informationalized commodities like digital writing. That is, while the use/exchange relation is very much alive in "informational capitalism" (Fuchs 2010), it has taken on new forms in a digital environment. As Marx (1990) reminds us in the early chapters of *Capital*, volume 1, the contradiction between use- and exchange value should not be confused with the *shape* this contradiction takes (commodity fetishism). Rather, we must see the use/exchange contradiction as forming out of the long history of exchange practices that have become the conditions for capital accumulation. All commodities carry the use/exchange tension, but the shape of this tension will be infinitely varied. It can only be so. In fact, for Marx, use-value, as the intrinsic *worth* of a commodity for fulfilling a human need, must *precede* the expression of exchange value. That is, an object must be useful enough to attract exchange value. Exchange value, then, is not simply the antithesis of use—it is also the extension and appropriation of useful objects into commodity relations to exploit their potential for creating surplus value.

The Internet and Web 2.0 are currently undergoing this process. The Internet, from its inception in the early 1960s through its development in the 1990s, was largely funded by taxpayers and developed under the auspices of several public universities and government agencies (Hauben and Hauben 1997). By the mid-1990s, the National Science Foundation, which had managed the "backbone" of the Internet for the previous decade, opened the door for privatization, and thus the public utility of the Internet gave way to capital, transforming this once publicly owned space into one for business and commerce. So, whether we are talking about the expensive hardware needed for digital writing or the toll to get online, the use-value of the writing we do in Web 2.0 *already* carries exchange value (see Harrison 2005; Ryan 2010).

This appropriation by capital of the time, materials, and labor of the Internet has led to new forms of value production, the most conspicuous being the enormous amount of data our digital writing produces. The rise in the exchange value of digital data exposes another oversight in Web 2.0 writing theory. When we look back at O'Reilly's (2005) original definition of Web 2.0, it's bubbling with a rhetoric of business and innovation—a vision of the web as the perfect balance of neoliberal ideology and communitarian responsibility. Exchange value is not just present in "What is Web 2.0?"—it is very much a driving force, one that fundamentally depends on the massive production and collection of digital data. O'Reilly (2005, 9) is clear on this point:

> One of the key lessons of the Web 2.0 era is this: *Users add value*. . . . The key to competitive advantage in internet applications is the extent to which users add their own data to that which you provide. . . . Therefore, Web 2.0 companies *set inclusive defaults for aggregating user data and building value as a side-effect of ordinary use of the application.*

Thus, the "secret of the web 2.0 dynamic" isn't simply a thriving use-value driven economy of writing; it is also the *latent* potential of exchange value that can be siphoned from user-created content. The companies that emerged from the dot.com crash figured out that producing value was not going to happen in ways typical of twentieth-century print capitalism. The enigma to be solved by Google, Amazon, Facebook, and other Web 2.0 companies was how to build web applications that would attract a core base of users with "free," simple, and "functional" (Dilger 2010) tools for communication, consumption, and information management. By building a useful application for easy social and semiotic production, these platforms could then become hubs for the creation of several layers of exchange value. I call this the process of *ascendant exchange value*, and in the context of Web 2.0, it emerges in full force in the transition from a centralized, manufacturing-based economy to the informationalized economies we have today (Brandt 2005; Castells 2010; Jameson 1984). Viable models of Web 2.0 writing theory that recognize ascendant exchange value must struggle with the context of globalized, commodified information and its relation to user-created content. At the center of this is the "currency of the web" (D. Harris 2011): digital data. Understanding emerging Web 2.0 writing practices requires a deeper engagement with digital data—the conditions of its production and use as well as its circulation through culture.

CIRCULATION IN WEB 2.0 WRITING THEORY

The idea of circulation is integral to Web 2.0 writing theory. Many in the field have found it to be a useful metaphor for thinking about the fluid nature of digital textuality (Eyman 2007; Porter 2010; Rice 2005; Trimbur 2000; Yancey 2004). In "Made Not Only in Words: Composition in a New Key," Yancey (2004, 312–15) outlines three ways we think about circulation in the field: *textual circulation*, *genre circulation*, and *media circulation*. *Textual circulation* is what we would associate with the intertextuality of quoting and paraphrase. *Genre circulation* centers on the generative ways texts organize human relations. And *media circulation* refers to the ways old and new media converge to create new semiotic forms in a digital environment. These are helpful guides for understanding the circulation of digital texts in lived culture. At the same time, there is a disconnect similar to the one encountered in Web 2.0 writing theory's inversion of the exchange/use relation—that is, the three types of circulation Yancey cites (all common in the field) bracket digital literacy practices from their constitutive role as circulators of capital. Thus, while Web 2.0 writing theory has been quick to pick up on the metaphorical power of circulation to help theorize digital literacies, it has also been quick to divest it of Marxian analysis and the circulation of capital. Trimbur's (2000) work is an exception here. As he points out, "The question to begin with is not so much where the commodity goes as what it carries in its internal workings as it circulates" (209). When commodified writing circulates, not only does it carry rhetorical, semiotic meaning (which makes it a unique type of commodity), it "also reproduces the prevailing and contradictory social and economic relations of capitalism" (208).

From a Marxian point of view then, circulation is not simply about tracing written artifacts as they move from writers to readers. Rather, it's about understanding this movement in relation to the circulatory demands of capital and how this process conditions our literate activity.

DIGITAL WRITING AND THE INDUSTRIAL CIRCUIT OF CAPITAL

One way we can begin to articulate the ascendance of exchange value in Web 2.0 writing is to bring Marx's theorization of the industrial circuit of capital more fully into our discussions of digital writing. This macro view of capital circulation comprises the sphere of production and the sphere of circulation (sometimes called *sphere of exchange*), as expressed in the following diagram (Figure 13.1):[2]

Despite the static depiction, this circuit should be seen as the dynamic, material social production of surplus value. The M at the circle's zenith stands for money in motion, or capital. Money is used to purchase C (commodity) in the form of MP (means of production—technology, machinery, etc.) and LP (labor power). MP and LP then enter into the sphere of production, P, and emerge from this process changed as C* a new, "altered" commodity that now embodies the labor

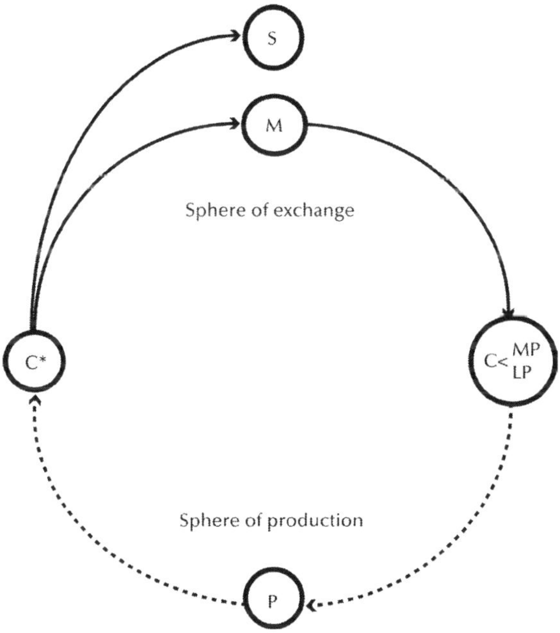

Figure 13.1. The circuit of capital.

and technologies used to produce it, which makes it "swollen" with surplus value (Marx 1990, 298). C* enters into the sphere of circulation and will, ideally, complete the circuit by being sold on the market. Once sold, the labor power congealed in the commodity is set free in the form of *s*—surplus value. In completing the circuit, capital has regenerated and *increased* in size.[3]

While Marx had industrial capitalism in mind when he conceived of the industrial circuit, he was well aware that communication technologies matter to the circulation of capital.[4] This truth becomes even more prominent in informational capitalism and Web 2.0, in which our writing practices take on a primary role as engines of capital circulation and accumulation. Critical media theorists Vincent Manzerolle and Atle Kjøsen frame it this way: "Media enable capital to move as an iterative process and are therefore the key component for capital's circulation; and it is media . . . that are the means by which capital communicates itself to itself in and through society" (Manzerolle and Kjøsen 2012, 216). Manzerolle and Kjøsen use the general term *media* here, but in the context of this discussion, we are specifically focused on the writing that takes place in and through digital media and how our digital literacy practices contribute to the circulation of capital.

THE SPHERE OF DIGITAL PRODUCTION—THE DATA MINE AND THE RISE OF BIG DATA

As a dialectical relation, the sphere of circulation can only be understood in interaction with the sphere of production. That is, in order for circulation to occur and for value to accrue, there must be something to circulate. In an industrial economy, these were tangible, manufactured commodities. In the context of Web 2.0 and informational economies, it's digitized data of all kinds. While Web 2.0 writing theory has certainly recognized the productive capacities of Web 2.0 writing, it hasn't taken the next step to connect this growth in writing production with processes of capital accumulation. This kind of value creation is evident in practices of data mining and surveillance that have become standard for both governments and corporations (Andrejevic 2012; McKee 2011; Turow 2011). We can take the online advertising industry as an example. According to the *Wall Street Journal*'s series "What They Know" (Angwin, July 30, 2010), "The largest U.S. websites are installing new and intrusive consumer-tracking technologies [cookies, beacons] on the computers of people visiting their sites—in some cases, more than 100 tracking tools at a time." This kind of consumer surveillance has spawned a multibillion-dollar-a-year online advertising industry that sells user data on several flourishing exchanges.[5] Research from the IAB (Interactive Advertising Bureau) shows that revenue from online advertising has grown no less than 10 percent a year since 2000, with some years reaching 20 to 30 percent growth. In 2012, ad revenue reached $36.6 billion (IAB 2013).

Keeping in mind O'Reilly's (2005) emphasis on data management, we shouldn't be too surprised that Web 2.0 companies are becoming savvier in their collection and use of user-created data. According to IBM (Zikopoulos et al. 2012), the world generates 2.5 exabytes of data every day—the equivalent of two and a half billion gigabytes. By 2020, they estimate the world will be producing 35 zetabytes of data annually.[6] This large-scale industrial production of data comes from all kinds of sources, but a good percentage of it comes from our writing online—e-mails, tweets, reviews, posts, and comments. The information-technology industries have labeled this deluge *big data*, and it has become the raw material of informational capitalism. Big data, in addition to being another clever marketing phrase, is the kind of bulk information that cannot be analyzed by human beings. It requires the combined power of networked servers and algorithmic programming to sift through data streams looking for the telltale signs of human patterns and social trends (see Dumbill 2012).

Understandably, big data has raised a few eyebrows, and several scholars have expressed doubts about its overblown claims (see Boyd and Crawford 2012; Gomes 2012). But as critical media scholar Mark Andrejevic (2012, 74) stresses, we should make no mistake—large-scale, extensive data collection is

> at the core of the economic model upon which Web 2.0 services and platforms are being constructed. That the business literature is hyping the model and businesses are staking billions of dollars in building the databases and developing the hardware and software for storing and sorting data may not mean that the model will work, but that it is worth considering the consequences.

Although O'Reilly (2005) had made his own predictions regarding the centrality of data in Web 2.0, the rhetoric and activities of big data are definitively more aggressive in tone and style. Expanding practices of data mining and data commodification are particularly virulent for the way they turn Web 2.0 writers into "double objects of commodification" (Fuchs 2010, 57), as our writing, and the digital detritus we leave, is collected, sold, then doubled back upon us through an "intensified exposure to commodity logic" (Fuchs 2010, 57) and the use of targeted marketing and advertising (Turow 2011). This is what it means for exchange value to be ascendant—the moment exchange value is "in the air," heightening the single-minded effort on the part of Web 2.0 corporations to actively seek out vibrant spaces of use-value that can then be leveraged for capital circulation and production.

DIGITAL WRITING AND ACCELERATION

The evolution of Web 2.0 demonstrates how processes of value creation take up and get intertwined with our digital literacies. One of the outcomes of this relation is *acceleration*—digital writing technologies are a key means for accelerating the circuit of capital accumulation. As Marx (1993a, 185) makes clear, the circulation of capital must be understood as a process, one incessantly trying to speed up and shorten the time of the circuit and secure surplus value:

> Capital, as self-valorizing value, does not just comprise class relations, a definite social character that depends on the existence of labor as wage-labor. It is a movement, a circulatory process . . . [that] can only be grasped as a movement, and not as a static thing.

Marx draws our attention to two fundamental aspects of the circulation process of capital. First, circulation is shaped by the insatiate need for capital to "self-valorize" and regenerate itself; and second, this need to regenerate *conditions* the social relations that emerge in support of capital's circulation. What this suggests is rather striking in terms of the circulation of Web 2.0 writing. If writing, in all its digital iterations, is fundamental to the circulation of capital (as I've been arguing), then the growth of the digital writing public is also, in part, a manifestation of capital's need to grow. The *movement* is the emphasis here—the "suspended animation" Trimbur notes at the beginning of this chapter. From the perspective of the industrial circuit of capital, capital's incessant need to regenerate itself is the force that drives capital circulation. As David Harvey (2010) puts it, "If capital flow stops then the body politic of capitalist society dies." Our digital literacies are essential for this movement to occur.

As our day-to-day experiences tell us, completing the circuit of capital is a process of struggle, one continually confronted by what Marx (1993b) calls "barriers" to and "interruptions" (Marx 1993a) of profit. Such barriers come in many forms—market competition, bad weather, government regulations, illiteracy—but the two fundamental barriers slowing capital's circuit are *time* and *space*; or, in other words, materiality itself. Christopher Arthur (1988, 117) notes that the first obstacle to capital's circulation is that "capital must *invest itself in matter*" in the shape of a material commodity. For capital to be realized, it needs a transport vessel—some *thing* that must be produced and then circulated socially in order to acquire value. Once the circuit is complete, surplus value precipitates out and the process repeats.

But what if there were a way to accelerate this process and skip the transformation into a tangible commodity? What is needed is a technology that *dematerializes* objects in time and space—the exact thing computerized, digital writing technologies are designed to do. It's critical to note that this process of dematerialization is through and through a *written* process in which human-made writing technologies are used to *codify* material social phenomena into binary mathematics and electric pulses. Thus, when we talk about the "speed" of digitized life and the "logic" of acceleration, we are intuiting the ways digital media help to create the conditions for capital accumulation "through progressive reorganizations of space and time and the adoption of newer and faster media such as . . . transportation[,] . . . digitization, [and] telecommunications" (Manzerolle and Kjøsen 2012, 219). The acceleration of commodity exchange enabled by digital media, by collapsing time and the material spaces through which capital must travel, plays a defining role in the digital literacies of Web 2.0.

RECOGNIZING THE TENSIONS

One of the strongest aspects of Marxian analysis is its emphasis on contradiction. I find it helpful to think of contradiction as a tension. The shift is useful for the way it pulls the semantic meanings of contradiction into the experience of the body. We *feel* contradiction in our day-to-day tensions, the in-betweenness of twenty-first-century life. When we experience the dis-ease that comes with commodified social relations, we are often experiencing a contradiction in capitalism. I've tried to explore one such contradiction here—the historical moment when exchange value is on the ascent. As scholars and teachers of writing, it is within our interests to recognize these moments and their relations with emerging forms of digital literacy. When we fail to recognize the exchange value of our digital writing, we lose an important vantage point from which to study and understand contemporary digital technology, digital literacies, and their complex relationship with the production of surplus value.

We are living in an exciting time to study writing, one fraught with the tensions that come with the space and spread of digital media. The tensions seem particularly acute right now, when such clearly useful technologies are being turned against the best hopes of the early visionaries of the Internet and the promises of Web 2.0. Thus, as our writing tools evolve and new textual forms emerge, our ways of studying and theorizing about writing must evolve, too. The posts we make to connect with friends and family, the comments we leave online, the websites we read, and the e-mails we send are, in a sense, written twice—that is, not only are they alphabetic expressions necessary for human communication, but they are also inscribed in the subtext of the digital data they generate. This layered nature of digital texts compels us to reconsider many of our assumptions about what writing is, the purposes it serves, and the kinds of value it creates. Amidst the mountains of data and the speed at which they move, we must continue to keep our study and analysis of writing embedded in a late-capitalist mode of informational production. It is here, at the juncture of use and exchange, where we can fight out the struggles that keep alive the possibility of economies of writing driven by use-value.

Notes

1. In Marxian terms, use represents "production for human needs" and exchange represents "production for profit" (Trimbur 2000).
2. Image is taken from *Marx's "Capital"* (Fine and Saad-Filho 2004, n.p.). Reproduced with permission from Pluto Press.
3. Marx's shorthand version of this formula is M—C . . . P . . . C*—M*.

4. Although Marx (1990, 1993a) spends little time discussing communication technologies in *Capital*, the references he does make suggest that he grouped the means of communications with other technologies (steam, large-scale machinery) as essential for circulating and accumulating capital.
5. To see how many third-party companies are tracking you online, try Mozilla Firefox's add-on Collusion at http://www.mozilla.org/en-US/collusion/.
6. The numbers I've cited vary, and the only available data come from corporate research by companies like IBM and the IDC (International Data Corporation) (IDC 2013).

14

WWW.ENGL.ISH

Internationalized World Wide Web Domains and Translingual Complexities

Jay Jordan

At an October 2009 meeting in Seoul, the Internet Corporation for Assigned Names and Numbers (ICANN), a US-based nonprofit entity that oversees the allocation of Internet addresses, announced its approval of a fast-track process for creating newly "internationalized" country-code top-level World Wide Web domains (ICANN 2016).[1] The process involves a technical workaround through which creators and consumers of web content can, for the first time, generate and access web addresses using characters from a variety of written codes other than English. In an online video presentation based on the Seoul meeting, several ICANN staffers and administrators praised the emergence of internationalized domain names (IDNs) as a key moment in the roughly 20-year history of the World Wide Web (Chen 2009). In fact, Peter Dengate Thrush, ICANN chairman, asserted that the development of IDNs represents "the biggest change to the underlying structure of the Internet since its creation forty years ago." Alongside this claim about the technical evolution that IDNs supposedly represent, Thrush asserted that the projected proliferation of websites "will mean people can get their names in their languages to experience their Internet" (ICANN 2016).

While IDNs do mark a key evolution in how the World Wide Web can be accessed and used, the change is not as fundamental or as straightforward as Thrush's celebratory comments suggest. It is true that web users may now create and type web addresses in an increasing number of scripts, including Arabic, Chinese, Cyrillic, and Hangeul. But the "underlying structure" of the Internet itself—including its most basic software layers—carries the clear linguistic legacy of its largely US-based invention as well as the economic legacy of English's role as

DOI: 10.7330/9781607325239.c014

an international language of commerce, education, and political control (Cerf 2012; Danet and Herring 2003; Dor 2004; Luke, Luke, and Graham 2007). In specific terms, "If one wants to do so much as put up a webpage on a server, one must learn a set of English-based acronymic mnemonics (HTML tags) to properly format the page and a cryptic operating system with English-mnemonic commands in English syntax to host it (e.g., Unix/Linux) and manage a browser with English commands in the menus to view it (e.g., Mozilla)" (Paolillo 2007, 425). But as entrenched as English is in the history and evolution of the Internet, English itself changes as it spreads globally. And English does not remain hermetically sealed from other languages. In one example, Robert Holland (2002) observes that English lexical items appear in Indonesian syntax in print ads that seem to appeal to high economic classes. More broadly, as Daniel Dor (2004, 114) argues, a proliferation of languages—especially online—does not mean resistance to the economic forces that have entrenched English as a lingua franca; instead, such proliferation evinces an economic logic in which "the agents of economic globalization have realized that adapting to local cultures and languages is a necessary component of staying competitive." So the promise of IDNs is that web users may now create and access content in "their [own] languages," but the content actually populating IDNs prompts further questions about the complexities of language ownership, contact, and use, even (especially) in traditionally English-dominant environments.

This chapter introduces the technical and social contexts of IDNs and connects the IDNs' development to a nexus of linguistic and economic conditions in which English and other languages interanimate. My specific focus is on websites that, despite the evolution of newer forms of online media, remain highly visible and highly valuable sites of information, negotiation, and commerce. I describe three websites that have already appeared in newly internationalized domains: one each in the People's Republic of China, the Republic of Korea, and the Russian Federation. My analysis of these emerging sites draws on scholarship in translingualism and in scholarly and professional discussions of web-page layout and generic design conventions. I argue that websites appearing in internationalized domains, to the extent that they feature mixtures of otherwise apparently discrete linguistic codes stretched across web-page elements, are important exemplars of translingual production that expand scholarly attention beyond examples of traditional academic writing and into a growing/diversifying global writing economy.

HISTORY AND TECHNICAL CONTEXT

In a message board posting on August 6, 1991, Tim Berners-Lee, a scientist in residence at the European Center for Nuclear Research (commonly known by its French acronym, CERN) wrote what has popularly become the World Wide Web's birth announcement. Berners-Lee, a computer engineer, had spent time at CERN developing schemes to allow computers to address, recognize, and share hypertext documents over hardware networks. He also created HTML, the hypertext markup language that standardized these documents, and WorldWideWeb, the first-of-its-kind client software that allowed users to retrieve and view them. While Berners-Lee would go on to build the first World Wide Web server at CERN, the organization's initial response to his work was cool: his supervisor at CERN responded that his proposal for information management was "vague but exciting" ("Tim Berners-Lee's Proposal" 2008). So he turned to Internet-based newsgroups, announcing his inventions and distributing both his client and server software based on the philosophy that "much academic information should be freely available to anyone" and that it should be shared by "internationally dispersed teams."

In the two decades since Berners-Lee's announcement and call for participation, the web has grown well beyond its initial and projected user bases, incorporating a variety of online communities for whom English is not a first or even a dominant language.[2] Just as crucially, it has evolved qualitatively as well. The vast majority of present-day websites and pages exist for purposes that could loosely be called *secondary*: in fact, the web's growth as a communication medium was relatively slow and restricted largely to academic contexts until 1993, when the National Center for Supercomputing Applications at the University of Illinois at Urbana-Champaign released Mosaic, a graphical web browser that directly influenced the development of Netscape Navigator and Microsoft Internet Explorer—products that marked the web's transition from a scholarly to a largely commercial platform (National Center for Supercomputing Applications 2013). Most recently, the web has evolved to support a variety of previously discrete functions: it is now common to use programs such as Chrome and Firefox not only to browse and create web-specific content but also to send and receive e-mail messages; to compose, revise, and share more traditional (word-processed) documents; to upload and download work files from remote servers; and to manage professional and social relationships. So ubiquitous is the web as a computing platform that Google, one of the most successful companies ever to capitalize on the development of Internet-based technologies, now distributes a personal computer operating system that is little more than a web browser.

In spite of its proliferating functionality, however, the web retains a key technical limit that is a product of its early development. While it is possible (and increasingly common) to author web content in multiple languages and scripts, the web continues to rely on hardware and software technologies that were built in English-dominant environments and that continue to have compelling legacy effects on the ways users author, access, and locate content.[3] The most salient such effect for this chapter is the web's built-in requirement that web addresses include only characters from the American Standard Code for Information Interchange (ASCII)—a scheme based on the English alphabet (Figure 14.1).

To contextualize this limitation and the function and implications of IDNs, some further technical description is called for. The roughly 2.4 billion global web users (Internet World Stats 2013) are already familiar with how to access web content—that is, by using a browser, a software application that allows users to view/interact with web-based content regardless of computer platform or operating system by entering linguistically meaningful strings of characters corresponding to website addresses. What many users may not realize, however, is that what happens *after* they press Enter is complicated, if largely transparent. First, the string of alphanumeric characters that makes up a web address (the uniform resource locator [URL]) is transmitted by the browser via an Internet connection to the nearest computer server that is part of the domain name system (DNS), essentially a vast phone book of web addresses. The characters are matched against the DNS server's database of addresses until the correct match is found, and then the address is converted to a string of numbers separated by periods—the internet protocol (IP) address. Only then is the original computer's request for the relevant website and page transmitted to the target server, which may then permit access to its content. It is certainly possible for users to type IP addresses into browser address bars directly, but 74.125.224.72 is unwieldy for most users to remember, especially compared with www.google.com.

In order for this translation process to work, a browser must send ASCII characters to compare with the DNS's list of natural language addresses. That is, only characters from the ASCII set are valid as part of DNS queries: if a browser sent non-ASCII characters, it would be doing the equivalent of typing letters directly into a telephone system instead of matching letters to their corresponding keypad numerals (as in trying to dial 1–800-PAINTER instead of 800–724–6837). Thus, the DNS system cannot support the written codes used by the majority of the planet's

	0	1	2	3	4	5	6	7
0	NUL	DLE	space	0	@	P	`	p
1	SOH	DC1 XON	!	1	A	Q	a	q
2	STX	DC2	"	2	B	R	b	r
3	ETX	DC3 XOFF	#	3	C	S	c	s
4	EOT	DC4	$	4	D	T	d	t
5	ENQ	NAK	%	5	E	U	e	u
6	ACK	SYN	&	6	F	V	f	v
7	BEL	ETB	'	7	G	W	g	w
8	BS	CAN	(	8	H	X	h	x
9	HT	EM	)	9	I	Y	i	y
A	LF	SUB	*	:	J	Z	j	z
B	VT	ESC	+	;	K	[	k	{
C	FF	FS	,	<	L	\	l	|
D	CR	GS	-	=	M	]	m	}
E	SO	RS	.	>	N	^	n	~
F	SI	US	/	?	O	_	o	del

Figure 14.1. American Standard Code for Information Interchange (ASCII Table: Your Web Reference 2013).

population. IDNs provide a workaround by adding an additional step to the DNS name/IP address resolution process. When a user with an IDN-supporting web browser enters a URL containing at least one non-ASCII element (such as http://παράδειγμα.δοκιμή), the user's browser translates the URL into a non-human-friendly string of ASCII characters (such as http://xn-hxajbheg2az3al.xn-jxalpdlp, the ASCII equivalent of the human-readable address immediately above), which is then resolvable by DNS to a unique IP address—returnable in this case as the Greek-language example.test page currently maintained by ICANN.

Thus, despite Peter Dengate Thrush's statement that IDN development is "the biggest change to the underlying structure of the Internet since its creation forty years ago," it is not clear that IDNs represent a structural change at all (ICANN 2016). English—represented most visibly by the practical ASCII limit in DNS—is still at the heart of the Internet and its associated technologies, including the nearly ubiquitous hypertext transfer protocol (http), which undergirds the web's global use as a collection of linked content. To be sure, though, IDNs do represent significant investment in the web as a multilingual medium. The complexity they demonstrate in the relationship between English as a legacy and continuing key language and other codes carries over to the content that increasingly populates the IDNs.

THEORIES AND METHODS

My analysis of example web pages in emerging IDNs is guided by two bodies of theory and practice: genre and layout in online settings and translingual approaches to composition.

Layout

Following Janet Giltrow and Carolyn Miller, Doreen Starke-Meyerring (2008, 401) refers to genre as a "relatively durable archive of cultural knowledge." Far from remaining static, however, genres may be significantly affected by social changes, including technological evolutions. The web, while not the first medium to permit or encourage nonlinear reading, marks just such an evolution, allowing "the inclusion of several functions or several texts with different communicative purposes in a single document" (Santini 2007, 2). Specifically, researchers of genre in computing environments note that web pages add to the typical genre attributes of "content" and "form" a third one—"functionality"—that indexes the presence of executable code, including navigation and other interactive affordances (Dong et al. 2008; also see Shepherd and Watters 1998, 1999). While there are no compelling technical restrictions on web-page layout, the durability of print genres and the growth of the web as a commercial medium have affected web-page design, positioning websites as points of market-oriented generic negotiation between producers and consumers of web content. Luc Pauwels (2012, 255) observes that layout choices are simultaneously "tools used to attract, direct[,] and invoke the desired effect on, or response from, website visitors" and signifiers of "producer-related ideas, opinions[,] and aspirations." Such choices, realized specifically in a range of elements such as background, color schemes, left-right or right-left orientation, and symmetry, may contribute to a "very rigid structure . . . or embody a more open space to wander around" (255).

While Pauwels calls particular attention to legacy generic forms, such as family albums and scrapbooks, that can provide templates for

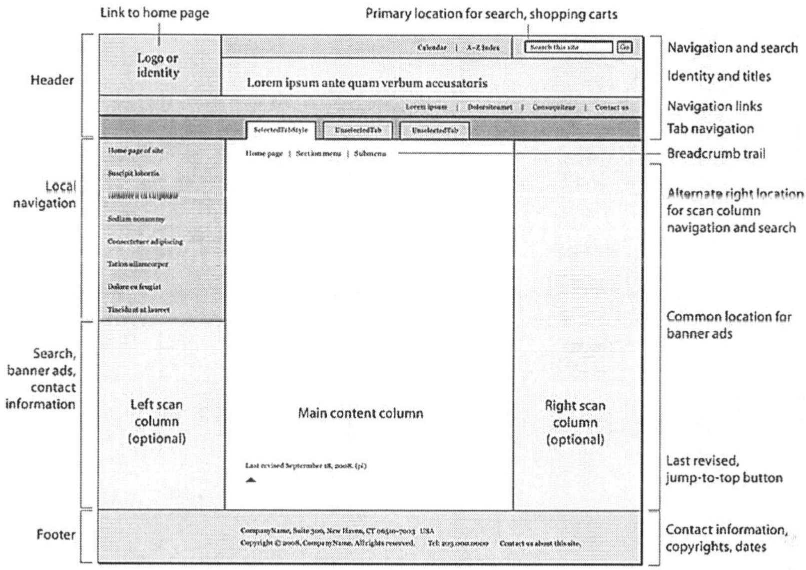

Figure 14.2. Canonical page layout (Lynch and Horton 2011).

contemporary web authors, web pages do not need to conform to legacy layouts in order to exemplify design durability and predictability—even across cultural, language, and national bases of users. In several studies, Michael Bernard (2000, 2001, 2002) and Bernard and Sheshadri (2004) have demonstrated consistency in international web users' expectations of placement/layout of conventional e-commerce web-page elements, such as advertisements, internal and external links, and the "shopping cart," with 76 percent of 258 participants in Bernard and Sheshadri's study reporting that their layout expectations overall conformed to their preferences. These page-layout-level user expectations appear consistent with the symbolic trends that Joel Spring (2006, 251) believes are part of "global consumerism," in which brand names and icons are recognizable across apparently disparate cultural and language groups. And such expectations track very closely with the "canonical page design" introduced in the *Web Style Guide Online* (Figure 14.2), in which "content" and "functionality" elements recur in consistent areas, as authors Patrick J. Lynch and Sarah Horton observe (Lynch and Horton 2011).

Consistent with findings in Bernard (2000, 2001, 2002) and in Bernard and Sheshadri (2004), the "canonical" layout here locates typically dynamic "content" elements near the center of the page and more static "functionality" elements around its periphery, concentrating the most expected and permanent navigational elements along the top and left sides, search utility at top right, and logo and branding information (including a link back to the local homepage) at top left.

Translingual Approaches to Composition

While research on web genres and website layout has contributed to an understanding of how content, functionality, and related visual-design decisions travel across international contexts, recent scholarship in applied linguistics and in rhetoric and composition addresses how communicative acts can be meaningful—even innovative—in linguistically complex settings. Emerging translingual approaches (Horner, Lu, Royster, and Trimbur 2011; Horner, NeCamp, and Donahue 2011) shift the focus on uses of language from compliance with particular and/or preestablished codes to the pragmatics of situationally dynamic code-meshing (Canagarajah 2006; Young 2009; Young and Martinez 2011). Suresh Canagarajah (2013, 19–20) concisely and critically summarizes traditional perspectives on language contact, arguing that Western European Enlightenment intellectual and economic movements gave rise to a "monolingual paradigm" in which languages are assumed to operate according to efficient, controllable, durable standards. Further, monolingualism and associated beliefs that languages are discrete as well as ontologically prior to language-in-use assume that "the locus of language [is] cognition rather than social context" and that "communication [is] based on grammar rather than practice" (20). A corollary to such assumptions is the implicit claim that multilingual contact leads either to the collapse of discrete language differences into a comfortably preestablished lingua franca or to the realization that communication is simply not possible because of irresoluble codes. However, examples of communication among nonnative and indeed arguably nonfluent English-language users demonstrates that preestablished codes may matter less than the unestablished and unestablishable uses of those codes to address global and local conditions of linguistic complexity (see, e.g., Crystal 1997, 2006; Facchinetti, Crystal, and Seidlhofer 2010; House 2003; Jenkins 2009; Meierkord 2012; Pennycook 2007; Rubdy and Saraceni 2006).

Codes themselves certainly retain and will continue to retain prominence, but the daily use of those codes will (continue to) reflect the agency of diverse users, who are usually more interested in strategizing with codes to accomplish goals than they are in aligning themselves with supposedly correct varieties. Multilingualism on the web, like generic evolution on the web, is not a wholly new phenomenon divorced from print and oral uses. However, studying translingual production on the web potentially benefits scholarship on translingualism in two ways. First, the web's flexible layout and formatting permit producers of content—whether in ASCII or internationalized domains—significant control over how their diverse uses of code are shown to prospective audiences. That control in turn allows scholars to view the web as a rich environment for studying how multiple codes might inhabit the same spaces/occasions—a central preoccupation of the translingual approach. Second, as I relate above, ICANN believes its rollout of IDNs represents a high-water mark in the development of a truly world-wide (read: discretely multilingual) web. To the extent that the content populating IDNs is not as unproblematically multilingual as ICANN expects, studying IDNs provides scholars a chance to examine convergences and divergences between an international *policy* of multilingualism and an international *practice*. So far, such practice appears complex enough to call for nuanced description and analysis. In the few examples I have analyzed so far, the ways in which codes differently inhabit layout distinctions between content and functionality areas of web pages highlight *both* how codes can be used for discrete purposes on sites that anticipate linguistically complex audiences *and* how uses of codes exceed such distinctions.

EXAMPLES

To select the examples in this section, an undergraduate research assistant[4] and I used idnsearch.net, a crowdsourced and socially tagged clearinghouse of links to sites in internationalized domains. Employing keyword searches on *chinese*, *korean*, and *russian*, we further filtered results to those sites that appeared to include both English and at least one other code in the bodies of their homepages. At several points before we finally settled on the three sites described and analyzed here, we rechecked sites' availability, understanding that the web's instability as an archive is, if anything, exacerbated by the novelty and uncertainty of emerging IDNs.

Russian Federation: гигабайт.рф

It is difficult to explore emerging IDNs without encountering Russian-language websites. Indeed, the United Nations Educational, Scientific, and Cultural Organization (UNESCO) and EURid—the registry for the .eu country-level Internet domain—jointly report (EURid-UNESCO 2012, 41) that the Cyrillic code .рф IDN has been the most successful so far: registries in the new domain grew by 54 percent during 2011, and monthly growth has been roughly equivalent to the popular ASCII .ru domain. At least some of the growth in .рф domain sites is likely attributable to the national status of the Russian language. Citing UNESCO statistics, the joint report observes that 80 percent of Russian residents speak Russian natively and that there is relatively little in- or outmigration of people or importation of foreign-language media.

Gigabyte Technology, a personal computer hardware company based in Taiwan, maintains one mirror of its Russian-language site in the .рф domain. The company distributes and sells its components globally through a widely dispersed network of distributors and partner retailers, including over 14 hundred in the Russian Federation alone ("Where to Buy" 2013). Given the company's large Russian footprint and its implicit desire to retain and build connections with the relatively linguistically homogeneous Russian market, it makes sense for it to have a .рф web presence.

Gigabyte's Russian-language homepage (Figure 14.3) clearly follows a variation of the "canonical" e-commerce layout described by Lynch and Horton. Even with little or no knowledge of written Russian, a site viewer could identify the prominent branding at top left, topside navigational elements, and the more dynamic content in the middle of the homepage, much of which is headed by dates in a kind of newsfeed format. Most of the page's dynamic and static content appears in Cyrillic script. The most prominent English-language element is the company logo itself—again, at top left and, in keeping with canonical layout and coding, serving double duty as a clickable homepage link. English/ASCII is also visible at page bottom, where the canonical model locates copyright and contact information. Indeed, here, Gigabyte's page includes an English-language reference to "GIGABYTE TECHNOLOGY CO., LTD," the full legal name of the site owner. In addition, the page bottom includes a collection of (Russian) links that appear to duplicate other page links (such as Mobile Version) as well as an English-language reference to RSS. That link, along with the familiar orange-square logo, denotes the availability of consistently updated information readable by a newsfeed or blog aggregator. While it is feasible to assume that "really simple syndication" or "rich site summary" could be translated and rendered in Russian, much as other content on the page is, *RSS* appears here in ASCII characters likely as a testament both to the common use of *RSS* as a pseudoacronym (which, like *SAT* or *KFC*, no longer stands for a fuller term) and

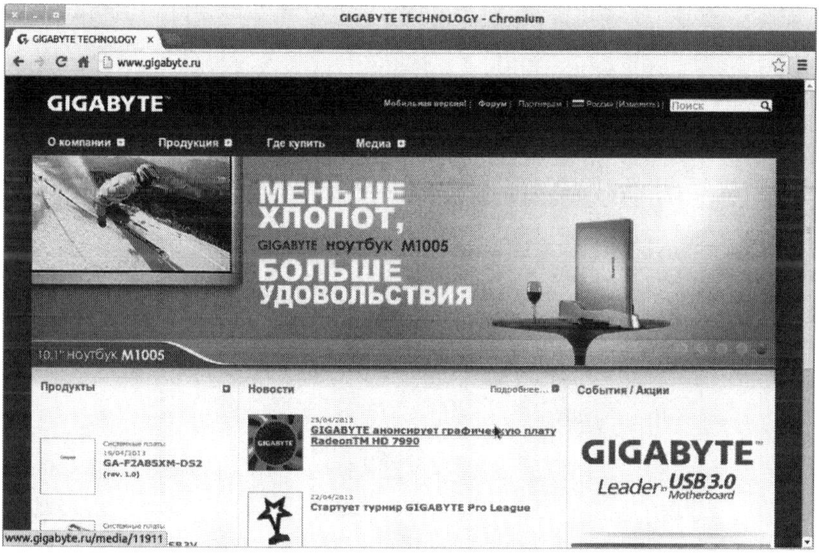

Figure 14.3. *гигабайт.рф* (Giga-Byte Technology Co. 2013).

to RSS's reliance on web-based technologies that retain English-language legacy effects. In fact, following Joel Spring's (2006, 251) argument about the ubiquity of "brand icons" across languages, *RSS* may also be readable as a symbolic element of a growing global consumerist culture that freely adopts, adapts, and combines "local" and "global" languages.

Outside the peripheral functionality areas, other English-language and/or ASCII items appear in dynamic content areas of Gigabyte's homepage. In the large dynamic rotating-content area just below the topside navigation, several items include ASCII references to Gigabyte trademarks—especially model names of hardware components. And a number of English-language items are clearly present because they are US-based trademarks (such as Intel and Nvidia). Evident in these examples is not only the ongoing effect of the role English has played in some of the foundational software technologies of the web (such as RSS) but also the economies that surround related hardware. Many government and private-sector entities remain concerned about how data and computing technologies circulate among the United States and other countries that, like Russia, prompt concerns for trademark holders about intellectual property infringement. It is no surprise that the linguistic environment of even a single company's Russian homepage would reflect this economic, legal, and technological complexity.

Republic of Korea: 부산디지털대학.kr/

Ethnologue reports that the Republic of Korea, or South Korea, is among the most linguistically homogeneous countries in the world, with a near-zero probability that any two residents speak different first languages (Lewis, Simons, and Fennig 2016). Also notable is its Internet saturation—greater than 100 percent coverage (owing to the expansion of smartphone usage; see Moran 2012) and the highest percentage of fiber optic cable-to-home connections in the world, according to Mark McDonald in a *New York Times* article published February 21, 2011. According to the EURid-UNESCO (2012) report, South Korea's combination of national-language pride and investment, cultural and linguistic homogeneity, and Internet saturation/use positions the country as a leading creator of IDN content for the foreseeable future.

However, this twin allegiance to the Korean language and to Internet development does not exclude the presence of English or the complexities of online translingual production. Nor does it mean Korea could or does attempt to limit Korean content producers' connections to a globalizing economy. The internationalized homepage of Busan Digital University is exemplary (Figure 14.4).

According to the "About BDU" pages at the ASCII (http://www.bdu.ac.kr) site, the university is a Christian institution offering online courses in "social welfare, management, hospitality and tourism, and digital media." Founded as Dongseo Cyber University in 2002, its name was changed by university administrators the following year in a bid to represent more clearly its physical location in Busan, South Korea's second-largest city. While pride in this location is apparent, BDU's self-regard as a "worldwide on-line education leader" is also explicit, suggesting a complex online identity that tries to represent itself as both Korean and international.

This complexity carries over into the layout, content, and functionality of BDU's internationalized site. As with explicitly e-commerce sites described by Lynch and Horton's (2011) model, this university site has a conventional layout that assigns functional/navigational components to the periphery and more dynamic/newsfeed-type content to the center. Ewa Callahan (2005) points to compelling reasons for educational institutions to adopt e-commerce-oriented layout models: "international" universities in particular have clear imperatives to market themselves to a wide, globally dispersed potential student body. And even in cases in which a country may not attract many foreign students—owing perhaps to students' perception that that country's language may be too difficult to learn or not prominent

Figure 14.4. 부산디지털대학.kr (Busan Digital University 2010).

enough—universities still tend to publish at least some English-language web content owing to English's global status as a language of academic and commercial exchange (Luke, Luke, and Graham 2007). BDU's homepage appears to follow suit. While the page's content is overwhelmingly rendered in Hangeul, English/ASCII does congregate in functional areas, including the top-left university logo, where it appears (as both "Busan Digital University" and as "BDU") alongside the Hangeul-character full name. The bilingual logo appears again at the left side of page bottom alongside an English-language copyright notice. At the right side of the bottom of the homepage, bilingual logos for two other nearby universities appear, including Dongseo University and Kyungnam College of Information and Technology.

A few other English/ASCII items appear elsewhere on the BDU homepage, occupying locations and apparently fulfilling purposes that make them more difficult to classify. On the right side of the page at the edge of a dynamically scrolling set of content-related images are two small areas labeled (in English) Quick Link and Popup Zone. Clicking on Quick Link causes a list of links to slide out from the right side of the page, including an ASCII-labeled FAQ link. (Here, as with ASCII-coded RSS links, it is probable that the term *FAQ* now functions as a pseudo-acronym, thus no longer prompting a translation of the full term *frequently asked questions.*) Clicking Popup Zone pulls up a horizontal bar at a slightly lower position on the page, which includes manually scrollable, exclusively Hangeul-coded content. Last, and also notable, is a small area just below the middle-page content-related images, which is labeled "10th Anniversary." Other page areas include references to the university's anniversary, including, prominently, the top-left logo area, in which the bilingual logo alternates appearing with a large red "10." However, none of the other homepage anniversary references include English/ASCII content. Further research with Korean-language experts on BDU's site and on other sites in ASCII and internationalized .kr domains could further explore these spatially dispersed examples of English/ASCII-Hangeul contact. For now, it seems probable that, given a number of South Korean universities' explicit desires to assert both national status (in a homogeneous country) and *inter*national status, these universities will promote themselves, even in successful Korean-language IDNs, through linguistically diverse online presentations.

People's Republic of China: 钢板库. 中国

China is the most populous country on the planet. It is also notable for its authoritarian control of information channels and networks, including domestically and internationally accessible websites registered in Chinese-language and Chinese-managed domains or in domains outside the country. This control has prompted conflict between ICANN's explicitly international but subtly US-dominant internationalization scheme and the state-centered policy orientation of the Chinese Internet registrar, the China Internet Network Information Center (CNNIC). This conflict simmered for 13 years as different stakeholders positioned themselves as gateways to China's massive online population and market. Hong Xue (2004, 563) notes that Chinese users began complaining about English and ASCII dominance in Internet resources as early as 1997—the same year Chinese institutions, including the nascent CNNIC, began experimenting with their own home-grown Chinese-character domains. By 2000, as Xue reports, ICANN was asserting that local internationalization experiments that did not conform to its emerging standards must give way—a directive that did not sit well with Chinese registrars, who considered the DNS system "west-centric" (565) and who expressed significant national-security-related concerns about ICANN's ties to the US Department of Commerce (580). CNNIC did dedicate itself to working actively with ICANN, and, by May 2010, secured fast-track approval for the .中国 (Simplified) and .中國 (Traditional) domains.

Figure 14.5. 钢板库.中国 *(Anyang Dazheng Steel Silo Co. 2013).*

Given Chinese Internet authorities' sometimes troubled history with ICANN, and given the early beginnings of Chinese efforts to develop homegrown Chinese-language support for Internet users, it may be expected that emerging Chinese IDNs would host much clearly local and exclusively Chinese-language content—perhaps serving as ultimate examples of ICANN's claim of "one Internet; many languages." To be sure, the size of China's Internet presence means that broad claims about linguistic trends online must be well supported with significantly more exemplification. However, in the case of one e-commerce example, translingual complexities comparable to those in Korean and Russian IDNs do surface.

Anyang Dazheng Steel Silo Co., Ltd., is an Anyang (He'nan Province), China-based manufacturing company specializing in silos and other agricultural structures. The English-language version of its website references projects in Southeast Asia and East Africa in addition to its Chinese domestic work. The cross-border durability of Lynch and Horton's canonical layout is visible. In contrast to Korean and Russian examples, however, periphery/functionality areas in the Chinese-language version (Figure 14.5) include virtually no English/ASCII content.

Anyang Dazheng's corporate logo (rendered exclusively in Chinese script) is top left, common site navigation is top center, and the footer area includes legal and contact information. In fact, the only ASCII code apparent on the periphery is the ".com" in contact e-mail addresses at page bottom—evidence that the internationalization represented by IDNs is not yet emergent in Internet protocols outside the web. English/ASCII material is quite apparent, though, in canonically dynamic content areas down the homepage's center. Perhaps most obvious—just above the footer—are scrolling English/ASCII links, complete with extremely familiar logos, to Google and BaiDu, the popular Chinese search site.

But other examples prompt questions about the reasons for English inclusion. Just below the topside navigation, content rotates through a set of images, two of which (as of April 2013) include manipulated photos of steel building projects as well as English-language taglines: "Business Goals Create the Future of Industry Development" and "Altogether Wins." Further down the page center, several newsfeed-style link categories are bilingually titled: Company News, Industry News, and Work View. Just below those are undated link categories bilingually titled Superiority, Principle, and Equipment. There is an English-language direct translation of the default Chinese-language site—prominently linkable from the top center of the homepage. However, the circulation of English-language items on the default page strongly suggests Anyang Dazheng's awareness that its international marketing has linguistic stakes. Any Chinese company could count on the regional and growing global prominence of Chinese languages to warrant the assumption that prospective Asian clients could find Chinese content accessible, but, in Anyang Dazheng's case, its work in East Africa warrants its engagement of English as a lingua franca. If the company relies on its web presence for promotion across borders, it is certainly aware that website visitors may not immediately land on the homepage most linguistically familiar to them. Despite China's long investment in a Chinese-language web, then, Anyang Dazheng demonstrates that English remains a key default language for a complex web audience.

CONCLUSION

This chapter adopts considerations of web-page layout and translingual composition to describe and analyze a very small selection of web pages in Chinese, Korean, and Russian IDNs. It suggests a clear need for ongoing research that further tests and refines the analysis and that takes up additional relevant topics. To be sure, more work could be done to expand comparative analysis across more IDNs/languages, including fast-growing Arabic domains in Middle Eastern and Asian nations. More focused analysis could also be done within IDNs, which can and should employ collaborations with language experts. While emerging translingual scholarship expresses considerable agnosticism about the switching or meshing of discrete codes, the growing number of internationalized websites strongly suggests that at least the visual representation of multiple codes will continue to have symbolic significance, especially considering the ongoing role e-commerce websites play in international commercial negotiations.

Ongoing scholarship should also respond to other potentially related computing developments to gauge their impact on internationalization as well as their implications for translingual contact: for instance, recent decisions by ICANN to open generic top-level domains (gTLDs) beyond .com and .edu to (largely English-language) terms such as *.design* and *.music* potentially retrench the primacy of ASCII characters in top-level domains even though emerging TLDs could be highly attractive to web producers globally (EURid-UNESCO 2012, 27). Global content producers may, then, need to manage the increased complexity of web addresses that, themselves, present users with more than one code before they even reach page content. Beyond the "traditional" web, social media platforms such as Facebook, Instagram, Tumblr, and Twitter now commonly give new and experienced web users the primary means by which they constitute personal and professional online identities and contact others. The ease with which a user—whether individual or corporate—can create such identity trades off with the fixity that proprietary templates impose on layout and other design considerations (Arola 2010): that is, users may easily populate predesigned Twitter bios but have little or no control over how Twitter renders that important form of self-expression. Extending research on translingual production outside e-commerce-related web content and into more personal/social content could reveal whether and how translingual production is affected by more locked-down design environments and by the considerably more diverse genres of social media. At least as compelling as the development of the social web has been the proliferation of devices used to access any and all web content. One estimate places the global number of mobile cellular/data subscriptions at roughly 6 billion by the end of 2011 ("Global" 2013). More devices mean more form factors and, thus, even more potential layout and other design variables, which could clearly affect the evolution of the canonical model I have employed here: if the layout distinctions between functional and dynamic/content areas are reorienting themselves to accommodate four-inch, seven-inch, and 10-inch screens, for instance, what are the implications for how different codes interact spatially?

There are significant pedagogical implications as well, especially for students and teachers in composition programs, which have long organized themselves—at least implicitly—as monolingual spaces. Websites such as the ones I have featured here represent exemplars of translingual production online that can model the complexities of such production and also prompt students' questions about the motivations behind specific linguistic decisions. More broadly, IDN development offers composition curricula a ready-made, student-accessible research context in which students can use resources such as idnsearch.net to survey both the geographic spread of IDNs and the translingual evolution of specific sites. Along the way, instructors might engage students in exploring the affordances and constraints that computing technologies present to those who need or want to write translingually: different language settings for hardware and software are available, but the ease with which composers may change settings varies considerably. If the promise of IDNs—and, indeed, of the World Wide Web—is more and more fluidity among apparently discrete codes, it is worth asking with students how the tools composers must employ to manipulate those codes might be made more useful. It is also worth asking with students how existing- and emerging-language work connects to broader questions about globalization: as Luke, Luke, and Graham (2007) argue, global economies seem to function at simultaneously huge and individual scales at which their operations seem either too big to comprehend or so small that they appear to be the product of individual talent or genius. I hope I have shown that the visible uptake of multiple codes in emerging IDNs provides a record—one that scholar-teachers and students can use as a powerful heuristic in asking not only *how* languages appear to interact but also *why* and *for which producers and consumers.*

While this chapter cannot reach firm conclusions about how English and other apparently discrete codes will continue to interact on the increasingly world-wide and increasingly design-diverse web, it certainly confirms that such interactions will occur. The increasing use and presence of non-ASCII codes will not mean, contrary to ICANN's assumptions, that the web shifts in many locations from a discrete English condition to a discrete other-than-English state. In fact, English will continue to be a dominant web language, owing in part to its presence in the web's computing infrastructure and to its dominance of available web programming languages, especially html. But English's presence will also continue in web-page content itself—even on pages accessible at addresses using non-ASCII characters. Producers of web content will thus do what language users have always done: attempt to self-represent, connect to others, and make meaning with linguistic codes and with other available symbolic resources in ways both wholly expected and complexly innovative.

Notes

1. Thirty-one countries have so far substantially completed the process: Algeria, Bangladesh, China, Egypt, Georgia, Hong Kong, India, Iran, Jordan, Kazakhstan, the Republic of Korea, Malaysia, Mongolia, Morocco, Oman, Pakistan, the Palestinian Territory, Qatar, the Russian Federation, Saudi Arabia, Serbia, Singapore, Sri Lanka, the Syrian Arab Republic, Taiwan, Thailand, Tunisia, Ukraine, the United Arab Emirates, and Yemen (ICANN 2016).
2. Internet World Stats (2013) estimates that, by the end of 2011, Chinese languages were nearly at parity with English online and that Arabic, Chinese, and Russian each demonstrated four-digit growth in their appearance on the web between 2000 and 2011.
3. English's ubiquity in the web's and the Internet's software and hardware layers closely resembles what Luke, Luke, and Graham (2007) observe about English's ubiquity in other international technocratic domains, such as finance and law.
4. I am grateful for Laurel Baeder's detail-oriented assistance and to the University of Utah's Undergraduate Research Opportunities Program for funding her work.

PART IV

Public Writing Economies

15

HABERMASOCHISM

The Promise of Cyberpublics in an Information Economy

Donna LeCourt

This chapter emerges out of what seems to me an odd gap in the scholarship around the public sphere in our field: a failure to attend to the role of the Internet. Despite claims of the "public turn," most theories of the public make little mention of the Internet as a viable public sphere (e.g., Rivers and Weber 2011; Weisser 2002; Welch 1997; Wells 1996). On the other hand, the public seems to function as a "given" in much digital scholarship, where more attention is given to the process of composing than to its distribution and circulation (see Trimbur 2000). The idea of the *public sphere* (i.e., the potential for the text to initiate discussion, interaction, and collective action) is less emphasized; even when the public is considered, as in Dubisar and Palmeri's (2010, 89) compelling piece on students producing political remix videos, the Internet is seen as a "significant vehicle for *delivering arguments*" (italics added) with little consideration of the kind of interaction one seeks to initiate with others. While there are exceptions (e.g., Jackson and Wallin 2009; M. Johnson 2008), most digital models of public action adopt more of a "prosumer" model, locating political action in how the consumer of media becomes a producer. Prosumers are imagined to engage in "semiotic guerrilla warfare" in which writers intervene by offering up new multimodal texts that disrupt mass-market ones by "directly changing the semiotic fabric itself" (Sheridan, Ridolfo, and Michel 2005, 827). Despite the desire for political action in such prosumer models, the public is positioned primarily as a venue for distribution and the audience reduced to a consumer, albeit of alternative meanings. In sum, despite the Internet's potential to encourage participatory interactions in public space within various publics and

DOI: 10.7330/9781607325239.c015

counterpublics, that potential has largely remained unexplored (Ede and Lunsford 2009, 43).

I find this gap between the potential of digital public spheres and its treatment in our public sphere theories and digital pedagogies troubling as someone deeply invested in seeking out places where we can imagine a role for citizens as actors with agency in discursive arenas. Troubling, but understandable. Given our initial techno-utopic hopes for global public spheres and collective action in the early 1990s, a certain amount of skepticism seems in order. So many of those early hopes were dashed as we quickly realized that power inequities offline reproduced themselves online—that factors like race, class, and gender were not going to disappear. As the Internet grew more commercial, many abandoned the idea of public spheres, seeing the net taken over by economic exchange. Concerns about commercialization, advertising, and the ownership of new media have been particularly prominent in communication studies, leading some to reject the Internet as a potential public sphere because it fails to separate citizenship from consumer culture, understood by these scholars as a basic Habermasian requirement for public spheres. (See Goode 2005, 107–8; Papacharissi 2013, 123–25). Some communication scholars interested in the public sphere, as a result, turned their attention to the local, the use of civic space by local governments, nonprofits, and NGOs (e.g., Bohman 2004; Notaro 2006). The hope of the average citizen engaging in multiple public spheres and taking action gave way to a fear that the web was mainly used to purchase things and that user-generated content only encouraged individuals to deepen their original opinions by finding other like-minded people in enclaved discourse (Sunstein 2007) or to turn their attention to social interactions rather than civic ones in an "expressive-cultural" sphere rather than a "deliberative-civic" one (e.g., Goode and McKee 2013; Roberts-Miller 2004). Those who did not give in to such limited uses, including many in digital composition, turned instead to the Internet's potential for publication and thus equated social action with the circulation of individual voices.

Although I can certainly argue that there is more going on in cyberspace, my goal in this chapter is to explore each side of this debate: that public spheres are impossible within information capital or that social action is limited to offering venues for individual voices/texts to circulate widely. I suggest that the "problem of digital public spheres" may not lie so much with the information economy as with our own sense of agency, or lack thereof, within it. Indeed, rather than seeing the information economy as a detriment to the development of digital public spheres, I suggest that our potential civic agency may lie not simply with opinion formation or disruption but with a more direct influence on markets through the very means by which many see our agency reduced: the immaterial labor and information we provide as fodder for this economy through our digital production.

ECONOMY AND COMMODITY IN PUBLIC SPHERES: A TURN TO HABERMAS

I am certainly not the first in our field to ask whether the Internet can function as a public sphere. I suspect that part of the reason we have not furthered this line of inquiry is that we have too faithfully sought out deliberative models based in a Habermasian concept of critical-rational debate (e.g., Barton 2005; Jackson and Wallin 2009; Roberts-Miller 2004; Rodman 2003; I. Ward 1997) as have many in communications who similarly focus on deliberative reciprocity and role-taking as necessary, following Jürgen Habermas, for public spheres (e.g., Dahlberg 2001; Goode and McKee 2013; Poster 1995). In contrast, I find Habermas much more interesting for his insights into how particular cultural-historical-economic *conditions* can foster the emergence of public spheres. Habermas is, admittedly, a problematic touchstone given the binary he creates between private and public, the presumption of equality among all reasonable beings, and the problematic focus on a single public sphere. Yet his analysis of the historical conditions that led to an active public sphere in the long eighteenth century is worth reexamining for what it may reveal about the digital age. For my purposes here, then, I table these critiques and turn my attention to two of his central insights about the preconditions for public spheres—the circulation of information and the centrality of the bourgeois class—to examine what they might offer for an analysis of the Internet's potential for fostering new public spheres. I focus on these concepts for two reasons. First, they align well with the debate with which I began in that the circulation of voice associates well with Habermas's claims about information. Second, the centrality of the bourgeoisie as actors with influence over the state connects to questions of our potential agency within an information economy. More important, given that these two points speak directly to the relations between citizen discourse and the economy necessary for public spheres, they also provide the basis for considering the distinctiveness of the digital age and the potential that might lie within it.

The proliferation of multiple information sources, Habermas (1962) claims, was a necessary precursor to a public sphere. Whereas information had previously been controlled by the monarchy, with early capitalist long-distance trade, beginning in the late sixteenth century, "the traffic in commodities and news" became possible (15). Traffic in trade required traffic in news and mail necessary for exchanging market and credit information. Habermas links such developments to the emergence of the modern nation-state, as private financing of the monarch could not keep up with demand, and local markets expanded such that local regulation was insufficient. A more centralized authority and system of taxation helped locate authority in the state, and a tax-based system developed to meet that state's demand for capital. These changes also expanded the need for news and information:

> Commercial news reporting was therefore subject to the laws of the same market to whose rise it owed its existence in the first place. It is no accident that printed journals often developed out of the same business correspondence that already handled hand-written newsletters. Each item of information contained in it had its price; it was therefore natural to increase the profits by selling to more people. (21)

Notice that information is not unaffected by market forces; rather, it is a commodity. The spread of information was both necessary to and part of the market.

News and information, along with literature, became the subject of the public sphere as "the private people for whom the cultural product became available as a commodity profaned it inasmuch as they had to determine its meaning on their own (by way of rational communication with each other), verbalize it, and thus state explicitly what precisely in its implicitness for so long could assert its authority" (37). Information flow, in this way, was necessary to develop a public sphere, but information existed apart from the state:

> In this stratum, which more than any other was affected and called upon by mercantilist policies, the state authorities evoked a resonance leading the publicum, the abstract counterpart of public authority, into an awareness of itself as the latter's opponent, that is, as the public of the now emerging public sphere of civil society. For the latter developed to the extent to which the public concern regarding the private sphere of civil society was no longer confined to the authorities but was considered by the subjects as one that was properly theirs. (23)

The public sphere Habermas locates in the eighteenth century was also intimately connected to the rise of the bourgeois class as the local burghers were replaced by emerging companies tied to the state for broader trade both within and between nation-states. Such connections also forced the need for information to spread to this class, who now saw themselves as needing to monitor the state and their own capital interests.

Literary discussions in coffee houses and salons took on a decidedly political turn as the aristocracy mixed with business owners, craftsmen, and shopkeepers (Habermas 1962, 33). The nature of discussion changed when those engaging in dialogue saw themselves as both impacted by and impacting the health of the state through their commerce. In Habermas's terms, "As soon as privatized individuals in their capacity as human beings ceased to communicate merely about their subjectivity but rather in their capacity as property-owners desired to influence public power in their common interest, the humanity of the literary public sphere served to increase the effectiveness of the public sphere in the political realm" (56). The bourgeoisie, in short, required information to conduct business but also desired information to protect their interests from the state. As a result, the public sphere of the eighteenth century relied heavily on the emergence of the bourgeoisie, a class of people capable of influencing the state in that their productivity and capital were now necessary to its functioning. Information alone does not create a public sphere; the active public spheres in Habermas's analysis require, first, the use of that information in ways that serve those now constituting "the public" and, second, a public with enough economic clout to influence the state. In such a scenario, neither information nor participants exist outside of relations of capital. Information is a commodity, and the influence of the public is constructed in economic terms.

If information flow is a defining feature of the possibility for public spheres, then the web certainly meets this criterion, albeit in very different market terms. Yet the influence the bourgeoisie wielded seems noticeably absent. What I'd like to suggest in the rest of this essay is that if we situate both these questions—the nature of information and the citizenry's ability to influence matters of public concern—within an information economy, then we see that, while information obviously functions differently than it did in the eighteenth century, it does so in ways that possibly lend more influence to the public than in recent history. Information in Web 2.0, I argue, may well be a commodity, but it is not necessarily commodified. That is, user-generated content may accrue surplus value for corporations who exploit that labor, but this very form of exploitation points to a kind of influence in the economy and government that's rarely acknowledged.

THE PROLIFERATION OF INFORMATION: CITIZEN VOICE OR HABERMASOCHISM?

Within an information economy, the proliferation of information is admittedly a proliferation of capital. But it also indicates a multiplicity of information sources, interpretations, and opinions that parallels the Habermasian salons of the eighteenth century. The expanding number of blogs, social networking sites (SNS), Indymedia sites, YouTube videos, Twitter feeds, and electronic publications certainly brings us back to a public where, in Habermas's terms, "the private people for whom the cultural product became available as a commodity profaned it inasmuch as they had to determine its meaning on their own" (Habermas 1962, 37). In fact, communication scholar Luke Goode (2005) finds this self-reflexivity via new media to offer Habermasian hope for digital public spheres. But perhaps the greatest similarity to Habermasian information flows lies in how mass media sources have lost some of their corporate control, as more and more news stories are "breaking" on the net first. However, the sheer volume of information, no matter who produces it, does not ensure emerging public spheres, as those who locate the hope of public spheres in democratic voice posit. Despite disagreements over whether the quality of information or online deliberative exchanges justifies calling the Internet a Habermasian public sphere, communication and political science research clearly shows that "greater access to information and communication channels does not ensure increases in civic engagement" (Papacharissi 2013, 121; see also Dahlgren 2005).

While a vibrant flow of information may be a prerequisite of emerging public spheres, it cannot be equated with them. Access to information just as often becomes a substitute for dialogue and collective action when we take consumption or circulation to be communicative action. Cultural theorist David Golumbia, in a June 24, 2009, post to the *Harvard University Press Blog*, usefully comments on this kind of information misunderstood as action in reference to the Iranian protests in 2009, during which Westerners watched the protests, leaked through YouTube and twitter feeds as US commenters lauded the way the Internet allowed the protesters to gain a much larger audience. What, Golumbia rightly asks, was the result of more information for the protesters soon arrested and silenced? Not much:

> At the very least, the failure of the Iranian revolution shows that the thesis that "network openness" leads automatically or directly to democracy is false—we have plenty of network openness, we keep celebrating it, and yet all we saw in practice was a near-revolution very similar to hundreds we have seen in the past.

We may feel as if we have acted because we are better informed, but we merely watched the protests with no visible result. Consumption masqueraded as action. The WikiLeaks controversy even more clearly illustrates the failure of information to incite action. Julian Assange, founder of WikiLeaks, has said many times that what has disturbed him the most about the controversy over the leaked documents is that they elicited so little reaction from the public. As political scientist Alasdair Roberts (2011) explains,

> WikiLeaks is predicated on the assumption that the social order—the set of structures that channel and legitimize power—is both deceptive and brittle: deceptive in the sense that most people who observe the social order are unaware of the ways in which power is actually used, and brittle in the sense that it is at risk of collapse once people are shown the true nature of things. The primary goal, therefore, is revelation of the truth.

Such presumptions assume that publics emerge only when a "secret" is revealed, basing the emergence of publics on the revelation of information alone. Yet information as a panacea for social inaction only works when the public believes the truth is being withheld, not a likely scenario in the self-reflexive, skeptical mediaverse of the twenty-first century.

To presume that information is all a public sphere needs is to engage in what political theorist Jodi Dean (2002) calls "Habermasochism," from which my title is drawn. For Dean, the assumption that the "secret" must be revealed before public spheres can emerge is precisely what keeps public spheres from emerging in the digital age. Following Habermas, Dean locates the concept in the relocation of sovereign power that was supported by secrecy to the deliberative decision making of supposedly autonomous, rational subjects. Our inherited concept of public spheres, she posits, is precisely what keeps the public from being able to intervene effectively in public affairs. The ideology of the secret is what keeps the information economy (what she terms "communicative capital") operating so well. We produce more and more information under the belief that we are acting in our own best interests. The myth of the secret—the idea that we need only to expose to others the information, analysis, or opinion they have not yet accessed—undergirds what I have been calling the *circulation-of-voice* perspective on digital publics. From Golumbia's and Dean's perspectives, however, this position misrecognizes circulation as democratic action with disastrous results as it fuels the information economy and prevents citizens from seeking other approaches to action.

This is what I find to be the great insight of Dean's analysis: how the desire for democracy and the public sphere actually subjects us to the insidiousness of communicative capital. The promise of the public sphere, as Dean (2002) explains, continues to have great currency. All it needs, seemingly, is more information, more access, more knowledge: in short, more publicity. It becomes a fantasy, "the empty signifier of desire" for democracy. Within this symbolic field, the secret "marks the constitutive limit of the public, a limit that the public sphere cannot acknowledge. . . . How do we know when we have enough information, when the ultimate secret has been revealed? We don't. We can't—the secret is a matter of form, not content, so it can never fully or finally be revealed" (42). Instead, we keep searching for information that will ultimately speak to a collective truth, to a critical judgment that can provide the basis for action. In this continual search, the activity of knowing substitutes for action; we search for and/or produce that one piece of information that will lead to action, never finding it, and thus never interacting with each other in our continual search for the secret. Participation with others is forestalled by the search. In Dean's (2002, 119) formulation, the "economies of drive and desire . . . explain why communicative reflection provides not a mode of democratic freedom but a more insidious basis for global capitalism. . . . Communicative capitalism, we might say, relies on publicity without publics." In this light, relying overly much on information as the key element of public spheres reinforces relations of capital. By producing what we hope is action as communication, we just power the information economy, circulating yet more content by which our labor can be converted to exchange value for others. In such a scenario, even production or prosumer action fails as "messages are contributions to circulating content—not actions to elicit responses" (Dean 2008, 107).

Information is no more "free" from the commodity relation on the web than it was in the eighteenth century, a point that democratic-voice perspectives often overlook. While users generating content may not be seeking monetary reward, such content nevertheless participates in the information economy. User-generated content contributes to what marketers refer to as *data*, the currency of the web. In an age of what economist Phil Graham (2006) has called "hypercapitalism," the knowledge economy has dematerialized many areas of material and social experience into data. As Graham writes, "More abstract forms of value have become dominant sources of commodities. These trends rely on new media, and are defining features of hypercapitalism, a political economic system in which products of the most intimate aspects of human activity can be technologized, alienated, and sold as commodities" (ix). Data become the raw material of the information economy, much like natural resources were the raw material of an industrial economy. Calling data the collective commodity of the information economy is more than a metaphor; according to an article by Steve Lohr in the *New York Times* on February 11, 2012, a report by the forum Big Data, Big Impact declared data "a new class of economic asset, like currency or gold." Yet in this new economy, unlike that of the eighteenth century, the consumer is also producing the commodity rather than simply purchasing it. In this way, value is extracted from our immaterial labor. Vincent R. Manzerolle and Atle Mikkola Kjøsen perhaps present this reading most succinctly: "Social networks . . . leverage the social work of users to subsume them, turning them into a means of piggybacking the circulatory requirements of capital onto the social relationships . . . of communicating subjects" (Manzerolle and Kjøsen 2012, 224).

This understanding of capital is quite different from the commercialization concerns in communication studies modeled on older versions of capital accumulation in its focus on advertising and ownership of media. Communicative capital looks, instead, at how information itself undergirds the economy—that is, how information becomes the raw material that gains surplus value through distribution networks beyond its production, implicating the multiplicity of information sources central to public spheres within the capitalist cycle of production, distribution, and consumption and the corresponding cycles of circulation, exchange, and value. How this occurs is probably nowhere more evident than in data mining of the web conducted by marketers. Techniques of what is called *dataveillence,* a term coined in 1994 by computer scientist Roger Clarke for "the systematic use of personal data systems in the investigating and monitoring of the actions or communications of one or more persons" (quoted in Elmer 2004, 74), have expanded exponentially with Web 2.0 to support the need to cater to the individual consumer rather than a mass market (54). Some of these data are collected directly through the information we all use to register for various Web 2.0 platforms, but more often, marketers purchase such data from these very platforms, which now own our information under the frequently hidden terms we accede to when registering. The point is not simply to track certain data points but to track interactions, conversations, and relationships: in other words, content and meaning. Bill Tancer (2008, 50), general manager of the global Internet research company Hitwise, writes that "as the Internet moves from a vast group of static pages we did little but read, to an environment where users are posting volumes of data about their personal lives, I have an ever-growing, rich database from which to understand our society, or more specifically, what people are thinking about collectively at any given moment." More than simply information, our user-generated content is selling our thoughts and relationships as well as our data. Christian Fuchs (2010, 191) perhaps summarizes this point best, explaining that the market share of companies like Facebook can only be explained by a new commodity relation wherein the users don't buy products; rather, "the users themselves are sold as a commodity."

When we produce what we hope is communicative action within such an economy, we are, in Dean's (2008, 104–5) terms, simply acceding to the ideologies and material needs of that economy, circulating yet more content by which our labor can be converted to exchange value for others. As a result, the potential for action is undercut as "changing the system . . . seems to require strengthening the system." It is this sense that all content is ultimately commodified that leads others to reject any possibility for digital public spheres in an information economy that partially operates on the backs of the surplus labor of average users.

THE PROMISE OF DIGITAL PUBLIC SPHERES

Where Dean's argument goes awry is in the assumption that recognizing information as a commodity automatically means it is commodified, that user-generated content has no value beyond its exchange. Failing to distinguish between commodity and commodification is the chief mistake, in my view, of those who reject the possibility of digital public spheres by pointing to the Internet as overly embedded in capital relations. To understand information as a commodity does speak to its implication in exchange and labor, but its status as a commodity need not undercut the potential use-values such content has for the producer. Use and exchange cohere in any commodity. Citizens, as the democratic-voice arguments accurately assume, also receive benefits from sharing this information; otherwise, the economy would not work. In his analysis of Facebook, Eran Fisher (2012, 179), drawing on the work of Jodi Dean (2010), demonstrates this point, arguing that, while social networking sites are more exploitative of labor than mass media, they actually produce less alienation through their participatory functions and social uses: "In order for Facebook to exploit the work of its users, it must contribute to the de-alienation of their users, propagating the ideology that de-alienation can in fact (and solely) be achieved by communicating and socializing on SNS, an ideology of communication, networking, and self-expression. . ." There must be a *use-value* to our immaterial labor; if what we produce were only fodder for an information economy, there would be no motivation to produce it as unpaid labor.

To understand our potential agency in this economy, it is helpful to distinguish between information and knowledge. What I have been calling *information* here is not the conversion of data into knowledge. The exchange relation in which others extract from our data information that can be made meaningful in a specific context powers the knowledge economy. Graham (2006, 4) locates a knowledge economy, for example, in the production of certain kinds of expertise, "a political acknowledgement that certain classes of meaning are privileged; that access to these meanings is restricted; and that meanings can in fact be owned and exchanged, if not entirely consumed." An information economy, however, puts the focus on data, on how the information we so freely produce drives part of the economy through which others derive profit. Information, then, is what we produce that is then converted into data to be sold. Data emerges as a commodity purchased by others who convert it into knowledge, thus commodifying it beyond its original purposes by rematerializing it within a new context of exchange. In short, data is not in itself commodified; it is "mined" through the process of dataveillance to produce the commodity.

Acknowledging the difference between information and knowledge economies does little to reduce exploitation; web writers are not sharing in the surplus value their information, as data, generates. But this is also not the classic definition of alienated labor, as one's labor does not negate the use-value one attains through Web 2.0 interfaces even if others take up its exchange value. Use and exchange both exist in the commodity, but seemingly in separate spheres in which one group sees production as primarily use (and thus are less alienated) and the others as primarily exchange. In Graham's (2006, x) terms, "Any knowledge economy based on the logic of capitalist commodity production must involve specific forms of labor the products of which can be owned separately from the people that produce them." Labor, in this view, is still exploited, but separating use and exchange in this way also points to the flexibility of data. It need not only be processed to produce the commodity; as data, it is not yet commodified. There are multiple potential use-values for the writer, including interacting with the information produced in favor of social action and forming multiple publics. The fact that others can extract exchange value from those materials, can commodify that knowledge, does not mean the data itself is commodified or only seen in terms of its exchange value. This point is what Jodi Dean misses; the economy may run on information, but that does not mean information's only use is economic. Just as the profit motive drove the production and circulation of information in Habermas's analysis, the information economy benefits from user-generated production, but this does not mean the product is reducible to its exchange value; it is not already commodified.

If the knowledge economy is located in the manipulation of data into socially useful (or economically valuable) knowledge, then it is also a relation in which we can play a role. How we circulate that information, use it collectively with others, and leverage it to form collectivities may produce another exchange relation. If all people are producers of information (data), then all "are potential producers of knowledge commodities, that is, creators of value in a knowledge economy" (Graham 2006, x). The commodity circulates freely (thus the surplus value others can accrue from it) and is open to a fluid set of uses, but only, I argue, if we see what we *do with information in our activity with others* as part of the function of the Internet rather than imagining our role as only producers and consumers of information. Publishing alone does not equate with social action; it simply plays into the cycle of production from which the information economy can manipulate its value into exchange. But circuits of distribution and circulation can also be applied to the commodity whose goal is the sharing of expertise for socially progressive goals, for the basis of collective action, for the more traditional goals of the public sphere.

Ironically, dataveillance and other forms of information collection may also be where we can locate our influence and agency in relation to the market and the state. Information mining suggests citizens have economic influence that, while not equivalent to that of the bourgeoisie, can give us more power than we recognize. While analyses of how surplus value and exchange value benefit all but the producer are certainly accurate in a strict economic sense, there is also a form of power here. As the raw material of the information economy, the average user does have control over what kind of content is produced. If market forces follow that content, as dataveillance suggests, then it also suggests that our content matters. And it matters not just to marketers but to the mass media outlets that track content just as assiduously for different purposes, such as for political campaigns seeking to take the measure of the electorate, and the varied uses to which dataveillance can be put. Much like coal can't be made into bread, no matter the labor and conversions applied to it, not all content produced need only serve the interests of capital accumulation. If information is the conductor of the new economy train, then it suggests a quite powerful role for producers as more than just potential consumers of content and marketing tactics. Although this is not the same kind of influence the bourgeoisie had as leaders of industry, it does suggest an economic role that can be leveraged toward more effective public spheres.

CONCLUSION

A certain exhaustion inheres in claims that the web's role in economic relations means citizens cannot be influential and use it toward civic ends. Even in the "ideal" moment of the eighteenth century, public spheres emerged precisely because of economic change. There is no reason to assume such is not possible in an information economy unless we continue to believe that acting as a public simply means consuming and producing information without the necessary interaction and building of coalitions upon which social action relies. The information economy does not necessarily exclude the possibility of digital public spheres; in fact, this economy may be what can help writer-citizens achieve influence. But if we see our only function as providing information, then we do fall prey to Dean's communicative capital, to equating information production with action in ways that forestall other democratic uses. Value is not necessarily in the information itself; it is in the use to which we put that information—how it is circulated, engaged, taken up, responded to—that matters. When we see information equating with action, we open up our content to nothing other than the commodity relation. We need, instead, to imagine the function of our user-generated content and interactions on the web differently: we are not seeking the truth but seeking to alter it, to alter the world around us. But we can't do it alone by circulating one more message we hope others will read or only by being "better informed." Information capital need not be the death knell of public spheres any more than information as commodity was for the eighteenth century; it is in the circulation and use of that commodity that writer-citizens can intervene and that the potential for public spheres may be located.

16

TIERRA CONTAMINADA

Economies of Writing and Contaminated Ground

Jason Peters

Everyone feels stuck. That's the dominant impression I'm left with after talking with Amelia, a community activist and founder of the Rhode Island Environmental Justice League, about a local controversy in Providence. In 2005, the city had tried to build a public high school on an urban brownfield site without seeking the proper environmental permits. The RI Department of Environmental Management sued the city (D. Fisher 2010). The situation is complex because it involves multiple layers of history, economics, politics, and the lived experiences of area residents in a multilingual neighborhood. Many residents' properties abut the brownfield, their backyards marked off with chain-link fencing and bilingual signs warning of contaminated ground. Frustrations have run so high that some believe the delay in remediating the site is deliberate. They accuse lawmakers and corporate executives of a conspiracy of silence motivated by racism. My conversation with Amelia fades into a thoughtful silence for a moment, and I wonder if she's wondering whether there is some truth to the accusations. Finally, she says, "Everybody wants the land to be cleaned up. It's not like the politicians are trying to be evil" (A. Rose, pers. comm.).

Since 2011, I've been peripherally involved in the environmental remediation efforts at this site, popularly known as Mashapaug Pond. I've attended stakeholder meetings, visited residents' houses, participated in community arts-education workshops, served on planning committees, and helped to organize events. I've analyzed dozens of scientific documents and transcripts of meetings collected by Rhode Island's Department of Environmental Management, and I've interviewed some of the leading activists on the issue. Through this work, I've come to identify a sedimented set of economic and rhetorical patterns—an

DOI: 10.7330/9781607325239.c016

economy of writing—that operates at this site. This economy consists of the production and circulation of knowledge in the form of texts and social scripts that, taken together, have profound implications for the identity construction and discursive maneuvering of individuals variously labeled *stakeholders, residents, experts, politicians, consultants, property owners,* and *neighbors.* In this chapter, I'll first trace some of these sedimented economic and rhetorical patterns. Then, through a close analysis of two public hearings concerning the contested high-school construction project, I'll examine how these economic and rhetorical patterns cohere in an economy of writing. Finally, I'll propose that translation is the means through which environmental activism can make (and in fact already is making) a critical intervention into this economy; translation can be seen as a kind of currency exchange that makes different kinds of work possible.

ECONOMIC PATTERNS: MASHAPAUG POND AND ECONOMIC DEVELOPMENT

Mashapaug Pond, a small, urban freshwater pond in the center of a mixed-use neighborhood, is on the state's "impaired-waters" list, meaning it's not safe for human recreation. Its eastern cove and a large swathe of adjoining land is an EPA-designated brownfield site. A brownfield is defined by the 2002 Small Business Liability Relief and Brownfields Revitalization Act as "real property, the expansion, redevelopment, or reuse of which may be complicated by the presence or potential presence of a hazardous substance, pollutant, or contaminant" (US Environmental Protection Agency 2011). The pond waters suffer from large blooms of toxic blue-green algae, low levels of oxygen for supporting plants and other aquatic life, and the presence of dioxin, a highly toxic industrial by-product. The groundwater contains a large shifting plume of perchloroethylene (PCE), the vapors of which emanate from the soil in potentially toxic concentrations. The surrounding soil also contains high levels of heavy metals such as copper and lead.

Four economic developments have led to these conditions. The first was the nineteenth-century construction of Providence's municipal water infrastructure, a complicated set of underground channels called a *combined sewage overflow* (CSO) system. CSOs are common in older, industrialized cities in the United States. They work by draining the flow of raw sewage and the flow of rainwater through separate channels; however, when rainfall exceeds one-half inch, the storm runoff overflows the system, combining sewage with rainwater, which in effect dumps raw sewage into the watershed's rivers and ponds. The Narragansett Bay Commission, an NGO formed to address the water quality of the state's bay, has spearheaded the development of a decades-long $342 million project to replace the outdated CSOs, which are partially responsible for the "impaired" status of the pond's waters.

The second development was the establishment and operation of the Gorham Manufacturing Company on the eastern cove of the pond from 1890 to 1987. For many years, Gorham was one of the largest sterling-silver manufacturers in the world. Chemical waste from the industrial processing of silver still contaminates the soil and groundwater. Gorham's operations are largely responsible for the presence of dioxin in the water, the groundwater plume, and the heavy metals in the soil. In 1987, Gorham was bought by Textron, the industrial conglomerate and Fortune 500 company, and the factory was closed. Shortly afterward, a number of sealed 55-gallon drums of industrial solvent were discovered and excavated from the bottom of the pond. Textron is now officially responsible for funding the environmental remediation of the Gorham-related contamination, though the land itself has been parceled out to developers, one of which is the City of Providence.

The third major development was the 1960 construction of the Huntington Expressway, Rhode Island State Highway 10, which disrupted the flow of natural underground channels that connect the pond to the larger Pawtuxet River watershed (Office of Water Resources 2007). Left to their own devices, these groundwater channels would continuously flush the pond with fresh water following rainstorms. Their disruption has created a kind of clogging and sedimenting effect. Following rainstorms, contaminants like lawn fertilizer and sewage now collect in the pond and stay there, feeding the algae blooms and depleting oxygen levels. The fourth development was the construction in the 1960s of the Huntington Industrial Park on the pond's western side. The industrial park covers most of the surrounding soil with impervious surface—the asphalt of the parking lots and the roofs of the buildings—which impedes the soil's natural ability to filter various chemicals out of the water. Now storm water from the parking lots and roofs drains directly into the city's CSOs.

From this discussion, we can see that the economic patterns present at this site have literally been etched into the landscape. These patterns have so affected the land that the pond watershed no longer follows the topography of the area, the way land would naturally shed water, from the highest geographical points down to the lowest. Instead, the watershed has shifted westward, following the drainage patterns of the built environment. Although there are multiple sources of contamination, and although they are interrelated, I focus in this chapter only on the Gorham brownfield because that is where, in 2005, the City of Providence illegally broke ground on the construction of the Jorge Alvarez High School. The DEM lawsuit forced the city to stop construction, conduct a site investigation, and draft a remediation plan. This incident set in motion a highly contentious series of interactions and confrontations among city and state agencies, the residents of the area, and the general public, which taken together throw a stark light on the economy of writing that operates on such contaminated ground.

RHETORICAL PATTERNS: ENVIRONMENTAL COMMUNICATION AND PUBLIC HEARINGS

By 2007, the city had obtained the necessary clearances and Jorge Alvarez High School opened on the brownfield, outfitted with a subslab ventilation system that removed soil vapor from beneath the building and monitored air quality within the building itself. As part of the remediation process, two state-mandated public hearings were held in 2005 to discuss the "technical adequacy" of the city's six-month assessment of the site and the "technical feasibility" of the remediation and construction plans (Providence Redevelopment Agency 2005). Transcripts from these hearings reveal a tension between the terms *public* and *technical*. In fact, the hearings constitute a contact point for two different discourses embodied by those terms. Each discourse valorizes different forms of reason, produces different knowledges from the same material circumstances, and has different techniques for authorizing and reifying those knowledges.

One discourse valorizes the procedures of technical reason over social reason; it authorizes itself through what Jeanne Gunner (2012, 627), citing Bruce Horner (2007), describes as "professionalization," the accumulation of credentials and the acquisition of specializations and narrowly defined expertise; and it is reified, in the form of written documents, as legal procedure and technical knowledge. The other discourse valorizes the procedures of social reason over technical reason; it authorizes itself through what Jennifer Peeples and Kevin DeLuca call "body knowledge"—the emotional and physiological experience of personally living at or near a brownfield site; and it is reified, in the form of social scripts, as cultural practice (Peeples and DeLuca 2006, 76). It is important to note that these discourses do not neatly correspond to the social roles of expert and public at public hearings. That is to say, members of the public may deploy the rhetorical strategies of technical reason, while an environmental scientist may enact one of the social scripts produced by social reason. The discourses are simultaneous, overlapping, and they circulate to varying degrees through the language practices of all of the public-hearing participants.

Two specific rhetorical patterns emerge from the interaction of these discourses at public hearings. One concerns the problematic location of authority as a function of the writing practices supporting technical reason. Though the public hearing is ostensibly mandated to give members of the public an opportunity to occupy the role of rhetorical agent on environmental issues that potentially impact them, that rhetorical agency is represented in the form of written documents—transcripts of hearings, environmental impact statements, and legally mandated agency responses—all of which are designed by and circulated among governmental and technical experts. Thus, the public hearing itself becomes a stage in the writing practices that support technical reason, and discursive authority over the hearing itself is invested in the agencies that organize and manage the public comments in written form.

The technical management of public comment leads to a valuation of individual comments as either normal or aberrant, rational or irrational, according to the criteria of technical reason. In their study of emotion in environmental discourse, Killingsworth and Palmer (1995, 2) note how the label of *hysteria* has been applied to emotional discourse that falls outside the norms of technical reason. However, the hysterical response is often a calling to attention of parts of technological practice that technical reason itself turns away from, those "shortcomings or 'side effects' of technological practice" (3). Thus, "hysterical" responses to environmental degradation "seem irrational" because "rational public discourse" is defined by inattention to the side effects of technological practice, except as those side effects provide further opportunity for rational, technological response (3).

Katz and Miller (1996, 123) have described the control exerted over public participation through such technical management of public comment, in which technical expertise "set[s] the agenda" of the hearing and decides when the public [speaks] and when they just [listen]." The public is asked to speak, but technical expertise is empowered to shape the rhetorical situation and to authorize which public comments merit written responses. This technical management is evident in the city's initial notice announcing the meetings, which narrowly sets the terms for the hearing and limits public comment to a discussion of "the technical feasibility of the proposed remedial alternative" (Providence Redevelopment Agency 2005). A second notice emphasizes that, in accordance with state law, "the legal purpose of public comment is to allow input on the 'technical feasibility' of the proposed remedial alternative" (Providence Redevelopment Agency 2005).

The second rhetorical pattern concerns what Nelta Edwards (2002, 109) calls a "familiar story line" in environmental rhetoric, and what I call a *script of suspicion*, a particular set of actions and attitudes produced by social reason in response to its interactions with technical reason. Thomas Farrell and Thomas Goodnight's account of the communication practices at Three Mile Island provide a dramatic example of the conditions in which this script is activated (Farrell and Goodnight 1981). At Three Mile Island, misrepresentations, misunderstandings, and silences pervaded official communications with the public. "Some representatives of the nuclear power industry," they write, "made misleading statements. Still others did not speak at all. The people of Middletown and Londonderry did not know whom to believe. Many simply fled. . . . No one understood all that was going on" (273). As we'll see, the script of suspicion operates in this context, actively seeking to fill in gaps in communication by interpreting silences and attempting to reconcile conflicting reports through the procedures of social reason.

The script of suspicion can also develop when scientific analyses run counter to community belief or when technical knowledge fails to corroborate body knowledge. Edwards (2002, 109) says that from the point of view of residents in contaminated communities, scientific "studies often 'prove' that there is no environmental problem. However, people in the local community still believe that their health is being affected and may believe that the agencies that are supposed to protect and aid them fail to do so." The script is characterized by a distrust of scientific studies whose conclusions or recommendations seem instead to support government and corporate interests. Stuart Blythe, Jeffrey, Grabill, and Kirk Riley note that "some citizens assume that government reports represent bogus science designed to convince citizens of the value of an agency's preferred solution" (Blythe, Grabill, and Riley 2008, 279). The script can take the form of spontaneous community resistance to policymaking, it can appear in the formulation of conspiracy theories, or it can take the form of citizens co-opting for themselves the procedures of technical reason and hiring independent consultants to either gather alternate data or to corroborate the data analyses published in official agency reports (Rhode Island Department of Environmental Management 2007).

In sum, the public hearing constrains social reason to fit the demands of technical reason and the discourses of development, what Farrell and

Goodnight (1981, 274) refer to as the "visions of the public" implied by "technical communicative discourse." At public hearings, those individuals who speak as members of the public unwittingly end up embodying two contradictory visions of the public implicit in the two discourses that circulate. One is of a "mythical" public, free to "exchange ideas and to influence policy on equal terms" with officials (McComas 2003, 165). The other is of a public that has allowed itself to be constituted by the processes of representative legislation and technocratic governance. In other words, this public represents social reason as invented by technical reason. This public has already consented to the superiority of technical reason to determine right action and has given itself over to technical reason as "the warrant and benefactor" (Farrell and Goodnight 1981, 272) of analyses only possible through the procedures of technical reason.

An examination of the transcripts from two public hearings held in 2005 reveals the way these rhetorical patterns operate at Mashapaug Pond. The hearings were held in response to a written report that detailed the environmental contaminants found at the proposed construction site for Alvarez High School. The circulation of the written report at the hearing, the various public and official responses to that circulation, and the very act of composing the hearing into a written transcript as part of the authorization of the redevelopment project highlight the way technical reason's problematic location of authority and the resulting activation of a social script of suspicion constitute an economy of writing at this site.

CASE STUDY OF AN ECONOMY OF WRITING

On October 5, 2005, Peter Grivers, an engineer contracted by the city to manage the site remediation, offers opening remarks. He says, "The purpose of tonight's meeting is to present the site investigation that was performed on the parcel piece of the former Gorham Manufacturing site. At this time we will accept verbal and written comments on the site investigation and the technical aspects of the proposed remedial action" (Providence Redevelopment Agency 2006, 17). Grivers opens the meeting by setting the agenda, defining what topics and forms of expression will constitute public interaction. However, these terms prove impossible for the audience to adhere to. The site investigation report is a highly technical document, and Grivers's presentation is not effectively designed to communicate its technical aspects in layman's terms. Plus, the meeting is conducted in English without an interpreter, which precludes the non-English-speaking residents of the neighborhood from participating. The result is a narrow authorization of public participation that erases differences of linguistic, cultural, and socioeconomic status at the same time that it inscribes a hierarchy that valorizes the technical over the bodily and experiential.

The impact of this authorization can be seen in the way the written report circulates at the hearing. For example, at one point Grivers attempts to explain what contaminants were found at the site:

> MR. GRIVERS: What I would like to point out is that we have identified chemicals or compounds if you will that consist of metals, total petroleum hydrocarbons, something called PAHs or polycyclic aromatic hydrocarbons and volatile organic compounds. Some of you may be wondering what that means. Well, total petroleum hydrocarbon, the TPH is just a general name for just what it says, petroleum hydrocarbon. (Providence Redevelopment Agency 2006, 24)

A member of the audience immediately interrupts this awkward attempt to describe TPH:

> MS. DIPRETE: Excuse me. Is this in the report? You're using technical terms and it's not in the report.
>
> MR. GRIVERS: The Site Investigation Reports are submitted to DEM. DEM has environmental experts that review these. Typically, they're not written for a level of understanding to the general public. I'm doing my best to explain it. We'll answer any questions that you have and we'll be happy to take those question [*sic*]. (25)

District Senator Juan Pichardo, who is also in the audience, then protests the terms of the meeting:

> SENATOR PICHARDO: Is this a real forum to inform the public? They're going to walk away from this hearing with no real information. Yes, [more information is] in the library, again, probably the technical part, but [this meeting could be] more on the level of where people could understand. (26)

At this point, Allan Sepe, acting director of public property for the City of Providence and one of the organizers of the hearing, intervenes in order to reassert the purpose of the meeting and the way in which audience participation will be managed:

> SEPE: The forum here is you do have questions, you can ask them. There's another meeting on the 19th. That would be answered. If you get [questions] now, from the 19th, your questions will be answered. (26)

The presentation returns to the prescribed format for a moment, only to be interrupted before Grivers has a chance to resume his attempted explanation of TPH. An unidentified speaker asks, "Do you have an interpreter, Spanish interpreter" (29)? After a short debate over whether the city has a legal obligation to provide a Spanish interpreter, Sepe interjects, "Why don't we get through the presentation. There will be another meeting. If we have to have another meeting after that, we will. Let's get through the presentation" (29).

Here we see a key difference in the way authority operates at this hearing compared to the way it is described in the literature on environmental rhetoric. Rather than exert control over public participation through management of the hearing, Grivers and Sepe respond to the challenges to their authority by dispersing it, at first between themselves and then ultimately by abdicating it to nobody in particular. At first, Grivers is presented as the authority on the Gorham site remediation. However, when his inability to appeal to audience members leads them to contest his authority, that authority transfers to Sepe, who asserts himself as the agent who sets the terms and manages the interactions among audience, speaker, and subject. In order to circumvent the obviously unresolvable tensions of this rhetorical situation, Sepe resorts to invoking a future rhetorical situation that will be more informative and effective—a second public hearing to be held on October 19. The result of this exchange is that authority at this meeting becomes unverifiable; it becomes impossible to identify the terms for negotiating the differences articulated, to identify whose agenda is being enacted through the erasure of difference, and for what purposes those differences are being erased.

The dispersal of authority leads the DEM and city representatives to interact with the audience in ways that seem to devalue the experiential knowledge of living at the site. Questions and criticisms voiced at the hearing meet with silence or deferral, what Toni Morrison calls a "stressed absence." Morrison (1989, 11) writes, "Certain absences are so stressed, so ornate, so planned, they call attention to themselves; arrest us with intentionality and purpose, like neighborhoods that are defined by the population held away from them." The silences in the public hearings become viewed as rhetorical strategies that control the terms of the meeting, the ways in which speaker, audience, and subject are allowed to interact with one another. The public senses the intentionality of these silences and activates a script of suspicion in response. They interpret silence as evidence of a hidden agenda, in part because they recognize that their own silence in public discourse is enforced on them as a way of erasing their very real concerns about living around the contaminated site.

Silence, then, circulates in these channels and accumulates symbolic value. For the expert with technical knowledge, silence is equated with a lack of authority to speak "beyond the margins of his or her own discipline" (Farrell and Goodnight 1981, 287). For the nonexpert with experiential knowledge, silence is equated with a strategic circumvention of the idealized democratic goals of public participation in municipal policymaking. This articulation of rhetorical silence as a conspiracy is a version of what Wayne Campbell Peck, Linda Flower, and Lorraine Higgins call "the literacy of social and cultural critique," which "openly addresses issues of power, defining social relationships in terms of ideological and economic struggle" (Peck, Flower, and Higgins 1995, 204). Amelia Rose's formation of the Environmental Justice League after 2005 was itself a rhetorical act that performed this kind of critique but in a way that legitimized the critique from the point of view of the technical expert so that it moved through the same channels as technical reason and government policymaking, affixing the same values to discursive silences (pers. comm.). An earlier environmental activist group, the Adelaide Avenue Environmental Coalition, practiced a more radical version of social critique, actively seeking to verify conspiracy theories by independently hiring engineering firms to double-check the site investigations of Providence's and Textron's engineers (Rhode Island Department of Environmental Management 2007).

I want to present two examples of these conspiracy theories in order to illustrate the depth of public concern over the meaning of the city's and the DEM's rhetorical silences. One theory held that two 15-thousand-gallon underground storage tanks filled with flammable naphthalene were buried on the former Gorham site. There were in fact two large buried tanks, but nobody knew their contents. In 1995, the DEM hired an engineering firm to investigate. They reported that the tanks were filled with water, that they had been connected to a sump pump in the basement of one of the Gorham buildings, and that their function was probably to provide an immediate water source in case of a fire (Rhode Island Department of Environmental Management 1995). The report includes the raw data of a number of tests for VOCs in the water of the tanks. Despite this thorough report, the naphthalene theory persisted for more than 12 years. The speculation was that the city did not want to pay to have the tanks removed and to test and remediate the site for naphthalene, which would further delay development of the land parcel, so the engineering firm was paid to fudge the data (Rhode Island Department of Environmental Management 2007). The Adelaide Avenue Environmental Coalition hired an independent engineering firm to replicate the tests in the report, writing to a senior engineer at the DEM that "the community is still of the belief that these two fifteen thousand gallon tanks were used at some time for storing Naphtha and/or other solvents. We are continuing to research this fact and are trying to verify this for future presentation" (Rhode Island Department of Environmental Management 2007, 5). These tests, however, yielded the same results as the DEM's.

At the October 19, 2005, public hearing, Stephanie Kennedy, a member of the audience, describes the hidden agenda she believes underlies the decision to build the high school in the first place. She compares the decision to a "story" she "read a long time ago" (Providence Redevelopment Agency 2006, 99) about a plantation owner named William Lynch who, Kennedy reports, devised a strategic plan for controlling slaves in the West Indies, and whose name was the source of the term *Lynch law.* According to *Wikipedia,* the Lynch story was a hoax, but it circulated on the Internet in the 1990s and was referenced by Louis Farrakhan in an open letter to the Million Man March in 2005 ("William Lynch Speech" 2011). In her public comments, Kennedy calls the high-school siting controversy a modern iteration of Lynch's "plan." She says, "Back then they did what they called lynching people out of a tree. That's what you're doing to us lynching us with chemicals. You don't have the noose around my neck because the noose is going to be in my nose and in my chest" (Providence Redevelopment Agency 2006, 99).

The paranoia and sensationalism of these theories threaten to distract us from a key insight: that these theories are linguistic products of a particular interaction of the discourses that give rise to them. The distortions in knowledge and information contained in them are part of the same economy of writing as the DEM site-investigation report. The conspiracy theories are among the discursive "side effects of technological practice" (Killingsworth and Palmer 1995, 3) in that they are produced by the same writing practices that produce the written documents that support technical reason: transcripts of public comments, site-investigation reports, and legally sanctioned environmental remediation and redevelopment plans. In addition to producing technical reason, these writing practices also produce irrationality and suspicion but locate these technological "side effects" among the aberrations and failures of social reason. These public comments are easily dismissed as ignorant or ill informed; but on the contrary, these are bodies speaking history, participating in a single economy of writing etched into the landscape that assigns differential values to different discursive roles and to the different knowledges capable of being produced by those roles. The effect is to privatize some knowledges as expert even as this economy divests itself of others labeled ignorant.

We need to recall that these scripts of suspicion are activated in response to the problematic location of authority between two discourses that have historically operated to construct a particular version of Mashapaug Pond as a place. The discourse of technical reason demands that expert knowledge remain silent when it lacks the authority to speak, while the discourse of social reason defines silence as strategy. The legal mechanism of the public hearing constitutes a rhetorical situation in which these competing discourses come into contact but provides no guidance on how to negotiate that contact. Further, the legal procedures for writing the public hearing require that the DEM and city representatives record the comments of the audience, publish a transcript, and draft and publish a response to selected comments. This displacement of the writing process from its original rhetorical situation leaves intact the hierarchies that valorize technical knowledge over experiential knowledge and valorize the technical expert's interpretations of silence. This displacement also leaves intact the interpretation of those silences as sinister, as the writing practices of technical reason cannot erase the experiential knowledge of participants even when that experience cannot be verified through technical procedures of knowledge formation.

ENVIRONMENTAL ACTIVISM AS INTERVENTION INTO ECONOMIES OF WRITING

The transcripts of the 2005 public hearings reveal intense public outrage percolating under the surface of the high-school siting controversy, outrage that extends past the controversy itself to an entire system of interaction between technical and social reason. The authority of city officials is so blatantly interrupted by the emotionally charged speech of the audience that it seems clear the issues being contested are neither the findings of the investigation report nor even the cleanup of the pond. The citizens who self-identify as members of the public, and who speak on behalf of the public, seem to want the pond never to have been contaminated in the first place, and if it were contaminated, they want not to have lived near it. They take advantage of state-mandated public participation in policymaking as an available forum for directly voicing these desires without representation—which is to say, with misrepresentation and misrecognition—as congressional constituents in a system that never seems to work in their favor.

Everybody knows this. The city officials, the engineers, and the directors of the DEM all know that public hearings don't work the way they were intended. But everybody is stuck. And the only promise for revamping the system seems to lie with the development of NGOs. In the case of Mashapaug Pond, the leading NGOs are the Environmental Justice League of Rhode Island (EJLRI) and the Urban Pond Procession (UPP), which have pursued a collaborative and decentralized engagement with citizens that is part political activism, part environmental science curriculum, part social advocacy, and part event planning. The success of these two organizations depends on a strong volunteer base and on their ability to secure grant funding, which requires that they frame their projects in such a way as to make development appear to be redevelopment when seeking support from their congressional representatives.

I'm thinking, for example, of a joint project between EJL and UPP, funded by a $317,000 EPA Urban Waters Small Grant, that includes a plan to encourage businesses at the Huntington Industrial Park to depave sections of their parking lots in order to reduce the amount of impervious surface surrounding the pond. At the ceremony to award the grant, Rhode Island's then-governor, Lincoln Chafee, called the rehabilitation of Rhode Island's freshwater ponds the preservation of an important natural resource for future economic development, with no hint of irony in his voice. The work of these NGOs is largely the work of translation. They translate environmental science from English into Spanish and Cambodian; they translate technical reports into lay terms; and they translate the discourse of social and cultural critique into the discourse of development. The possibilities for change here on one hand seem enormous because this translation work has dissolved the percolating tensions of the 2005 public hearings and has mobilized people; on the other hand, this work risks "repurpos[ing]" activism and protest into the "social entrepreneurship . . . of a revamped NGO sphere" (Trimbur 2012, 726) that is itself complicit in political economies that continue to disadvantage the very people the NGOs purport to help.

There seem to be few alternatives, however. In *Natural Discourse*, Sidney Dobrin and Christian Weisser identify discourse as the site of oppression (Dobrin and Weisser 2002). They argue that "oppressive hegemonies manifest themselves in discourse; racial, cultural, sexist, classist oppression recurs through discourse. How we transgress those oppressive constructs, how we survive in them is a matter of discursive maneuvering" (9). Critiques of resistance and activism are made on the grounds that they don't do enough for real change because they rely on a "politics of the impossible" (Lamsal and Paudel 2012, 764).

Such critiques clamor for a term capable of transcending the terms set by oppressive discourse. There seems to be no way to outmaneuver oppression other than to work gradual transformation through translation and stylistic play (764). The use of federal money to teach neighborhood residents how and why we should tear up a parking lot strikes me as evidence of "the small meso-level changes" that Lamsal and Paudel recommend (765). Writing studies, particularly studies of writing as an economy, can perform similar work, in effect tearing up the parking lots of the discourses of development. Writing studies can make visible both the socially repressed strategies that legitimate and valorize some knowledges over others and the full consequences of those strategies. Such work opens a discursive space through which we can remake the places we inhabit so that one knowledge is not erased in favor of another; so that the past is not constantly being left behind; and so that it becomes possible to think of change in terms of the small accruals, exchanges, and sedimentations of everyday life rather than in terms of transcendence.

17

DEMOCRATIC RHETORIC IN THE ERA OF NEOLIBERALISM

Phyllis Mentzell Ryder

A market-infused attitude toward public decision making has become prevalent around the world. At its roots, the argument suggests that a civil society is most democratic and prosperous when it yields the places and commonplaces of civil discourse to capitalist logic. Proponents of this sort of market democracy see it as *more* democratic than traditional liberal democracy because it removes the potentially elitist, potentially distorted role of government. Instead, a "neutral" market arbitrates public needs. Political scientist Benjamin Barber (2001, 59), who argues vociferously against this sort of democracy, explains that its reach extends far into civil society: "The myth of the markets," he says, advances the "zany and overblown claim that wholly unregulated markets are the sole means by which we can produce and distribute everything we care about, from durable goods to spiritual values, from capital development to social justice, from profitability to sustainable environments, from private wealth to the essential commonweal." This sort of market democracy has been termed *neoliberalism.*[1]

Neoliberalism has been critiqued on both economic and political grounds by economists, political scientists, labor activists, and public intellectuals across the world. Many have outlined the terrible consequences of neoliberal policies, which drain money from the poor and deliver it to the wealthy. I am deeply concerned about these consequences of neoliberalism, but for this chapter, I want to address an equally important, if more abstract, concern: the consequences for public rhetoric. Proponents of neoliberalism appropriate the rhetoric of democracy. By redefining democracy in the image of the market, they gain control of the material and rhetorical spaces of democracy and stifle alternative democratic visions. For public intellectual Henry Giroux (2005b), the outlook is dire:

DOI: 10.7330/9781607325239.c017

> Neoliberalism has become one of the most pervasive, if not, [*sic*] dangerous ideologies of the 21st century. Its pervasiveness is evident not only by its unparalleled influence on the global economy, but also by its power to redefine the very nature of politics itself. Free market fundamentalism rather than democratic idealism is now the driving force of economics and politics in most of the world, and it is a market ideology driven not just by profits but by an ability to reproduce itself with such success that, to paraphrase Fred Jameson, it is easier to imagine the end of the world than the end of neoliberal capitalism.

The very idea of democracy is at risk.

Invoking a crisis is a common rhetorical device. Democracy, working well, is always in crisis. Because there is no single definition of democracy, competing ideals circulate constantly; they clash constantly; and each time, one side or the other declares democracy under siege. I consider such clashes an important, inevitable move in democratic rhetoric: they agitate and motivate publics to engage. One of the dangers of neoliberal rhetoric, however, is how smoothly it disguises its own rhetoricity. Even as it appropriates democratic commonplaces, neoliberalism is convinced it can do without rhetoric. The realism of "the market" is enough; it sees itself as grounded in "human nature." Economic laws of capitalism are made parallel to physical laws, as unquestionable as gravity. Any sense of public purpose, public agency, or public capacity is set forward in terms of the market. From this premise, advocates for neoliberalism erase the entry points for public debate about the relationship of democracy and capitalism. The challenge for public rhetoric, then, is to resist and expose this appropriation of democratic commonplaces.

To make visible the rhetoricity of neoliberalism, I'll provide a rubric of the commonplaces of democracy and examine how neoliberalism has appropriated this discourse, devolving from "of the people, by the people, for the people" into "of the market, by the market, and for the market." I'll illustrate with examples from contemporary arguments in favor of neoliberalism. While such arguments are embedded in everyday conversations and speeches, they surface most explicitly in the mission statements and policy papers of think tanks, so I will draw from the first-principle statements of the Heritage Foundation and publications of scholars at the American Enterprise Institute. In choosing these examples, I don't mean to suggest that only people on the right of the political spectrum advocate for neoliberalism, as I hope you'll hear how the logic of such positions is rather commonplace these days. Rather, I choose them because they illustrate most clearly the rhetorical mechanisms that combine economic and democratic logic, moves more subtly enthymematic elsewhere. Finally, I'll examine some responses of groups like Occupy Wall Street. My conclusion is cautiously optimistic: yes, democracy can be wrested away from neoliberalism, but it won't be easy, and it may not look like the standard, representative democracy that many imagine democracy "should" be.

THE MATRIX OF DEMOCRACY: FOR THE PEOPLE, OF THE PEOPLE, BY THE PEOPLE

To begin, I offer a diagram I call the *Matrix of Democracy* (Figure 17.1),[2] which represents available means of persuasion, or commonplaces, in democratic rhetoric. Like Ralph Cintron (2010, 110), I see *commonplaces* (a term I use interchangeably with *topoi)* as very potent. Aristotle would say that commonplaces are stock arguments readily at hand, but Cintron goes further: commonplaces are saturated with world-views; they are arguments about how to *be*. Cintron says, "If we think of *topoi* as storehouses of social energy, we might also think of *topoi* as organizing our lifeworlds—including our economies, our very materiality—according to social energies." As "storehouses of energy," topoi are volatile things.

To motivate people to action, public rhetors contrast what they say is actually existing democracy ("the world as it is," to use Saul Alinsky's [1971] phrase) against the ideal they think the public should strive for ("the world as it should be"). They do so by implying or declaring a purpose, actors, and actions for democracy. These commonplaces of *for the people, of the people, by the people* are represented as the three axes of the matrix. Each holds a continuum of democratic arguments; each point on the matrix is a vibrant, righteous declaration about how democracy works. Whether or not public rhetors call explicit attention to a point on the matrix, the rhetoric itself is infused with a democratic vision about the purpose, actor, and action of democracy, and this vision gives energy and power to their claims.

For the people: Arguments along the horizontal axis concern *the purpose of government.* Should government protect individual property and individual rights (over to the right), or should it facilitate the inherent interconnectedness among citizens, a more communitarian view over on the left?

Of the people: The vertical axis asks *who should govern?* Who are the deciders? Arguments near the top of the axis posit that a small group of people is suited to govern in the interests of the rest; those near the bottom, that more people should have more direct influence. Where we place ourselves on the vertical axis is often bound up with where we stand

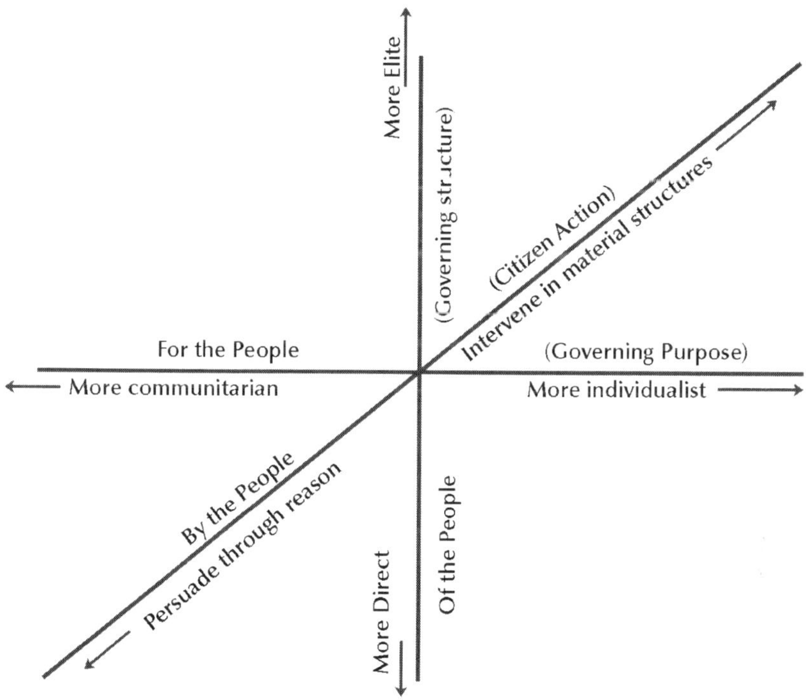

Figure 17.1. Matrix of Democracy

on the horizontal one: Who is best suited to protect private property—can the masses be trusted? Won't they become greedy mobs? Who is best suited to create community—can the elite understand the rest of us?

By the people: Imagine the diagonal line as coming straight out of the page. It posits *how* "the people" should engage in democracy. What are the appropriate tools of public democratic action? Those who position themselves near the point out in front (which shows up on the bottom left in a two-dimensional model) trust more in reason and deliberation; for them, the right course of action for citizens is a Habermasian model of the public sphere, where we meet and deliberate to identify a right action. The audience for those arguments changes, depending on where you are on the vertical axis. You might write a reasoned letter to your congressional representative (front, midtop on the matrix) or engage in reasoned discussion in a binding town-hall meeting (front, near the bottom).

Those who position themselves at the far end of the axis have no hope that reasoned argument can create the change they want. What action does one take if all of society is thoroughly saturated with the ideology one opposes? Reason doesn't work here; instead, the actors must break people from their habits so they see how they're being manipulated. They must interrupt the systems that undergird the ideology before any change can happen. Think Earth Liberation Front. Think Occupy.

As members of a public saturated with democratic discourse, we feel the pull of the commonplaces from all over the matrix. On one day, I might rally with women at the National Mall to pressure government to protect my right to birth control and abortion. On another day, I might disrupt an annual shareholder meeting to pressure a paper company to clean up public waterways. My purpose, target, and mode of action shift in each setting, yet I engage both scenes in the name of democracy. To put it another way, the topoi offer no clear direction for what counts as *the* democratic response in a given situation (see Cintron 2009; Rai 2010). If scholars limit "real" democratic action to only one point on the matrix, we lose the big picture. *Every* point on the grid reverberates with righteousness. *Every* point pulses with the moral energies of the topos of the people, by the people, for the people.

Many critics of neoliberalism position it in a particular point on the matrix of democracy (individualist, elitist, nonrational) and then seek to demonstrate how these are not truly democratic categories. My project is different. I want to understand how neoliberalism moves around on the matrix—indeed, how it tries to dissolve the matrix—and how opponents of neoliberalism fight to keep the whole matrix, with its multitude of public arguments, available for democratic discourse.

Rhetorics of Neoliberalism

This is not the first time our country has experienced a consolidation of wealth wrapped up in arguments for elite, market-focused democracy. Former US Labor Secretary Robert Reich (2010, 2) notes that the first stage of American capitalism in 1870–1929 paralleled the situation leading up to the recent economic crisis. Public support for that earlier vision gave way after the Great Depression to a period (1947–1975) when the role of government was understood as checking the excesses of capitalism (2). History might suggest that we're merely swinging the same pendulum.

Yet the current moment is not a national one; indeed, as international corporations and transnational finance absorb physical and virtual public spaces, the nation has become a weaker and weaker player. Some argue that the solution is to extend the matrix and substitute *transnational* governing bodies for the national government. Habermas and others seek to hold international governing bodies such as the IMF or the World Bank to standards based on political (rather than economic) topoi, chastising them for being nonrepresentative (Ryder 2011, 182–83). But while such an argument rightly reorients the analysis to a political stage, it may not go far enough in considering how that political stage itself has been reconfigured.

Neoliberal "For the People": What Is the Purpose of Government?

The neoliberal commonplace is that governments exist to support free-market capitalism by protecting individual property rights and individual choice in economic matters. This role is seen as integral to democracy. We can find examples of this rhetoric within the "First Principles" of the Heritage Foundation (2013). Note how the topoi of democracy—freedom, liberty, and choice—are detached from government and attributed to free enterprise:

> Economic freedom is *necessary* for the protection of liberty. Liberty without economic freedom is not true liberty and will inevitably become tyranny. As Friedrich Hayek once observed: "To be controlled in our economic pursuits means to be controlled in everything." If government controls a citizen's basic economic decisions—where to work, what to buy, how much to sell for—it controls, as a practical matter, most aspects of a citizen's life.

This stance maps onto the right side of the horizontal axis of the matrix, where the government's purpose is to protect property, a security central to capitalism—and, by extension, democracy itself. Another Heritage Foundation "First Principles" page, under the link What Are Property Rights?, explains,

> The right to property is the natural right to acquire, own, and use property. Property rights form not only the basis for a free market economy, but also for republican self-government, deeply intertwined as they are with human liberty. To be free is to exert one's talents in the pursuit of happiness, and property rights are a fundamental requirement for securing the just rewards of one's labor. According to the Founders, property rights also formed the cornerstone of a commercial republic: When a man has a bit of property—a home, a piece of land, his own source of food and security—he can be independent, and therefore free.

Property rights, then, are imbued with the full, moral righteousness of the Declaration of Independence and the approval of the Founding Fathers. The purpose of government is to protect private enterprises.

The link between liberty and capitalism rests in the claim that free-market capitalism, rather than democratically elected representatives, is the best mechanism for ascertaining public desires. Any attempt to regulate or direct the market through government action is seen as distorting the real workings of the market, and therefore, the real desires of the people. The communitarian side of the axis is abhorrent because it suggests that the government knows more than the market. As critic David Harvey (2005, 2) explains, "State interventions in markets (once created) must be kept to a bare minimum because, according to the theory, the state cannot possibly possess enough information to second-guess market signals (prices) and because powerful interest groups will inevitably distort and bias state interventions (particularly in democracies) for their own benefit." I'll say more about the rhetoric that positions capitalism as the best decider in the next section. The point here is that, while neoliberalism would diminish government's role in anything that could be handed over to the market, its proponents are also aware that some government must exist to provide the security and structure for that market. For the government to do so is vital; for it to do anything more is undemocratic.

In neoliberal discourse, all actions and decisions are understood as market decisions. Public education is turned over to the marketplace through vouchers for charter schools; prisons are contracted out to private companies; and all manner of daily choices are framed within a logic of free-market competition. Political scientist Wendy Brown (2005, 41) explains that within neoliberalism, the economy must be "directed, buttressed, protected by law and policy as well as by the dissemination of social norms designed to facilitate competition, free trade, and rational economic action on the part of every member and institution of society."

A clash of visions about the purpose of government is, in itself, nothing new. We can trace communitarian and individualist tensions in the United States back before the Constitution, as *Washington Post* columnist E. J. Dionne (2012) has done in his book *Our Divided Political Heart.* What's new about the neoliberal reading of the purpose of government is that it becomes the foundational argument that erases the other two axes on the matrix of democracy. When government is in the support role, serving as a watchdog and cheerleader for the market, the public has no say in *who governs* and *how.*

Neoliberal "Of the People": Who Governs?

The vertical axis on the matrix represents arguments about who is best suited to make decisions on behalf of the public. The axis stretches from elite to direct democracy and concerns itself with the human frailty of those to whom we entrust our political will. Deciders must be distant enough from the populace to see the big picture, unswayed by special interests—including their own—and able to arbitrate fairly for the good of the whole (the value at the top of the axis). Yet they also must be immersed in the populace so they understand the very real conditions of people's lives; indeed, at the very bottom of the axis, people directly govern themselves. The vertical axis is about protecting the public against selfishness, greed, and fear mongering.

Neoliberalism acknowledges human frailty and sees capitalism as the only system that truly accounts for it. The American Catholic philosopher Michael Novak (1982, 118), who has pushed the Democratic Party to embrace capitalism more fully, argues in *The Spirit of Democratic Capitalism* that the market is "proportioned to man as he is, not as dreams would have him be." Similarly, Allan Meltzer (2012, 6), who has served as visiting scholar at both the Hoover Institute and the American Enterprise Institute, proclaims early in his book *Why Capitalism* that "humans are morally imperfect, and so are their institutions," and he regularly refers to Kant's description of humanity as the fundamental problem with government: "'Out of timber so crooked as that from which man is made, nothing entirely straight can be carved'" (Kant 1784, quoted in Meltzer 2012, 5).

If we begin from the proposition that everything human is corrupt, the vertical line on the matrix of democracy isn't very compelling because every position on it is fraught with human weakness. Relying on people is dangerous: bureaucrats and public officials can be too easily persuaded to respond to special interests; government officials too often yield to their baser humanity and steal, lie, or manipulate the system. Better, instead, to ascertain and respond to public desires through competitive market exchange, where a seemingly nonhuman system of "natural" economic laws—disembodied and therefore free of human frailty—quickly accounts for and accommodates individual desires. Neoliberalism displaces human agency in public forums but celebrates it in private ones. The system of free enterprise is simultaneously a set of "natural" laws and "us" making individual, free choices through our roles as consumers and entrepreneurs. Thus, while remaining democratic, we do away with troublesome government.

We can see all of these moves in Meltzer's description of capitalism (Meltzer 2012, 16). First he gives a pretty standard explanation for how capitalism works. Note how capitalism is equated with freedom, while government is rendered as "official," "ordered," and ultimately aligned with losers:

> Capitalism allocates by letting relative prices adjust around the trade-offs expressed by buyers' individual expressed needs, which constitute their overall demand. Replacing consumer choices with an official decision fails to incorporate these accurate, individual, consumer buy-sell data into the system, thus distorting prices. At the set price, some will gain but others will lose. By contrast, a freer system allows market equilibrium prices to evolve based on the actual, accurate demands of all. Those who lose in the ordered system would have preferred to choose for themselves.

While such descriptions may seem restricted to consumer choices, Meltzer later extends consumer decisions to decisions about government itself.

As he equates capitalism with freedom and any alternative with coercion, Meltzer deploys the rhetorical moves that James Aune (2001, 40) identifies in *Selling the Free Market: The Rhetoric of Economic Correctness*: the perversity thesis—*things will inevitably go differently than intended*—and the futility thesis—*the attempt simply won't work*:

> Capitalism is not a utopian system, but there is no better system for providing growth and personal freedom. Capitalism's known alternatives offer less freedom and lower growth, and the "better alternatives" people imagine are almost always someone else's idea of utopia. Libraries are full of books on utopia and those that have been tried have either not survived or not flourished. The most common reason for failure is that one person or one group's utopian ideal is unsatisfactory for others who live subject to its rules. Either the rules change or they are enforced by authorities. Capitalism, particularly democratic capitalism, gains support because it provides a means for orderly change in government. Choice is one of freedom's most valued attributes. (Meltzer 2012, 27)

In the end, then, we hear two messages: radical individual choice trumps any sort of public decision making, and "there is no alternative" (to invoke Margaret Thatcher's famous phrase).

The vertical axis of the matrix of democracy dissolves because there is no longer a debate about whether to give decision-making power to elites or representatives or for people to govern themselves directly; nor is there any sense of whom to petition in such a debate. Opponents have nothing to argue and no one to persuade; they are seen as futilely fighting against "natural" economic "laws." Thus, in the name of freedom, the neoliberal public divests itself of its own role in governing. Benjamin Barber (2007, 120) puts it this way: "Nowadays, the idea that only private persons are free, and that only personal choices of the kind consumers make count as autonomous, turns out to be an assault not on tyranny but on democracy. It challenges . . . the legitimate power by which we try to rule ourselves in common."

While the neoliberal citizen is no longer self-governing, the topos of the patriotic citizen is still very much alive within neoliberal rhetoric. The role such a citizen would play, though, is very much transformed.

Neoliberal "By-the-People" Citizen Action: How Does the Public Effect Public Change?

The third axis of the matrix delineates how the public is supposed to act to convey its will to those who govern. Not surprisingly, because it has already removed the target for any such actions, neoliberalism does away with this axis, too. Instead of a collective identity of "the public" within a *political* system, individuals act within an *economic* system: "The market dissolves the very idea of a polity into itself, . . . turning citizens from rhetorical agents into economic atoms—investors, entrepreneurs, consumers, taxpayers" (Trimbur 2012, 726). Again, the market is seen as *more democratic* than the public sphere for arbitrating public desires because it treats each citizen the same way: one consumer dollar is the same as any other, and the market wants to reach everyone.

I'll elaborate on two central rhetorical moves by which neoliberals appropriate democratic language as they turn citizens into "economic atoms." First, they profess to have a more egalitarian and positive view of the citizen. Citizens are described as being fully capable of controlling their lives. They calculate carefully to ensure they receive maximum benefit from their choices; they try, fail, grow, and become more responsible in their future choices. Second, this emphasis on the cycle of failure and learning exempts the system itself from critique. In the end, when the only civic actions are economic actions, citizens do not develop any tools for political activity; they have no mechanism for introducing public concerns and needs that cannot be addressed by the market.

Capitalism is touted as a system that fully respects people, even while acknowledging that they will make some mistakes. The Reverend Robert Sirico (2010) highlights this positive citizen identity:

> Rightly understood, capitalism is simply the name for the economic component of the natural order of liberty. . . . Most of all, it means the economic application of the principle that every human person has dignity and should have that dignity respected.

Consumer-citizens are rational actors who weigh the "utility, benefit, or satisfaction" of a thing against a "microeconomic grid of scarcity, supply and demand, and moral value-neutrality" (W. Brown 2005, 40). Capitalism encourages consumers to do their research before making purchases; it encourages businesses to be what Sirico, drawing on theological vocabulary, calls "other-regarding" (2010), knowing their consumers well in order to meet their needs. Capitalism is applauded for encouraging risk taking and innovation and for allowing actors to learn from those choices. Moreover, capitalism encourages hard work and persistence: "The relation of reward to effort or achievement may not be precise, but it is positive" (Meltzer 2012, 4).

Neoliberalism prides itself on having the most respectful view of the citizen-consumer. Notice how the topoi of *coercion* versus *freedom* are used to argue that capitalism educates consumer-citizens without ever dictating their actions. "Democratic capitalism persists and spreads," Meltzer (2012, 52) tells us, "because it is not a system of imposed morality." At the same time, it provides some moral direction "because competition induces honest behavior more than other systems" (5). The system doesn't have to coerce morality because individuals will do so; customers will abandon unscrupulous businesses (Sirico 2010).

It might appear, given its language of individual rationality, that the neoliberal position could be pinpointed on the matrix at the intersection of individualism (right on the horizontal axis) and reason (on the points of the axis coming forward). But this view would be deceiving because the medium through which the individual *consumer* delivers the rational message—a purchase—is fundamentally different from when a *citizen* delivers a rational message—a letter, e-mail, or speech. "Asking what 'I want' and what 'we as a community to which I belong need' are two different questions," Barber (2007, 126) reminds us, "though neither is altruistic and both involve 'my' interest: the first is ideally answered by the market; the second must be answered by democratic politics." The market medium eclipses the option of those public deliberations. We can only *buy* or *not buy*, "as if consumers, one by one, spending their dollars and yen in accord with private wants, could somehow miraculously produce common goods and a healthy civic climate" (Barber 2001, 59).

A critical point for neoliberals in describing the role for citizens is that choice within free markets must include the choice to fail because failure is seen as a necessary teacher. To rescue people from failure is to deny them an opportunity to learn from their situations. It allows them to become complacent, to stop innovating. On a larger scale, the knowledge gained from struggling to overcome failure benefits the system: "Competition eliminates less efficient activities and strengthens survivors, encouraging them to adapt to change" (Meltzer 2012, 6).

A critical move happens in discussions of necessary failure. Because failure is the way capitalism teaches people to grow and adapt, people must accept responsibility for their failures. Stressing people's ability to choose also means that if they choose badly, the blame falls on them alone.

> In making the individual fully responsible for her/himself, neo-liberalism . . . carries responsibility for the self to new heights: the rationally calculating individual bears full responsibility for the consequences of his or her action no matter how severe the constraints on this action, e.g., lack of skills, education, and childcare in a period of high unemployment and limited welfare benefits. (W. Brown 2005, 42)

The logic applies both to describe those experiencing poverty and those who manage huge corporations and financial systems, whose actions might devastate the economy. Meltzer (2012, 17) admits, for example, that "greed produces Enrons and Worldcoms" but sees these examples as "less a characteristic of a system than a vice of individuals."

> By defining failure as a prerequisite to learning and by making the moral claim that people must be permitted to learn from their failures or they will never grow, neoliberalism neatly protects capitalism from critique. When members of the public are reduced to economic atoms, they lose opportunities to practice other modes of decision making. There is no forum for engaging the larger, systemic problems that might make the economic playing field unfair; anyone who attempts to explain a failure in such a way is called a *whiner* or a *crybaby*—someone unwilling to shoulder responsibility. As Wendy Brown (2005, 42) explains, "A 'mismanaged life' becomes a new mode of depoliticizing social and economic powers and at the same time reduces political citizenship to an unprecedented degree of passivity and political complacency."

By winning consent on the first premise—that the purpose of government is to clear space for the market—neoliberals set up a cascade of consequences that shift democratic agency and civic action outside the usual matrix of democracy. By attributing agency to a nonhuman "natural" force, neoliberalism claims to have solved the problems of human frailty and makes any attempt to fight its dictates seem silly. How do you fight the laws of nature? Whom would you fight? By enlisting government in promoting neoliberal policies, proponents of neoliberalism continue to extend its reach, appropriating public institutions and public spaces and creating the physical and rhetorical conditions to continue to spread the message of its "naturalness" and "inevitability."

Occupy Wall Street and the Rhetorics of Democracy

Those who resist neoliberalism work to define it as a *political* entity. To do so takes a massive collective gathering whose purpose is to put neoliberalism back on the matrix of democracy—to define the purpose, actors, and methods of neoliberalism as points within the domain of public deliberation. The message is not to replace Big Business with Big

Government; rather, the message is that neoliberalism has thoroughly saturated public discourse and must be exposed before we can move on. Naming and resisting neoliberalism means peeling back multiple layers and demands an awareness of the complex interconnections among all lives, across the world. No one person, no one group, can understand the extent of the web.

One set of responses to neoliberalism manifested in the Global Justice movement (whose members converged on meetings of transnational finance and global free trade, such as the World Trade Organization, the World Bank, and leaders of the G20) and the more recent Occupy camps around the world. In these spaces, feminists stand alongside union men; laid-off firefighters stand with anticapitalist anarchists; mothers of the disappeared stand next to environmentalists. They hold signs that point in many directions at once. Manifestos, written collaboratively, are not crisp demands but poetic world-views. There is no leader who can explain it all authoritatively to the reporters.

I have analyzed the rhetoric of the IMF/World Bank protests elsewhere,[3] so I won't repeat that discussion here. Instead, I'll briefly consider how some of the participants in the Occupy movement have articulated their purpose and strategy, as it ties to reclaiming democracy from neoliberalism. I draw on movement documents, stories, and analyses provided by participants and collected in Kate Khatib, Margaret Killjoy, and Mike McGuire's *We Are Many: Reflections on Movement Strategy from Occupation to Liberation* (Khatib, Killjoy, and McGuire 2012).

The Occupiers, mobilized by their belief that the existing and pervasive neoliberal democracy is not democracy at all, are united in a fight to reclaim the commonplaces of democracy. But because neoliberalism has altered the topoi so much, the democracy formed in response does not map smoothly onto the matrix, either. While neoliberalism asserts a foundational claim about the purpose of government—to serve the market—those who fight neoliberalism defer any articulation about the purpose of government. They do not make demands of any particular entity (governmental or otherwise). Instead, they operate as a prefigurative political space, trying out alternative democracies both tentatively and with great excitement.

Not articulating a common purpose is often seen as the greatest failing of antiglobalization protests and Occupy encampments. Unable to project a unified, positive vision for an alternative democracy, they instead seem to hold endless meetings, focusing on how to manage their camps day to day and occasionally foraying out to march, blockade, or take other actions. One of the common slogans—"Occupy Everything,

Demand Nothing"—seems mystifying, as there is no specific target or request; there are only people dissatisfied with the current state of things.

But this interpretation misses a deeper theoretical understanding about how (at least some of) the participants wish to develop a new vision of democracy. Decisions about the purpose of government are deferred so that the position, whenever it is made, can be most inclusive. In this sense, the lack of a clear articulation of an a priori purpose of government is precisely the point: in a fully democratic space, such decisions arise from the bottom up, as *people* listen to *people* and as a *public*. Joshua Clover (2012, 99), who was part of the Oakland commune, explains, "The fomenting of a new political hegemony allows for an endless array of individual grievances, but precludes any single demand to which everybody must submit, as its particulars might exclude some portion of the everybody hailed by the formula of 'the 99%.'" Occupation anticipates the possibilities of democracies to come, creating "a momentary opening in capitalist time and space, a rearrangement that sketche[s] the contours of a new society" ("Communique from an Absent Future," quoted in Clover 2012, 98).

Refusing to make demands has a second purpose as well: by not addressing anyone, protesters make the case that no entity has the capacity to act on behalf of neoliberalism (Clover 2012, 98). The Occupy public does not orient itself toward government through rallies, votes, or party activities, for example, because the government is already aligned with neoliberalism. In the first article of *We Are Many*, Vijay Prashad (2012, 15) explains that "[the Occupy movement] has refused to allow the political class to engage with it, largely because it does not believe that this political class will be capable of understanding the predicament of the 99%." Because neoliberalism is so extensive, so infused into political, cultural, and social institutions around the world, no one actor or institution has the power to transform it. It perpetuates in multiple forms, manifesting in different ways in different places.

Instead, Occupy spreads into as many pockets of neoliberal space as possible, demonstrating the extensive reach of both neoliberalism and the resistance. Occupying what is often privatized space, participants reclaim a critical infrastructure from neoliberalism: noncommodified public spheres, "those institutions engaged in dialog, education, and learning—that address the relationship of the self to public life, of social responsibility to the broader demands of citizenship, and provide a robust vehicle for public participation and democratic citizenship" (Giroux 2005a, 142). Many of the seemingly public places in neoliberal cities are designed and policed as places for entertainment, comfort, security, and orchestrated interactions—think of vibrant new city centers anchored with stores, where pedestrians stroll and shop under the gaze of security guards. In many such areas, political solicitation is barred because such discourse is unpredictable, chaotic, and sometimes confrontational.[4] It would dampen the buying mood. But the Occupy camps reclaimed these spaces, for a while, and redefined their public function as one of direct, participatory democracy, projecting their vision of the appropriate roles for citizens. In the process, as Prashad (2012, 18) writes, the movement "brok[e] the chain of despondency and allowed us to imagine new communities."

In the Occupy view of democracy, participation is the point. The new public is unified in a new type of class war that claims "a cultural identity [with] *a focus on one's available means for exercising a decision-making power* within and against privatization's strict limits on public right and voice, including in the workplace" (Welch 2008, 11; italics added). Occupy citizens are far from passive. Hundreds, sometimes thousands of people make decisions in general assemblies through a highly structured consensus process; together, they decide how to run the camps. The market economy there is bartering. The goal for those selling is to meet people's needs, not to accumulate profit for investors. Moreover, the buyers are not merely consumers; they also trade their talents and gifts. The Occupy camps made visible, for some time and for some people, the possibility of living outside of capitalist exchange. Participants enacted the society they wished to see (Cornell 2012, 177).

Accounts by participants at both Occupy Zuccotti Park and Occupy Oakland focus on participatory structures infused with a self-conscious meta-analysis about how well those methods include everyone. Occupy adopted a consensus model of decision making that experienced organizers brought with them from other movements (Cornell 2012, 165).[5] This model allows many participants to communicate in meetings—using hand signals—their agreement, disagreement, uncertainty, need for greater clarification, and so on. Most important, decisions are not made until everyone agrees—or a large portion of people do; Zuccotti Park adopted a 90 percent threshold of agreement (Cornell 2012, 164). General assemblies are time-consuming ways to arrive at decisions. At the same time, they can be energizing, providing a jolt of excitement when people experience a democracy that listens.

The literature written during and about Occupy demonstrates the careful, difficult work of acknowledging the histories of oppression in dominant society and previous social justice movements. Likewise, it seeks to understand how the violence of neoliberalism affects different groups differently, an investigation that not only pushes them to create alternatives within their own spaces but also provides a fuller picture of how neoliberalism operates. Occupy citizens understand movement building as a process of constant education and kairotic action.

Much more can be said about how Occupy struggles to define democracy and confront neoliberalism. My goal is not to be exhaustive but to provide a few examples to help illustrate how moments like these can be understood using the rhetorical topoi on the matrix of democracy.

Democracy Is Dead; Long Live Democracy

Because the concepts of neoliberalism and democracy are fluid, always adjusting to and appropriating the discourses they encounter, any analysis of neoliberalism or the responses to it is an ongoing project. At this juncture, the rhetorics of neoliberalism attempt to shift the common ground, redefining democratic topoi in market terms. But these moves, while extensive and powerful, are never complete. Though neoliberalism attempts to dissolve the public capacity of the matrix, those democratic commonplaces erupt and burst through the ruptures. They fade away. They erupt again. Despite the rhetoric of realism and inevitability, neoliberalism has not silenced all its critics.

It's not yet clear what the alternative looks like. We don't know if direct, participatory democracy as it was practiced in the general assemblies of the Occupy camps will be offered for broader, national, or international decision making. We don't know how an alternative democracy will link economic and political decisions. We don't know what mechanism an alternative democracy will use to wrest power away from political, cultural, and social institutions that continue to interpellate citizens in the neoliberal model. But I am made optimistic because the struggle remains. There remain pockets where the neoliberal values of efficiency and expedience hold no sway. The struggle will be long and messy, the outcomes not easily measurable but rather slow forays into public consciousness, small yet persistent reminders about the power of a public. I am optimistic because the very struggle to define democracy is a sign that democracy itself is alive and kicking.

Notes

1. The derivation of *neoliberal* is not political (as in liberal versus conservative) but economic. Classic *economic liberalism*, such as that proposed by Adam Smith (1776) in *The Wealth of Nations*, is a laissez-faire model in which governments do not intervene in markets but instead allow free competition. *Neo*liberalism keeps free trade

and competition but rejects the laissez-faire component. Instead, it enlists the state in advancing capitalist goals. Laws, police, and militaries help privatize public services and secure comfortable and nondisruptive space for commercial competition (Welch 2008, 7). Moreover, neoliberalism extends its market analysis into all parts of society. "Neo-liberal rationality . . . involves *extending and disseminating market values to all institutions and social action,* even as the market itself remains a distinctive player" (W. Brown 2005, 39–40; italics in original).

2. I provide a fuller discussion of the Matrix of Democracy in my book *Rhetorics for Community Action* (Ryder 2011).
3. See Phyllis Mentzell Ryder 2011, chapter 6.
4. For an excellent analysis of privatized public spaces, see Don Mitchell (1995, 2011).
5. As Andrew Cornell (2012) explains, the consensus model has a long history, going back to Quaker meetings and peace protests, winding through the Student Nonviolence Coordinating Committee (SNCC) in the civil rights movement, and most recently prevalent in the early 2000s Global Justice (anti-free-trade globalization) movements. The process gives a structure that attempts to overcome the exclusion seen to be inherent in decision-making models such as parliamentary procedure and majority-rule voting.

AFTERWORD
Lessons Learned

Deborah Brandt

Reading the instructive essays in this volume took me back to my first encounter with the idea of the speech economy. It was in Dell Hymes's 1974 *Foundations in Sociolinguistics: An Ethnographic Approach.* With the term *speech economy,* Hymes shows how we cannot communicate anything to anybody without activating and maneuvering the larger relational systems that condition life as we find it. When we speak or write to each other, we are dragged into—and must drag along—the weight of our worlds. Hymes provides analytical tools for seeing the means by which this happens: look for the setting, the scene, the participants, the purposes, the speech acts, the registers, the channels, the conventions, the styles, the genres of a discourse and you will see something of an operating speech economy and its grip. Attending to what Hymes calls the "context of situation" makes present the resources a person has for producing, valuing, and circulating language—as well as the purchase others have for taking up, judging, or suppressing that language. For Hymes, language competence lies in how we transact with and through the weight of our circumstances.

Three years later, in 1977, Pierre Bourdieu published "The Economics of Linguistic Exchanges." He goes even further than Hymes by implying that language is the first and fundamental economic system. It is the site where we learn the economic facts of life as we labor to produce, exchange, and profit from language but do so amid disparities in power, wealth, privilege, and reward. Before we can really make messages, Bourdieu reminds us, we must secure the authority to be heard. We need enough symbolic capital to complete the transaction. For Bourdieu, language competence requires management of power relations, especially "the capacity to command a listener . . . the power to impose reception" (Bourdieu 1977, 648). The trouble is that the authority to speak is not equally distributed and, in fact, like other material goods, can be scarce for most people. Linguistic insecurity,

DOI: 10.7330/9781607325239.c018

like food insecurity, is manufactured politically through the unjust manipulation of power.

In connecting language and economy, both Hymes and Bourdieu wanted to account for variance, stratification, and conflict in language and to underscore how values govern linguistic styles and the possibilities for meaning. Both of them also wanted to show that communication is far from the only function of language, far from the only deal going down or work getting done when we discourse. But writing studies has found it difficult, for various reasons, to take up this work in a full-fledged way. When we invoke *context of situation*, for instance, the economic connotations are too often attenuated, considered, if at all, as analogic or metaphoric rather than vital and constitutive. The context of situation tends to be treated as a site for making discourse rather than the material out of which it is made. Bourdieu's concept of symbolic capital also is too often stripped of its full material meaning, treated as if it is some weightless value that can be spun out of linguistic symbols rather than as the means by which material realities barrel through linguistic symbols. Maybe the failure to integrate economic relations into mainstream pedagogical or writing theory has to do with the difficulty of thinking past the abstractions that are the habit of academic disciplines. Or maybe it has to do with the insecurity of a field that undertakes a marginalized and suspect enterprise within the humanities. Maybe we have learned to be squeamish about, even hostile toward, the economic dimensions of literacy, afraid that such a focus would reduce our mission to the instrumental teaching of workplace skills and make us cave in to crass demands for practical education. Better to exaggerate the ideal side of literacy—its contribution to intellectual and personal development, its association with expression, agency, resistance, identity, its role in disinterested knowledge making or noble community building.

Yet this collection of essays demonstrates what writing studies can gain (and not lose) by making economic relations central to interpretation, analysis, and action. At the very least the essays show how terms like *resources, labor, production, circulation, use, value, exchange, commodification,* and *transfer* can be generative for understanding the processes and products of writing as well as its teaching and learning. These concepts provide alternatives to the static analytic terms inherited from formalism. They help to situate writing in a broader and potentially more dynamic framework and can alert us to the many agents, near and far, who jockey to gain from what our enterprise produces. These essays show us how much more there is to teach and learn in writing than audience awareness or genre conventions or figuring out what one has to say. They suggest why authority will not be found by hammering a ruling dialect into the brain. Rather, collectively, these essays locate literacy and the rhetorical arts in knowing every bit of what is useful in all of what one must handle when trying to make connections in the world; in being prepared for how the reach of such stable-seeming elements like self-presentation, language skill, pedagogical theory, or administrative structure can shift in the fluid and volatile contexts of value and authority in which they always move. The essays are a reminder that whatever truths or solutions we may discover as researchers, teachers, administrators, or writers, we must remember how contingent they are on the contexts they are made of and understand them in that way. If ever one is tempted to think otherwise, it will be time to read *Economies of Writing* again.

REFERENCES

Adams, Peter, Sarah Gearhart, Robert Miller, and Anne Roberts. 2009. "The Accelerated Learning Program: Throwing Open the Gates." *Journal of Basic Writing* 28 (2): 50–69.

Adams, Peter Dow. 1993. "Basic Writing Reconsidered." *Journal of Basic Writing* 12 (1): 22–36.

Adler-Kassner, Linda. 2008. *The Activist WPA: Changing Stories about Writing and Writers.* Logan: Utah State University Press.

Adler-Kassner, Linda, Robert Crooks, and Ann Watters, eds. 2006. *Writing the Community: Concepts and Models for Service-Learning in Composition.* Sterling, VA: Stylus.

Agee, Jane M. 1977. "The Realities of College Composition Courses." *English Journal* 66 (8): 58–60. http://dx.doi.org/10.2307/815899.

Alcorn, Marshall. 2002. *Changing the Subject in English Class: Discourses and the Constructions of Desire.* Carbondale: Southern Illinois University Press.

Alford, Barry. 2009. "DCM as the Assessment Program: Mid Michigan Community College." In *Organic Writing Assessment: Dynamic Criteria Mapping in Action,* ed. Bob Broad, 37–50. Logan: Utah State University Press.

Alinsky, Saul. 1971. *Rules for Radicals: A Practical Primer for Realistic Radicals.* New York: Random House.

ALP "ALP: Accelerated Learning Program." 2012. Community College of Baltimore County. http://alp-deved.org.

Andrejevic, Mark. 2012. "Exploitation in the Data Mine." In *Internet Surveillance: The Challenges of Web 2.0 and Social Media,* ed. Christian Fuchs, 71–88. New York: Routledge.

Anson, Chris M. 2008. "The Intelligent Design of Writing Programs: Reliance on Belief or a Future of Evidence." *WPA: Writing Program Administration* 32 (1): 11–36.

Anson, Chris M., and Robert A. Schwegler. 2011. *The Longman Handbook for Writers and Readers.* 6th ed. New York: Pearson.

Anyang Dazheng Steel Silo Co. 2013. Accessed Mar. 1, 2013.

Arola, Kristin L. 2010. "The Design of Web 2.0: The Rise of the Template, the Fall of Design." *Computers and Composition* 27 (1): 4–14. http://dx.doi.org/10.1016/j.compcom.2009.11.004.

Artemeva, Natasha. 2005. "A Time to Speak, a Time to Act: A Rhetorical Genre Analysis of a Novice Engineer's Calculated Risk Taking." *Journal of Business and Technical Communication* 19 (4): 389–421. http://dx.doi.org/10.1177/1050651905278309.

Artemeva, Natasha, and Janna Fox. 2010. "Awareness versus Production: Probing Students' Antecedent Genre Knowledge." *Journal of Business and Technical Communication* 24 (4): 476–515. http://dx.doi.org/10.1177/1050651910371302.

Arthur, Christopher. 1988. "The Fluidity of Capital and the Logic of the Concept." In *The Circulation of Capital,* ed. Christopher Arthur and Geert Reuten, 95–129. New York: St. Martin's.

ASCII Table: Your Web Reference. 2013. ASCII-table.com. Accessed Apr. 21, 2013.

Aune, James Arnt. 2001. *Selling the Free Market: The Rhetoric of Economic Correctness.* New York: Guilford.

DOI: 10.7330/9781607325239.c019

Barber, Benjamin R. 2001. "Blood Brothers, Consumers, or Citizens? Three Models of Identity—Ethnic, Commercial, and Civic." In *Cultural Identity and the Nation-State*, ed. Carol Gould and Pasquale Pasquino, 57–65. Lanham, MD: Rowman and Littlefield.

Barber, Benjamin R. 2007. *Consumed: How Markets Corrupt Children, Infantilize Adults, and Swallow Citizens Whole.* New York: Norton.

Barclay, Eliza. 2009. "Speaking the Same Language." *Washington Post.* April 21.

Bartholomae, David. 1979. "Teaching Basic Writing: An Alternative to Basic Skills." *Journal of Basic Writing* 2 (2): 85–109.

Bartholomae, David. 1985. "Inventing the University." In *When a Writer Can't Write: Studies in Writer's Block and Other Composing-Process Problems*, ed. Mike Rose, 134–65. New York: Guilford.

Bartholomae, David. 1993. "The Tidy House: Basic Writing in the American Curriculum." *Journal of Basic Writing* 12 (1): 4–21.

Bartholomae, David. 2005. "What Is Composition and (If You Know What That Is) Why Do We Teach It?" In *Writing on the Margins: Essays on Composition and Teaching*, ed. David Bartholomae, 327–42. Boston: Bedford/St. Martin's. http://dx.doi.org/10.1007/978-1-4039-8439-5_21.

Bartholomae, David, and Anthony R. Petrosky, eds. 1986. *Facts, Artifacts, and Counterfacts: Theory and Method for a Reading and Writing Course.* Portsmouth, NH: Heinemann.

Barton, Matthew. 2005. "The Future of Rational-Critical Debate in Online Public Spheres." *Computers and Composition* 22 (2): 177–90. http://dx.doi.org/10.1016/j.compcom.2005.02.002.

Bawarshi, Anis. 2010. "The Challenges and Possibilities of Taking Up Multiple Discursive Resources in U.S. College Composition." In *Cross-Language Relations in Composition*, ed. Bruce Horner, Min-Zhan Lu, and Paul Kei Matsuda, 196–203. Carbondale: Southern Illinois University Press.

Bazerman, Charles. 2013. "Predatory Open Access Journals." E-mail to WPA-L. May 25.

Beach, King. 2003. "Consequential Transitions: A Developmental View of Knowledge Propagation through Social Organizations." In *Between School and Work: New Perspectives on Transfer and Boundary-Crossing*, ed. Terttu Tuomi-Gröhn and Yrjö Engeström, 39–61. New York: Pergamon.

Beaufort, Anne. 2007. *College Writing and Beyond: A New Framework for University Writing Instruction.* Logan: Utah State University Press.

Belcher, Diane. 2009. "How Research Space Is Created in a Diverse Research World." *Journal of Second Language Writing* 18 (4): 221–34. http://dx.doi.org/10.1016/j.jslw.2009.08.001.

Bennett, Daniel L., Adam R. Lucchesi, and Richard K. Vedder. 2010. "For-Profit Higher Education: Growth, Innovation, Regulation." Center for College Affordability and Productivity. http://www.centerforcollegeaffordability.org.

Bereiter, Carl. 1995. "A Dispositional View of Transfer." In *Teaching for Transfer: Fostering Generalization in Learning*, ed. Anne McKeough, Judy Lupart, and Anthony Marini, 248–58. Mahwah, NJ: Lawrence Erlbaum.

Bergmann, Linda, and Janet Zepernick. 2007. "Disciplinarity and Transfer: Students' Perceptions of Learning to Write." *WPA: Writing Program Administration* 31 (1–2): 124–49.

Berlin, James. 1988. "Rhetoric and Ideology in the Writing Class." *College English* 50 (5): 477–94. http://dx.doi.org/10.2307/377477.

Bernard, Michael. 2000. "Examining User Expectations of the Location of Web Objects." ResearchGate. http://www.researchgate.net/publication/228894745_User_expectations_for_the_location_of_web_objects.

Bernard, Michael. 2001. "Developing Schemas for the Location of Common Web Objects." Software Usability Network Research Laboratory, Wichita State University. January 9. http://usabilitynews.org/developing-schemas-for-the-location-of-common-web-objects/. http://dx.doi.org/10.1177/154193120104501502.

Bernard, Michael. 2002. "Examining User Expectations for the Location of Common E-Commerce Web Objects." *Usability News*, July 29. http://www.gieger.com/site/research/webobject_placement.pdf.

Bernard, Michael, and Ashwin Sheshadri. 2004. "Preliminary Examination of Global Expectations of Users' Mental Models for E-Commerce Web Layouts." Software Usability Network Research Laboratory, Wichita State University July 12. http://usabilitynews.org/tag/global/.

Biber, Douglas. 2006. *University Language: A Corpus-Based Study of Spoken and Written Registers*. Philadelphia, PA: John Benjamins. http://dx.doi.org/10.1075/scl.23.

Biber, Douglas, and Edward Finegan, eds. 1994. *Sociolinguistic Perspectives on Register*. New York: Oxford University Press.

Bleich, David. 1999. "In Case of Fire, Throw in (What to Do with Textbooks Once You Switch to Sourcebooks)." In *(Re)Visioning Composition Textbooks: Conflicts of Culture Ideology, and Pedagogy*, ed. Xin Liu Gale and Fredric G. Gale, 15–42. Albany: SUNY Press.

Block, David. 2007. "Bilingualism: Four Assumptions and Four Responses." *Innovation in Language Learning and Teaching* 1 (1): 66–82. http://dx.doi.org/10.2167/illt043.0.

Blommaert, Jan. 2010. *The Sociolinguistics of Globalization*. Cambridge: Cambridge University Press. http://dx.doi.org/10.1017/CBO9780511845307.

Blythe, Stuart, Jeffrey T. Grabill, and Kirk Riley. 2008. "Action Research and Wicked Environmental Problems: Exploring Appropriate Roles for Researchers in Professional Communication." *Journal of Business and Technical Communication* 22 (3): 272–98. http://dx.doi.org/10.1177/1050651908315973.

Bohman, James. 2004. "Expanding Dialogue: The Internet, the Public Sphere and Prospects for Transnational Democracy." In *After Habermas: New Perspectives on the Public Sphere*, ed. Nick Crossley and John Michael Roberts, 131–55. Oxford: Blackwell. http://dx.doi.org/10.1111/j.1467-954X.2004.00477.x.

Bourdieu, Pierre. 1977. "The Economics of Linguistic Exchanges." *Social Sciences Information. Information Sur les Sciences Sociales* 16 (6): 645–68. http://dx.doi.org/10.1177/053901847701600601.

Bourdieu, Pierre. 1984. *Distinction: A Social Critique of the Judgment of Taste*. Trans. Richard Nice. Cambridge: Harvard University Press.

Bourdieu, Pierre. 1986. "The Forms of Capital." In *Handbook of Theory and Research for the Sociology of Education*, ed. John G. Richardson, 241–58. New York: Greenwood.

Bourdieu, Pierre. 1991a. *Language and Symbolic Power*. Trans. Gino Raymond and Matthew Adamson. Cambridge: Polity.

Bourdieu, Pierre. 1991b. "Language and Symbolic Power." In *The Discourse Reader*, ed. Adam Jaworski and Nikolas Coupland, 502–13. New York: Routledge.

Bousquet, Marc. 2008. *How the University Works: Higher Education and the Low-Wage Nation*. New York: New York University Press.

Bousquet, Marc, Leo Parascondola, and Tony Scott, eds. 2004. *Tenured Bosses and Disposable Teachers: Writing Instruction in the Managed University*. Carbondale: Southern Illinois University Press.

Boyd, Danah, and Kate Crawford. 2012. "Critical Questions for Big Data." *Information, Communication and Society* 15 (5): 662–79. http://dx.doi.org/10.1080/1369118X.2012.678878.

Bracher, Mark. 1999. *The Writing Cure: Psychoanalysis, Composition, and the Aims of Education*. Carbondale: Southern Illinois University Press.

Braddock, Richard A., Richard Lloyd-Jones, and Lowell Schoer. 1963. *Research in Written Composition*. Urbana, IL: NCTE.

Brandt, Deborah. 2001. *Literacy in American Lives*. Cambridge: Cambridge University Press. http://dx.doi.org/10.1017/CBO9780511810237.

Brandt, Deborah. 2005. "Writing for a Living: Literacy and the Knowledge Economy." *Written Communication* 22 (2): 166–97. http://dx.doi.org/10.1177/0741088305275218.

Brandt, Deborah. 2012. "Afterword: The Real and Fake Economies of Writing." *JAC* 32 (3–4): 769–78.

Bransford, John, and D. Schwartz. 1999. "Rethinking Transfer: A Simple Proposal with Multiple Implications." *Review of Research in Education* 24 (1): 61–100. http://dx.doi.org/10.3102/0091732X024001061.

Breneman, David W., Brian Pusser, and Sarah E. Turner, eds. 2006. *Earnings from Learning: The Rise of For-Profit Universities.* Albany: SUNY Press.

Brent, Doug. 2011. "Transfer, Transformation, and Rhetorical Knowledge: Insights from Transfer Theory." *Journal of Business and Technical Communication* 25 (4): 396–420. http://dx.doi.org/10.1177/1050651911410951.

Brent, Doug. 2012. "Crossing Boundaries: Co-op Students Relearning to Write." *College Composition and Communication* 63 (4): 558–92.

Bringle, Robert G., Julie A. Hatcher, and Richard N. Muthiah. 2010. "The Role of Service Learning on the Retention of First-Year Students to Second Year." *Michigan Journal of Community Service Learning* 16 (2): 38–49.

Broad, Bob. 2003. *What We Really Value: Beyond Rubrics in Teaching and Assessing Writing.* Logan: Utah State University Press.

Broad, Bob. 2009. "Organic Matters: In Praise of Locally Grown Writing Assessment." In *Organic Writing Assessment: Dynamic Criteria Mapping in Action*, ed. Bob Broad, 1–13. Logan: Utah State University Press.

Brodkey, Linda. 1992. "On the Subjects of Class and Gender in 'The Literacy Letters." In *Becoming Political: Readings and Writings in the Politics of Literacy Education*, ed. Patrick Shannon, 97–112. Portsmouth, NH: Heinemann.

Broudy, H. S. 1977. "Types of Knowledge and Purposes of Education." In *Schooling and the Acquisition of Knowledge*, ed. Richard Chase Anderson, Rand J. Spiro, and William Edward Montague, 1–17. Hillsdale, NJ: Erlbaum.

Brown, Stephen, and Sidney Dobrin, eds. 2004. *Ethnography Unbound: From Theory Shock to Critical Praxis.* Albany: SUNY Press.

Brown, Wendy. 2005. *Edgework: Critical Essays on Knowledge and Politics.* Princeton, NJ: Princeton University Press.

Bruffee, Kenneth. 1984. "Collaborative Learning and the 'Conversation of Mankind.'" *College English* 46 (7): 635–52. http://www.jstor.org/stable/376924. http://dx.doi.org/10.2307/376924.

Buell, Marcia. 2004. "Code-Switching and Second Language Writing." In *What Writing Does and How It Does It: An Introduction to Analyzing Texts and Textual Practices*, ed. Charles Bazerman and Paul Prior, 97–122. Mahwah, NJ: Lawrence Erlbaum.

Busan Digital University. 2010. Accessed Mar. 1, 2013.

Butler, Judith. 1997. *Excitable Speech: A Politics of the Performative.* New York: Routledge.

Cahill, Lisa, Susan Miller-Cochran, Veronica Pantoja, and Rochelle L. Rodrigo. 2008. "Graduate Student Writing Groups as Peer Mentoring Communities." In *Stories of Mentoring: Theory and Praxis*, ed. Michelle F. Eble and Lynée L. Gaillet, 153–8. West Lafayette, IN: Parlor.

Callahan, Ewa. 2005. "Cultural Similarities and Differences in the Design of University Web Sites." *Journal of Computer-Mediated Communication* 11 (1): 239–73. http://dx.doi.org/10.1111/j.1083-6101.2006.tb00312.x.

Cameron, Deborah. 2000. *Good to Talk?: Living and Working in a Communication Culture.* London: SAGE.

Canagarajah, A. Suresh. 1996. "'Nondiscursive' Requirements in Academic Publishing, Material Resouces of Periphery Scholars, and the Politics of Knowledge Production." *Written Communication* 13 (4): 435–72. http://dx.doi.org/10.1177/0741088396013004001.

Canagarajah, A. Suresh. 2006. "The Place of World Englishes in Composition: Pluralization Continued." *College Composition and Communication* 57 (4): 586–619.

Canagarajah, A. Suresh. 2011. "Codemeshing in Academic Writing: Identifying Teachable Strategies of Translanguaging." *Modern Language Journal* 95 (3): 401–17. http://dx.doi.org/10.1111/j.1540-4781.2011.01207.x.

Canagarajah, A. Suresh. 2013. *Translingual Practice: Global English and Cosmopolitan Relations.* New York: Routledge.

Carnegie Classification of Institutions of Higher Education. 2016. "Downloads: 2015 Update Public File." carnegieclassifications.iu.edu. Jun. 9, 2016. Accessed Oct. 7 2016. http://carnegieclassifications.iu.edu/downloads.php.

Carnicelli, Thomas. 1980. "The Writing Conference: A One-to-One Conversation." In *Eight Approaches to Composition,* ed. by Timothy Donovan and Ben McLelland, 101–32. Urbana: NCTE.

Casanave, Christine Pearson. 2002. *Writing Games: Multicultural Case Studies of Academic Literacy Practices in Higher Education.* New York: Routledge.

Castells, Manuel. 2010. *The Rise of the Network Society.* 2nd ed. Malden, MA: Blackwell.

Cenoz, Jasone, and Durk Gorter. 2011. "Focus on Multilingualism: A Study of Trilingual Writing." *Modern Language Journal* 95 (3): 356–69. http://dx.doi.org/10.1111/j.1540-4781.2011.01206.x.

Cerf, Vinton G. 2012. Foreword to *EURid-UNESCO World Report on Internationalized Domain Name Deployment 2012.* eu Insights. Accessed Mar. 10, 2013. https://www.icann.org/en/system/files/files/eurid-unesco-deployment-08nov12-en.pdf.

Chen, Dong Song. 2009. "Web Addresses in Multi Language." YouTube video, 6:47. October 30. Accessed Apr. 25, 2013. https://www.youtube.com/watch?v=NxVrr_zSYUI.

Cintron, Ralph. 2009. "Immigration, Minutemen, and the Subject of Democracy." Presented at the Western States Rhetoric and Literacy Conference, Salt Lake City, UT, October.

Cintron, Ralph. 2010. "Democracy and Its Limitations." In *The Public Work of Rhetoric: Citizen-Scholars and Civic Engagement,* ed. John Ackerman and David Coogan, 98–116. Columbia: University of South Carolina Press.

Clark, Irene L. 2003. *Concepts in Composition: Theory and Practice in the Teaching of Writing.* Mahwah, NJ: Lawrence Erlbaum.

Cleary, Michelle Navarre. 2011. "How Antonio Graduated On Out of Here: Improving the Success of Adult Students with an Individualized Writing Course." *Journal of Basic Writing* 30 (1): 34–63.

Clover, Joshua. 2012. "The Coming Occupation." In *We Are Many: Reflections on Movement Strategy from Occupation to Liberation,* ed. Kate Khatib, Margaret Killjoy, and Mike McGuire, 95–103. Oakland, CA: AK Press.

Conley, David T., and Paul L. Gaston. 2013. *A Path to Alignment: Connecting K–12 and Higher Education via the Common Core and the Degree Qualification Profile.* Lumina Foundation for Education. October. http://files.eric.ed.gov/fulltext/ED555855.pdf.

Connors, Robert J. 1985. "Mechanical Correctness as a Focus in Composition Instruction." *College Composition and Communication* 36 (1): 61–72. http://dx.doi.org/10.2307/357607.

Cope, Bill, and Mary Kalantzis, eds. 2000. *Multiliteracies: Literacy Learning and the Design of Social Futures.* New York: Routledge.

Cornell, Andrew. 2012. "Consensus: What It Is, What It Isn't, Where It Comes from, and Where It Must Go." In *We Are Many: Reflections on Movement Strategy from Occupation to Liberation,* ed. Kate Khatib, Margaret Killjoy, and Mike McGuire, 163–73. Oakland, CA: AK Press.

Covino, William. 1988. *The Art of Wondering: A Revisionist Return to the History of Rhetoric.* Portsmouth, NH: Boynton/Cook Heinemann.

Crawford, Ilene. 2010. "Growing Routes: Rhetoric as the Study and Practice of Movement." In *Rhetorica in Motion: Feminist Rhetorical Methods & Methodologies,* ed. Eileen Schell and K. J. Rawson, 71–87. Pittsburgh, PA: University of Pittsburgh Press.

Crystal, David. 1997. *English as a Global Language.* New York: Cambridge University Press.

Crystal, David. 2006. *Language and the Internet.* 2nd ed. Cambridge: Cambridge University Press.

Cushman, Ellen. 1999. "The Public Intellectual, Service-Learning and Activist Research." *College English* 61 (3): 328–36. http://dx.doi.org/10.2307/379072.

Cushman, Ellen. 2012. "Learning from the Cherokee Syllabary: A Rhetorical Approach to Media Research and Teaching." *JAC* 32 (3–4): 541–64.

Dahlberg, Lincoln. 2001. "Computer-Mediated Communication and the Public Sphere: A Critical Analysis." *Journal of Computer-Mediated Communication* 7 (1). http://dx.doi.org/10.1111/j.1083-6101.2001.tb00137.x.

Dahlgren, Peter. 2005. "The Internet, Public Spheres, and Political Communication: Dispersion and Deliberation." *Political Communication* 22 (2): 147–62. http://dx.doi.org/10.1080/10584600590933160.

Danet, Brenda, and Susan C. Herring. 2003. "Introduction: The Multilingual Internet." *Journal of Computer-Mediated Communication* 9 (1). http://dx.doi.org/10.1111/j.1083-6101.2003.tb00354.x.

Davis, Robert Con. 1987. "Freud's Resistance to Reading and Teaching." *College English* 49 (6): 621–35. http://dx.doi.org/10.2307/377798.

Davis, Vivian. 1990. "Paranoia in Language Politics." In *Not Only English: Affirming America's Multilingual Heritage,* ed. Harvey Daniels, 71–6. Urbana, IL: NCTE.

Dean, Jodi. 2002. *Publicity's Secret: How Technoculture Capitalizes on Democracy.* Ithaca, NY: Cornell University Press.

Dean, Jodi. 2008. "Communicative Capitalism: Circulation and the Foreclosure of Politics." In *Digital Media and Democracy: Tactics in Hard Times,* ed. Megan Boler, 100–19. Cambridge: MIT Press.

Dean, Jodi. 2010. *Blog Theory: Feedback and Capture in the Circuits of Drive.* Cambridge: Polity.

Dean, Terry. 1989. "Multicultural Classrooms, Monocultural Teachers." *College Composition and Communication* 40 (1): 23–37. http://dx.doi.org/10.2307/358178.

Deans, Thomas. 2000. *Writing Partnerships: Service-Learning in Composition.* Urbana, IL: NCTE.

DeGenaro, William, ed. 2007. *Who Says? Working-Class Rhetoric, Class Consciousness, and Community.* Pittsburgh, PA: University of Pittsburgh Press.

Deming, David J., Claudia Goldin, and Lawrence F. Katz. 2012. "The For-Profit Postsecondary School Sector: Nimble Critters or Agile Predators?" *Journal of Economic Perspectives* 26 (1): 139–64. http://dx.doi.org/10.1257/jep.26.1.139.

DePaul, Amy. 2010. "Why Is College So Expensive? The War on Public Universities." *Alternet,* September 9. http://www.alternet.org/story/147933/.

Detweiler, Jane, and Maureen McBride. 2009. "Designs on Assessment: University of Nevada, Reno." In *Organic Writing Assessment: Dynamic Criteria Mapping in Action,* ed. Bob Broad, 52–72. Logan: Utah State University Press.

Dews, C. L. Barney, and Carolyn Leste Law. 1995. *This Fine Place So Far from Home: Voices of Academics from the Working Class.* Philadelphia, PA: Temple University Press.

Dias, Patrick, and Anthony Paré, eds. 2000. *Transitions: Writing in Academic and Workplace Settings.* Creskill, NJ: Hampton.

Dilger, Bradley. 2010. "Beyond Star Flashes: The Elements of Web 2.0 Style." *Computers and Composition* 27 (1): 15–26. http://dx.doi.org/10.1016/j.compcom.2009.12.002.

Dionne, E. J. 2012. *Our Divided Political Heart: The Battle for the American Idea in an Age of Discontent.* New York: Bloomsbury.

Dobrin, Sidney I., and Christian R. Weisser. 2002. *Natural Discourse: Toward Ecocomposition.* Albany: SUNY Press.

Dong, Lei, Carolyn Watters, Jack Duffy, and Michael Shepherd. 2008. "An Examination of Genre Attributes for Web Page Classification." *Proceedings of the 41st Hawaii International Conference on System Sciences,* 1–10. New York: Wiley-IEEE Computer Society. http://dx.doi.org/10.1109/HICSS.2008.53.

Dor, Daniel. 2004. "From Englishization to Imposed Multilingualism: Globalization, the Internet, and the Political Economy of the Linguistic Code." *Public Culture* 16 (1): 97–118. http://dx.doi.org/10.1215/08992363-16-1-97.

Downing, David, Claude Mark Hurlbert, and Paula Mathieu, eds. 2002. *Beyond English, Inc.: Curricular Reform in a Global Economy*. Portsmouth, NH: Heinemann.

Driscoll, Dana Lynn, and Jennifer Wells. 2012. "Beyond Knowledge and Skills: Writing Transfer and the Role of Student Dispositions." *Composition Forum* 26 (Fall). http://compositionforum.com/issue/26/beyond-knowledge-skills.php.

Dryer, Dylan. 2007. "On Possibilities of Reading and Writing: Genre Uptake, Discursive Resources, and the Composition of Institutional Texts." PhD diss., University of Wisconsin-Milwaukee. ProQuest (3262955).

Dubisar, Abby, and Jason Palmeri. 2010. "Palin/Pathos/Peter Griffin: Political Video Remix and Composition Pedagogy." *Computers and Composition* 27 (2): 77–93. http://dx.doi.org/10.1016/j.compcom.2010.03.004.

Duff, Patricia. 2005. "Problematising Academic Discourse Socialisation." In *Learning Discourses and the Discourses of Learning*, ed. Helen Marriot, Tim Moore, and Robyn Spence-Brown, 1–19. Melbourne: Monash University Press.

Dumbill, Ed. 2012. "What Is Big Data?" *Strata: Making Data Work.* O'Reilly, January 11. https://www.oreilly.com/ideas/what-is-big-data.

Eagleton, Terry. 2011. *Why Marx Was Right.* New Haven, CT: Yale University Press.

Ede, Lisa. 2008. *The Academic Writer: A Brief Guide.* Boston: Bedford/St. Martin's.

Ede, Lisa, and Andrea Lunsford. 2009. "Among the Audience: On Audience in an Age of New Literacies." In *Engaging Audience: Writing in an Age of New Literacies*, ed. by M. Elizabeth Weiser, Brian M. Fehler, and Angela M. Gonzalez, 42–69. Urbana, IL: NCTE.

Edwards, Nelta. 2002. "Radiation, Tobacco, and Illness in Point Hope, Alaska: Approaches to the 'Facts' in Contaminated Communities." In *Environmental Justice Reader: Politics, Poetics and Pedagogy*, ed. Joni Adamson, Mei Mei Evans, and Rachel Stein, 105–24. Tucson: University of Arizona Press.

Elbow, Peter. 1973. *Writing without Teachers.* Oxford: Oxford University Press.

Elmer, Greg. 2004. *Profiling Machines: Mapping the Personal Information Economy.* Boston: MIT Press.

Emig, Janet. 1964. "On the Uses of the Unconscious in Composing." *College Composition and Communication* 15 (1): 6–11. http://dx.doi.org/10.2307/355938.

English, U. S. 2013b. "Multilingual Ballots: How Much Do They Cost?" http://www.us-english.org/userdata/file/CostofMultilingualBallots.pdf.

English, U. S. 2013a. "Facts and Figures." n.d. Accessed September 1, 2013. http://www.us-english.org/userdata/file/FactsandFigures.pdf.

"English Flow Chart." 2013. *Pre-Advising at Urban Community College.* Urban Community College [name changed to protect the institution]. Accessed April 29, 2013.

EURid-UNESCO World Report on Internationalized Domain Name Deployment 2012. 2012. eu Insights. https://www.icann.org/en/system/files/files/eurid-unesco-deployment-08nov12-en.pdf.

Executive Order No. 13166. 2000. 3 C.R.F. 50121–22.

Eyman, Douglass. 2007. "Digital Rhetoric: Ecologies and Economies of Digital Circulation." PhD diss., Michigan State University, East Lansing.

Facchinetti, Roberta, David Crystal, and Barbara Seidlhofer, eds. 2010. *From International to Local English—And Back Again.* New York: Peter Lang.

Farrell, Thomas B., and G. Thomas Goodnight. 1981. "Accidental Rhetoric: The Root Metaphors of Three Mile Island." *Communication Monographs* 48 (4): 271–300. http://dx.doi.org/10.1080/03637758109376063.

Fine, Ben, and Alfredo Saad-Filho. 2004. *Marx's "Capital."* 4th ed. London: Pluto.

Fisher, David. 2010. "City Slow to Warn Neighbors of Toxic Contamination." ecoRI News, 24 June. Accessed September 28, 2013. http://www.ecori.org/social-justice-archive/2010/6/24/city-slow-to-warn-neighbors-of-toxic-contamination.html.

Fisher, Eran. 2012. ""How Less Alienation Creates More Exploitation? Audience Labour on Social Network Sites." *Triple C: Cognition, Communication, Co-operation* 10 (2): 171–83.

Fishman, Joshua. 1992. "The Displaced Anxieties of Anglo-Americans." In *Language Loyalties: A Source Book on the Official English Controversy*, ed. James Crawford, 165–70. Chicago, IL: University of Chicago Press.

Ford, Julie Dyke. 2004. "Knowledge Transfer across Disciplines: Tracking Rhetorical Strategies from a Technical Communications Classroom to an Engineering Classroom." *IEEE Transactions on Professional Communication* 47 (4): 301–45. http://dx.doi.org/10.1109/TPC.2004.840486.

Fowler, H. Ramsey, and Jane E. Aaron. 2010. *The Little, Brown Handbook.* 11th ed. New York: Pearson.

Fox, Tom. 1990. *The Social Uses of Writing: Politics and Pedagogy.* Norwood, NJ: Ablex.

Fraizer, Dan. 2010. "First Steps beyond First Year: Coaching Transfer after FYC." *WPA: Writing Program Administration* 33 (3): 34–57.

France, Alan. 1993. "Assigning Places: The Function of Introductory Composition as a Cultural Discourse." *College English* 55 (6): 593–609. http://dx.doi.org/10.2307/378696.

Freud, Sigmund. 1964. *The Complete Psychological Works.* Vol. 22. Trans. James Strachey. London: Hogarth.

Fuchs, Christian. 2010. "Labor in Informational Capitalism and on the Internet." *Information Society* 26 (3): 179–96. http://dx.doi.org/10.1080/01972241003712215.

Gadzinski, Eric. 1997. "The Year of Living Dangerously; or Not Just an Adventure, but a Job." *ADE Bulletin* (117): 35–7. http://dx.doi.org/10.1632/ade.117.35.

Gale, Xin Liu, and Fredric G. Gale, eds. 1999. *(Re)Visioning Composition Textbooks: Conflicts of Culture, Ideology, and Pedagogy.* Albany: SUNY Press.

Galef, David. 2000. "Words, Words, Words." In *Day Late, Dollar Short: The Next Generation and the New Academy*, ed. Peter Herman, 161–74. Albany: SUNY Press.

Gallagher, Chris W. 2009. "What Do WPA's Need to Know about Writing Assessment? An Immodest Proposal." *WPA: Writing Program Administration* 33 (1–2): 29–45.

Gallagher, Chris W. 2011. "Being There: (Re)Making the Assessment Scene." *College Composition and Communication* 62 (3): 450–76.

Gibson-Graham, J. K. 2006. *The End of Capitalism (As We Knew It): A Feminist Critique of Political Economy.* Minneapolis: University of Minnesota Press.

Giga-Byte Technology Co. 2013. Accessed Mar. 1, 2013.

Gilyard, Keith. 2000. "Basic Writing, Cost Effectiveness, and Ideology." *Journal of Basic Writing* 19 (1): 36–42.

Gilyard, Keith. 2012. "Writing Economies, Activism, and Community Work." *JAC* 32 (3–4): 461–78.

Giroux, Henry. 2005a. "Globalizing Dissent and Radicalizing Democracy: Politics, Pedagogy, and the Responsibility of Critical Intellectuals." In *Radical Relevance*, ed. Laura Gray-Rosendale and Steven Rosendale, 141–59. Albany: SUNY Press.

Giroux, Henry. 2005b. "Neoliberalism and the Demise of Democracy: Resurrecting Hope in Dark Times." *Dissident Voice*, August 7. http://www.dissidentvoice.org/Aug04/Giroux0807.htm.

Gomes, Lee. 2012. "Is There Big Money in Big Data?" *MIT Technology Review*, May 3. http://www.technologyreview.com/news/427786/is-there-big-money-in-big-data/.

Goode, Luke. 2005. "Mediations: From the Coffee House to the Internet Café." In *Jurgen Habermas: Democracy and the Public Sphere*, ed. Luke Goode, 89–119. London: Pluto.

Goode, Luke, and Alan McKee. 2013. "Conflict and Seduction in the Public Sphere." *Media Culture & Society* 35 (1): 113–20. http://dx.doi.org/10.1177/0163443712464565.

Gorski, Paul C. 2009. "Insisting on Digital Equity: Reframing the Dominant Discourse on Multicultural Education and Technology." *Urban Education* 44 (3): 348–64. http://dx.doi.org/10.1177/0042085908318712.

Graff, Gerald. 1987. *Professing Literature: An Institutional History*. Chicago, IL: University of Chicago Press.

Graff, Gerald, and Cathy Birkenstein. 2010. *They Say/I Say: The Moves That Matter in Academic Writing*. 2nd ed. New York: Norton.

Graham, Phil. 2006. *Hypercapitalism: New Media, Language, and Social Perceptions of Value*. New York: Peter Lang.

Grego, Rhonda, and Nancy Thompson. 1996. "Repositioning Remediation: Renegotiating Composition's Work in the Academy." *College Composition and Communication* 47 (1): 62–84. http://dx.doi.org/10.2307/358274.

Grego, Rhonda, and Nancy Thompson. 2008. *Teaching/Writing in Thirdspaces: The Studio Approach*. Carbondale: Southern Illinois University Press.

Gross, Martin L. 1999. *The Conspiracy of Ignorance: The Failure of American Public Schools*. New York: HarperCollins.

Gunner, Jeanne. 1993. "The Status of Basic Writing Teachers: Do We Need a 'Maryland Resolution'?" *Journal of Basic Writing* 12 (1): 57–63.

Gunner, Jeanne. 2012. "Disciplinary Purification: The Writing Program as Institutional Brand." *JAC* 32 (3–4): 615–44.

Gutiérrez y Muhs, Gabriella, Yolanda Flores Niemann, Carmen G. González, and Angela P. Harris, eds. 2012. *Presumed Innocent: The Intersections of Race and Class for Women in Academia*. Logan: Utah State University Press.

Haas, Christina. 1996. *Writing Technology: Studies on the Materiality of Literacy*. Mahwah, NJ: Lawrence Erlbaum.

Habermas, Jurgen. 1962. *The Structural Transformation of the Public Sphere: An Inquiry into a Category of Bourgeois Society*. Trans. Thomas Burger. Cambridge: MIT Press.

Hacker, Diana, and Nancy Sommers. 2010. *The Bedford Handbook*. 8th ed. Boston, MA: Bedford/St. Martin's.

Hairston, Maxine. 1982. *A Contemporary Rhetoric*. 3rd ed. Boston, MA: Houghton Mifflin.

Hanson, Allan F. 1993. *Testing Testing: Social Consequences of the Examined Life*. Berkeley: University of California Press.

Harris, Derrick. 2011. "Dissecting the Data: 5 Issues for Our Digital Future." *GigaOM*, November 15.

Harris, Muriel. 2005. *Prentice Hall Reference Guide*. Upper Saddle River, NJ: Prentice-Hall.

Harrison, Stanley. 2005. "The Condition of the Writing Class: Capital, Composition, Writing, and the Proletariat." *JAC* 25 (3): 543–70.

Harvey, David. 2005. *A Brief History of Neoliberalism*. New York: Oxford University Press.

Harvey, David. 2010. "The Enigma of Capital and the Crisis This Time." American Sociological Association Meetings, Atlanta, GA, August 16. http://davidharvey.org/2010/08/the-enigma-of-capital-and-the-crisis-this-time/.

Haswell, Richard H. 2005. "NCTE/CCCC's Recent War on Scholarship." *Written Communication* 22 (2): 198–223. http://dx.doi.org/10.1177/0741088305275367.

Hauben, Michael, and Rhonda Hauben. 1997. *Netizens: On the History and Impact of Usenet and the Internet*. Los Alamitos, CA: Wiley-IEEE Computer Society.

Haven, Cynthia. 2009. "The New Literacy: Stanford Study Finds Richness and Complexity in Students' Writing." *Stanford News*, October 12. http://news.stanford.edu/news/2009/october12/lunsford-writing-research-101209.html.

Hawhee, Debra. 1999. "Composition History and the Harbrace College Handbook." *College Composition and Communication* 50 (3): 504–22. http://dx.doi.org/10.2307/358863.

Heller, Monica. 1999. "Alternative Ideologies of *la francophonie*." *Journal of Sociolinguistics* 3 (3): 336–59. http://dx.doi.org/10.1111/1467-9481.00082.

Heller, Monica. 2003. "Globalization, the New Economy, and the Commodification of Language and Identity." *Journal of Sociolinguistics* 7 (4): 473–92. http://dx.doi.org/10.1111/j.1467-9841.2003.00238.x.

Heller, Monica. 2010. "The Commodification of Language." *Annual Review of Anthropology* 39 (October): 101–14. http://dx.doi.org/10.1146/annurev.anthro.012809.104951.

Heller, Monica, and Alexandre Duchene. 2012. "Pride and Profit: Changing Discourses of Language, Capital, and Nation-State." In *Language in Late Capitalism: Pride and Profit*, ed. Alexandre Duchene and Monica Heller, 1–21. New York: Routledge.

Heritage Foundation. 2013. "First Principles: Economic Thought." September 12. http://www.heritage.org/initiatives/first-principles/economic-thought.

Hernandez-Zamora, Gregorio. 2010. *Decolonizing Literacy: Mexican Lives in the Era of Global Capitalism.* Clevedon: Multilingual Matters.

Hill, Jane H. 2001. "The Racializing Function of Language Panics." In *Language Ideologies: Critical Perspectives on the Official English Movement, Volume 2: History, Theory, and Policy*, ed. Roseann Dueñas González with Ildikó Melis, 245–67. Urbana, IL: NCTE.

Hobart and William Smith Colleges. 2013a. "Writing and Rhetoric." http://hws.edu/academics/curr_wrrh.aspx.

Hobart and William Smith Colleges. 2013b. "Community Engagement and Service Learning." http://hws.edu/academics/service/index.aspx.

Hobart and William Smith Colleges. 2013c. "Geneva 2020." http://www.hws.edu/about/geneva_2020.aspx.

Holder, Eric. 2011. "Federal Government's Renewed Commitment to Language Access: Obligations under Executive Order 13166." *Memorandum to Heads of Federal Agencies, General Counsels, and Civil Rights Heads.*

Holland, Robert. 2002. "Globospeak? Questioning Text on the Role of English as a Global Language." *Language and Intercultural Communication* 2 (1): 5–24. http://dx.doi.org/10.1080/14708470208668072.

Horner, Bruce. 2000. *Terms of Work for Composition: A Materialist Critique.* Albany: SUNY Press.

Horner, Bruce. 2007. "Redefining Work and Value for Writing Program Administration." *JAC* 27 (1–2): 163–84.

Horner, Bruce. 2012. "Introduction: Economies of Writing." *JAC* 32 (3–4): 453–60.

Horner, Bruce, Christiane Donahue, and Samantha NeCamp. 2011. "From Monolingualism to Translingualism in Writing Research." Paper presented at the Writing Research across Borders II Conference, George Mason University, Fairfax, VA, February 18.

Horner, Bruce, Min-Zhan Lu, Jacqueline Jones Royster, and John Trimbur. 2011. "Language Difference in Writing: Toward a Translingual Approach." *College English* 73 (3): 303–21.

Horner, Bruce, Samantha NeCamp, and Christiane Donahue. 2011. "Toward a Multilingual Composition Scholarship: From English Only to a Translingual Norm." *College Composition and Communication* 63 (2): 269–300.

Horner, Bruce, and John Trimbur. 2002. "English Only and U.S. College Composition." *College Composition and Communication* 53 (4): 594–630. http://dx.doi.org/10.2307/1512118.

Hourigan, Maureen M. 1994. *Literacy as Social Exchange: Intersections of Class, Gender, and Culture.* Albany: SUNY Press.

House, Juliane. 2003. "English as a Lingua Franca: A Threat to Multilingualism?" *Journal of Sociolinguistics* 7 (4): 556–78. http://dx.doi.org/10.1111/j.1467-9841.2003.00242.x.

Huebner, Thom. 1999. "Sociopolitical Perspectives on Language Policy, Politics, and Praxis." In *Sociopolitical Perspectives on Language Policy and Planning in the USA*, ed. Thom Huebner and Kathryn A. Davis, 1–16. Amsterdam: John Benjamins. http://dx.doi.org/10.1075/sibil.16.05hue.

Hyland, Ken. 2002. "Authority and Invisibility: Authorial Identity in Academic Writing." *Journal of Pragmatics* 34 (8): 1091–112. http://dx.doi.org/10.1016/S0378-2166(02)00035-8.

Hymes, Dell. 1974. *Foundations in Sociolinguistics: Ethnographic Approaches.* Philadelphia: University of Pennsylvania Press.

IAB (Interactive Advertising Bureau). 2013. December 15. http://www.iab.net.

ICANN (International Corporation for Assigned Names and Numbers). 2016. Accessed August 5, 2016. http://www.icann.org.

IDC (International Data Corporation). 2013. Accessed September 17. http://www.idc.com.

Institute of Medicine of the National Academies. 2002. *Unequal Treatment: Confronting Racial and Ethnic Disparities in Health Care.* Washington, DC: National Academic Press.

Internet World Stats. Usage and Population Statistics. 2013. Miniwatts Marketing Group. Accessed April 10, 2013. http://www.Internetworldstats.com/.

Jackson, Brian, and Jon Wallin. 2009. "Rediscovering the 'Back-and-Forthness' of Rhetoric in the Age of YouTube." *College Composition and Communication* 61 (2): W374–96.

Jacquemet, Marco. 2005. "Transidiomatic Practices: Language and Power in the Age of Globalization." *Language & Communication* 25 (3): 257–77. http://dx.doi.org/10.1016/j.langcom.2005.05.001.

Jameson, Fredric. 1981. *The Political Unconscious: Narrative as a Socially Symbolic Act.* Ithaca, NY: Cornell University Press.

Jameson, Fredric. 1984. "Postmodernism: Or, The Cultural Logic of Late Capitalism." *New Left Review* (146): 53–92.

Jarratt, Susan C., Katherine Mack, Alexandra Sartor, and Shevaun E. Watson. 2009. "Pedagogical Memory: Writing, Mapping, Translating." *WPA: Writing Program Administration* 33 (1–2): 46–73.

Jenkins, Jennifer. 2009. "English as a Lingua Franca: Interpretations and Attitudes." *World Englishes* 28 (2): 200–7. http://dx.doi.org/10.1111/j.1467-971X.2009.01582.x.

Johnson, Cheryl L. 1994. "Participatory Rhetoric and the Teacher as Racial/Gendered Subject." *College English* 56 (4): 409–19. http://dx.doi.org/10.2307/378335.

Johnson, Matthew. 2008. "Public Writing in Gaming Spaces." *Computers and Composition* 25 (3): 270–83. http://dx.doi.org/10.1016/j.compcom.2008.05.001.

Johnson, T. R. 2011. "How Student Writers Develop: Rhetoric, Psychoanalysis, Ethics, Erotics." *JAC* 31 (3–4): 533–77.

Johnson, T. R. 2014. *The Other Side of Pedagogy: Lacan's Four Discourses and the Development of the Student Writer.* Albany: SUNY Press.

Jones, Danell. 1997. "Crossing the Great Divide: From Manhattan to Montana." *ADE Bulletin* 117 (Fall): 42–4. http://dx.doi.org/10.1632/ade.117.42.

Kahneman, Daniel. 2011. *Thinking, Fast and Slow.* New York: Farrar, Straus and Giroux.

Kameen, Paul. 1995. "Studying Professionally: Pedagogical Relationships at the Graduate Level." *College English* 57 (4): 448–60. http://dx.doi.org/10.2307/378243.

Kant, Immanuel. 1784. "Idea for a Universal History with a Cosmopolitan Intent." In *Perpetual Peace, and other Essays on Politics, History, and Morals.* Trans. Ted Humphrey, 29–40. Indianapolis: Hackett.

Katz, Steven B., and Carolyn R. Miller. 1996. "The Low-Level Radioactive Waste Siting Controversy in North Carolina: Toward a Rhetorical Model of Risk Communication." In *Green Culture: Environmental Rhetoric in Contemporary America,* ed. Carl G. Herndl and Stuart C. Brown, 110–40. Madison: University of Wisconsin Press.

Khatib, Kate, Margaret Killjoy, and Mike McGuire, eds. 2012. *We Are Many: Reflections on Movement Strategy from Occupation to Liberation.* Oakland, CA: AK Press.

Killingsworth, M. Jimmie, and Jacqueline S. Palmer. 1995. "The Discourse of 'Environmentalist Hysteria.'" *Quarterly Journal of Speech* 81 (1): 1–19. http://dx.doi.org/10.1080/00335639509384094.

Kirsch, Gesa, and Joy Ritchie. 1995. "Beyond the Personal: Theorizing a Politics of Location in Composition Research." *College Composition and Communication* 46 (1): 7–29. http://dx.doi.org/10.2307/358867.

Kleine, Michael W. 1999. "Teaching from a Single Textbook 'Rhetoric': The Potential Heaviness of the Book." In *(Re)Visioning Composition Textbooks*, ed. Xin Liu Gale and Frederic G. Gale, 137–61. Albany: SUNY Press.

Krieger, Murray. 1994. *The Institution of Theory*. Baltimore, MD: Johns Hopkins University Press.

Kristeva, Julia. 1984. *Revolution in Poetic Language*. Trans. Margaret Waller. New York: Columbia University Press.

Krugman, Paul. 2007. *The Conscience of a Liberal*. New York: Norton.

Kuo, Chih-Hua. 1999. "The Use of Personal Pronouns: Role Relationships in Scientific Journal Articles." *English for Specific Purposes* 18 (2): 121–38. http://dx.doi.org/10.1016/S0889-4906(97)00058-6.

Kynard, Carmen, and Robert Eddy. 2009. "Toward a New Critical Framework: Color-Conscious Political Morality and Pedagogy at Historically Black and Historically White Colleges and Universities." *College Composition and Communication* 61 (1): W24–44.

Lamsal, Tika, and Hem Paudel. 2012. "Beyond the Politics of Despair: Imagining the Possibilities for Change." *JAC* 32 (3–4): 758–67.

Latour, Bruno. 2005. "From Realpolitik to Dingpolitik: Or How to Make Things Public." In *Making Things Public: Atmospheres of Democracy*, ed. Bruno Latour and Peter Weibel, 75–7. Cambridge: MIT Press.

Lau v. Nichols. 1974. 414 U.S. 563. LexisNexis Academic. Accessed April 15, 2013.

LaVeist, Thomas A., Darrell J. Gaskin, and Patrick Richard. 2009. *The Economic Burden of Health Inequalities in the United States*. Washington, DC: Joint Center for Political and Economic Studies; http://dph.illinois.gov/sites/default/files/publications/The_economic_burden_of_health_inequalities_US.pdf.

Lewis, M. Paul, Gary F. Simons, and Charles D. Fennig, eds. 2016. *Ethnologue: Languages of the World*. 19th ed. Dallas: SIL International; http://www.ethnologue.com.

Lillis, Theresa. 2012. "Economies of Signs in Writing for Academic Publication: The Case of English Medium 'National' Journals." *JAC* 32 (3–4): 695–722.

Lillis, Theresa, and Mary Jane Curry. 2010. *Academic Writing in a Global Context: The Politics and Practices of Publishing in English*. New York: Routledge.

Limited English Proficiency. n. d. "Commonly Asked Questions and Answers Regarding Limited English Proficient (LEP) Individuals." Frequently Asked Questions. LEP.gov. Last modified April 15, 2016. https://www.lep.gov/faqs/faqs.html.

Lindquist, Julie. 2012. "Time to Grow Them: Practicing Slow Research in a Fast Field." *JAC* 32 (3–4): 645–66.

Looker, Samantha M. W. 2011. "Enacting and Interrogating the 'Academic' in Undergraduate Language and Literacy Practices." PhD diss., University of Illinois at Urbana-Champaign. ProQuest (3479404).

Lu, Min-Zhan. 1994. "Professing Multiculturalism: The Politics of Style in the Contact Zone." *College Composition and Communication* 45 (4): 442–58. http://dx.doi.org/10.2307/358759.

Lu, Min-Zhan. 2004. "An Essay on the Work of Composition: Composing English against the Order of Fast Capitalism." *College Composition and Communication* 56 (1): 16–49. http://dx.doi.org/10.2307/4140679.

Luke, Allan. 1996. "Genres of Power? Literacy Education and the Production of Capital." In *Literacy in Society: Language Description and Language Education*, ed. Ruqaiya Hasan and Geoffrey Williams, 308–38. New York: Longman.

Luke, Allan, and Victoria Carrington. 2004. "Globalisation, Literacy, Curriculum Practice." In *The RoutledgeFalmer Reader in Language and Literacy*, ed. Teresa Grainger, 52–66. New York: Routledge.

Luke, Allan, Carmen Luke, and Phil Graham. 2007. "Globalization, Corporatism, and Critical Language Education." *International Multilingual Research Journal* 1 (1): 1–13. http://dx.doi.org/10.1080/19313150709336861.

Lunsford, Andrea. 2011. *The St. Martin's Handbook*. 6th ed. Boston: Bedford/St. Martin's.

Lynch, Patrick J., and Sarah Horton. 2011. *Page Structure and Site Design*. 3rd ed., Web Style Guide; http://www.webstyleguide.com/wsg3/6-page-structure/3-site-design.html, Accessed Mar. 1, 2012.

Lyons, Gene. 1976. "The Higher Illiteracy." *Harper's Magazine*, September, 33–40.

Malcolm, Katie. 2011. "Resurfacing: New Guides for Basic Writing." PhD diss., University of Wisconsin-Milwaukee. Proquest (1738077844).

Manzerolle, Vincent, and Atle Mikkola Kjøsen. 2012. ""The Communication of Capital: Digital Media and the Logic of Acceleration." *Triple C: Cognition, Communication, Co-operation* 10 (2): 214–29.

Martínez, Iliana A. 2005. "Native and Non-Native Writers' Use of First Person Pronouns in the Different Sections of Biology Research Articles in English." *Journal of Second Language Writing* 14 (3): 174–90. http://dx.doi.org/10.1016/j.jslw.2005.06.001.

Marx, Karl. 1990. *Capital: A Critique of Political Economy*. vol. 1. New York: Penguin Classics.

Marx, Karl. 1993a. *Capital: A Critique of Political Economy*. vol. 2. London: Penguin Classics.

Marx, Karl. 1993b. *Grundrisse: Foundations of the Critique of Political Economy*. London: Penguin Classics.

Matsuda, Paul Kei. 2003. "Coming to Voice: Publishing as a Graduate Student." In *Writing for Scholarly Publication: Behind the Scenes in Language Education*, ed. Christine Pearson Casanave and Stephanie Vandrick, 39–51. Mahwah, NJ: Lawrence Erlbaum.

Matsuda, Paul Kei. 2006. "The Myth of Linguistic Homogeneity in U.S. College Composition." *College English* 68 (6): 637–51. http://dx.doi.org/10.2307/25472180.

Matsuda, Paul Kei, Tanita Saenkhum, and Steven Accardi. 2013. "Writing Teachers' Perceptions of the Presence and Needs of Second Language Writers: An Institutional Case Study." *Journal of Second Language Writing* 22 (1): 68–86. http://dx.doi.org/10.1016/j.jslw.2012.10.001.

McComas, Katherine A. 2003. "Citizen Satisfaction with Public Meetings Used for Risk Communication." *Journal of Applied Communication Research* 31 (2): 164–84. http://dx.doi.org/10.1080/0090988032000064605.

McCurrie, Matthew Kilian. 2009. "Measuring Success in Summer Bridge Programs: Retention Efforts and Basic Writing." *Journal of Basic Writing* 28 (2): 28–49.

McGurl, Mark. 2009. *The Program Era: Postwar Fiction and the Rise of Creative Writing*. Cambridge, MA: Harvard University Press.

McKee, Heidi. 2011. "Policy Matters Now and in the Future: Net Neutrality, Corporate Data Mining, and Government Surveillance." *Computers and Composition* 28 (4): 276–91. http://dx.doi.org/10.1016/j.compcom.2011.09.001.

McNabb, Richard. 2001. "Making the Gesture: Graduate Student Submissions and the Expectations of Journal Referees." *Composition Studies* 29 (1): 9–26.

Meierkord, Christiane. 2012. *Interactions across Englishes: Linguistic Choices in Local and International Contact Situations*. New York: Cambridge University Press. http://dx.doi.org/10.1017/CBO9781139026703.

Meltzer, Allan H. 2012. *Why Capitalism?* Oxford: Oxford University Press.

Memering, W. Dean. 1978. "Forward to the Basics." *College English* 39 (5): 553–61. http://dx.doi.org/10.2307/376116.

Meyers, Walter E. 1971. "Handbooks, Subhandbooks, and Nonhandbooks: Texts for Freshman English." *College English* 32 (6): 716–24. http://dx.doi.org/10.2307/374333.

Micciche, Laura. 2009. "Rhetorics of Critical Writing: Implications for Graduate Writing Instruction." *College Composition and Communication* 60 (3): W35–48.

Micciche, Laura. 2011. "Toward Graduate-Level Writing Instruction." *College Composition and Communication* 62 (3): 477–501.

Mignolo, Walter D. 2011. *The Darker Side of Western Modernity: Global Futures, Decolonial Options.* Durham, NC: Duke University Press. http://dx.doi.org/10.1215/9780822394501.

Miles, Libby. 2000. "Constructing Composition: Reproduction and WPA Agency in Textbook Publishing." *WPA: Writing Program Administration* 24 (1–2): 27–51.

Miley, Michelle. 2013. "Thirdspace Explorations in Online Writing Studios: Writing Centers, Writing in the Disciplines, and First Year Composition in the Corporate University." PhD diss., University of Houston. ProQuest (3574470).

Miller, Abby, Chandra Taylor Smith, and Andrew Nichols. 2011. "Promising Practices Supporting Low-Income, First-Generation Students at DeVry University." http://www.pellinstitute.org/downloads/publications-Promising_Practices_at_DeVry_University_May_2011.pdf.

Miller, Thomas. 1997. *The Formation of English.* Pittsburgh, PA: University of Pittsburgh Press.

Milson-Whyte, Vivette. 2012. "Economies, Identities, and Perceptions of Writing: Self-Portraits and Academic Writing Performance among Jamaican Students." *JAC* 32 (3–4): 565–90.

Mitchell, Don. 1995. "The End of Public Space? People's Park, Definitions of the Public, and Democracy." *Annals of the Association of American Geographers* 85 (1): 108–33.

Mitchell, Don. 2011. "Homelessness, American Style." *Urban Geography* 32 (7): 933–56. http://dx.doi.org/10.2747/0272-3638.32.7.933.

Modern Language Association. MLA Office of Research. 2013. *Report on the MLA Job Information List, 2012–2013.* https://apps.mla.org/pdf/rpt_jil_1314web.pdf.

Moffett, James. 1988. "Writing, Inner Speech, and Meditation." In *Coming on Center: Essays in English Education,* by James Moffett 133–81, 2nd ed. Portsmouth, NH: Heinemann.

Moore, Cindy, Peggy O'Neill, and Brian Huot. 2009. "Creating a Culture of Assessment." *College Composition and Communication* 61 (1): W107–32.

Moran, Andrew. 2012. "OECD: South Korea High-Speed Internet Penetration Rate Tops 100%." *Digital Journal,* July 23. http://www.digitaljournal.com/article/329199.

Morrison, Toni. 1989. "Unspeakable Things Unspoken: The Afro-American Presence in American Literature." *Michigan Quarterly* 28 (1): 1–24.

Mortensen, Peter. 1999. "Of Handbooks and Handbags: Composition Textbook Publishing after the Deal Decade." In *(Re)Visioning Composition Textbooks: Conflicts of Culture, Ideology, and Pedagogy,* ed. Xin Liu Gale and Fredric G. Gale, 217–29. Albany: SUNY Press.

Mortensen, Peter, and Gesa Kirsch. 1996. *Ethics and Representation in Qualitative Studies of Literacy.* Urbana, IL: NCTE.

Mulroy, David. 2003. *The War against Grammar.* Portsmouth, NJ: Heinemann.

Murphy, Michael. 2000. "New Faculty for a New University: Toward a Full-Time Teaching-Intensive Faculty Track in Composition." *College Composition and Communication* 52 (1): 14–42. http://dx.doi.org/10.2307/358542.

Murray, Donald. 1968. "The Listening Eye: Reflections on the Writing Conference." In *The Writing Teacher's Sourcebook,* ed. Gary Tate and Edward Corbett, 232–7. New York: Oxford University Press.

Myers, D. G. 1996. *The Elephants Teach: Creative Writing since 1880.* Englewood Cliffs, NJ: Prentice Hall.

National Center for Supercomputing Applications. University of Illinois at Urbana-Champaign. 2013. "NCSA Mosaic." Last modified December 3, 2013. http://www.ncsa.illinois.edu/enabling/mosaic.

Nelms, Gerald, and Ronda Leathers Dively. 2007. "Perceived Roadblocks to Transferring Knowledge from First-Year Composition to Writing-Intensive Major Courses: A Pilot Study." *WPA: Writing Program Administration* 31 (1–2): 214–40.

New England Resource Center for Higher Education. 2016. "Carnegie Community Engagement Classification: Classified Campuses." nerche.org. Aug. 10. Accessed Oct.

7, 2016. http://www.nerche.org/index.php?option=com_content&view=article&id=341&Itemid=618#Classified.

Newfield, Christopher. 2008. *Unmaking the Public University: The Forty-Year Assault on the Middle Class.* Cambridge, MA: Harvard University Press.

Notaro, Anna. 2006. "The Lo(n)g Revolution: The Blogosphere as an Alternative Public Sphere?" *Reconstructions* 6 (4): 1–19.

Novak, Michael. 1982. *The Spirit of Democratic Capitalism.* New York: Simon and Schuster.

Nowacek, Rebecca. 2011. *Agents of Integration: Understanding Transfer as a Rhetorical Act.* Carbondale: Southern Illinois University Press.

NYC General Assembly. 2013. "Principles of Solidarity." http://www.nycga.net/resources/documents/principles-of-solidarity/.

O'Dair, Sharon. 2000. "Stars, Tenure, and the Death of Ambition." In *Day Late, Dollar Short: The Next Generation and the New Academy,* ed. Peter Herman, 45–61. Albany: SUNY Press.

O'Reilly, Tim. 2005. "What Is Web 2.0?" O'Reilly. September 30. http://www.oreilly.com/pub/a/web2/archive/what-is-web-20.html.

Oakeshott, Michael. 1962. *Rationalism in Politics and Other Essays.* London: Methuen.

Office of Water Resources. 2007. "Total Maximum Daily Load for Dissolved Oxygen and Phosphorous, Mashapaug Pond, Providence, Rhode Island." *RI DEM/Office of Water Resources—TMDL Program.* September. http://static1.squarespace.com/static/546d61b5e4b049f0b10b95c5/t/55073f59e4b0692c8417ef2a/1426538329758/mashpaug.pdf.

Ohmann, Richard. 1996. *English in America.* Hanover, NH: Wesleyan University Press.

Ollman, Bertoll. 1976. *Alienation: Marx's Conception of Man in Capitalist Society.* 2nd ed. New York: Cambridge University Press.

OMB (Office of Management and Budget). 2002. "Report to Congress. Assessment of the Total Benefits and Costs of Implementing Executive Order No. 13166: Improving Access to Services for Persons with Limited English Proficiency." March 14.

Paolillo, John C. 2007. "How Much Multilingualism? Language Diversity on the Internet." In *The Multilingual Internet: Language, Culture, and Communication Online,* ed. Brenda Danet and Susan C. Herring, 408–30. New York: Oxford University Press. http://dx.doi.org/10.1093/acprof:oso/9780195304794.003.0018.

Papacharissi, Zizi. 2013. *A Private Sphere: Democracy in a Digital Age.* Cambridge: Polity.

Park, Joseph Sung-Yul, and Lionel Wee. 2012. *Markets of English: Linguistic Capital and Language Policy in a Globalizing World.* New York: Routledge.

Pauwels, Luc. 2012. "A Multimodal Framework for Analyzing Websites as Cultural Expressions." *Journal of Computer-Mediated Communication* 17 (3): 247–65. http://dx.doi.org/10.1111/j.1083-6101.2012.01572.x.

Peck, Wayne Campbell, Linda Flower, and Lorraine Higgins. 1995. "Community Literacy." *College Composition and Communication* 46 (2): 199–222. http://dx.doi.org/10.2307/358428.

Peckham, Irvin. 2010. *Going North, Thinking West: The Intersections of Social Class, Critical Thinking, and Politicized Writing Instruction.* Logan: Utah State University Press.

Peeples, Jennifer A., and Kevin M. DeLuca. 2006. "The Truth of the Matter: Motherhood, Community and Environmental Justice." *Women's Studies in Communication* 29 (1): 59–87. http://dx.doi.org/10.1080/07491409.2006.10757628.

Pennycook, Alastair. 2007. *Global Englishes and Transcultural Flows.* London: Routledge.

Perkins, David N., and Gavriel Salomon. 1988. "Teaching for Transfer." *Educational Leadership* 46 (1): 22–32.

Perkins, David N., and Gavriel Salomon. 2012. "Knowledge to Go: A Motivational and Dispositional View of Transfer." *Educational Psychologist* 47 (3): 248–58. http://dx.doi.org/10.1080/00461520.2012.693354.

Petraglia, Joseph, ed. 1995. *Reconceiving Writing, Rethinking Writing Instruction.* Mahwah, NJ: Lawrence Erlbaum.

Porter, James. 2010. "Rhetoric in (as) a Digital Economy." In *Rhetorics and Technologies: New Directions in Writing and Communication,* ed. Stuart Selber, 173–97. Columbia: University of South Carolina Press.

Porter, James E., Patricia Sullivan, Stuart Blythe, Jeffrey T. Grabill, and Libby Miles. 2000. "Institutional Critique: A Rhetorical Methodology for Change." *College Composition and Communication* 51 (4): 610–42. http://dx.doi.org/10.2307/358914.

Poster, Mark. 1995. "The Net as a Public Sphere?" *Wired,* November 1. http://archive.wired.com/wired/archive/3.11/poster.if_pr.html.

Prashad, Vijay. 2012. "This Concerns Everyone." In *We Are Many: Reflections from Movement Strategy from Occupation to Liberation,* ed. Kate Khatib, Margaret Killjoy, and Mike McGuire, 9–19. Oakland, CA: AK Press.

Prendergast, Catherine. 2008. *Buying into English: Language and Investment in the New Capitalist World.* Pittsburgh, PA: University of Pittsburgh Press.

Prentice, Mary. 2009. "Service-Learning's Impact on Developmental Reading/Writing and Student Life Skills Courses." *Community College Journal of Research and Practice* 33 (3–4): 270–82. http://dx.doi.org/10.1080/10668920802580523.

Prior, Paul. 1998. *Writing/Disciplinarity: A Sociohistoric Account of Literate Activity in the Academy.* Mahwah, NJ: Lawrence Erlbaum.

Providence Redevelopment Agency. 2005. "Providence—Bilingual Notice of Public Meeting 10–5–05 & Public Hearing 10–19–05." October. http://www.dem.ri.gov/programs/benviron/waste/gorham/b510xxh1.pdf.

Providence Redevelopment Agency. 2006. "Providence—Response to Public Comments on the Site Investigation Report." *RIDEM/Waste Management—Gorham/Textron Site (Adelaide Avenue) Documents Index.* January 24. http://www.dem.ri.gov/programs/benviron/waste/gorham/b60124ea.pdf.

Racelis, Juval V., and Paul Kei Matsuda. 2015. "Exploring Multiple Identities of L2 Writing Teachers." In *Advances and Current Trends in Language Teacher Identity Research,* ed. Yin Ling Cheung, Selim Ben Said, and Kwanghyun Park, 203–16. London: Routledge.

Rai, Candace. 2010. "Power, Publics, and the Rhetorical Uses of Democracy." In *The Public Work of Rhetoric: Citizen-Scholars and Civic Engagement,* ed. John Ackerman and David Coogan, 39–55. Columbia: University of South Carolina Press.

Raimes, Ann, and Maria Jerskey. 2011. *Keys for Writers.* 6th ed. Boston, MA: Wadsworth.

Reich, Robert B. 2010. *Aftershock: The Next Economy and America's Future.* New York: Knopf.

Reichert-Powell, Pegeen. 2009. "Retention and Writing Instruction: Implications for Access and Pedagogy." *College Composition and Communication* 60 (4): 664–82.

Reiff, Mary Jo, and Anis Bawarshi. 2011. "Tracing Discursive Resources: How Students Use Prior Genre Knowledge to Negotiate New Writing Contexts in First-Year Composition." *Written Communication* 28 (3): 312–37. http://dx.doi.org/10.1177/0741088311410183.

Rendleman, Eliot Franklin. 2009. "Technological Performativity: Mapping the Rhetoric of Student Valuation and Identity in Composition Textbooks." PhD diss., University of Nevada, Reno. ProQuest (3355598).

Rendleman, Eliot Franklin. 2013. "Survey of Textbook Adoption Policies and Practices in First-Year Writing Programs." CompPile.org. http://compfaqs.org/textbooks/adoption/index.php.

Reynolds, Nedra. 2004. *Geographies of Writing: Inhabiting Places and Encountering Difference.* Carbondale: Southern Illinois University Press.

Rhode Island Department of Environmental Management. 1995. "ABB—Letter to RIDEM Re: Underground Storage Tanks (See RIDEM e-mail 10-19-06)." *RIDEM/Waste Management—Gorham/Textron Site (Adelaide Avenue) Documents Index.* March 27. http://www.dem.ri.gov/programs/benviron/waste/gorham/d95327ut.pdf.

Rhode Island Department of Environmental Management. 2007. "Community Letter to RIDEM—Re: Textron's Park Parcel Remediation Plan—Public Comments." RI DEM/ Waste Management—Gorham/Textron Site (Adelaide Avenue) Documents Index. September 5. Accessed September 28, 2013. http://www.dem.ri.gov/programs/benviron/waste/gorham/d70905lt.pdf.

Rice, Jenny Edbauer. 2005. "Unframing Models of Public Distribution: From Rhetorical Situation to Rhetorical Ecologies." *Rhetoric Society Quarterly* 35 (4): 5–24. http://dx.doi.org/10.1080/02773940509391320.

Ritter, Kelly. 2006. "Extra-Institutional Space and the Public Value of the WPA." *WPA: Writing Program Administration* 29 (3): 45–64.

Rivers, Nathaniel A., and Ryan P. Weber. 2011. "Ecological, Pedagogical, Public Rhetoric." *College Composition and Communication* 63 (2): 187–218.

Roberts, Alasdair. 2011. "The WikiLeaks Illusion." *Wilson Quarterly* (Summer). http://wilsonquarterly.com/quarterly/summer-2011-a-changing-middle-east/the-wikileaks-illusion/.

Roberts-Miller, Trish. 2004. "Parody Blogging and the Call of the Real." In *Into the Blogosphere: Rhetoric, Community, and Culture of Weblogs*, ed. Laura J. Gurak, Smiljana Antonijevic, Laurie Johnson, Clancy Ratliff, and Jessica Reyman. University of Minnesota Libraries. Digital Conservancy. http://conservancy.umn.edu/handle/11299/172812.

Rodman, Gilbert. 2003. "The Net Effect: The Public's Fear and the Public Sphere." In *Virtual Publics: Policy and Community in an Electronic Age*, ed. Beth Kolko, 11–48. New York: Columbia University Press.

Roen, Duane, Victor Villanueva, Stuart Brown, Gesa Kirsch, John Adams, Susan Wyche-Smith, and Sheri Helsley. 1995. "Revising for Publication: Advice to Graduate Students and Other Junior Scholars." *Rhetoric Society Quarterly* 25 (1–4): 237–46. http://dx.doi.org/10.1080/02773949509391047.

Roozen, Kevin. 2010. "Tracing Trajectories of Practice: Repurposing in One Student's Developing Disciplinary Writing Processes." *Written Communication* 27 (3): 318–54. http://dx.doi.org/10.1177/0741088310373529.

Rosa, Alfred, and Paul Eschholz. 2011. *The Writer's Brief Handbook*. 7th ed. Upper Saddle River, NJ: Pearson.

Rose, Mike. 1980. "Rigid Rules, Inflexible Plans, and the Stifling of Language: A Cognitivist Analysis of Writer's Block." *College Composition and Communication* 31 (4): 389–401. http://dx.doi.org/10.2307/356589.

Rose, Mike. 1981. "Sophisticated, Ineffective Books: The Dismantling of Process in Composition Texts." *College Composition and Communication* 32 (1): 65–74. http://dx.doi.org/10.2307/356346.

Rose, Mike. 1985. "The Language of Exclusion: Writing Instruction at the University." *College English* 47 (4): 341–59. http://dx.doi.org/10.2307/376957.

Rose, Mike. 2010. "Re-mediating Remediation." *Open Words: Access and English Studies* 4 (1): 5–10.

Rose, Mike, and Karen McClafferty. 2001. "A Call for the Teaching of Writing in Graduate Education." *Educational Researcher* 30 (2): 27–33. http://dx.doi.org/10.3102/0013189X030002027.

Rosen, Andrew S. 2011. *Change.edu: Rebooting for the New Talent Economy*. New York: Kaplan.

Rosenblatt, Louise. 1938. *Literature as Exploration*. New York: MLA.

Rounsaville, Angela. 2012. "Selecting Genres for Transfer: The Role of Uptake in Students' Antecedent Genre Knowledge." *Composition Forum* 26 (Fall). http://compositionforum.com/issue/26/selecting-genres-uptake.php.

Royer, Daniel, and Roger Gilles, eds. 2003. *Directed Self-Placement: Principles and Practices*. Cresskill, NJ: Hampton.

Royster, Jacqueline Jones, and Rebecca Greenberg Taylor. 1997. "Constructing Teacher Identity in the Basic Writing Classroom." *Journal of Basic Writing* 16 (1): 27–50.

Rubdy, Rani, and Mario Saraceni, eds. 2006. *English in the World: Global Rules, Global Roles.* London: Continuum.

Rubdy, Rani, and Peter Tan, eds. 2008. *Language as Commodity: Global Structures, Local Marketplaces.* New York: Continuum.

Russell, David. 1995. "Activity Theory and Its Implications for Writing Instruction." In *Reconceiving Writing, Rethinking Writing Instruction,* ed. Joseph Petraglia, 51–77. Mahwah, NJ: Lawrence Erlbaum.

Russell, David. 1999. "Activity Theory and Process Approaches: Writing (Power) in School and Society." In *Post-Process Theory: Beyond the Writing-Process Paradigm,* ed. Thomas Kent, 80–95. Carbondale: Southern Illinois University Press.

Ruszkiewicz, John, Christie Friend, Daniel E. Stewart, and Maxine Hairston. 2011. *The Scott, Foresman Handbook for Writers.* 9th ed. New York: Pearson.

Ryan, Johnny. 2010. *The History of the Internet and the Digital Future.* London: Reaktion Books.

Ryder, Phyllis Mentzell. 2011. *Rhetorics for Community Action: Public Writing and Writing Publics.* Lanham, MD: Lexington Books.

Santini, Marina. 2007. "Characterizing Genres of Web Pages: Genre Hybridism and Individualization." *Proceedings of the 40th Hawaii International Conference on System Sciences, Waikoloa, HI.* New York: Wiley-IEEE Computer Society. http://dx.doi.org/10.1109/HICSS.2007.124.

Schell, Eileen. 1998. *Gypsy Academics and Mother-Teachers: Gender, Contingent Labor, and Writing Instruction.* Portsmouth, NH: Boynton/Cook.

Schneiderman, Stuart. 1983. *Jacques Lacan: The Death of an Intellectual Hero.* Cambridge, MA: Harvard University Press. http://dx.doi.org/10.4159/harvard.9780674865761.

Scott, Tony. 2009. *Dangerous Writing: Understanding the Political Economy of Composition.* Logan: Utah State University Press.

Segal, Judy Z. 1995. "Textbooks and Subtexts or How to Choose a Handbook." *Journal of Teaching Writing* 14 (1–2): 111–27.

Selfe, Cynthia. 1999. *Technology and Literacy in the Twenty-First Century: The Importance of Paying Attention.* Carbondale: Southern Illinois University Press.

Selfe, Cynthia L., and Gail E. Hawisher. 2006. "Methodologies of Peer and Editorial Review: Changing Practices." *College Composition and Communication* 63 (4): 672–98.

Shapiro, Shawna. 2011. "Stuck in the Remedial Rut: Confronting Resistance to ESL Curriculum Reform." *Journal of Basic Writing* 30 (2): 24–52.

Shaughnessy, Mina. 1977. *Errors and Expectations: A Guide for the Teacher of Basic Writing.* New York: Oxford University Press.

Sheils, Merrill. 1975. "Why Johnny Can't Write." *Newsweek,* December 8, 58–65.

Shepherd, Alan, John McMillan, and Gary Tate, eds. 1998. *Coming to Class: Pedagogy and the Social Class of Teachers.* Portsmouth, NH: Heinemann/Boynton Cook.

Shepherd, Michael, and Carolyn Watters. 1998. "The Evolution of Cybergenre." *Proceedings of the 31st Hawaii International Conference on System Sciences, Waikoloa, HI.* New York: Wiley-IEEE Computer Society.

Shepherd, Michael, and Carolyn Watters. 1999. "The Functionality Attribute of Cybergenres." *Proceedings of the 32nd Hawaii International Conference on System Sciences, Waikoloa, HI.* New York: Wiley-IEEE Computer Society.

Sheridan, David, Jim Ridolfo, and Anthony Michel. 2005. "The Available Means of Persuasion: Mapping a Theory and Pedagogy of Multimodal Public Rhetoric." *JAC* 25 (4): 803–43.

Shor, Ira. 1997. "Our Apartheid: Writing Instruction and Inequality." *Journal of Basic Writing* 16 (1): 91–104.

Sirico, Robert A. 2010. "The Moral Basis for Economic Liberty." Heritage Foundation First Principles Series Report #30. http://www.heritage.org/research/reports/2010/07/the-moral-basis-for-economic-liberty.

Sledd, James. 1993. "Anglo-Conformity: Folk Remedy for Lost Hegemony." In *Eating on the Street: Teaching Literacy in a Multicultural Society*, ed. David Shaafsma, 87–95. Pittsburgh, PA: University of Pittsburgh Press.

Slomp, David. 2012. "Challenges in Assessing the Development of Writing Ability: Theories, Constructs, and Methods." *Assessing Writing* 17 (2): 81–91. http://dx.doi.org/10.1016/j.asw.2012.02.001.

Smit, David. 2004. *The End of Composition Studies.* Carbondale: Southern Illinois University Press.

Smith, Adam. 1776. *The Wealth of Nations, Books I–III.* Ed. Andrew Skinner. New York: Penguin.

Smith, David, and Phil Evans. 1982. *Marx's Kapital for Beginners.* New York: Pantheon.

Soliday, Mary. 2002. *The Politics of Remediation: Institutional and Student Needs in Higher Education.* Pittsburgh: University of Pittsburgh Press.

Spear, Karen. 1997. "Controversy and Consensus in Freshman Writing: An Overview of the Field." *Review of Higher Education* 20 (3): 319–44. http://dx.doi.org/10.1353/rhe.1997.0005.

Spolsky, Bernard. 2004. *Language Policy.* Cambridge: Cambridge University Press.

Spring, Joel H. 2006. *Pedagogies of Globalization: The Rise of the Educational Security State.* New York: Routledge.

St. Germain-McDaniel, Nicole. 2010. "Technical Communication in the Health Fields: Executive Order 13166 and Its Impact on Translation and Localization." *Technical Communication (Washington)* 57 (3): 251–65.

Starke-Meyerring, Doreen. 2008. "Genre, Knowledge, and Digital Code in Web-Based Communities: An Integrated Theoretical Framework for Shaping Digital Discursive Spaces." *International Journal of Web Based Communities* 4 (4): 398–417. http://dx.doi.org/10.1504/IJWBC.2008.019547.

Steen, R Grant. Apr 2011. "Retractions in the Scientific Literature: Is the Incidence of Research Fraud Increasing?" *Journal of Medical Ethics* 37 (4): 249–53. Medline:21186208 http://dx.doi.org/10.1136/jme.2010.040923.

Steinmetz, George. 2011. "Bourdieu, Historicity, and Historical Sociology." *Cultural Sociology* 5 (1): 45–66. http://dx.doi.org/10.1177/1749975510389912.

Sternglass, Marylyn. 1997. *Time to Know Them: A Longitudinal Study of Writing and Learning at the College Level.* London: Routledge.

Stygall, Gail. 1994. ""Resisting Privilege: Basic Writing and Foucault's Author Function." *College Composition and Communication* 45 (3): 320–41.

Sullivan, Patricia. 1991. "Writing in the Graduate Curriculum: Literary Criticism as Composition." *JAC* 11 (2): 283–300.

Sunstein, Cass. 2007. *Republic.com 2.0.* Princeton: Princeton University Press.

Tancer, Bill. 2008. *Click: What Millions of People Are Doing Online and Why It Matters.* New York: Hyperion.

Tassoni, John, and Cynthia Lewiecki-Wilson. 2005. "Not Just Anywhere, Anywhen: Mapping Change through Studio Work." *Journal of Basic Writing* 24 (1): 68–92.

Taubman, Peter. 2012. *Disavowed Knowledge: Psychoanalysis, Education, and Teaching.* New York: Routledge.

Thaiss, Chris, and Terry Myers Zawacki. 2006. *Engaged Writers, Dynamic Disciplines: Research on the Academic Writing Life.* Portsmouth, NH: Boynton/Cook.

Thompkins, Kenya MaKonnen. 2007. "One Size Doesn't Fit All: A Descriptive Study of First-Year Writing at Selected Florida Colleges and Universities." PhD diss., Florida State University. ProQuest (3301602).

Thompson, Clive. 2009. "Clive Thompson on the New Literacy." *Wired*, August 24. http://archive.wired.com/techbiz/people/magazine/17-09/st_thompson.

Thorndike, E. L. 1999. *The Principles of Teaching: Based on Psychology*. London: Routledge.

Tierney, William. 2011. "Too Big to Fail: The Role of For-Profit Colleges and Universities in American Higher Education." *Change* 43 (6): 27–32. http://dx.doi.org/10.1080/00091383.2011.618079.

Tighe, Donald J. 1963. "The Shame of Freshman English." *College Composition and Communication* 14 (1): 32–5. http://dx.doi.org/10.2307/355296.

"Tim Berners-Lee's Proposal." 2008. https://www.w3.org/History/1989/proposal.html.

Tobin, Lad. 1991. "Reading Students, Reading Ourselves: Revising the Teacher's Role in the Writing Class." *College English* 53 (3): 333–48. http://dx.doi.org/10.2307/378108.

Trimbur, John. 2000. "Composition and the Circulation of Writing." *College Composition and Communication* 52 (2): 188–219. http://dx.doi.org/10.2307/358493.

Trimbur, John. 2012. "Writing after Print Capitalism." *JAC* 34 (3–4): 723–31.

Troyka, Lynn Quitman, and Douglas Hesse. 2009. *Simon & Schuster Handbook for Writers*. 9th ed. Upper Saddle River, NJ: Pearson.

Tuomi-Gröhn, Terttu, and Yrgo Engeström, eds. 2003. *Between School and Work: New Perspectives on Transfer and Boundary-Crossing*. New York: Pergamon.

Turkle, Sherrie. 1979. *Psychoanalytic Politics: Jacques Lacan and Freud's French Revolution*. New York: Basic Books.

Turow, Joseph. 2011. *The Daily You: How the New Advertising Industry Is Defining Your Identity and Your World*. New Haven: Yale University Press.

Uluave, Luana. 2005. "The Revolving Door: Teaching and Not Teaching Writing at a For-Profit University." *Works and Days* 45/46 (1–2): 121–49.

US Department of Education. 2012. "Title III Part A Programs: Strengthening Institutions: Awards.". http://www2.ed.gov/programs/iduestitle3a/awards.html.

US Department of Health and Human Services. 2001a. *Cultural Competence Works: Using Cultural Competence to Improve the Quality of Health Care for Diverse Populations and Add Value to Managed Care Arrangements*. Substance Abuse and Mental Health Services Administration.

US Department of Health and Human Services. 2001b. *National Standards for Culturally and Linguistically Appropriate Services in Health Care: Executive Summary*. Office of Minority Health. http://minorityhealth.hhs.gov/assets/pdf/checked/finalreport.pdf.

US Department of Health and Human Services. 2003. "Guidance to Federal Financial Assistance Recipients Regarding Title VI Prohibition Against National Origin Discrimination Affecting Limited English Proficient Persons." HHS.gov. Accessed October 3, 2013. http://www.hhs.gov/civil-rights/for-individuals/special-topics/limited-english-proficiency/guidance-federal-financial-assistance-recipients-title-VI/.

US Department of Health and Human Services. 2010. "Think—Speak—Act Cultural Health: Part 1." Video. Office of Minority Health. https://www.thinkculturalhealth.hhs.gov/content/clas.asp.

US Department of Health and Human Services. 2013a. "About HRSA." Health Resources and Services Administration. Accessed March 18, 2013. http://www.hrsa.gov/about/.

US Department of Health and Human Services. 2013b. "What Are the National CLAS Standards?" Health Resources and Services Administration. https://www.thinkculturalhealth.hhs.gov/content/clas.asp.

US Department of Justice. 2002. "Guidance to Federal Financial Assistance Recipients Regarding Title VI Prohibition Against National Origin Discrimination Affecting Limited English Proficient Persons." *Federal Register* 67 (177): 41455–72.

US Department of Management and Budget, Office of Information and Regulatory Affairs. 2002. "Report to Congress: Assessment of the Total Benefits and Costs of Implementing Executive Order No. 13166; Improving Access to Services for Persons with Limited English Proficiency." March 14. Whitehouse.gov.

US Environmental Protection Agency. 2011. "Brownfields." Accessed October 4. https://www.epa.gov/brownfields/brownfield-overview-and-definition.

Uzuner, Sedef. 2008. "Multilingual Scholars' Participation in Core/Global Academic Communities: A Literature Review." *Journal of English for Academic Purposes* 7 (4): 250–63. http://dx.doi.org/10.1016/j.jeap.2008.10.007.

Verhaege, Paul. 2004. *On Being Normal and Other Disorders: A Manual for Clinical Psychodiagnostics.* Trans. Sigi Jottkandt. New York: Other Press.

Ward, Irene. 1997. "How Democratic Can We Get? The Internet, the Public Sphere, and Public Discourse." *JAC* 17 (3): 365–79.

Ward, Jay A. 1981. "Changes in the Training of Writing Teachers." *JAC* 2 (1–2): 153–60.

Wardle, Elizabeth. 2007. "Understanding 'Transfer' from FYC: Preliminary Results of a Longitudinal Study." *WPA: Writing Program Administration* 31 (1–2): 65–85.

Wardle, Elizabeth. 2012. "Creative Repurposing for Expansive Learning: Considering 'Problem-Exploring' and 'Answer-Getting' Dispositions in Individuals and Fields." *Composition Forum* 26 (Fall). http://compositionforum.com/issue/26/creative-repurposing.php.

Wardle, Elizabeth, and Doug Downs. 2011. *Writing about Writing: A College Reader.* Boston, MA: Bedford/St.Martins.

Watkins, Evan. 1989. *Work Time: English Departments and the Circulation of Cultural Value.* Palo Alto, CA: Stanford University Press.

Webb-Sunderhaus, Sara. 2010. "When Access Is Not Enough: Retaining Basic Writers at an Open-Admissions University." *Journal of Basic Writing* 29 (2): 97–116.

Wee, Lionel. 2003. "Linguistic Instrumentalism in Singapore." *Journal of Multilingual and MulticulturalDevelopment*24 (3): 211–24. http://dx.doi.org/10.1080/01434630308666499.

Weisser, Christian R. 2002. *Moving beyond Academic Discourse: Composition Studies and the Public Sphere.* Carbondale: Southern Illinois University Press.

Welch, Nancy. 1997. *Getting Restless: Rethinking Revision in Writing Instruction.* Women in History Series. Portsmouth, NH: Heinemann.

Welch, Nancy. 2008. *Living Room: Teaching Public Writing in a Privatized World.* Portsmouth, NH: Heinemann.

Wells, Susan. 1996. "Rogue Cops and Health Care: What Do We Want from Public Writing?" *College Composition and Communication* 47 (3): 325–41. http://dx.doi.org/10.2307/358292.

"Where to Buy." 2013. gigabyte.com.

Wible, Scott. 2013. *Shaping Language Policy in the U.S.: The Role of Composition Studies.* Carbondale: Southern Illinois University Press.

"William Lynch Speech." 2011. *Wikipedia.* May 7. https://en.wikipedia.org/wiki/William_Lynch_speech.

Williams, Jeffrey. 2013. "The Great Stratification." *Chronicle of Higher Education,* December 2, 1–10. http://chronicle.com/article/The-Great-Stratification/143285.

Williams, Raymond. 1977. *Marxism and Literature.* New York: Oxford University Press.

Xue, Hong. 2004. "The Voice of China: A Story of Chinese-Character Domain Names." *Cardozo Journal of International and Comparative Law* 12 (2): 559–92.

Yancey, Kathleen Blake. 2004. "Made Not Only in Words: Composition in a New Key." *College Composition and Communication* 56 (2): 297–328. http://dx.doi.org/10.2307/4140651.

Yancey, Kathleen Blake. 2008. *Writing in the 21st Century: A Report from the National Council of Teachers of English.* www.ncte.org/library/NCTEFiles/Press/Yancey_final.pdf.

Young, Vershawn Ashanti. 2009. "'Nah, We Straight': An Argument against Code Switching." *JAC* 29 (1–2): 49–76.

Young, Vershawn A., and Aja Y. Martinez, eds. 2011. *Code-Meshing As World English: Pedagogy, Policy, Performance.* Urbana, IL: NCTE.

Zebroski, James. 2002. "Composition and Rhetoric Inc.: Life After the English Department at Syracuse University." In *Beyond English, Inc.: Curricular Reform in a Global Economy,* ed.

David Downing, Claude Mark Hurlbert, and Paula Mathieu, 164–80. Portsmouth, NH: Heinemann.

Zelnick, Stephen. 1983. "Student Worlds in Student Conferences." In *Writing Talks: Views on Teaching Writing from across the Disciplines*, ed. Muffy E. A. Siegal and Toby Olson, 47–58. Upper Montclair, NJ: Boynton-Cook.

Zikopoulos, Paul C., Chris Eaton, Dirk deRoos, Thomas Deutsch, and George Lapis. 2012. *Understanding Big Data: Analytics for Enterprise Class Hadoop and Streaming Data*. http://www-01.ibm.com/common/ssi/cgi-bin/ssialias?infotype=SA&subtype=WH&htmlfid=IML14296USEN.

ABOUT THE AUTHORS

Bruce Horner is Endowed Chair in Rhetoric and Composition at the University of Louisville, where he teaches courses in composition, composition theory and pedagogy, and literacy studies. His recent books include *Crossing Divides: Exploring Translingual Writing Pedagogies and Programs* (Utah State UP, forthcoming), *Reworking English in Rhetoric and Composition: Global Interrogations, Local Interventions* (Southern Illinois UP, 2014), and *Rewriting Composition: Terms of Exchange* (Southern Illinois UP, 2016).

Brice Nordquist is Assistant Professor of Writing and Rhetoric at Syracuse University, where he teaches courses in composition, literacy studies, language politics, and ethnographic methods. He is the author of *Literacy and Mobility: Complexity, Uncertainty, and Agency at the Nexus of High School and College* (Routledge, 2017). His current book project investigates global proliferations and local implementations of concurrent enrollment writing courses.

Susan M. Ryan is Associate Professor of English at the University of Louisville. She is the author of *The Grammar of Good Intentions: Race and the Antebellum Culture of Benevolence* (Cornell UP, 2003) and *The Moral Economies of American Authorship: Reputation, Scandal, and the Nineteenth-Century Literary Marketplace* (Oxford UP, 2016). Her current project addresses how India figured into the nineteenth-century American imaginary.

* * * *

Anis Bawarshi is Professor of English at the University of Washington, where he specializes in the study and teaching of writing, rhetorical genre theory, writing program administration, and research on knowledge transfer. He is co-managing editor of the journal *Composition Forum* and coeditor of the book series Reference Guides to Rhetoric and Composition. His publications include *Genre and the Invention of the Writer: Reconsidering the Place of Invention in Composition*; *Genre: An Introduction to History, Theory, Research, and Pedagogy* (with Mary Jo Reiff); *Scenes of Writing: Strategies for Composing with Genres* (with Amy Devitt and Mary Jo Reiff); *Ecologies of Writing Programs: Profiles of Writing Programs in Context* (coedited with Mary Jo Reiff, Christian Weisser, and Michelle Ballif); and *Genre and the Performance of Publics* (coedited with Mary Jo Reiff).

Deborah Brandt is Professor Emerita of English at the University of Wisconsin–Madison. Her research focuses on social and economic contexts for literacy and literacy learning. She is author most recently of *The Rise of Writing: Redefining Mass Literacy* (Cambridge UP, 2015), which won the 2017 Mina P. Shaughnessy Prize from the Modern Language Association, and *Literacy in American Lives* (Cambridge UP 2001).

Jenn Fishman is Associate Professor of English at Marquette University, where she teaches courses in rhetoric and composition/writing studies and directs the First-Year English Program. Her scholarship includes special issues of *CCC Online* and *Peitho*, *REx 1*, and "Performing Writing, Performing Literacy," which received the Richard

C. Braddock Award for Outstanding Article on Writing or the Teaching of Writing. Her current grant-supported work includes Kenyon Writes and the Undergraduate Research Impact Project (with Dominic DelliCarpini and Jane Greer). She is also the Immediate Past President of the Coalition of Feminist Scholars in the History of Rhetoric and Composition.

T. R. Johnson is Professor of English and Weiss Presidential Fellow at Tulane University, where he served as Director of Freshman Writing for thirteen years. His books include *The Other Side of Pedagogy: Lacan's Four Discourses and the Development of the Student Writer* (SUNY 2014) and *A Rhetoric of Pleasure: Prose Style and Today's Composition Classroom* (Heinemann 2003). He has also taught at Boston University and the University of Louisville. He has been a contemporary jazz disc-jockey at WWOZ 90.7 FM in New Orleans since 2001.

Jay Jordan is Associate Professor and Chair of Writing and Rhetoric Studies and Associate Professor of English at the University of Utah. He is author of *Redesigning Composition for Multilingual Realities* and has co-edited collections on second language writing. His work has also appeared in *Across the Disciplines, College Composition and Communication, College English, Composition Studies, Computers and Composition, Rhetoric Review,* and several other collections. He is working on projects related to WAC in transnational settings and related to the circulation of rhetorical theory in multilingual composition.

Kacie Kiser attended Arizona State University as a PhD student in rhetoric and composition. Now a full-time mother of two, she supports local nonprofit organizations within her community through her writing.

Steve Lamos is Associate Professor in the Program for Writing and Rhetoric at the University of Colorado–Boulder. His publications include *Interests and Opportunities: Race, Racism, and University Writing Instruction in the Post–Civil Rights Era* (University of Pittsburgh Press, 2011), articles in *CCC, CE, JBW,* and *WPA,* and several book chapters. Lamos's current book project examines the role of non-tenure-track writing instruction in the neoliberal academy.

Donna LeCourt is Associate Professor of English at the University of Massachusetts Amherst. She is the author of *Identity Matters: Schooling the Student Subject in Academic Discourse* (2004) and co-editor with Carrie Leverenz and Amy Goodburn of *Rewriting Success in Composition Studies* (2012). Her current project is on the promise of digital writing for social change within an information economy.

Samantha Looker is Assistant Professor of English and Director of First-Year Writing at the University of Wisconsin Oshkosh. Her work on writing pedagogy and linguistic variation has appeared in *Teaching English in the Two-Year College* and *English Teaching: Practice and Critique.* Her first-year composition reader *Language Diversity and Academic Writing,* part of the Bedford/St. Martin's Spotlight series, is coming in late 2017.

Rebecca Lorimer Leonard is Assistant Professor in the Department of English at the University of Massachusetts Amherst. She has published in *College English, Research in the Teaching of English,* and *Written Communication,* among others. Her current book, *Writing on the Move: Migrant Women and the Value of Literacy,* is in production with the University of Pittsburgh Press. She is currently at work on *Transfer: An Introduction to History, Theory, Research and Pedagogy* with Rebecca Nowacek and Angela Rounsaville for the Reference Guides to Rhetoric and Composition Series with Parlor Press.

Katie Malcolm is an instructional consultant at the University of Washington's Center for Teaching and Learning, where she consults with faculty and TAs across the university on teaching, particularly developing and assessing writing assignments for multilingual students. Previously she spent four years as an English faculty member in the Seattle

Community Colleges teaching basic writing and composition courses. She received her PhD in Rhetoric and Composition from the University of Wisconsin–Milwaukee and currently researches translingual writing pedagogies across the curriculum and internationally.

Paul Kei Matsuda is Professor of Writing, Rhetoric, and Literacies and Director of Second Language Writing at Arizona State University. He is founding chair of the Symposium on Second Language Writing and editor of the Parlor Press Series on Second Language Writing. He has published widely on issues related to identity, language, and writing. His most recent publications include *Exploring Composition Studies: Sites, Issues, Perspectives* (2012) and *Handbook of Second and Foreign Language Writing* (2016). More information can be found at http://pmatsuda.faculty.asu.edu.

Joan Mullin is Professor of English and Executive Director of the University of North Carolina Charlotte's University Writing Program. Her co-authored book *ARTiculating: Teaching Writing in a Visual Culture* and published chapters focus on the visual (in *The Routledge Companion to Research in the Arts*) and on cross-cultural writing theories (in *Reworking English in Rhetoric and Composition: Global Interrogations, Local Interventions*). Currently, she interrogates academic definitions of research through *The Research Exchange: A Research Database of Writing Studies.*

Jason Peters is Assistant Professor of English at California Polytechnic State University, San Luis Obispo. He is currently working on a book project about language politics in twentieth-century North America.

Christian J. Pulver is Assistant Professor of Writing Studies at Roger Williams University in Bristol, Rhode Island. His work focuses on the cultural and historical formation of information economies, materialist ecologies of writing, literacy, and visual rhetorics. He is currently working on a book-length project that explores the economic and ecological implications of online writing and consumer data collection.

Kelly Ritter is Professor of English, Director of Undergraduate Rhetoric, and Provost Fellow for Undergraduate Education at the University of Illinois Urbana-Champaign. Her most recent books are *To Know Her Own History: Writing at the Woman's College, 1943–1963* (University of Pittsburgh Press, 2012), *Reframing the Subject: Postwar Instructional Film and Class-Conscious Literacies* (University of Pittsburgh Press, 2015), and, with Melissa Ianetta, the forthcoming *Landmark Essays in Writing Program Administration* (Routledge). Through July 2017, Ritter is also editor of *College English*, the flagship journal for the college section of the National Council of Teachers of English (NCTE).

Phyllis Mentzell Ryder is Associate Professor of Writing at the George Washington University. Her book, *Rhetorics for Community Action,* analyzes the rhetoric of democracy in the era of globalization and proposes a community-based pedagogy for teaching public and academic writing. Her research examines the public rhetoric of local community organizations, the rhetorics of social protests, and the rhetoric of neoliberalism; she has been published in *Rhetoric Review*, *Reflections*, *JAC,* and the *Community Literacy Journal*, among others.

Tony Scott is Associate Professor in the Department of Writing Studies, Rhetoric and Composition at Syracuse University. His scholarship includes *Dangerous Writing: Understanding the Political Economy of Composition* (Utah State University Press, 2009) and the co-edited collections *Tenured Bosses and Disposable Teachers: Writing Instruction in the Managed University* (Southern Illinois University Press, 2004) and Composition in the Age of Austerity (Utah State University Press, 2016). His articles have appeared in *College Composition and Communication, College English, Composition Studies, Computers and*

Composition, and *Written Communication*. In 2014, Tony and co-author Lil Brannon won the Richard Braddock award for "Democracy, Struggle, and the Praxis of Assessment."

Scott Wible is Associate Professor of English and director of the Professional Writing Program at the University of Maryland, College Park. His research on public policy, linguistic diversity, and rhetorical education has appeared in *College Composition and Communication*, *College English*, *Rhetoric Society Quarterly*, and *Cultural Studies*, and his book *Shaping Language Policy in the U.S: The Role of Composition Studies* (Southern Illinois UP, 2013) earned the 2014 CCCC Advancement of Knowledge Award. His current book project invents strategies for rhetoric and writing studies to engage entrepreneurship and innovation initiatives now emerging in higher education.

Yuching Jill Yang is a PhD candidate in Writing, Rhetorics, and Literacies at Arizona State University. Her research interests are L2 writing, rhetoric and composition, second language acquisition, and learner belief. Her dissertation is on L2 writers' beliefs in multilingual composition classrooms. She is the co-author of the book chapter "Professional Development by Doing Real Research Collaboratively" in *Doing Real Research in Applied Linguistics* (Routledge, forthcoming).

James T. Zebroski is the senior composition faculty person at University of Houston. The focus of his scholarship over the last thirty-five years has been critical theory and writing. This work has centered on many forms of unauthorized writing. In over fifty published essays, he has explored various dimensions of unauthorized writing—including Vygotsky's theories of writing, social class and writing, alternative histories of rhetoric and composition, ethnographic writing, and post-Stonewall gay literature. His book *Thinking through Theory: Vygotskian Perspectives on the Teaching of Writing*, published in 1994, is still in print. It is the first and only book-length treatment of the work of Lev Vygotsky in rhetoric and composition. Zebroski came to University of Houston in 2007 to put into place a new PhD program in Rhetoric, Composition, and Pedagogy, which now has more than twenty-five students.

INDEX